FEMINISM IN COALITION

Feminism

LIZA TAYLOR

in Coalition

Thinking with US Women of Color Feminism

DUKE UNIVERSITY PRESS
Durham and London
2022

Designed by A. Mattson Gallagher
Typeset in Chaparral Pro by Westchester Publishing Services

Library of Congress Cataloging-in-Publication Data
Names: Taylor, Liza, [date] author.
Title: Feminism in coalition : thinking with US women of color
feminism / Liza Taylor.
Description: Durham : Duke University Press, 2022. | Includes
bibliographical references and index.
Identifiers: LCCN 2022020478 (print)
LCCN 2022020479 (ebook)
ISBN 9781478016519 (hardcover)
ISBN 9781478019152 (paperback)
ISBN 9781478023784 (ebook)
Subjects: LCSH: Womanism. | Womanism—United States. |
Feminism—United States. | African American feminists. | Feminist
theory—United States. | BISAC: SOCIAL SCIENCE / Feminism &
Feminist Theory | SOCIAL SCIENCE / Black Studies (Global)
Classification: LCC HQ1197 .T395 2022 (print) |
LCC HQ1197 (ebook) | DDC 305.420973—dc23/eng/20220705
LC record available at https://lccn.loc.gov/2022020478
LC ebook record available at https://lccn.loc.gov/2022020479

Cover art: Darius Quarles, *Coalition*, 2022. Acrylic on canvas,
30 × 40 inches. Courtesy of the artist.

To the students who took Feminism in Coalition at LMU (spring 2016 and spring 2018) and Elon (spring 2020). This is for you.

Contents

Contents

Acknowledgments

Thank you to the Women of Color feminist authors of the texts referenced throughout this book. I'm deeply indebted to all of you for your willingness to share your lived experiences and for your brilliant conceptual and political formulations. Writing a "political theory" doctoral dissertation that aimed to center the concepts and theories of US Women of Color feminism was no small feat. I could not have completed it without the help of several people. Thank you to Geoffrey Whitehall and Lori Marso for helping to put back together the pieces of my work when I encountered intense resistance. Thank you to my dissertation committee (Carole Pateman, Joshua Dienstag, Juliet Williams, and Ray Rocco) for passing an unconventional political theory dissertation, with a special thanks to Juliet for encouraging me to name these authors and texts as primary. Thank you to the Women of Color feminism fellow travelers who sustained me and this project beyond the University of California at Los Angeles. Without you, this book never would have come to fruition. A special thanks to Zein Murib. Upon discovering our shared interest in coalition politics and Women of Color feminism at a 2014 Western Political Science Association panel, we set out to find other political science scholars working in this area. A year later, our first "Feminism in Coalition" panel was born. Thank you to Juliet Hooker,

Cynthia Burack, Katherine Knutson, Wendy Sarvasy, and Cricket Keating for joining us on the WPSA 2015 panel, and to Karma Chávez and Shireen Roshanravan for joining us for the 2016 NWSA iteration. I am deeply grateful to Jocelyn M. Boryczka at *New Political Science* for encouraging Zein and me to turn our evolving panel into a published symposium. I am equally grateful to Courtney Berger at Duke for her enthusiasm for this intervention, for showing me that there is an audience for this work, and for sharpening my contribution. Thank you to the anonymous readers of the manuscript. Your insights encouraged me along the way and enriched the overall argument. Cricket, your careful attention to this manuscript has made the project what it is. Thinking *with you* over the years has sustained me on so many levels. Through it all, thank you to Lori Marso. Your imprint is on everything I write. I would not be here without you.

To the students who took A People's History of Democratic Thought while at UCLA (spring 2011 and spring 2012), thank you for encountering Women of Color feminism with such enthusiasm and for letting it change you. Thank you to the Bellarmine Society of Fellows at Loyola Marymount University, where my political science colleagues, especially John Parrish and Andrew Dilts, encouraged me to design my own senior seminar class in my first year as a postdoctoral teaching fellow. To the students who took Feminism in Coalition at LMU and later at Elon, my gratitude is beyond words. Thank you for embracing the coalition simulation with such courage and vulnerability. Thank you also for your brilliant questions and provocations. Many key analytical moves, insights, and concepts in this book crystallized in conversation with all of you.

To the local Durham, North Carolina, self-taught artist who created the painting depicted on the cover of this book, Darius Quarles, thank you for your vision, your enthusiasm and care, and your exceptional talent in translating the spirit of this project into a piece of visual art.

Finally, thank you to my family for believing in me and for tolerating the amount of time I spend working. To Shawn, your love, acceptance, patience, and kindness is a constant source of sustenance. Thank you from the bottom of my heart.

Introduction

A Discipline in Need of Feminist Refinement:
Obscuring the "Politics" of Intersectional Group Activism

Though research on progressive coalition politics is notably limited among many mainstream contemporary political theorists—noteworthy exceptions include Anna Carastathis (2013), Ange-Marie Hancock (2011), Edwina Barvosa (2008), and Cricket Keating (2005, 2018), among others[1]—when attention has veered in this direction in the past decades, a curious and troubling pattern has emerged. In addition to looking to a narrow set of political thinkers, much contemporary analysis tends to obscure the concrete politics of coalition activists in favor of densely philosophical accounts fixated on the discursive unfixity, improbability, and unpredictability of coalitional activism.

Take for example the 2012 supplementary issue of *Theory and Event* that focused on the student coalition that emerged as part of Quebec's Maple Spring, in which a student strike against rising tuition fees grew into a broader people's struggle against neoliberal policies that pushed austerity measures and weakened democratic institutions. In response to the announcement made by the Parti libéral du Québec in early 2010 of its intention to raise tuition fees by seventy-five percent over five years beginning in 2012, a handful of Quebec student associations formed the Coalition large de l'Association pour une solidarité syndicale étudiante (CLASSE), which represented half of the striking students and was considered to be the most radical of the student groups in its commitment to free postsecondary education and an egalitarian internal decision-making structure. Offering a chronology of events, thirteen articles, and the CLASSE Manifesto itself, the *Theory and Event* issue sought to explain and interpret the events of the Maple Spring as they had unfolded up to the point of the issue's publication (summer 2012). Remarkably, most of the contributing authors were from art, art history, communications, and philosophy departments. Given that *Theory and Event* self-identifies as a journal committed to the fields of "political theory and political science," it is curious that only one self-identified "political theorist" appeared in a special issue on an explicitly political event. On a more generous reading, one might welcome *Theory and Event*'s commitment to interdisciplinarity in its treatment of political activism. Such an interpretation, however, is complicated by the fact that the dominant analytical lens used by this seemingly diverse set of authors was one informed narrowly by poststructuralist philosophical commitments to ontological unfixity, epistemological undecidability, and political indeterminacy, and particularly by the work of a handful of theory titans in this area: Jacques Rancière, Jacques Derrida, Gilles Deleuze, Félix Guattari, Alain Badiou, Slavoj Žižek, and, of course, Judith Butler. As Butler has argued in her most recent lectures on the topic of coalition, what brings people together in the space of coalition is not a shared political commitment to, say, dismantling the neoliberal structures that drive austerity measures and the antidemocratic policies unfolding in Quebec in 2012. No, what brings people to progressive coalitions, Butler maintains, is the unpredictability of ethical encounter—the fact that we do not know with whom we will find ourselves in the space of coalition—or, as she has also put it, the "unchosen dimension" of our solidarity work (Butler 2015, 152). With theorists such as Butler as their guides, the contributing authors emphasized the unpredictability, uncertainty, unimaginability, and undecidability of this moment of coalitional activism.

Such an interpretative frame, however, was particularly odd given the remarkable decisiveness and, dare I say, *decidability* of CLASSE itself.

Whereas the scholarly interpretations of the Maple Spring were replete with unknowns—and with an emphasis on undecidability as a site of productive political engagement—CLASSE's manifesto was explicit in outlining its own set of knowable problems and political goals. The problem, it asserted, was neoliberal capitalism and the corresponding undemocratic form of politics it both engenders and relies on. The goal, it insisted, was a more participatory democratic order. The most concrete act CLASSE called for in the manifesto was the strike itself, hoping that this action would incite a groundswell of support from students and nonstudents alike in their shared political commitment to contesting a social order that guaranteed unequal access to public services leading to increased wealth for a small number of people and corporations (CLASSE 2012). One of the only pieces published within this special issue that explicitly takes up these concrete political reasons for the formation of the strike is the CLASSE manifesto itself. Are we therefore left to believe that political theorists have no insightful interpretative frames to apply to the unfolding of coalitional events? And if it seems that activists may be the best theorists of the concrete politics that incite and guide coalitional activism, then why weren't their theoretical insights foregrounded in the special issue? The dissonance between the concrete politics articulated by CLASSE and the insistence by contemporary theorists on the complete undecidability and political indeterminacy of coalition events reflects the severe limitations of a theoretical framework that proceeds from these poststructuralist theoretical influences instead of from the accounts of activists on the ground.

Fast-forward five years. In the wake of the 2016 US presidential election, many political scientists scrambled to make sense of a campaign season and electoral outcome that defied much of the established knowledge on the logic behind successful election campaigns and voter behavior. To others, especially to the variety of nonwhite minorities, women, and others targeted by Donald Trump's shockingly offensive campaign rhetoric, the outcome simply laid bare to the unknowing portion of white America—those not subject to Trump's hourly Twitter vitriol—what those who were subject to his racist, xenophobic, misogynist, and otherwise distasteful comments had known for quite some time: America was becoming increasingly polarized by racial and misogynist attitudes. To a handful of political science scholars, this outcome was also not unexpected. It simply confirmed what Michael Tesler had discovered in the years leading up to the 2016 election: rather than indicating the end of hostile race relations in America, Barack Obama's presidency ignited increasing racial resentment, the effects of which we can see in the public's response to Trump's racially hostile campaign rhetoric (see Tesler 2016a, 2016b; Sides, Tesler, and Vavreck 2016). Tesler's findings in relation to the effect of racial attitudes on the 2016 presidential election—the fact that those with stronger racial resentment and ethnocentric beliefs were more likely to support Trump than other Republican candidates (Tesler 2016b)—have been corroborated and expanded by other scholars interested in the "cultural backlash" explanation for Trump's successful presidential bid: the fact that the 2016 election was unusually influenced by hostile attitudes toward progressive viewpoints about people of color, the LGBTQ community, and women (see Inglehart and Norris 2019; Turney et al. 2017).

This analysis bears a striking resemblance to the analysis given to explain Ronald Reagan's victory in the 1980 presidential election. In the same way that backlash to growing progressive attitudes and the shifting demographics in the United States that played a part in electing our first Black male president gave us Donald Trump, scholars in the 1980s showed that growing resentment toward the progressive gains of the civil rights movement (Edgar 1981; Cook 2015) and women's liberation (Eisenstein 1981; Edgar 1981, 225) set the stage for Reagan's successful presidential bid and the policies that defined his presidency: a "war on drugs" that put a disproportionate number of young Black men behind bars, a return to family values policies that threatened feminist gains on workplace and reproductive justice, and Reaganomics policies that reduced domestic government spending on programs that would help minority and poor Americans while granting multibillion dollar tax cuts for the rich and big business. With the multipronged attack on women, people of color, and the poor that was the result of many of Reagan's policies, any effective response from the Left at the time would have to be similarly multifaceted.

The need for a multifaceted and coalition response to diverse oppressions was already a familiar fact for many Women of Color feminists of the time. Following Chela Sandoval (2000) and Chandra Mohanty (2003), I understand Women of Color not as an ontological category describing a certain identity related to being a woman of color but instead as a way of understanding or as an analytic—that is, a theoretical and political orientation characterized by a critical awareness of oppressions as mobile and interlocking and a critical orientation toward monolithic understandings of "women." I am following Shireen Roshanravan (2014) in capitalizing *Women of Color* when referring to texts and authors adopting this particular political and theoretical feminist orientation (when referring to women who simply hold the identity women of color, I refrain from capitalizing the term). While most Women of Color feminist scholars are indeed nonwhite, understood as an "analytic," Women of Color feminism can accommodate white feminist activist-theorists as well. Minnie Bruce Pratt's influential 1984 essay, "Identity: Skin Blood Heart," is exemplary here.

In a number of interviews in the 1980s and 1990s, Angela Davis had asserted that women of color and other subjugated people would have to come together in coalitions if they ever hoped to effectively dismantle the interlocking oppressive forces that shaped their lives (Davis 1989; Davis 1998; Davis and Martínez 1994; Davis and Bhavnani 1989). In fact, this theme of coalition politics has been central to Women of Color feminist activism since Shirley Chisholm first championed it in her 1972 bid for the presidential nomination of the Democratic Party wherein she advised diverse subjugated people to unite in coalitions committed to undermining the interlocking oppressive forces that were gaining traction in the backlash to the civil rights movement of the 1960s (Chisholm 1972). Even before Chisholm's urgent call to intersectional coalition politics, members of what came to be known as the Third World Women's Alliance (TWWA) gestured in a similar direction in the late 1960s (see Beal in Morgan 1970; Burnham 2001).[2] Throughout the 1970s and 1980s, influential activist theorists such as Bernice Johnson Reagon, Audre Lorde, Sandoval, the TWWA, and the cofounders of the Combahee River Collective (Combahee) as well as activist editors such as Barbara Smith, Gloria T. Hull, Patricia Bell Scott, Cherríe Moraga, and Gloria Anzaldúa (who compiled a range of Black and Women of Color feminists anthologies in this period) all echoed Chisholm's call, consistently maintaining that the only way to effectively undermine oppression was in coalitions across seemingly intractable race, class, gender, sexuality, and other divides. As Davis declared in 1989, "this is the era of coalitions" and specifically "multiracial" social justice coalitions committed to tackling intersecting forms of oppression and subordination (Davis and Bhavnani 1989, 71). In line with her contemporaries, Davis envisioned a form of unity that would compel people "to look at many different issues in a qualitatively different way" (Davis and Bhavnani 1989, 78). When asked in an interview on PBS's *Frontline* to specify what she meant by "coalition," Davis clarified that what is needed are "politically based coalitions" that are more focused on the issues than progressive movements had been in the past and that are defined by coalitional strategies that "go beyond racial lines. We need to bring black communities, Chicano communities, Puerto Rican communities, Asian American communities together" (Davis 1998).

By the mid-1990s, a much broader range of white, postmodern, and Third World feminists also began discussing coalition. As Linda Nicholson argued in 1994, coalition politics is "not something merely external to feminist politics but [is] that which is also internal to it" (Nicholson 1994, 102). Feminist politics, she insisted, had been "exhibiting internal coalitional strategies" since the late 1960s (103). While the work of Women of Color feminists is no doubt at the forefront of this history, Nicholson proposed that many other white feminists were also, and had been for decades, interested in coalition politics. Charlotte Bunch confirmed this only two years later by stating that while the "women's movement" may be dead, "the women's coalition is (or maybe coalitions of women are) alive and well" (Bunch et al. 1996, 934). By 2000, a consensus across feminist theory had emerged: the way forward for feminism was coalition. The 2000 *Signs* special issue, "Feminism at a Millennium," is indicative of this. Almost all of the fifty-plus articles published in this special issue "attest to the urgency of coalitions" (Howard and Allen 2000, xxiv, xxix). The practice of coalition, both the editors and many of the contributors (Stimpson, O'Barr, Ransby, Brodkin, Laslett and Brenner, and Bauer and Wald) argued, is crucial to feminism's future (Howard and Allen 2000, xxx). This consensus remains strong today.

When asked to speak at the University of Chicago only weeks after Trump's election, Davis again attested to the need for progressives to engage in "radical activism" that would build and strengthen "community" and that would be defined by collective "struggle" against intersecting, oppressive forces in the form of multiracial coalitions (Davis and Taylor 2016). What is needed in our contemporary moment, Davis implored the crowd, is a truly intersectional approach to undermining oppression, one that is led by younger social justice activists informed by the lessons learned from the Women of Color feminist activists who have been engaging in effective coalitional organizing since the 1970s. Davis's call to progressive activism in the form of intersectional coalition politics is unambiguous. Still, it is yet to be taken up by many mainstream political theorists.

In the January 2017 supplementary issue of *Theory and Event*, devoted to questions on how progressives might respond to a Trump presidency, no time is devoted to progressive *coalition* politics as a possible answer. In comparison with the 2012 supplementary issue on CLASSE, the selection of authors appearing in the January 2017 issue of *Theory and Event* had shifted decisively toward political theory and political science orientations (almost all of the scholars are situated in political science departments or social justice centers). But what had dropped from the conversation was the need for progressive alliances in the form of "coalition."[3] Given the urgent need to shift our thinking to progressive coalition politics in light of Trump's multipronged attack on diverse subjugated people, patterns such as this leave me worried that many contemporary scholars are ill-equipped to take on our current set of challenges.

With Women of Color feminists' continued insistence (since at least the late 1960s) on the importance of coalition politics to any successful progressive movement to dismantle interlocking oppressive forces, why haven't political theorists on "the Left (minus the feminist political theorists listed at the start of the introduction) taken up this line of thinking more often? And when they do engage with coalition politics, why do they treat coalition as an unimaginable, unpredictable, and politically indeterminate phenomenon? The disjuncture between what coalition activists report in the trenches and what many mainstream political theorists theorize about in academic writing troubles me and not just because of the charge that it widens the theory-practice divide (which, indeed, it does) and thus delegitimates political theory as a vocation. My concerns run deeper. Dominant strands of contemporary political theory (including, among others, those shaped by poststructuralist influences), I fear, are stymied by this growing dissonance, leaving them ill-prepared to conceive of effective intersectional collective responses necessary in a Trump United States. (It's important to note that "Trump America" began before Trump was elected and will likely continue long after he leaves office.) This is so because they find themselves confounded by what Ernesto Laclau and Chantal Mouffe have labeled the "crisis" of post-Marxist collective politics.

In *Hegemony and Socialist Strategy* (1985), Laclau and Mouffe argue that the twentieth century, particularly the movements of the 1960s, has exploded the Marxist notion that *class* is the primary marker of forms of social injustice. What is now in "crisis" is a vision of the Left that relies on the Marxist ideas of the ontological centrality of the category of the "working class" and the supposed homogeneity of a "collective will" (Laclau and Mouffe 1985, 2). The proliferation of struggles by feminists, sexual minorities, racial minorities, religious minorities, ethnic minorities, and so on reflects what they call a "surplus of the social" in relation to what might have previously been thought of as the organized structures and categories of society (1). In simple terms, narrow class, race, or gender politics alone fail to capture the breadth of devastation brought on by the neoliberal policies of Reaganomics.

What concerns me here is not just the implication of this so-called crisis—that intersectional social justice struggles are incapable of forming a united coalitional front—but rather, that for Laclau and Mouffe and other influential coalition thinkers such as Deleuze, Guattari, and Butler this crisis is shaped by a concurrent shift at a more theoretical level toward poststructuralist philosophical and political reflections on difference and the implications they carry for collective politics (see Coles 1996, 375). Laclau and Mouffe best articulate this shift in their appeal to what I will present as a multilayer crisis reflecting the poststructuralist theoretical orientations that I find troubling: (1) the assumption of the supposed incompatibility between intersectional social justice struggles and Marxist collective organizing (the intersectionality crisis); (2) the inclination toward the ontological unfixity of all social categories such as "workers" and "women" (the ontological crisis); (3) the proclivity toward epistemological *un*decidability as the accepted framework for making sense of the movement of power and oppression (the epistemological crisis); and (4) the insistence on political indeterminacy as the basis of coalitional activism (the political crisis).

For Laclau and Mouffe and for other contemporary scholars informed by the theoretical orientations named above, all categories are thought to be forever unstable or "unfixed" due to their ongoing *discursive* production— that is, their ongoing production in and through language that leaves categories such as "class," "women," or "workers" forever unfinished (Laclau and Mouffe 1985, 85, x). In addition to challenging fixed ontological categories, Laclau and Mouffe argue that discursive unfixity has devastating implications for modes of *understanding* built on structural determinism, or the notion that society and the forces of oppression operating in it are intelligible structures that could be fully grasped through scientific rationalism or other identifiable modes of understanding. If the perceived ontological crisis is marked by a "surplus" of the social, we might understand the epistemological crisis to be marked by a perceived *deficit* of knowledge, or "structural *un*decidability" (Laclau and Mouffe 1985, xii). If we cannot rely on our old ways of knowing and understanding social forces, how are we to identify the power structures that we hope to challenge politically? Thus the practical politics dimension of the crisis emerges, the perceived political indeterminacy that is thought to be the necessary complement to discursive unfixity and epistemological undecidability. In essence, thinkers such as Laclau and Mouffe (1985, 109, 176), Deleuze and Guattari (1987, 469–70) and Butler (1990, 20–22) try to match the unfixity of the social with an equally indeterminate left-oriented (the lowercase *l* in *left-oriented* is meant to signal a lack of clear political directionality in such formulations) coalition politics. As many mainstream contemporary authors attempt to confront and work through the layers of this crisis, they encounter several tensions, roadblocks, and conundrums, which are what concern me here.

Specifically, when influential contemporary political theorists, such as Butler, have attempted to maneuver around the tension that results from simultaneously adopting a philosophical commitment to discursive unfixity and a political commitment to a *determinate* Left-oriented agenda, they have succeeded in doing so only by sacrificing the politics of coalition in favor of either problematic notions of ontological disturbance, in the form of *coalition as spectacle* (made popular by Butler's collective drag argument), or apolitical and highly unlikely aspirations to universal ethical community, in the form of *coalition as ethical community* (made popular by Butler's more recent work). In what I call *coalition as spectacle*, Butler's commitment to discursive unfixity shapes a congruous form of politics in the form of collective parodic repetition (Butler 1990, 43–44, 186–88). In this formulation of "antifoundational" coalition politics (20–22, 45), the goal and direction of a coalitional assemblage remain as uncertain as the signifying process that produces the individuals therein (23). Coalition emerges here *as spectacle* wherein sexual minorities find themselves performing unplanned disruptive acts of gender and sexuality defiance, such as collectively dressing in drag. The very purpose of the coalition thus reveals itself in a spectacular performance of gender and sexuality parody.

In a second formulation (though incongruous with Butler's first), politics as ontological disruption is replaced by politics in the form of *ethical orientation*. Politics is eclipsed here by a shared ethical commitment that is itself rooted in our universally shared "condition of primary vulnerability" wherein we are all, as infants, at the mercy of others to keep us alive (Butler 2004, 31). According to Butler, this primary vulnerability, the fact of our shared precariousness, can form the basis of a universal community committed to tackling the uneven precarity of the *most* vulnerable (certain bodies are more vulnerable to the forces of global market capitalism than others). Instead of outlining a Left-oriented coalition politics built around the experience of a particular social group, such as the proletariat, in her formulation of what I am calling *coalition as ethical community*, Butler expands the very notion of class to include *all* people. In such an understanding, however, the very real danger of coalition politics across intractable race, class, gender, and other differences vanishes from view. Thus, despite their incongruity, both formulations share one thing: the concrete politics of progressive coalitions—that is, the goal or purpose of the coalition and the arrangements of power that situate and frustrate all collective efforts—becomes obscured in the process.

The chokehold of these poststructuralist philosophical influences on contemporary theorizing about progressive coalition politics has led to markedly narrow depictions of collective politics (when a concrete politics is even articulated). It is this, and not the simple fact of the widening divide between theory and practice, that deeply troubles me. Is it possible to foreground the politics that demands intersectional coalitions in the first place and both situates and frustrates encounters within coalitional spaces while also attending to the multiplicity, heterogeneity, and complexity that mark our contemporary social world? Yes, I will argue; a possible way out of this impasse between unfixity and fixity emerges most prominently within early US Women of Color coalitional feminism. Though I will focus primarily on texts that emerged in the 1970s and 1980s, many of the key ideas surfacing here exist within a longer genealogy of US Black and Women of Color feminism beginning as early as the nineteenth century and continuing into the present. I engage texts from this longer genealogy throughout my discussion. I specify the context of the United States (*US* Women of Color feminism) not to signal a shared nationality among the different activist-scholars engaged here but rather to locate the scholarly and publishing context wherein their major works first appeared.

Thinking with and through the Concept of Coalition with Women of Color Feminism

Feminism in Coalition: Thinking with US Women of Color Feminism is thus an invitation to more of my colleagues within contemporary political theory to *think with* US Women of Color coalitional feminist theory. Heeding Davis's call, it implores political activists and theorists alike to take cues from some of our most rigorous political theorists on collective intersectional group politics. Recall that for Chisholm, uniting fractured social justice movements was a *challenge* (not a crisis) that she and contemporaneous Women of Color coalition feminists met with a notion of coalition politics centered on dismantling interlocking oppressive structures. While many scholars since Laclau and Mouffe have taken for granted the relationship between the proliferation of social justice struggles and discursive unfixity, I contend that there are alternative ways to accommodate multiplicity and complexity without subscribing either to discursive unfixity in the form of coalition as spectacle or to ethical commitment in the form of coalition as ethical community. To arrive at these alternative understandings, we must turn to alternative voices that will lead us to new concepts, specifically to ones not limited to the theoretical straitjacket of poststructuralist influences.

My impetus in turning to alternative voices is shaped by an interest in thinking differently and better about effective intersectional group politics in a demographically shifting and politically divided United States. The insights of these voices point toward possible ways out of the impasses faced by contemporary European/US political theorists who are stymied by poststructuralist philosophical reflections on difference. Feminist, especially Women of Color, coalitional activists and theorists have been actively working through these problematics since the late 1960s. Thus, one of the major claims of this book is that contemporary political and feminist theorists who have not yet engaged this rich body of work would do well to turn toward these activists and theorists instead of away from them, as have certain prominent feminist theorists such as Butler (1990 and 1995) and Jasbir Puar (2007 and 2012).

By "intersectional" group politics I mean a form of collective group politics that attends to multiple "intersecting" (Crenshaw 1991), "interlocking" (Combahee 1983), or "intermeshing" (Lugones 2003) social justice concerns—assaults on reproductive autonomy, contesting neoliberal policies that benefit the rich and corporations at the expense of the middle and working classes, separating children from their parents at the US-Mexico border, forms of structural racism including the disproportionate imprisonment of Black and Brown people, police brutality against Black and Brown people, using welfare policies as a way to police the reproductive autonomy of Black and Brown women, the disappearance of Black, Brown, and Indigenous women, and so many others. While such injustices may be of primary concern to corresponding identity groups (women, the working class, people of color, women of color, prisoners, Indigenous people, and so on), when I speak frequently of *intersectionality*, I resist speaking of actual identity groups. Rather, I am speaking to a particular "analytic," or way of understanding systems of domination and oppression (Crenshaw 2015). Though *intersectionality* as a term emerged formally with Kimberlé Crenshaw's 1989 article "Demarginalizing the Intersection of Race and Sex," the concept and analytical practice had been in circulation well before Crenshaw's coinage.

Sojourner Truth's work is exemplary here. In her "Ain't I a Woman?" speech—delivered to the Women's Rights Convention in Akron, Ohio, in 1851—Truth challenges both the racial violence of slavery and the rigid gendered stereotypes of Southern, aristocratic femininity in her provocative and repeated question, "Ain't I a woman?" Within a context of a convention devoted to the situation of "women," Truth challenges both the women and men present to consider whether a Black slave such as herself, who defies traditional notions of white femininity by working in the fields and stepping out of carriages and over ditches without the help of a man, is still a "woman." Through this simple question, Truth positions herself at the intersection of white supremacy and patriarchy, forcing her audience to begin to acknowledge the existence of two systems of oppression simultaneously (2004, 128). Frances Beal elaborates a similar argument in her famous 1969 pamphlet, "Double Jeopardy: To Be Black and Female," wherein she highlights the "slave of a slave" (Beal in Morgan 1970, 385) status of Black women on account of their double marginality in relation to both racist and sexist capitalism. Her claim is an analytical one that carries clear political implications. Like Truth, the analytic she adopts is that of intersectionality wherein she insists that to make sense of the effects of racist capitalism, one must analyze its connection to sexist capitalism. Not only do multiple systems of oppression exist simultaneously, but these systems interact with one another. The implication that this analytic carries for group politics was rather straightforward for Beal: "Any white woman's group who does not have an anti-imperialist and anti-racist ideology has absolutely nothing in common with the black woman's struggle" (Beal in Morgan 1970, 393). Indeed, this became the rallying call behind the activist work she did as part of the TWWA and as editor of the TWWA's journal, *Triple Jeopardy*.

When I use *intersectionality*, then, I am speaking to this evolving sense of the ways in which multiple systems of domination exist in society simultaneously and are mutually reinforcing. I am crediting US Black and Women of Color feminism with bringing this to the fore. Thus, when I position this project as one invested in exploring the possibilities for intersectional collective group politics, I mean to signal an interest in exploring possibilities of alliances across race, class, gender, sexuality, faith, ethnicity, and other differences for the sake of tackling intersecting systems of domination and oppression. What version of progressive collective group politics might an intersectionality analytic inform? While this question is posed as a live and pressing one in contemporary feminist studies, one of my central claims is that this "politics" question was settled long ago with early US Women of Color coalition feminists such as Combahee, the TWWA, Reagon, and many others.[4] For the feminists who developed the analytic of intersectionality, the corresponding politics was always coalition politics. Part of my aim here is to make this claim unequivocally clear so that contemporary theorists and activists might move on to the next question of how we might utilize the savvy coalitional strategies of US Women of Color coalitional feminism in the context of our contemporary social justice struggles.

When using the formulation *Women of Color*, I resist any connection to Puar's treatment of *women of color* in her 2012 article, "'I Would Rather Be a Cyborg Than a Goddess.'" When Puar uses either the phrase "women of color," or its acronym, WOC, she treats it as an identity category that has become "simultaneously emptied of specific meaning in its ubiquitous application and yet overdetermined in its deployment" insofar as it is the "difference of African American women that dominates this genealogy of the term women of color" (Puar 2012, 52). For an incisive critique of Puar on this point, see James Bliss (2016). Not only does Puar problematically limit *women of color*'s usage to an identity category, but, as Bliss points out, her critique of intersectionality, and necessarily also of women of color, exhibits an anxiety in Puar's work that "manifests as hostility toward the project of radical Black feminism" (Bliss 2016, 734, 738). My project therefore proceeds in the opposite direction of Puar's insofar as it welcomes theoretical engagement with the radical Black and Women of Color feminists who gave us the sophisticated analytic of intersectionality and its corresponding politics of coalition.

Though the conversation about coalition politics within US Women of Color feminism is an ongoing one, my focus is primarily on the early generative texts written in the 1970s and 1980s, both because of the crucial importance of these texts and because of the historical resonance of their time to ours: a time of backlash to progressive gains. While there are differences between the activist-scholars from this period, I will instead highlight the ways in which they converge on using the *concept* of coalition not only as a practical solution to questions related to collective feminist organizing across difference but also as a theoretical apparatus for examining the very philosophical questions and puzzles that have perplexed many contemporary European/US political theorists. The variety of ways in which US Women of Color coalition feminists think with and through the concept of coalition enlivens broader conversations within contemporary political theory on theorizing political subjectivity and consciousness in spite of both ontological and epistemological fluidity and theorizing a version of progressive coalition politics that foregrounds the politics of coalitional work while also accommodating this fluidity.

Thinking with US Women of Color coalition feminists, this book thus traces a constellation of concepts orbiting the notion of "coalition" emerging in the early generative texts by the TWWA, Combahee, Chisholm, Reagon, Smith, Lorde, Moraga, Anzaldúa, Pratt, Sandoval, María Lugones, Mohanty, and the many authors appearing in *This Bridge Called My Back*. At various points throughout the book, I follow this conversation into the 1990s and early 2000s by reading a selection of texts by Crenshaw, Linda Alcoff, Edwina Barvosa-Carter, Cynthia Burack, Mohanty, Lugones, and Sandoval—and even into the present with works by Keeanga-Yamahtta Taylor, Erica Townsend-Bell, Karma Chávez, Carastathis, Keating, Roshanravan, Ashley Boher, and Zein Murib. The concepts that surface here are shaped by the analytic of intersectionality emerging out of an even longer genealogy of US Black and Women of Color feminism that begins with activists such as Truth. While tracing this conceptual genealogy, *Feminism in Coalition* challenges its political theory readers not yet familiar with US Women of Color coalitional feminism to enter unfamiliar territory, wherein the concept of coalition will emerge in unconventional and perhaps perplexing ways. In addition to uncovering more concrete notions of activist coalition politics—in the form of what I call "politico-ethical coalition politics"—I will invite readers to entertain notions of coalitional identity, coalitional consciousness, and coalitional scholarship. By challenging the chokehold that notions of undecidability, unfixity, and indeterminacy have over contemporary political thought, these more peculiar adjectival formulations of coalition will offer creative and ultimately promising ways out of the tensions and conundrums articulated above.

Concrete coalition politics, early US Women of Color coalition feminists maintain, requires an appreciation of interlocking oppressions, which not only produce what they conceive as "coalitional" understandings of collective group politics, identity, consciousness, and even scholarship, but also reshape the very stakes of Laclau and Mouffe's so-called crisis. Challenging the presumed intersectionality "crisis" of post-Marxist group politics, activist-scholars such as Smith and the other cofounders of Combahee show that for them there was never any "crisis" between Marxism and intersectionality. As we learn in a recent interview between Keeanga-Yamahtta Taylor (2017) and the cofounders of Combahee, their intersectional commitments and their Marxist commitments were clear and congruous from the start. As they put it, all that was required was an extension and reworking of Marxism, not an abandonment of Marxism. This presumption of the possible compatibility between Marxism and intersectional social justice concerns is further explored in Bohrer's *Marxism and Intersectionality: Race, Gender, Class, and Sexuality under Contemporary Capitalism* (2019). As my engagement with her text will reveal, while such a presumption is explicitly stated by the Combahee cofounders, it was also implied in accounts by Women of Color feminists appearing as early as the mid-nineteenth century. I take this shared presumption as my starting place so that I may reframe Laclau and Mouffe's so-called crisis of Marxism as a *challenge*, not a crisis—a challenge that Women of Color feminists such as Combahee and many others have met and worked through since the nineteenth century.

The ability to do this is captured in the formulation "politico-ethical coalition politics," a distinctive understanding of coalition located in early US Women of Color coalitional feminism and vividly on display in Reagon's 1981 coalition speech, "Coalition Politics: Turning the Century." I engage in a close examination of this speech alongside contemporaneous work by Smith and the other cofounders of Combahee; Chisholm; Lorde; Anzaldúa; the authors appearing in Moraga and Anzaldúa's (1983a) coedited anthology, *This Bridge Called My Back*; and Sandoval's account of the unique consciousness formed among the members of the US Third World feminist consciousness-raising (CR) group at the National Women's Studies Association (NWSA) annual conference in 1981. This undertaking reveals that politico-ethical coalition politics embodies three distinguishing characteristics: an emphasis on coalition as a dangerous and even life-threatening *struggle*; an understanding that coalition is generated out of a shared *self-reflexive political commitment* to undermining oppression; and an emphasis on *existential transformation* as inherent to the very process of coalescing. While I will demonstrate that the notion of politico-ethical coalition politics on offer from this rich body of work is uniquely *political* insofar as it foregrounds the decidable and goal-oriented politics of coalitional activism rooted in a shared political commitment to undermining oppression, I reveal that this form of collective political engagement is best thought of as politico-*ethical* insofar as the political commitment to undermining interlocking oppressive forces grounding their efforts is overtly self-reflexive, thereby encouraging an ethical sensibility characterized by love and existential transformation.

It is precisely this understanding of coalition politics that resonates across the 2017 Women's March on Washington's (WMW) unity principles, notably written and conceptualized by a national team composed primarily of Women of Color feminists. An unprecedented success in its ability to mobilize a diverse population for an intersectional social justice platform, this event offers an excellent opportunity to examine the extent to which this constellation of concepts might prove instructive for contemporary activists. Notwithstanding the various controversies that erupted leading up to and in the wake of the 2017 WMW, I will show that the key values and principles guiding the march, shaping the convictions of various speakers and attendees at the march, and even propelling some of the most heated controversies surrounding the march demonstrate the necessity and promise of politico-ethical coalition politics.

This form of coalition politics is made possible for Women of Color coalition feminists by reconfiguring notions of political subjectivity, political consciousness, and collective authorship in "coalitional" terms. By locating a "coalitional" understanding of identity within this literature, wherein Women of Color feminists are thought to be internally heterogeneous and complexly situated and nevertheless in a constant struggle toward ontological wholeness and unity, I show that thinking with these authors will offer creative alternatives to the emphasis on ontological unfixity and the subject-in-process characteristic of poststructuralist attempts to theorize multiple and fluid conceptions of identity within political theory. Through this process of internal struggle toward coalitional identity, the authors I examine show us, women of color acquire a "coalitional consciousness"; that is, a tactical epistemological awareness and acuity for navigating complex (though nevertheless identifiable) social systems of oppression and for assuming tactical political subjectivities for the sake of collective group action. The skills that they acquire by navigating their own coalitional identities and struggling toward ontological wholeness as coalitional selves, this *thinking with* reveals, prepares them for the difficult work of coalition politics with other subjugated peoples and across at times conflicting or hostile differences. Their ability to map potential lines of collective activism from *within* the space of lived oppression and marginalization, we will find, offers creative alternatives to the dominant mode of bird's-eye view theorizing typical of approaches within political theory as dissimilar as Lenin's scientific socialism and Deleuze and Guattari's unpredictable "minoritarian becomings" (Deleuze and Guattari 1987, 469–70).

I recognize that to use the concept of coalition in such unconventional ways will likely puzzle some readers. I will demonstrate that the multidimensionality that this concept holds for US Women of Color coalition feminists need not trouble us. Arriving at these imaginative concepts, however, is no easy task. To get there, these activist-theorists have also profoundly reshaped how they *do* political theory. To be sure, the unique contribution of US Women of Color coalitional feminism to the study of intersectional coalition politics does not end with its strong appeal to politico-ethical coalitions as the best way to unite diverse subjugated groups working to undermine oppression. While attention to coalition building and coalition politics is perhaps one of the most celebrated aspects of US Women of Color feminism among contemporary political and social theorists interested in progressive group politics (see Burack 2004, 159), the true sophistication in their notion of coalition lies in its multidimensionality. For these authors, coalitions were not simply "indispensable instrumental tools" of minority politics (159). Following Burack (2004), Sandoval (2000), and Townsend-Bell (2012), I will demonstrate that US Women of Color coalitional feminism also functions as a kind of coalitional discourse that not only arrives at coalition as the answer to the progressive politics question provoked by the perceived crisis of Marxism but also enacts a form of *coalitional scholarship*. This new understanding of what is entailed in the very *process of theorizing* coalition has led contemporary scholars such as Townsend-Bell to describe Women of Color feminist anthologies such as *This Bridge Called My Back* as "written" or "textual" coalitions (Townsend-Bell 2012, 130). While attempting to understand a material object such as a book as a "coalition" no doubt poses a hefty set of challenges, to pass off this final formulation of coalition as too strange or less than rigorous would be to miss one of US Women of Color feminism's most important contributions to both contemporary political theory and to contemporary feminist studies.

In order to effectively theorize coalition politics, these authors show that a more collaborative mode of scholarship is absolutely essential. I call this mode of scholarship *coalitional* because it is not just collaborative, it is also unambiguously political and is grounded in an activist and self-reflexive social justice mission. The insights emerging out of this coalitional scholarship and the urgency with which it pushes toward workable and practical solutions provide a stark contrast to the impasses and deadlocks that shape scholarship within dominant strands of contemporary political theory. First, it moves us in the direction of collective and even coalitional conversations as opposed to master narratives that grant authority to a handful of canonical male thinkers and comprehensive rational, or scientific, theories. Across the chapters that follow, I take no one, single theorist as my primary theorist. While I do select certain authors and pieces in order to illustrate certain points, many of the points I make by way of one text or one thinker are echoed across many other texts and authors. Furthermore, the texts I engage here mostly include a range of shorter essays, speeches, stories, poems, streams of consciousness, personal reflections, movement documents, and manifestos written by a range of US Women of Color coalition feminists, and they often appear in anthologies as opposed to single-authored books that attempt to outline a comprehensive theory of collective progressive politics. Much of early US Women of Color coalitional feminism in fact comes to us through anthologies or coauthored articles (see Lugones and Spelman 1983). By their very nature, anthologies create the opportunity for "a print-based collective space" (Norman 2006, 39). When such anthologies also self-reflexively engage the challenge of working across differences and for the sake of undermining interlocking oppressions, then they also have the potential to enact the very coalitions they seek (39). The coalitional discourses activated within these anthologies are overtly political, rooted in an activist social justice mission, and intensely self-reflexive. The authors are aware of the challenges inherent in the coalitional goals they hope to achieve and spend much time—in conversation with one another through printed interviews or explicit references to one another across the pages of the anthology—working toward solutions to the challenge that difference poses to collective intersectional politics. Women of Color feminist anthologies such as Smith's (1983a) *Home Girls*, Hull, Scott, and Smith's (1982) *All the Women Are White, All the Blacks Are Men, But Some of Us Are Brave*, and Moraga and Anzaldúa's (1983a) *This Bridge Called My Back* exemplify this collectively self-reflexive and overtly political character. Many of the authors I engage here (Smith, Moraga, Anzaldúa, and Lorde) were actively involved in bringing these anthologies to print.

Ideas presented in the handful of single-authored texts that I engage have also emerged out of coalitional conversations. For example, the linchpin of Sandoval's (2000) argument in *Methodology of the Oppressed*—which I will position as the bedrock of US Women of Color feminist understandings of coalitional consciousness—was developed in conversation with other Women of Color feminists in 1981 as they collectively reflected on their marginalization within mainstream academic feminism. As secretary to the US Third World feminist consciousness-raising (CR) group, a group that formed within the space of the 1981 NWSA Annual Meeting due to feelings of severe marginalization as women of color within the space of the conference, Sandoval's 1982 report, "Feminism and Racism: A Report on the 1981 National Women's Studies Association Conference," documents, summarizes, and reflects on the proceedings of the conference and the experiences of the US Third World feminist CR group. By assuming the role of "secretary," as opposed to primary "author," of this report, Sandoval places herself in a coalitional conversation with the other women at the conference. As such, she documents, rather than develops, a unique epistemology—or consciousness—of US Third World women that moves unequivocally toward coalition. Though I have never shared a common physical space with all of the Women of Color coalitional feminists whom I engage throughout this book, *Feminism in Coalition* similarly attempts to document the evolving sense of coalition emerging among these authors and texts. Coalition thus operates on two levels across Sandoval's work. The notion of the "methodology of the oppressed" that she develops in her 2000 book not only relies most fundamentally on the coalitional consciousness that is typical of US Women of Color feminism, but the very idea itself emerges out of the coalitional space of the 1981 meetings of the US Third World feminist CR group.

Both Lugones's and Mohanty's single-authored texts continue this trend toward coalitional scholarship. In the preface to *Pilgrimages* (2003), Lugones writes that the book "represents" an "attempt to grasp a thematic" for "many years of theoretical reflection within grass-roots radical political work" (ix). Ultimately, she asserts, the book is the outcome of "shaping ground together" (x). The book is "neither a contemplative, nor a visionary, nor a programmatic work"; instead, it "*takes up, from within, a feel for collectivity*" (ix; my emphasis). Not only will Lugones ultimately arrive at coalition as an indispensable tool for minority group politics, the book itself also attempts to embody many key components of coalitional thinking. It takes concrete encounters with difference as its starting place, and it creatively and collectively thinks through how such differences may provide the basis for collective emancipatory politics. In the introduction to *Feminism without Borders* (2003), Mohanty makes a similar declaration in relation to the collective thinking that went into the production of her book: "While many of the ideas I explore here are viewed through my own particular lenses, all the ideas belong collectively to the various feminist, anti-racist, and anti-imperialist communities in which I have been privileged to be involved. In the end, I think and write in conversation with scholars, teachers, and activists involved in social justice struggles. My search for emancipatory knowledge over the years has made me realize that ideas are always communally wrought, not privately owned" (1). Like Sandoval and Lugones, Mohanty positions her text within a coalitional conversation among Women of Color feminists and other social justice activists who are collectively committed to undermining and resisting interlocking oppressions. Not only is the book fundamentally preoccupied with elaborating visions of feminist political solidarity, but the text itself is born out of "a self-reflexive collective process" (8). Like Sandoval and Lugones, Mohanty thus situates her theoretical contributions as in conversation with, and indebted to, early US Women of Color feminists such as Smith, Lorde, and Reagon (4).

A second component of coalitional scholarship is the propensity to theorize from *within* lived struggle instead of from abstract principles. All the authors that I engage here theorize from within grassroots activist work. It is this experience of struggle, and not a theoretical framework rooted in either rational choice theory or discursive unfixity, that shapes their theory of coalition politics. In so doing, these authors dispense with a certain style of political theory that focuses either on rational argumentation or on poststructuralist tendencies toward discursive unfixity, and instead they favor innovative and creative modes of storytelling, polemical prose, rousing speeches or manifestos, and intensely personal reflections on encountering and working through multiple levels of difference. With this unique methodological approach to political theory, the US Women of Color coalition feminists I *think with* here spend time tracing both individual and group journeys toward coalition. Through such endeavors, the very notion of coalition—that is, of self-reflexively struggling across differences for the sake of a shared political commitment to undermining all forms of oppression—inflects the full life of their work.

These themes also arise in contemporary feminist scholarship on coalition. For instance, in *Wealth of Selves: Multiple Identities, Mestiza Consciousness, and the Subjects of Politics* (2008), Barvosa uses Anzaldúa's unique conception of identity to demonstrate how identity may be reconceived simultaneously as multiple *and* as cohesive and whole (11). Vital to the possibility of feminist alliance, Rowe argues in the same year, is the notion of a "coalitional subject" (2008, 3). Curiously, however, Aimee Carrillo Rowe ultimately turns explicitly to the language of "alliance" in place of "coalition" due to her belief (following Albrecht and Brewer 1990, 304) in its ability to signal a longer lasting and deeper political relationship built on trust. Coalition, on the other hand, is a short-lived and strictly strategic relationship. Following this distinction, Rowe argues that an "alliance analytic" will prove most useful to a project of theorizing possibilities for feminist solidarity and feminist politics (Rowe 2008, 5). My analysis, however, forces the question: Why this turn away from coalition, especially when we already know that Rowe contends that the "coalitional subject" is central to the subject of feminist alliance? My intervention thus departs slightly from Rowe's due to my interest in retaining the language and conceptual purchase of coalition not just as a practical answer to the question of collective progressive politics but also as a sophisticated concept in its own right.

My willingness to hold on to the concept of coalition and to explore it in its more curious adjectival forms is reflected in recent work by Chávez.

To call something "coalitional," Chávez argues in her 2013 book, is to imply an "intermeshed understanding of identity, subjectivity, power, and politics located on the dirt and concrete where people live, work, and play" (7). Absolutely crucial to both concrete coalition politics and coalitional understandings of identity, consciousness, and scholarship, my and Chávez's analyses both contend, is an appreciation of struggling against interlocking oppressions, which also produce what we might call intermeshed (pace Lugones) understandings of identity, power, politics, and subjectivity. Such an understanding accommodates complexity without insisting on fragmentation. Instead, it invokes a sense of wholeness or coherence in complexity and multiplicity. The ability to do this, I am suggesting, along with Chávez, is captured in the adjectival formulation, *coalitional*.

While Rowe, Barvosa, and Chávez all remain open to theorizing notions of subjectivity and consciousness that correspond (and for Rowe and Chávez explicitly so) with the notions of coalitional identity and coalitional consciousness that I will develop here, my analysis pushes *coalitional* into new territory with the notion of coalitional scholarship. Chávez gestures toward this idea in her definition of *coalitional* as involving a type of understanding that one acquires on "the dirt and concrete where people live, work, and play" (2013, 7). Here Chávez advocates "theory in the flesh" (7), drawing from Moraga and Anzaldúa's understanding of the phrase in *This Bridge Called My Back*, as a way in which activists-theorists bring the concrete material experiences of their lived struggles to their writing. Lugones's notions of "pedestrian" and "streetwalker" theorizing accomplish something similar (Lugones 2003, 5, 207–37). The emphasis in both approaches is on the idea of theorizing from below and from within lived struggle. Though overlooked by Chávez here, what is also central to these concepts and is exemplified in Moraga and Anzaldúa's *This Bridge Called My Back* is how such approaches to theory activate a coalitional discourse that becomes the basis of coalitional scholarship.

To return briefly to Rowe's analysis, it seems the notion of coalitional scholarship that I offer here may incline scholars such as Rowe to rethink the value of a "coalition analytic" over an "alliance analytic." The approach to collective politics on offer by early US Women of Color coalitional feminist theory, I will show, was clearly on display in the approach they took to their scholarship in the form of textual coalition. While Chávez, too, is aware of something unique to the way in which Women of Color feminists *do* political theory, my analysis demonstrates that it is worthwhile to actually name this unique methodology "coalitional scholarship" precisely because it points to the creative potential of coalition not only as a thing or practice on the ground (Chávez 2013, 146–47) or as a way of rethinking important related concepts (identity, consciousness) but also as a way of doing political theory. If the notion of politico-ethical coalition politics that I have developed here corresponds with Rowe's understanding of feminist alliance, then why not emphasize the remarkable continuity of thought found within early US Women of Color coalitional feminism by foregrounding the promise of this term, *coalition*? This is precisely what I set out to do.

Outline of Chapters

To accomplish these tasks, the book is staged around four moments of intervention in contemporary political thought that such a *thinking with* provokes, followed, in chapter 5, by an application of lessons learned through these encounters to the 2017 WMW and, in the conclusion, by takeaways for contemporary and future activists. Each of the first four chapters of the book is organized around accomplishing three main tasks, though not always sequentially: (1) presenting a central problematic in contemporary political or feminist theory encouraged by poststructuralist philosophical commitments to ontological unfixity, epistemological undecidability, or political indeterminacy; (2) reengaging the key concepts and components shaping each problematic through the lens of *thinking with*, depending on the chapter, intersectional feminist precursors to US Women of Color coalitional feminism, the key authors and texts from the early decades of the 1970s and 1980s, or other important texts from the 1990s and early 2000s; and finally (3) situating each chapter's conceptual intervention within more recent contemporary feminist scholarship in order to identify both what is unique to early US Women of Color coalitional feminism and how the concepts forged there continue to shape contemporary feminist studies in productive ways. Across these chapters, my intended audience includes both contemporary European/US political theorists as well as contemporary feminist theorists and activists. The work of *thinking with* US Women of Color coalitional feminism to revisit key problematics within contemporary political theory will prove particularly salient to contemporary political theorists who have yet to turn toward US Women of Color coalitional feminism and find themselves grappling with theorizing collective progressive activism beyond the theoretical straitjacket of poststructuralist theoretical influences. The variety of practical politics questions and philosophical puzzles that I explore along the way should be of particular interest to

feminist theorists invested either in celebrating the sophisticated theoretical reflections of early US Women of Color coalitional feminism, or in
critically reexamining trends within contemporary feminist scholarship on
the topics that I explore here—revisiting the subject of feminism through
the conceptual framework of multiple and fluid identity, developing an
intersectional feminist consciousness that might guide collective activism, exploring the relationship between the ethics and politics of feminist
activism, and engaging in activist feminist scholarship. Situating these
interventions within contemporary feminist activism through the case
study of the 2017 WMW and the concluding takeaways will appeal most
directly to feminist, ethnicity, and critical race studies activists interested
in engaging in intersectional collective politics in a contemporary moment
marked by proliferating attacks on intersectional social justice.

   Chapter 1, "From Rosa Luxemburg to the Combahee River Collective:
Spontaneous Coalition as a Precursor to Intersectional Marxism and Politico-
Ethical Coalition Politics," sets out to dissolve the premise of the so-called
crisis of post-Marxist collective politics (what I call the intersectionality crisis)
by putting Rosa Luxemburg's version of Marxism, as presented in "The Mass
Strike, the Political Party, and the Trade Unions" (1906), in conversation
with a genealogy of US Women of Color feminists beginning with Maria
Stewart in the first half of the nineteenth century and continuing through
Combahee and the TWWA. Both of these 1960s and 1970s Women of Color
feminist activist groups—Combahee in their "Black Feminist Statement"
(1977) and the TWWA in their *Black Woman's Manifesto* (compiled in the
late 1960s–1970)—and the lineage that came before them display a commitment to what contemporary scholars such as Bohrer understand as
intersectional Marxism. Such a commitment, I will show, might be productively read as a conceptual precursor to the notion of politico-ethical coalition politics emerging in the 1970s and 1980s. The problematic introduced
here is Laclau and Mouffe's starting place, namely, the assumption that
attention to intersectional social justice struggles and Marxism is necessarily
incompatible. By *thinking with* Combahee and the TWWA about Marxism,
we find that the version of Marxism that precipitates Laclau and Mouffe's
crisis is that of Vladimir Lenin. When putting Combahee, the TWWA, and
a genealogy of US Women of Color feminism in conversation with Luxemburg, we find that Lenin's rigid scientific socialism, which relies on Communists to shape the proletariat's class consciousness and corresponding
politics, might be replaced with a theory of spontaneous coalition politics
that emerges neither out of the precision of natural science (pace Lenin)

nor out of the morass of theories of discursive unfixity (pace Laclau and Mouffe) but instead out of the school of lived struggle.

Luxemburg's approach to Marxism was unique in her insistence that workers living and working in oppressive conditions would develop their own sophisticated understanding of oppression. It was this political consciousness, she insists, and not one imparted on them by school masters or party leaders, that would guide their activist efforts (Luxemburg 2004a). It is on this methodological point—theorizing from *within* lived struggle—that a fruitful conversation between Luxemburg and Women of Color feminist activists might begin. Though Luxemburg does not explicitly advocate an approach that could be called "intersectional," when reading her emphasis on theorizing from inside a space of lived struggle alongside Stewart, Truth, Ida B. Wells-Barnett, Combahee, and the TWWA, an *intersectional wedge* is opened in Marxism that not only dissolves the crisis of post-Marxist collective politics but also sets the stage for a theory of spontaneous though nevertheless united and directed coalition politics equipped to take on intersectional social justice concerns.

Building on the notion of intersectional Marxism developed in chapter 1, chapter 2, "Women of Color Feminism and Politico-Ethical Coalition Politics: Recentering the Politics of Coalition with Reagon, Smith, Combahee, and Lorde," develops the key components of "politico-ethical coalition politics" by thinking again with Combahee and with Reagon's 1981 coalition speech; Chisholm's 1972 article; the collection of essays, poems, stories, letters, speeches, and polemical appeals appearing across Lorde's 1984 work, *Sister Outsider*; and a selection of early 1980s pieces by Smith. The problematic explored here is the tendency among contemporary scholars such as Butler and those influenced by her work to obscure the politics that demand and situate coalitional activism in favor either of ontological disruption (in the form of *coalition as spectacle*) or ethical community (in the form of *coalition as ethical community*). In both formulations, the politics of coalition fades from view as attention either to antifoundational and politically indeterminate group spectacle or to apolitical and naively optimistic aspirations to ethical community takes center stage.

After outlining this problematic, the chapter proceeds to *think with* early US Women of Color coalition feminists in order to develop a theory of politico-ethical coalition politics that recenters the politics of coalition through three distinguishing features: an emphasis on coalition as a dangerous and even life-threatening *struggle*; an understanding that coalition is generated out of a shared *self-reflexive political commitment* to undermining oppression; and an emphasis on *existential transformation* as inherent to the very process of coalescing. Turning to Reagon's speech, the chapter soberly confronts the very real challenge of intersectional coalitional activism, an endeavor that Women of Color feminists insist is marked by continuous *struggle*. Such an emphasis, I will show, immediately calls into question naive aspirations on the part of Butler and other contemporary authors to a shared ethical orientation as the cementing force behind coalition efforts. I make this argument by resituating Reagon's oft-cited coalition speech outside of contemporary misinterpretations of this text that read into it an ethical orientation toward receptive generosity (see Coles 1996). By putting Reagon in conversation with her contemporaries, I reveal, instead, a nascent theory of coalition as politico-ethical encounter. While Romand Coles reads an ethical orientation in Reagon as the cementing force behind coalition politics, I instead read a *self-reflexive* political commitment to undermining all forms of oppression, and particularly those that emerge within coalitional spaces, as the cementing force behind coalition politics.

As I demonstrate across the chapter, thinking with early US Women of Color coalition feminists about coalition politics helps us to think differently about the conundrums shaping both of Butler's formulations of coalition politics. Unlike Butler's formulation of coalition as spectacle, Reagon, Smith, Lorde, and others show us that coalitional activism is uniquely *political* insofar as it foregrounds the decidable and goal-oriented politics of coalitional activism rooted in a shared political commitment to undermining interlocking oppressive forces. Unlike Butler's formulation of coalition as ethical community, it further reveals the important ethical dimension of coalition work without letting it eclipse the political basis of coalitional activism. This unique relationship between politics and ethics resonates across contemporary feminist engagements with questions of feminist alliance and solidarity. By contrasting arguments made by Mohanty in *Feminism without Borders* and taken up by authors in the *New Political Science* "Feminism in Coalition" symposium (2018),[5] with Butler's recent lectures on the topic, Puar's work on assemblage theory, and *Theory and Event*'s special CLASSE issue, I show the continued salience of politico-ethical coalition politics to contemporary political theory and feminist studies, while warning against a trend that moves decisively away from intersectionality and toward poststructuralist philosophical reflections on difference.

Chapter 3, "Coalition from the Inside Out: Struggling toward Coalition Identity and Developing Coalitional Consciousness with Lorde, Anzaldúa, Sandoval, and Pratt," grounds politico-ethical coalition politics in coalitional understandings of identity and consciousness that accommodate multiplicity and fluidity while resisting ontological unfixity and epistemological unde-cidability, thus presenting two more instructive concepts emerging out of this literature and introducing the third key component of politico-ethical coalition politics: an insistence on opening oneself to *self-transformation* as part and parcel to the process of coalescing. In relation to developing a notion of *coalitional identity*, the problem confronted is the philosophi-cal straitjacket of ontological unfixity, which has led Butler, Moya Lloyd, Diana Fuss, Puar, and many others to the complete disavowal of any form of identity-based group politics and to the outright dismissal of Women of Color feminists who seek to recuperate some notion of identity-based group action.

Offering a useful alternative to theorizations of the subject-in-process rooted in permanent discursive unfixity, the chapter seeks to celebrate the distinct advantages of an identity-based group politics, especially when "identity" is reconceived in coalitional terms. Returning to Lorde's *Sister Outsider* (1984f) and putting her in conversation with Anzaldúa's influential *Borderlands/La Frontera: The New Mestiza* (1987), Carmen Vázquez's account of working in a multiracial women's coalition in San Francisco in the 1980s (captured in Carastathis 2013), Combahee's nuanced rendering of identity politics in their 1977 "Black Feminist Statement," Mohanty's (1991) and Alcoff's (1997) brilliant treatments of such nuances in their discussions of positionality in the 1990s, and more recent work by Carastathis (2013), the chapter revisits questions centering on critiques of monolithic understand-ings of identity categories and the extent to which a more fluid conception of identity might nevertheless provide a basis for effective intersectional coalition politics. By thinking with a genealogy of US Women of Color coalitional feminism beginning with the early pivotal texts in the 1970s and 1980s and continuing with texts produced throughout the next three decades, the chapter develops a notion of *coalitional identity* conceived as an internal political process, or struggle, toward ontological wholeness that mirrors the external political process of struggling across difference that is required for successful politico-ethical coalition politics for these activist-theorists.

The chapter thus challenges contemporary engagements with Anzaldúa presented by feminist thinkers such as Cristina Beltrán (2004), wherein Anzaldúa's willingness to challenge unfixity is scrutinized. While Beltrán is reluctant to concede that a mestiza might have a special role to play in guiding collective politics due to her position as a border woman, I argue that it is precisely her unique ontological existence as a coalitional self that positions her and other Women of Color feminist activist-theorists from this period as our most promising guides in Trump's United States. When understanding identity in coalitional terms, we begin to appreciate how a focus on identity might lead us in the direction of critical self-awareness rather than essentialist identity politics.

In relation to developing a notion of coalitional consciousness, the problem confronted in the second half of the chapter builds from the epistemological "crisis" of Marxism. While Laclau and Mouffe's impetus in theorizing the social world as "unfixed" rests on their desire to avoid the epistemological decidability characteristic of Lenin's Marxism in the form of scientific socialism and top-down party politics, contemporary attempts to maneuver outside of this rigidity struggle to move away from bird's-eye view theorizing. Exemplary here is Deleuze and Guattari's theory of diagramming minoritarian becomings. Deleuze and Guattari break the rigidity of Lenin's scientific socialism through their account of the social world as a "machine assemblage" wherein the movement of oppression and groups existing within society follows a fluid rhizomatic, rather than arborescent, formation (Deleuze and Guattari 1987, 140, 358–61). Despite this injection of fluidity and movement into previously rigid and striated understandings of oppression and society, they nevertheless adopt a bird's-eye view of the social that, while it will not, in this case, *pre*scribe political activism in the way it did for Lenin, it is nevertheless locked into *de*scribing the fluid movements of collective group resistance as they unfold from a removed (bird's-eye view) perspective. While this move toward diagramming minoritarian resistances accommodates the smooth space of intermeshed and mobile forces of oppression, it is ill-equipped to guide coalitional activism. Politics here assumes a descriptive mode of mapping oppression and group resistance from above and after the fact, rather than attempting to prescribe the creation of future coalitional disturbances.

By putting Anzaldúa's conception of mestiza consciousness in conversation with Sandoval's articulation of "oppositional consciousness" and Lugones's conceptualization of "pedestrian theorizing," this chapter goes on to develop an account of mapping oppression that tactically *prescribes* collective political action without falling into a top-down approach. Specifically, recalling Luxemburg's approach to Marxism, it explores the possibility of theorizing oppression from *within* oppression through the notion of *coalitional consciousness*: a tactical epistemological awareness and acuity for navigating complex and fluid (though nevertheless identifiable) social systems of oppression and assuming tactical collective political subjectivities for the sake of collective group action. I'm indebted to both Sandoval (2000, 71) and Keating (2005) for their uses of the phrase "coalitional consciousness." In thinking especially with Sandoval here (I think more directly with Keating in the conclusion), I show that US Women of Color coalition feminists such as Anzaldúa, Vázquez, and others acquire this unique mode of understanding through the process of internal struggle toward coalitional identity. The skills they procure by navigating their own coalitional identities and struggling toward ontological wholeness as coalitional selves not only prepares them for the difficult work of coalition politics with other subjugated peoples and across, at times, conflicting or hostile differences but also equips them to practice prescriptive coalition politics from a collective position from *within* the map.

To return briefly to Beltrán's criticism of Anzaldúa (Beltrán 2004), this chapter therefore clarifies that the reason the unique coalitional consciousness of Anzaldúa and other "border women" might be valuable to collective organizing is not rooted in facile understandings of "standpoint" theory that treat Anzaldúa as possessing "right" or more "accurate" epistemology but in the practical know-how she has acquired through the process of "traveling," in Lugones's (1987) sense of the word, across her multiple identities and positionalities. Such journeys equip her and other women of color to engage in effective coalitional activism. As such, thinking with Anzaldúa, Sandoval, Lugones, and Vázquez, I will show, helps us to see how embracing fluidity and movement in our depiction of power and oppression does not necessarily wed us to a diagrammatic mode of descriptive politics. By theorizing from within the map, we avoid the dangers of bird's-eye view theorizing while still elaborating a decidable epistemology that might guide a politically fluid yet determinate form of coalitional activism. By turning in the final pages to Pratt's autobiographical essay, "Identity: Skin Blood Heart" (1984), in which she recounts her own coming to consciousness (as a white, Southern, Christian, middle-class lesbian woman), the chapter demonstrates that coalitional identity and coalitional consciousness are not capacities reserved only for nonwhite women. On the contrary, it argues that white people interested in engaging in politico-ethical coalition politics and taking seriously the task of confronting "white privilege" can and must develop these capacities (a theme I return to in chapter 5).

Chapter 4, "Writing Feminist Theory, Doing Feminist Politics: Rethinking Collective Feminist Authorship with *This Bridge Called My Back*," presents a uniquely "coalitional" way of engaging in feminist political theory distinctive to the Black and Women of Color feminist anthologies emerging in the early 1980s (though containing pieces written or delivered in the 1970s). The collaborative, unambiguously political, and intensely self-reflexive collective authorship practices of Women of Color feminists in this period such as Smith, Scott, Hull, Moraga, and Anzaldúa usher in promising alternatives to the problematic feminist collective authorship models offered in the decades immediately before and after the 1980s. Specifically, the chapter presents Moraga and Anzaldúa's coedited anthology, *This Bridge Called My Back*, as an exemplary depiction of *coalitional scholarship* insofar as it both arrives at and enacts politico-ethical coalition politics in the form of "textual" or "written" coalition. I'm indebted here to Burack and Townsend-Bell for their uses of phrases such as "coalitional discourse" (Burack 2004, 159) and "written" or "textual" coalitions (Townsend-Bell 2012, 130, 133, 144–45). It was in thinking with these formulations that I developed the notion of co-alitional scholarship, and it is precisely this mode of collective authorship, the chapter contends, that enables US Women of Color feminism to arrive at a politico-ethical understanding of coalition politics.

The chapter makes this argument by juxtaposing *This Bridge Called My Back* with two other groundbreaking attempts at collective feminist scholar-ship: Robin Morgan's 1970 anthology, *Sisterhood Is Powerful: An Anthology of Writings from the Women's Liberation Movement*, and Rebecca Walker's 1995 anthology, *To Be Real: Telling the Truth and Changing the Face of Feminism*. Insofar as feminist anthologies are thought to enact the collectivity for which they call, this juxtaposition reveals the danger in relying on either *ethical* notions of textual "sisterhood" (as found in *Sisterhood Is Powerful*), or *ontological* visions of lifestyle feminism in the form of textual mosaic (as found in *To Be Real*), as the cementing force behind social justice coali-tion politics. Only *This Bridge Called My Back*, I argue, emerges as a truly coalitional text, thus deepening the diverse ways in which the concept of coalition operates across this period and offering a creative alternative to problematic forms of single- and collective-authorship models dominant in political and certain feminist theory circles.

If feminist political theory is now moving unequivocally in the direction of coalition, which I contend that it is, then theorists interested in theo-rizing coalitional possibilities would do well to embrace new, coalitional, ways of thinking. By turning to more recent experiments with coalitional modes of engaging in collective scholarship, such as that undertaken by the Sangtin Writers and Richa Nagar in *Playing with Fire: Feminist Thought and Activism through Seven Lives in India* (2006), the chapter ends by demonstrating the continued relevance of the unique scholarly practices of early US Women of Color coalitional feminism. In my view, the concept of politico-ethical coalition politics is not only an improvement on other contemporary attempts to theorize Left-oriented intersectional politics insofar as it exposes the myth of the crisis of Marxism and effectively dissolves the tension between unfixity and fixity, but it also encourages this kind of methodological rethinking.

Chapter 5, "The Women's March on Washington and Politico-Ethical Coalitional Opportunities in the Age of Trump," turns to a practical application of the constellation of concepts developed in the first four chapters of the book. Specifically, it argues that the 2017 WMW offers a compelling account of the promise of politico-ethical coalition politics in the contemporary United States. At a time when the undiscriminating hatred politics of the Trump administration demands a united front to stand in opposition to a variety of oppressive policies and rhetoric, the post-Marxist challenge of re-envisioning progressive group politics outside of class-only, women-only, Black-only, and so on identity politics seems ever more pressing. On this front, contemporary scholars and activists have much to learn from the savvy coalitional strategies of early US Women of Color coalitional feminism, many of which were utilized to shape the core unity principles of the 2017 WMW. Rooted in a clear political commitment to undermining interlocking oppressions and driven by a critical self-awareness of the potentially oppressive and exclusionary internal dynamics that have haunted feminist organizing since the 1960s, the 2017 WMW national team succeeded in putting effective politico-ethical coalitional organizing into practice. Rather than speaking to the impossibility of realizing intersectional political commitments on a mass scale, the various controversies surrounding the march that erupted across news platforms in the weeks leading up to and in the months following the march reflect the strength of a coalitional strategy rooted in struggle, self-reflexive political commitment, and existential transformation. The one misstep of the march was the ontological entrapment staged by centering "women" in the chosen name for the march. Doing so muddled the clarity and blunted the strength of the message of self-reflexive political commitment otherwise espoused in the unity principles and statements coming from the core national team. It is precisely such a dogged political commitment that is urgently needed for progressive intersectional activism in an age of increasingly hostile race relations, persistent economic precarity, and emboldened misogyny.

In the conclusion, I consolidate lessons learned and takeaways for practical next steps on how to unite across difference for the sake of intersectional social justice struggles. In the spirit of the central political, philosophical, ethical, and scholarly orientations presented and celebrated across the book, my final remarks are deeply textured by the most recent insights of some of the earliest theorists of US Women of Color coalitional feminism, including Barbara Smith, Chandra Mohanty, Minnie Bruce Pratt, Angela Davis, María Lugones, and Cherríe Moraga, as well as by some of their contemporary fellow travelers, most prominently Keeanga-Yamahtta Taylor, Cricket Keating, and Sara Ahmed.

1

From Rosa Luxemburg to the Combahee River Collective

Spontaneous Coalition as a Precursor to Intersectional Marxism and Politico-Ethical Coalition Politics

In a recent interview with Keeanga-Yamahtta Taylor, Barbara Smith, one of the cofounders of the Combahee River Collective (Combahee)—a Black feminist lesbian group active in Boston from 1974 to 1980—reflects on why the Black feminism shaping the politics of Combahee remains valuable to contemporary social justice struggles forty years after Combahee's original founding. In so doing, she cites their socialist and anticapitalist origins. One would expect, she explains, a Black feminist group to be both anti-racist and opposed to sexism; what gave them their edge, thoroughness, and timeless relevance, she asserts, was their anticapitalist commitments. Indeed, for all of the founders interviewed for Taylor's edited book, *How We Get Free: Black Feminism and the Combahee River Collective*, the unique oppression experienced by Black women (and men) was firmly rooted in capitalism. As the founders explicitly state in Combahee's "Black Feminist Statement": "We realize that the liberation of all oppressed peoples necessitates the destruction of the political-economic systems of capitalism and imperialism as well as patriarchy. We are socialist because we believe the work must be orga-nized for the collective benefit of those who do the work and create the products, and not for the profit of the bosses" (Combahee 1983, 213). As we learn in their accounts of what brought them to activism and precipitated the founding of Combahee, all three—Barbara Smith, Beverly Smith, and Demita Frazier—found their way to Black feminist politics through a close engagement with and a commitment to Marxism (K.-Y. Taylor 2017, 6–7).[1] However, and as was the case with their engagement with other movements of the time (civil rights, women's liberation, and Black nationalism), they found Marxism limited as an analytical framework insofar as it failed to examine the intersection of race, class, and patriarchy. Sexual politics, they asserted, is just as pervasive in the lives of Black women as is the politics of race and class, leading them to insist that a "socialist revolution that is not also a feminist and anti-racist revolution will [fail to] guarantee [their] liberation," clarifying that while they are in "essential agreement with Marx's theory as it applied to the very specific economic relationships he analyzed ... his analysis must be extended further in order ... to understand [the] specific economic situation [of] Black women" (Combahee 1983, 213).

Thus, despite their critical awareness of the limitations of a Marxist analytic, the Black feminist politics of Combahee is best understood as an extension of, rather than a departure from, Marxism (K.-Y. Taylor 2017, 6–7; Bohrer 2019, 72–74). Smith reports that Combahee's best feminist allies were always the socialist feminists (Smith in K.-Y. Taylor 2017, 50). She also insists that it is the centrality of anticapitalism that makes the Black feminism of Combahee a powerful and relevant framework for social justice activism today. While most readers of the Combahee statement will cite it as an important text establishing the usefulness of identity politics or as a precursor to intersectionality, Smith invites us in another direction, specifically to consider how the politics of Combahee reflects a firm com-mitment to what we might understand as *intersectional Marxism*—that is, a version of Marxism that attends to multiple, intersecting, and mutu-ally reinforcing forms of oppression. Such a claim resonates with Ashley Bohrer's recent argument in *Marxism and Intersectionality: Race, Gender, Class, and Sexuality under Contemporary Capitalism* (2019). By tracing the shared history of Marxist and intersectionality traditions, Bohrer argues that "race, class, sexuality, and gender are completely inseparable systems" (16) and that Black women Communists, as well as other intersectionality activist-theorists, have been attentive to how capitalism is complicit in and structured by multiple interlocking oppressive forces since as least as early as an 1833 speech delivered by Maria Stewart, the first Black woman to lecture publicly about politics in the United States (Bohrer 2019, 37).

I find this juxtaposition between intersectionality and Marxism thought provoking, especially when positioned against the first layer of Ernesto Laclau and Chantal Mouffe's crisis of post-Marxist collective organizing. In the wake of the civil rights, women's liberation, and peace and environmental movements, Laclau and Mouffe concede that progressives must relinquish class as the articulatory core of Left politics (1985, 2). However, letting go of this category, they insist, throws Left politics into crisis. The first layer of the multilayer crisis they speak of, then, centers primarily on the challenge that intersectional social justice struggles pose to a unified Left-oriented politics. Understood this way, we are led to wonder whether "intersectional" Marxism is even possible. Marxism is often thought to be singularly focused on class as the articulatory core of progressive collective politics. Can Marxism then provide a useful analytic for the intersectional group politics that are demanded by the "surplus of the social" (1)? I believe it can, but it matters very much which tradition of Marxism we look to when making this pairing.

For the founders of Combahee there was never any crisis at all. Their intersectional commitments and their Marxist commitments were clear and congruous from the start. As they put it, all that was required was an extension of Marxism, not an abandonment of Marxism. Combahee's unproblematic commitments to both Marxism and intersectionality are best thought of as the logical *outcome* of an intersectional Marxist trajectory that has gone largely unnoticed, at least until the publication of Bohrer's 2019 book. Specifically, when contemporary political theorists such as Laclau and Mouffe have attempted to theorize progressive collective politics outside the category of class, they have done so against the backdrop of a *perceived* rather than an *actual* crisis of Marxism. The purpose of this chapter is to critically interrogate this backdrop through an examination of the varied Marxist theories of progressive coalition politics on offer by Vladimir Lenin and Rosa Luxemburg in an attempt to locate a version of Marxist coalition politics that might dissolve this crisis. I locate such a version in Luxemburg's theory of spontaneity and argue that the smooth juxtaposition between Combahee's intersectional and Marxist commitments is easily explained when appropriately positioned within this trajectory.

To fully understand the nuances of this trajectory, let us return briefly to Laclau and Mouffe. While they name the "surplus of the social" and the "proliferation of struggles" as the impetus for the crisis of Marxism (1985, 1), we would be remiss to assume that their only or primary concern had to do with the potential messiness of group politics of multiple subjugated groups. As Romand Coles has noted, their practical politics concern must be understood alongside their neo-Nietzschean philosophical commitments (1996, 375). The crisis of Marxism for Laclau and Mouffe is best understood as playing out on four levels. The challenge of intersectional Marxist politics (the first layer of the crisis) is shaped by coinciding ontological (second layer), epistemological (third layer), and political crises (fourth layer). Ontologically, this crisis is rooted in the "surplus of the social" that Laclau and Mouffe argue is brought on not just by the presence of many different subjugated groups all fighting for social justice but rather by the "discursive unfixity" of all social categories due to their production in and through ongoing and infinitely unstable linguistic forces (1985, x, 85). The epistemological component of the crisis is rooted in the "structural undecidability" that discursive unfixity is thought to engender once binary antagonisms are complicated by unstable identity categories (x–xii, 1–4). Politically, the crisis is rooted not just in the messiness of intersectional group politics but in the perceived political *indeterminacy* that is thought to result.

In an attempt to avoid the political impasse of this crisis and through an engagement with Louis Althusser and Antonio Gramsci, Laclau and Mouffe develop a notion of what I will call *coalition as Left hegemony*, wherein coalition politics takes the form of "hegemonic articulation" (1985, 7). Their intention is to move beyond a narrow Marxist class politics and to describe a form of collective Left politics that incorporates the "proliferation of struggles" (1) characteristic of their contemporary moment while avoiding the crisis of Marxism. A "hegemonic relation" emerges, they tell us, when a "set of particularities"—social actors occupying different positions "within the discourses that constitute the social fabric"—establishes "relations of equivalence between themselves" vis-à-vis oppressive forces, and then one of those particularities succeeds in representing the "totality of the chain" (xiii). Different particularities separately concentrating on, say, race, class, or gender, see the equivalences in their struggles and come together around one of those particularities. The creation of this "chain of equivalence among the various democratic struggles against different forms of subordination" provides the basis for their theory of coalition in the form of Left hegemony (xviii).[2] Laclau and Mouffe thus converge with activists and theorists in their shift toward coalition politics as the most viable way forward for post-Marxist progressive group politics. However, this progressive political project rests on enormously complicated philosophical terrain that results in a number of inconsistencies. First, despite their professed commitment to move completely away from fixed identity as the articulatory core of collective progressive politics, their notion of hegemonic articulation retreats, in the final instance, to fixed hegemonic identity as the basis of collective politics. Second and even more puzzling, despite their willingness to retreat ultimately to *fixed* identity—which is particularly mystifying given their strong commitments to ontological *unfixity* (Laclau and Mouffe 1985, 85, 128, 170, 176) and epistemological *undecidability* (144, 152, 186)—their philosophical commitment to *unfixity* reemerges in their so-called Left-oriented politics when they insist that the political direction of a "Leftist" hegemony (their version of a Left-oriented coalition) remains politically *indeterminate*. (I purposefully placed *Leftist* in scare quotes above due to the uncertainty they are introducing in relation to what it means to adopt a *Left*-oriented politics.)

Before exploring these inconsistencies, the chapter begins by exposing the rigidity of Lenin's version of scientific socialism as the basis for the perceived crisis of Marxism articulated by Laclau and Mouffe. It is only Lenin's version of Marxism that precipitates a "crisis." I then take up a critical examination of the philosophical inconsistencies that accompany Laclau and Mouffe's attempt to get around this crisis through a conception of progressive coalition politics in the form of Left hegemony. Often overlooked by contemporary coalition theorists, Luxemburg's version of Marxist coalition politics in the form of spontaneous worker's coalitions is offered as an alternative both to Lenin and to Laclau and Mouffe. In contrasting Luxemburg's Marxism with Lenin's, I aim to reveal a less rigid version of Marxist ontology, epistemology, and politics that succeeds in both breaking the ontological and epistemological rigidity of Lenin's Marxism and avoiding the perceived crisis of Marxism, while also avoiding the political indeterminacy and philosophical contradictions of coalition in the form of Left hegemony. Luxemburg does his by replacing Lenin's rigid *scientific* materialism with a supple version of *dialectical* materialism that emerges out of the school of lived struggle and shapes a spontaneous form of proletarian coalition politics.

On this methodological point we might begin a fruitful conversation between Luxemburg and US Women of Color feminism. Luxemburg's approach to Marxism was unique in its insistence that workers living and working in oppressive conditions would develop their own sophisticated understanding of oppression. It was this political consciousness, she insisted, and not one imparted to them by school masters or party leaders, that would guide their activist efforts. Though Luxemburg does not explicitly advocate an approach that can be called "intersectional," when reading her emphasis on theorizing from inside a space of lived struggle alongside works by early Black intersectional feminists as well as by Combahee and the Third World Women's Alliance (TWWA), an *intersectional wedge* is opened in Marxism that not only dissolves the "crisis" of post-Marxist collective politics but also sets the stage for a politically *determinate* form of progressive coalition politics that is equipped to take on intersectional social justice concerns.

Precipitating a Crisis: Lenin's Scientific Socialism

The best example of the *rigid* aspect of Marxist theory can be seen in Lenin's version of scientific socialism.[3] Marxist theory, for Lenin, involves not only an understanding and acceptance of the social ontology of class antagonism (the ontological component) but also a strict scientific materialism (the epistemological component) that ultimately requires the adoption of Communist ideology (the political component) rooted in strict and uncompromising goals: to abolish the bourgeois state and bourgeois property (see Lenin 1978, 8–9, 20–23). I aim to capture the ontological, epistemological, and political components in the phrase *scientific socialism*.

The ontological component of scientific socialism reduces to the notion that oppression in society manifests in a rigid class binary between the oppressed (the proletariat) and the oppressors (the bourgeoisie). Lenin takes this idea directly from Marx. As Marx states in the preface of *A Contribution to the Critique of Political Economy*, the "anatomy" of "civil society" must be "sought in political economy" (Marx 1970, 20). The economic structure, which we may come to understand through the study of political economy, determines all relations in civil society. Marx is uncompromising on this point. This strict social ontology is, as he puts it, the "guiding principle" of his studies (20). According to Marx, "the *economic structure* of society," made up of the totality of relations of production, is the "real foundation" of human society. The "legal and political superstructure," which determines forms of "social consciousness," arises from this base (20; my emphasis). Quite simply, the base determines the superstructure. Any change in the economic structure will lead to "transformation of the whole immense superstructure" (21). As such, all relations in society, including relations of oppression, are fixed by the economic structure. The current manifestation of the economic structure at the time that Marx and Friedrich Engels wrote *The Communist Manifesto* (industrialized capitalism) generated a specific form of class antagonism: one wherein the bourgeoise emerged as the oppressor class and the proletariat emerged as the oppressed class (see Marx and Engels 2004, 158–69). Any other forms of oppression appearing in society were thought to originate in this fundamental class antagonism.

This rigid social ontology—that the social world is determined or *fixed* by economic modes of production and results in a fundamental class antagonism—is informed, according to Lenin's interpretation of Marx, by an equally rigid scientific epistemology, scientific materialism. As Marx suggests, because the economic structure determines the superstructure, the only way to understand, evaluate, or examine society is by turning to the material conditions that determine relations of production (1970, 20). Any transformation of these material conditions, he insists, can be explained scientifically insofar as they follow certain rules of "natural science" (21). These scientific rules also determine corresponding "ideological" transformations—that is, transformations of the legal, political, religious, artistic, or philosophic forms by which people become conscious of and fight the conflict arising from these material conditions. Even something as immaterial as "consciousness," we find, is determined by the material conditions of life (21). Strict rules of natural science therefore determine social ontology, consciousness, ideology, and politics.

This scientific materialist approach is a historical approach insofar as Marx and Engels maintain that these scientific material conditions can be identified and understood only through extensive historical analysis. They outline this history in the first section of *The Communist Manifesto*, arguing that the material conditions that determine social existence are those of class antagonism, manifested in a variety of relations throughout history: between "freeman and slave, patrician and plebian, lord and serf, guild-master and journeyman, in short, oppressor and oppressed" (Marx and Engels 2004, 62). "The history of all society hitherto," they conclude, "is the history of class struggle" (62). Thus, Marxism according to Lenin, as a scientific and materialist methodology (expressed in historical materialism), does not rely on utopian experiments or abstract speculation (Lenin 1978, 35–36); it relies on learning, scientifically, from experience. And specifically, it is invested in empirically examining the "process of natural history" through "the *birth* of the new society *from* the old" (42); in short, it examines the dialectical evolution of Communism from capitalism (70).

In addition to scientifically knowing its origin, Lenin's take on Marxist epistemology (his reading of the Marxist dialectic) allows for scientific knowledge also of the direction this evolutionary process *will* take—toward inevitable collapse, out of which Communism *will* be born (Lenin 1978, 71).

In this way, Lenin's reading of the dialectic falls on the side of certainty. Not only is the final end, or telos, known—Communism—but the material conditions of the transition period, manifested in the temporary revolutionary dictatorship of the proletariat, are also known (73). However, while Lenin's version of scientific materialism insists that the current manifestation of class antagonism is knowable through scientific precision, he is adamant that only certain people are capable of acquiring this scientific understanding. Indeed, Lenin insists that this dialectical process will not necessarily move in the "right" direction unless the Communist Party directs it there. Because party leaders have a clear understanding of society and the forces that shape it, they know with scientific certainty in which direction this unfolding must go, thus setting the stage for rigid scientific socialism.

Lenin's version of scientific socialism is thus premised not only on a rigid understanding of Marxist ontology—that is, the *existence* of the necessarily oppressive relationship between the proletariat and the bourgeoisie under modern capitalist modes of production—it also depends on an equally rigid understanding of Marxist epistemology in the form of scientific materialism, wherein true "scientific understanding" is acquired only by the Party leaders and not by the workers. Indeed, Lenin insists that whereas Communists acquire *scientific understanding*, workers only ever arrive at *spontaneous sensing*. What fundamentally distinguishes a Communist epistemology from a workers' epistemology is the "theorizing edge" acquired by the Communists (Marx and Engels 2004, 74). Whereas the "social" consciousness of workers is marked by a "sense of" class antagonism, the "political" consciousness of Communists is marked by a "theorizing edge," or a scientific understanding not only of the class antagonism between the proletariat and the bourgeoisie but of historical materialism as a scientific process of class antagonism, an ideological commitment to abolish bourgeois private property, and a practical know-how in terms of leading a political movement (Marx and Engels 2004, 74; Lenin 1975, 24–25). Lenin thus contrasts a *social* epistemology of the workers—their "sense" of the antagonistic social relationship between workers and employers—with a *political* epistemology of the Russian Social Democrats—their "understanding" of the base-superstructure dialectic, what Lenin calls "scientific socialism" (Tucker 1975, 24–25).

Real politics in the form of scientific socialism, for Lenin, involves scientific strategic planning, not spontaneous, unplanned, or haphazard reaction. Though workers are capable of staging "spontaneous" struggles and revolts on their own, a clear Communist consciousness does not guide these actions. It appears only in its nascent or "embryonic" form there (Tucker 1975, 24).

Lenin follows Karl Kautsky in maintaining that true consciousness arises only out of "scientific knowledge," and as such, any true "consciousness" of the proletarian workers must be introduced to them "from without" (Kautsky in Tucker 1975, 28). It cannot, they both assert, arise from within spontaneously. Without consciousness, there is no ideology; without ideology, there is no politics. According to Lenin, the workers are not capable of true party consciousness or real politics; they are only ever involved in "spontaneous" movement. As such, Lenin's understanding of politics is as equally rigid as his understanding of ontology and epistemology. The only form of *coalition* politics permitted in Lenin's version of scientific socialism is one wherein the Communist Party chooses to temporarily align with other struggling groups. In such instances, Lenin's approach to coalition politics remains rigid in its purpose and direction but flexible in the "tactics" used to achieve these goals—that is, open to altering tactics on the ground and working with other groups depending on shifting circumstances (Marx in Tucker 1975, 78, 81). Thus, while an element of flexibility emerges in Lenin's understanding of tactics, this flexibility is always in the service of rigid party dogma. Lenin's emphasis on shaping workers' class consciousness from without and denigrating spontaneous workers' demonstrations, we will see shortly, contrasts sharply with Luxemburg's emphasis on political consciousness emerging out of the lived struggle of the workers.

An Unworkable Solution: Laclau and Mouffe's Coalition as Left Hegemony

When Laclau and Mouffe speak of the rigidity of Marxist thinking that has created a crisis of Marxist collective politics, I believe it is Lenin's version of Marxism that they have in mind. As one might expect, Laclau and Mouffe's alternative approach to collective Left politics attempts to break the rigidity of Lenin's Marxism, and they do this by appealing to the notion of discursive unfixity (Laclau and Mouffe 1985, x). Laclau and Mouffe turn to the "Althusserian complexity" inherent in the process of "overdetermination" in order to outline a picture of ontological *unfixity* (97). Following Althusser, they maintain that "everything existing in the social is overdetermined," because the "social constructs itself as a symbolic order" (97). By this, they mean that because all categories and identities are constructed symbolically through language—the category "class," for instance, gains meaning only in a particular historical location that has attributed certain meanings to it through language—they are always in the process of potentially changing meaning.

The state of something being infinitely open to new meaning, according to Laclau and Mouffe, is the same as being "overdetermined" in language. According to them, once we accept that categories and social relations are "symbolic" and therefore "overdetermined," we necessarily also accept their discursive unfixity (97). Unlike the Marxist base-superstructure logic, the logic of overdetermination is rooted in a "critique of every type of fixity, through an affirmation of the incomplete, open and politically negotiable character of every identity" (104). This would suggest that we can no longer rely on categories such as "women" or "workers" to unite us in political action precisely because these categories are already overdetermined—meaning there is no way to know in advance the content of these categories because the meaning is constantly evolving through language. Only "'mythical' fixations" of a determinate social ontology emerge, and such fixations, they argue, depend on political struggle (41–42).

Understanding all social categories as "symbolic" or "overdetermined," they believe, necessarily inserts an element of undecidability into the base-superstructure model that loosens the rigidity of Marxist ontology, epistemology, and politics (Laclau and Mouffe 1985, x, xii, 58). It introduces a *"logic of the social"* that, they argue, is no longer rooted in social foundations characteristic of the rigid base-superstructure model (3). Instead this "logic of hegemony," as they call it, is rooted in a fundamental "structural undecidability," or the fact that all social categories are forever unfixed (xii). As Laclau and Mouffe put it, the logic of hegemony is not "the majestic unfolding of an identity" but the "contingent" "response to a crisis" (7). It is not something that is predetermined by mathematical or scientific precision. Relations of modes of production do not simply determine social relations and social identities. Instead, because the social is marked by a fundamental "unfixity," it is equally undecidable (85).

In order to understand concrete "social" formations, they tell us, we must appeal to a "political" concept (139) called "hegemonic articulation" (7). Laclau and Mouffe develop "hegemonic articulation" by combining two important concepts: Althusser's concept of articulation (Althusser 1965, 1971) and Gramsci's concept of hegemony (Gramsci 1971, 1995). Following Althusser, Laclau and Mouffe understand discursive "structures" or "formations"—the only "structures" that emerge in their social ontology—as "articulatory practices" (Laclau and Mouffe 1985, 105). By this they mean that the structures themselves, which are only moments of *perceived* or *mythical* fixity, are always contingent because they emerge as a result of a political practice that is external to the pieces that make up the structure.

No discursive formation—no mythical identity category—they argue, can be thought of as a "sutured totality" precisely because it only ever comes into being through an articulatory, or political, process (106–7); discursive formations are not ontological facts but political creations.

What is possible, they maintain, are "partial fixations" that enable social subjects to form contingently and momentarily in relation to other social subjects (112). The *"practice of articulation,"* they tell us, *"consists in the construction of nodal points which partially fix meaning; and the partial character of this fixation proceeds from the openness of the social* [a social ontology of unfixity], *a result, in its turn, of the constant overflowing of every discourse* [overdetermination] *by the infinitude of the field of discursivity"* (113). Instead of simply *describing* an ontological fact of the social, for Laclau and Mouffe—following Gramsci, and now putting him in conversation with Althusser—hegemony is best thought of as a purposeful (read, political) practice. Replacing the principle of representation, which depends on representing ontologically fixed social identities, Laclau and Mouffe argue that hegemonic articulation is instead the "result of a political construction and struggle" that produces not an ontological category that can be represented by a political party but "chains of equivalence" that form to contest different forms of subjugation (65).

If their goal was to move away from the ontological fixity of stable identity categories, they seem to have succeeded. Hegemonic articulations are not rooted in a shared ontology (i.e., a shared identity as "women" or "workers"). They are instead based on chains of equivalences that come together as a result of *political struggle.* Thus, while a chain of equivalence *may* form around a "class" subject, it need not do so (65). Similarly, there are no necessary ontological links between, for instance, workers and women; any unity between them must be understood as a political (as opposed to an ontological) unity, and as such it must be the result of a hegemonic articulation, a political struggle (178). While hegemonic struggles may appear from the outside to reflect an antagonism between two stable social positions—between, for instance, men and women or whites and nonwhites or workers and capitalist owners—they insist that this sutured space (wherein a binary antagonism momentarily emerges as hegemonic) is always political and therefore contingent; it is never, strictly speaking, ontologically stable. The perceived closure of this space is therefore only necessary for the sake of the construction of the antagonism and the momentary "division of this space into two camps," resulting only in the *perceived* autonomy of the particular social movement (132).

Understanding such "mythical" fixations as political in this way seems to offer a viable way out of the problems that accompany approaches to collective politics that rely on ontologically fixed categories such as "women" or "workers." While contesting these stable and potentially exclusionary categories, Laclau and Mouffe nevertheless articulate a form of collective progressive politics that remains committed to contesting hegemonic oppressive forces by shifting from an ontological to a political basis for collective group action that is rooted in collective struggle. What becomes curious and indeed problematic at this point is their willingness to quickly reconceive this articulatory core in ontological terms.

Despite what appears to be the total displacement of fixed identity, Laclau and Mouffe retreat to identity in the final moment of articulation. Though chains of equivalence form when a set of particularities—"women," "workers," or Black people—identify a shared antagonism (perhaps, in this case, vis-à-vis corporate capitalism), in order to represent "the totality" of this "chain of equivalences" (xiii), it is necessary, they tell us, for one of the three particularities to *emerge as hegemonic* with a *split identity* as both its particularity (e.g., as "workers") and as the totality of the chain itself, representing the universal struggle of all women, workers, and Black people against corporate capitalism. Thus, an ontological category (a "split" identity) nevertheless emerges as hegemonic. I find this move at best puzzling and at worst deeply troubling. It is not clear to me why one stable particularity would need to emerge in this way at all, nor is it clear why such groups would not simply unite around a shared political commitment to, say, fighting interlocking oppressions rather than around an ontological category, even if this category is conceived as temporary or "mythical." Why not dispense altogether with the ontological base and embrace, instead, a political base rooted in a shared political commitment to struggle against interlocking oppression, much in the way Combahee had already done when Laclau and Mouffe were writing this? While one might understand the next move in their argument—their appeal to a "discursive exterior"—as an attempt to do precisely this, this, too, runs into dicey terrain.

In order for a semisutured hegemonic group to form—and this is the last component of hegemonic articulation—Laclau and Mouffe assert that a "discursive 'exterior'" must emerge (154). According to Laclau and Mouffe, a hegemonic articulation is always external to the fragments (particularities or marginalized groups) that compose it (94). They tell us that there is no "logical and necessary" relation between "socialist objectives and the positions of social agents in the relations of production." Any "articulation" that may result between them is "external and does not proceed from any *natural* movement of each to unite with the other" (86). What they mean by this is that there is nothing about social group identities that ontologically predetermines a site of political articulation between them; instead, these momentarily sutured groups form through a process of political struggle that ultimately results in a "'collective will' that is laboriously constructed from a number of dissimilar points" (from a number of dissimilar struggles) (87). The "collective will" that results from this struggle is not, they maintain, predetermined by the ontological positions of each of its elements. Diverse subjugated people do not, in such moments, come together around a shared identity; instead, the collective will originates in an *external democratic discourse* that may be summarized in the "democratic principle of liberty and equality" (154–55). This discourse, they argue, will form the basis of a new Left-oriented hegemonic articulation manifested in a chain of equivalences among a variety of struggles against oppression (176). As such, the multiple subordinated groups come together because of a common external discourse that connects their diverse struggles.

If one could interpret this "external democratic discourse" as a shared commitment to undermine all forms of oppression, then it would hold much promise for collective progressive politics across diverse subordinated groups. As I will argue in later chapters, a collective commitment to fighting interlocking oppressive forces is the basis of politico-ethical coalition politics for US Women of Color coalition feminists writing in the 1970s and early 1980s, including Combahee and the TWWA, and this provides an excellent way around the dangers of essential identity politics. Unfortunately, Laclau and Mouffe do not locate an external democratic discourse in the principle of undermining interlocking oppressions; they instead root it in the Enlightenment principles of equality and liberty. While only a cursory glance at the feminist and critical race interventions into so-called Enlightenment commitments to upholding equality and liberty "for all" reveals the danger in equivocating Enlightenment liberty and equality with undermining *all* forms of oppression, the problems with their appeal to a discursive *exterior* run deeper than this.[4] To begin with, why must this common discourse be thought of as *external* to the particularities themselves? Is it really necessary that one must adopt an "external" democratic discourse rooted in Enlightenment notions of equality and liberty in order to be compelled to fight against one's own oppressive circumstances? Would not the material conditions of enduring oppression provide their own impetus for generating an *internal* democratic discourse centered on liberation from oppressive forces? As I will demonstrate shortly, this is precisely what Luxemburg's version of Marxist epistemology opens up, something largely overlooked by Laclau and Mouffe and something that puts Luxemburg in fruitful conversation with US Women of Color feminism.

The peculiarity (a potentially dangerous one) of Laclau and Mouffe's appeal to an *external* democratic discourse grows deeper when juxtaposed against their insistence that the content of this discourse must remain unfixed. Laclau and Mouffe assert that "the *meaning* of liberal discourse on individual rights is not definitely fixed" and it is precisely this "unfixity" that makes this new articulation possible (176). The discursive unity that inheres in any hegemonic articulation, they insist, is not to be understood as "the teleological unity of a project" (109). We are thus led to believe that there is no predetermined direction, end, or telos to liberal-democratic ideology. Indeed, they distinguish their notion of ideology (borrowing from Gramsci) from a Marxist "superstructuralist" reading of ideology wherein the scientific calculability of economic relations determines ideology and politics.

While I find myself largely in agreement with Laclau and Mouffe in their insistence that the basis of collective Left-oriented politics be reconceived not as the "unfolding of an identity" but rather as a "response to a crisis" (Laclau and Mouffe 1985, 7), I find it problematic that they ultimately retreat from this assertion in their repositioning of a semi-fixed or momentarily fixed ontology as the basis of politics, and then reinsert unfixity at the level of political commitment and direction.[5] In these final moves, it seems to me that they have misconstrued the appropriate sites for fixity and unfixity. While an insistence on something *like* unfixity in relation to identities and categories seems right to me—many US Women of Color feminists have also challenged the notion of stable identities such as "women" as inherently exclusionary (I turn to this in later chapters)—the insistence on unfixity in relation to political commitments and ideals seems unnecessary and carries considerable baggage. Doing so, I demonstrate below in my discussion of Luxemburg, vastly underestimates the political *determinacy* that would likely result from moments of crisis brought on by enduring oppressive material conditions. While Laclau and Mouffe insist that their formulation of collective progressive politics in the form of hegemonic articulation is a necessary answer to the ontological, epistemological, and political crises of Marxism, I argue that a careful reading of Luxemburg's theory of spontaneity, and especially when contrasted with Lenin's scientific socialism, suggests that the *perceived* crisis of Marxism emerges only for certain versions of Marxism. Luxemburg's understanding of "dialectical"—in place of Lenin's "scientific"—materialism ushers in a form of spontaneous coalition politics that remains compatible with both a more fluid picture of "the social" than what we saw in Lenin's definition and a determinate progressive agenda that avoids the tensions and inconsistencies of Laclau and Mouffe's Left hegemony.

The Overlooked Alternative: Theorizing from within Lived Struggle with Luxemburg

The difference between Lenin's and Luxemburg's theories of Marxist coalition politics comes down to two markedly different interpretations of Marx and Engels's understanding of historical materialism and the dialectic. Whereas Lenin's understanding is rooted in a rigid *scientific* version of historical materialism, Luxemburg's understanding is rooted in a *dialectical* version of historical materialism that, in Luxemburg's interpretation, disavows the rigidity of Lenin's interpretation of historical materialism and thereby also disavows the ontological rigidity that Laclau and Mouffe insist is necessarily characteristic of Marxism. The divergence between Lenin and Luxemburg in their interpretations of historical materialism also informs two competing Marxist epistemologies. As we saw earlier, Lenin's scientific materialism informs a strictly *scientific understanding* of social phenomena and particularly of class oppression. As I will demonstrate here, Luxemburg's dialectical materialism informs a much more fluid and unpredictable *sensing* of class oppression rooted in the experience of lived struggle. These different epistemologies, finally, shape two competing versions of Marxist coalition politics. While Lenin presented a rigid scientific socialism that informed a tactical party coalition politics that allows for flexibility only in the service of strategic Communist goals, Luxemburg's dialectical materialism points the way toward a more flexible and reactive version of spontaneous worker's coalition politics, wherein a unique kind of unfixity emerges at the level of both epistemology and politics.[6] This sort of unfixity, I argue, should not be interpreted as discursive unfixity in the way Laclau and Mouffe might understand it; instead, it is rooted in the unpredictability that is inherent to coalition politics born out of lived struggle. It is precisely this methodological emphasis on lived struggle as the source of epistemology and politics, I assert, that opens an intersectional wedge in Marxism and puts Luxemburg in conversation with a long tradition of Women of Color feminists.

To make these arguments, I return again to Marx's preface to *A Contribution to the Critique of Political Economy* (1970) and Marx and Engels's *The*

Communist Manifesto (2004). In the preface, Marx distinguishes the "material transformation of the economic conditions of production, which can be determined with the precision of natural science" from the "legal, political, religious, artistic or philosophic—in short, ideological forms in which men become conscious of this conflict and fight it out" (Marx 1970, 21). While a transformation in social consciousness is inevitable once material conditions have shifted, Marx is less clear on how one may identify and predict such ideological transformations. Something other than the precision of natural science, he implies, is called for. This is where the dialectic as a more unpredictable process of unfolding emerges.

According to Marx and Engels, the dialectic functions alongside historical materialism. Following G. W. F. Hegel, they understand the history of society as an "unfolding," marked by a series of conflicts that ultimately result in revolutions that bring about a fundamental transformation of society; this new society will ultimately unfold in a similar way. The outcome of every new social transformation, every new "synthesis," is inevitably a fundamental transformation (Hegel 1988, 58–60, 67, 75, 78, 81, 82). Marx and Engels part ways with Hegel insofar as they understand this dialectical process to be a *material* process, meaning it unfolds according to the shifting material conditions of class antagonism.[7] Marx and Engels outline the transformations in material conditions that have unfolded in modern bourgeois society in the first part of *The Communist Manifesto*. Transformations in the means of production—the establishment of big industry and the world market—have necessarily affected corresponding transformations in the social reality of the bourgeoisie and the proletariat classes, social transformations that correspond to political transformations of, at first, the political advancement of the bourgeoisie, followed quickly by their political decline and the advancement of the proletariat.

When outlining this process, Marx and Engels present the dialectic as an independent, self-perpetuating process that unfolds without help from the outside (see Marx and Engels 2004, 66–67). The history of human society is not directed or governed by any external force. If society is a "sorcerer," the dialectic is the power of the "nether world" that is "summoned" by the material conditions of the present society (the sorcerer), a power that that very society is incapable of ultimately governing, directing, or controlling (66–67). As such, the dialectic process is not only determined by material conditions; it also is made manifest through the shifting material conditions defining each historical moment. Thus, the process itself is beyond our control; it is simply "going on before our eyes" (75). When exactly each step of the dialectic process will occur, how it will occur, and the details of its unfolding, Marx and Engels imply here, cannot be known in advance. The infinite unfolding of this process therefore inserts an element of uncertainty into historical materialism. Despite their shared commitment to Marxist materialism, Lenin plays off of the certainty of the Marxist dialectic while Luxemburg, I will show, plays off of its simultaneous unpredictability and inevitability.

Unlike Lenin, Luxemburg's materialism may be located not in the precision of scientific understanding, but in her critique of abstract theory and her preference for theory rooted in lived experience. No true understanding, she insists in "The Mass Strike, the Political Party, and the Trade Unions," can come from "abstract logical analysis," because just as surely as it might tell us that the mass strike is "absolutely impossible," it will also show us that it is "possible" and that "its triumph cannot be questioned" (Luxemburg 2004a, 171). In place of abstract logical analysis, Luxemburg prefers historical analysis of the material conditions perpetuating worker discontent.

> If, therefore, the Russian revolution teaches us anything, it teaches above all that the mass strike is not artificially "made," not "decided" at random, not "propagated," that it is an historical phenomenon which, at a given moment, results from social conditions with historical inevitability. It is not therefore by abstract speculations on the possibility or impossibility, the utility or the injuriousness of the mass strike, but only by an examination of those factors and social conditions out of which the mass strike grows in the present phase of the class struggle—in other words, it is not by *subjective criticism* of the mass strike from the standpoint of what is desirable, but only by *objective investigation* of the sources of the mass strike from the standpoint of what is historically inevitable, that the problem can be grasped or even discussed. (170–71)

According to Luxemburg, and in stark contrast with Lenin, the mass strike can be neither predicted nor planned with scientific precision. While certain material conditions—specifically, unbearable working conditions under capitalism—make its occurrence historically inevitable, it does not follow strict logical or scientific rules. Luxemburg's strong materialism—in this instance, in the form of learning from the material conditions that shape one's lived experience—is therefore accompanied by a version of the dialectic rooted simultaneously in inevitability and unpredictability. Through her unpredictability, she parts ways from Lenin.

Luxemburg describes the inevitability of the unpredictable unfolding of the proletarian revolution in a literary style reminiscent of Marx and

Engels's "sorcerer" passage. For Luxemburg, the dialectic is a "pulsating life of flesh and blood ... connected with all parts of the revolution by a thousand veins" (191). It does not follow a rigid or scientific scheme or program. The revolution itself represents the entire movement of the dialectical process in the shifting material, social, and political conditions that punctuate it. It does not unfold linearly or predictably; instead, it flows "like a broad billow over the whole kingdom"; at times it "bubbles forth from under the ground like a fresh spring," at others it is "completely lost under the earth." It is a "ceaselessly moving ... changing sea of phenomena" (191). The law of motion guiding it is a dialectical one, not governed by the precision of scientific materialism. As such, the revolution cannot be understood and analyzed in advance, nor can it be perpetuated or reproduced in the details of its unfolding, but rather emerges in the "political and social proportions of forces of the revolution" that influence it in a "thousand invisible and scarcely controllable ways" (192). Strike action cannot be meticulously planned, even if these plans leave room for tactical contingency in the way that they did for Lenin. The revolution itself cannot manifest in a program or plan at all, according to Luxemburg; instead it simply is the "method of motion of the proletarian mass" (192).

Luxemburg's more fluid understanding of social forces shapes a markedly different vision of Marxist epistemology than what we saw in Lenin. Challenging Lenin's reliance on the Communists to shape the proletariat's class consciousness and corresponding politics, Luxemburg argues that the "political education" of the Russian proletariat was not something imparted on them through "pamphlets and leaflets" or by a "schoolmaster" (198). Instead, it emerged through the fight itself, in and through struggle, in the "continuous course of the revolution," through the "actual" or "living" school of experience (182). As such, for Luxemburg, the political epistemology underpinning proletarian politics relies on spontaneous awakening that occurs within lived struggle, as opposed to planned or rational "understanding." We see this in her choice of words, such as "instinct" and "electric shock," to describe this coming to consciousness (171, 181). Whereas Lenin presents "sense" as an incomplete (embryonic) epistemology, Luxemburg presents sense or "instinct" as a reliable epistemology that will manifest both in sophisticated political consciousness and in concrete political action. Unsurprisingly, given the epistemological commitments outlined here, for Luxemburg, workers gain a "theoretical edge" not with scientific precision but instead with the lived experience of oppression. On this point, her Marxism aligns with that of Georg Lukács who similarly argues that the working class has an *epistemic* privilege over removed party leaders and the bourgeoise insofar as they understand both how capitalism operates from the position of the oppressed and how the bourgeoise systematically denies the reality of this position (Lukács 1968; Bohrer 2019, 64).

This notion of dialectic spontaneity, not scientific socialism, shapes Luxemburg's understanding of coalition politics. A mass strike, according to Luxemburg, cannot simply be placed "on the calendar on an appointed day" (Luxemburg 2004a, 169). We cannot do this because a mass strike is not a "purely technical means of struggle," guided by rational tactical planning and "'decided' at pleasure" (169). For Luxemburg, proletarian politics do not unfold according to a "predetermined plan" or "organized action" at all (180). Proletarian politics, she tells us, are born out of *"coalescing wage struggles* which, in the general temper of the revolutionary situation and under the influence of the Social Democratic agitation, rapidly became *political demonstrations"* (180; my emphasis). "Coalescing wage struggles" are not governed by a particular party ideology but emerge out of reactions against the material conditions of the workers (180). While in time they may acquire a "political direction," she insists that they originate in spontaneous struggle. Whereas "demonstration strikes" (political demonstrations) exhibit "the greatest mass of party discipline, conscious direction and political thought," "fighting strikes" (coalescing wage struggles) originate "for the most part spontaneously, in every case from specific local accidental causes, without plan and undesignedly" (192–93). Because every act of struggle is marked by a variety of economic, political and social, general and local, and material and psychical factors, Luxemburg insists that "no single act can be arranged and resolved as it if were a mathematical problem" (198). Spontaneity guides proletarian politics, Luxemburg argues, not because workers are "uneducated" but because revolutions "do not allow anyone to play the schoolmaster with them" (198).

As we can see here, Luxemburg offers a helpful alternative to the rigid class politics of Lenin's scientific socialism. Yet, her reading of Marxism is often overlooked in contemporary theorizations of progressive social justice coalition politics. While Laclau and Mouffe, for instance, engage Luxemburg on some of these points, they quickly dismiss her due to what they falsely perceive as an inconsistency in her approach. They argue that her appeal to a "class unity" contradicts her own logic of spontaneity that would require that the "type of unitary subject" to emerge out of spontaneous struggle remain "largely *indeterminate*" (Laclau and Mouffe 1985, 11; my emphasis). Luxemburg's logic of spontaneity, they insist, subscribes her to a discursive understanding of class unity wherein it is best understood as only ever a symbolic unity that will ultimately "overflow its own literality" (11). For Luxemburg to speak in terms of "class" unity at all, they argue, is to violate her own logic of spontaneity.

There is no reason, however, to insist that Luxemburg's logic of spontaneity moves in this direction at all. While her notion of spontaneity accommodates complexity, movement, fluidity, and change, it does so without subscribing to political indeterminacy, and unlike Laclau and Mouffe, I see no reason why it must. Luxemburg, unlike Laclau and Mouffe, is not informed by discursive commitments to unfixity, undecidability, or indeterminacy. While I have shown that her understanding of ontology is more fluid than Lenin's rigid ontology of class antagonism, there is no reason to believe that Luxemburg attributes this fluidity to what Laclau and Mouffe understand as *discursive* unfixity. Instead, Luxemburg's understanding of dialectical materialism is informed by an epistemology shaped by coming to political consciousness in and through lived struggle. As such, her notion of spontaneity accommodates a purposeful direction toward emancipation, broadly speaking, and while this spontaneous coming together may have occurred in certain instances of coalescing wage struggles in the form of worker's unity, there is no reason to believe that within other contexts it would not take the form of other and perhaps even more complex forms of coalitional unity—such as some combination of race, class, and gender unity at once. Luxemburg was, for instance, quite aware of the connection between women's struggle and class struggle. The lack of rights for women in Germany, she argues in "Women's Suffrage and Class Struggle," "is only one link" in a chain of oppression "that shackles people's lives" (Luxemburg 2004b, 239). Her logic of spontaneity therefore leaves room for the possibility of political unity and determinacy across diverse subjugated groups.

Similarly, recall that Luxemburg's appeal to what Marx and Engels refer to as "scientific socialism" falls much more heavily on the side of *dialectical* materialism than on the side of *scientific* materialism. The distinction here is important. While Luxemburg asserts that the discontent of the workers is inevitable, we do not get a strong sense that their political consciousness develops with the help of scientific precision or party dogma. Rather, it is inevitable because it emerges out of their experience of lived struggle as workers; the conditions of capitalism would necessarily lead workers to a place of resistance. This is why she insists on calling them "purely economic partial wage struggles" brought on by truly "intolerable working conditions" that workers sustain for a while before an "apparently trivial circumstance fill[s] the cup to overflowing" (Luxemburg 2004a, 174). She is adamant that these coalescing wage struggles do not arise out of any "preconceived" plan (176). Indeed, in Nicholaiev (a city in southern Russia at the time), she notes that they culminated in the general strike without the guidance of the Social Democratic Committee at all and even in opposition to the timeline preferred by the Communist Party (178). Because the Social Democratic Committee members were not the ones on the ground enduring the oppressive conditions of capitalism, they simply could not predict, plan, or shape when these seemingly trivial moments would occur (180). As she puts it, "The appeals of the parties could scarcely keep pace with the spontaneous risings of the masses"; they have "scarcely the time to formulate the watchwords of the onrushing crowd of the proletariat" (180).

Hastened by the material conditions endured by the workers, while such uprisings are surely inevitable, Luxemburg insists that the timing of their occurrence remain completely unpredictable and, once in motion, "incalculable" (181). This sense of unpredictability, let me be clear, parts ways with the sense of ontological unfixity and political indeterminacy found in Laclau and Mouffe. When Luxemburg tells us that "coalescing wage struggles" are "unpredictable," she means that they cannot be planned or programmed *from the outside*, by the Communist Party (180). For Luxemburg, there is no way to predict when someone, let alone a group of people, will have the "awakening" that leads them to coalition politics. This awakening cannot be predicted, planned, or imposed from the outside. However, the formation of such coalitions is nevertheless inevitable precisely because of the kind of political consciousness that is born out of collective and individual struggle (170). It is the "worker's condition of ceaseless economic struggle with the capitalist," Luxemburg maintains, that "keeps their fighting energy alive" and "forms ... the permanent fresh reservoir of the strength of the proletarian classes, from which the political fight ever renews its strength" (195). For Luxemburg, workers' coalitions are unpredictable (or "spontaneous") for the same reason that they are inevitable. It is the material conditions that both ensure their emergence while simultaneously prohibit their careful planning.

It is curious that Laclau and Mouffe are critical of Luxemburg for relying only on a "class" unity. Arguably, Luxemburg is not actually describing the formation of a *class* consciousness at all. To have a class consciousness, the Social Democrats would need to be involved. What is forming here is more accurately thought of as a worker's consciousness, and this kind of consciousness forms the basis of coalition politics in the form of coalescing wage struggles. It is a critical consciousness born out of lived struggle, and it is the basis of the unique form of social justice coalition politics engaged in by the workers, which is markedly different from the party coalition politics engaged in by the Social Democrats. Thus, the unity of the workers that Luxemburg describes, in the form of coalescing wage struggles, is not the rigid unity that Laclau and Mouffe fear it to be. Rather, it is just as fluid as the shifting material conditions that give rise to it, and herein lies the beginning of the intersectional wedge.

One important implication of an ontology rooted in a dialectical unfolding of material oppressive relationships and an epistemology rooted in lived experience of oppression is the inevitability of a coming to consciousness of intersecting oppressive forces, at least for those who find themselves complexly situated at the intersection of multiple forms of oppression. Luxemburg, as a woman and a labor activist, occupied just such a position. As she declares in her "Women's Suffrage and Class Struggle" speech in 1912, her understanding of "scientific socialism" (what I call dialectical materialism) tells her that injustices emerge as the result of lived experiences of a variety of oppressive material conditions. Those suffering these material conditions, she is certain, will inevitably rise up to contest them; such an occurrence is as equally inevitable as its timing is unpredictable. "If, however, there is a feeling of injustice in large segments of society— says Friedrich Engels, the co-founder of scientific socialism—it is always a sure sign that the economic bases of society have shifted considerably, that the present conditions contradict the march of development. The present forceful movement of millions of proletarian women who consider their lack of political rights a crying wrong is such an infallible sign, a sign that the social bases of the reigning system are rotten and that its days are numbered" (Luxemburg 2004b, 242). The shift in the base Luxemburg references here occurs at the intersection of multiple oppressive systems—in this instance, at the intersection of patriarchy and capitalism. The simple acknowledgment of multiple oppressive forces necessarily challenges Lenin's rigid Marxist ontology of a binary class antagonism between the proletariat and the bourgeoisie. However, and to be sure, the existence of this more fluid depiction of the social is *not* rooted in discursive unfixity. Luxemburg says nothing about resisting, permanently, the notion of social categories or identifiable oppressive forces; she simply acknowledges that, when rooted in lived experience, the political unities that form to contest such forces will change with the shifting material conditions that give rise to multiple oppressive forces. She acknowledges that women workers have already begun to contest an intersecting oppressive force that has necessarily troubled the rigid Marxist binary between worker and capitalist. The reality that women are contesting these two oppressive systems simultaneously is evidence enough for Luxemburg that the base has shifted away from a rigid binary.

Thus, not only does my reading of Luxemburg challenge Laclau and Mouffe's insistence that the only political unity Luxemburg accommodates is a "class" unity; it also necessarily locates the origin of ontological fluidity not in the discursive unfixity of all categories but rather in the shifting material conditions of interlocking oppressive forces, which is something that is brought to our attention, as both activists and theorists, through a lived experience of interlocking oppressions. As such, Luxemburg parts ways with Laclau and Mouffe by moving in the direction of fluidity and spontaneity without subscribing to political indeterminacy. The direction of coalescing wage struggles in "The Mass Strike" was determinable for Luxemburg. All she had to do was look at the concrete demands of the workers to determine what they were after politically. They moved unequivocally in the direction of contesting the oppressive working and living conditions of capitalism. Similarly, Luxemburg also identified a concrete political direction for women workers, challenging the oppressive material conditions of both patriarchy and capitalism, manifested in a clear demand for a concrete commitment on the part of labor activists to also fight for women's suffrage.

Opening an Intersectional Wedge in Marxism: Putting Luxemburg in Conversation with Women of Color Feminists

Luxemburg is far from alone in offering a version of Marxism that effectively breaks the ontological and epistemological rigidity of Lenin's Marxism without following Laclau and Mouffe into the abyss of political indeterminacy. Though I do not intend to claim that Luxemburg is an "intersectional" theorist, putting her in conversation with the women of color named in Bohrer's tracing of the "shared history" of intersectional and Marxist traditions certainly reveals the intersectional possibilities that follow from a methodological orientation toward theorizing out of lived experience. In "Chapter Zero" of *Marxism and Intersectionality*, Bohrer breaks down this historical recuperation into three periods: the nineteenth century, wherein she recovers the voices of Stewart, Sojourner Truth, and Ida B. Wells-Barnett to show how figures central to the development of the intersectional tradition were also "significantly interested in themes that have strong resonances with Marxist concerns of labor, class, capitalism, and political economy" (Bohrer 2019, 35); the first half of the twentieth century, wherein she recovers the voices of "black women communists" such as Louise Thompson and Claudia Jones, whose "pioneering work dealt with the interaction between race and gender under capitalism" (35); and the period between 1960 and 1980, wherein she recovers the voices of the Women of Color feminists who gave us theories of double jeopardy (Francis Beal), triple jeopardy (Deborah King), standpoint theory (Patricia Hill Collins), and racist sexism (Elizabeth "Betita" Martínez and Anna Nieto-Gómez), showing the ways in which "prominent intersectional theorists are specifically concerned with class and capitalism" (Bohrer 2019, 35).

Of particular interest to me are the voices recovered in the nineteenth century, insofar as these activist-theorists exemplify the potential of intersectional analysis when theorizing from lived experience decades before Luxemburg's pamphlet on the mass strike in Russia came to print. Though Bohrer rightly notes that it would be quite a stretch to claim that these women were "Marxists" (some of their works, for instance, appear decades before Marx elaborated his theories of surplus value and economic exploitation unique to industrialized capitalism), she makes a compelling case for the claim that their thinking was nevertheless "grounded in a perspective that could be described as historical-materialist" (36), which, I will suggest, puts them in conversation with Luxemburg's dialectical materialism. As I sketched above, Luxemburg's central claim is that oppressed people will come to consciousness of their own unique situation of oppression through the living school of experience. When one finds herself complexly positioned at the intersection of multiple oppressions, she will come to consciousness of this multipronged oppressive structure. This is precisely what we find in accounts of US Women of Color feminism from the nineteenth century.

As early as the first half of the nineteenth century, Stewart speaks to the connections among race, gender, and class. Her analyses were particularly sharp in their ability to connect race and gender to class oppression. As quoted in Bohrer, Stewart explains in an 1833 speech: "We have pursued the shadow, they have obtained the substance; we have performed the labor, they have received the profits; we have planted the vines, they have eaten the fruits of them" (Stewart in Bohrer 2019, 37). Two decades before Marx, Stewart effectively "elaborate[d] the outline of a theory of surplus value" (37), astutely capturing the intersection of a capitalist system that depended on exploited labor and a political-social system that depended on the denigration of Black bodies. Wells-Barnett's groundbreaking investigative reporting half a century later on lynching in the US South similarly showed the strong connection institutionalized racism has to capitalism by revealing that lynching was "predominantly a tool of economic control" of Black people, ensuring through intimidation and terror that Black people who were acquiring wealth and property would be kept down (Bohrer 2019, 40). Such "tactics of economic subordination," Megan Ming Francis notes in relation to Wells-Barnett, were "used to protect white economic power and to ensure a captive black labor force" (Megan Ming Francis in Bohrer 2019, 41–42). The "logic of lynching," in Wells-Barnett's estimation, was therefore "economic" not "criminal" (41).

About two decades after Stewart and three decades before Wells-Barnett, Truth (2004) delved deeper into the connections among race, class, and especially gender in her now famous "Ain't I a Woman?" speech. Speaking specifically to the kinds of productive and reproductive labor that were the conditions of enslaved Black women, Truth exposes the intersectional oppressive nature of the institution of slavery under capitalism through recalling the conditions of her own personal experience as an enslaved Black woman. Not only does she differentiate the experience of being a Black enslaved woman from the experience of being a white woman, thereby exposing the way in which sexism is "not constructed uniformly" (Bohrer 2019, 38)—*she* was never helped over ditches and in and out of carriages—Truth also differentiates the experience of being a Black enslaved woman from the experience of being a Black enslaved man (Truth 2004). While Black men and women both suffered under the racist institution of slavery, sexist stereotypes and institutionalized patriarchy operated to further oppress enslaved Black women who were treated as if they were not as valuable field hands as Black men, something they made up for with their reproductive capacity: "Enslaved women produce enslaved *people*, who are themselves bought and sold" (Bohrer 2019, 39). Like Stewart and Wells-Barnett, Truth perceptively captures the unique position of enslaved Black women, who sit at the intersection of multiple, intertwined systems of oppression. Thus, decades before Luxemburg's historical account of the coalescing wage struggles that culminated in the 1905 Russian Revolution, these women of color demonstrate precisely the kind of intersectional analysis that might emerge from complexly positioned individuals whose struggles are shaped by the interactions among racism, patriarchy, and capitalism. Their "school of lived experience" revealed to them an intersectional oppressive structure wherein capitalism emerges as one of many mutually reinforcing systems of domination.

This emphasis on the interconnected forces of capitalism, racism, and sexism was further explored only decades after Luxemburg's passing by pioneering Black women Communists such as Thompson and Jones, who develop theories of "triple exploitation" and "superexploitation," respectively. Drawing a connection between slavery under capitalism and the low wages of Black women's domestic labor under capitalism post-emancipation in the "Bronx 'slave market,'" Thompson develops the concept of the "triple exploitation" of Negro women, "as workers, as women, as Negroes" (Thompson in Bohrer 2019, 47). In so doing, she names the "racial-gendered" division of labor that confines Black women to domestic service work and the institutionalized and individual racist discrimination that both prevents Black people from attaining social benefits and ensures the underfunding and underprovisioning of Black neighborhoods, all as manifestations of this triple exploitation (Bohrer 2019, 47). As Bohrer notes, Thompson's account was particularly remarkable insofar as it named racism and sexism as forms of exploitation and not simply as oppressions used in order to justify or maintain exploitation.

In addition to popularizing the notion of "triple oppression," Jones conceptualized the notion of the "superexploitation" of Black women in her 1949 article, "An End to the Neglect of the Problems of the Negro Woman!" Building on Thompson's notion of triple exploitation, she writes, "Negro women—as slaves, as Negroes, and as women—are the most oppressed stratum of the whole population" (Jones in Bohrer 2019, 49). As Bohrer notes:

> According to Jones' biographer, Carol Boyce Davies, several aspects of Jones' thinking "advanced Marxist-Leninist positions beyond their apparent limitations" in conceiving the unique position of black women under capitalism. Her use of superexploitation was influential in disseminating the idea that black women's situation under capitalism was *something more* than mere exploitation, which was the dominant interpretation in certain Marxist circles at the time, and indeed, still is. The "super" of "superexploitation" suggests not only that black women are exploited as workers, often in significantly more precarious positions than their white and male counterparts, but also that their exploitation is structured differently, through the production and maintenance of both a segregated labor market *and* through racists and sexist ideas of their place in society. . . . For Jones, black women's position as superexploited people uniquely placed them as "the most revolutionary segment of the U.S. working class, thereby challenging orthodox Marxist postulations that industrial (white male) workers represented the [revolutionary] vanguard." (Bohrer 2019, 49–50)

Moving beyond Luxemburg's account of the situation of woman workers, Jones not only names a triple-pronged system of oppression, but she insists even more fervently than Luxemburg ever did (in relation to women) that the oppression of Black women was of a fundamentally different kind than that of other workers and women. As such, she dispenses completely with the notion that the source of all oppression is rooted only in class oppression, and she names Black women as the new revolutionary vanguard precisely because of their unique position at the intersection of all three of these exploitative systems—capitalism, racism, and sexism.

It is precisely this emphasis on the simultaneity of multiple interlocking forms of oppression that forms the bedrock of important late 1960s and 1970s US Women of Color feminist organizations such as the TWWA and Combahee. Such an understanding, both groups insist, comes to them from their lived experiences as women of color. Indeed, the common thread across the Women of Color feminists engaged here—from Stewart all the way through Combahee—is that a lived experience of intersectional oppression will shape a corresponding consciousness of intersectional oppression, which will, in turn, shape an intersectional politics, often in the form of coalition. Both the TWWA, as seen in the *Black Woman's Manifesto*, and Combahee, as seen in the "Black Feminist Statement," theorize about oppression from their lived experience at the intersection of multiple oppressions. Combahee is most explicit in naming this methodology. They build this case carefully, noting first:

> Above all else, our politics initially sprang from the shared belief that Black women are inherently valuable, that our liberation is a necessity not as an adjunct to somebody else's but because of our need as human persons for autonomy. This may seem so obvious as to sound simplistic, but it is apparent that no other ostensibly progressive movement has ever considered our specific oppression as a priority or worked seriously for the ending of that oppression.... We realize that the only people who care enough about us to work consistently for our liberation is us. (Combahee 1983, 212)

As Combahee members make explicit here, they cannot rely on others to speak for them. They must speak for themselves and theorize from within their lived experience of oppression, in order to accurately name the forms of oppression operating in their lives. This starting point shapes their appeal to "identity politics": "We believe that the most profound and potentially the most radical politics come directly out of our own identity, as opposed to working to end somebody else's oppression" (212). When they say that "the most radical politics *come directly out of our own identity*," they are speaking to this methodological commitment to theorizing out of lived experience. Their politics are shaped by their experience of oppression; this *experience* is what they mean to reference when they speak of their *identity*. Because they are complexly situated at the intersection of multiple oppressive forces, they believe that they are best positioned, by way of this intersectional social, political, and economic location, to name and dismantle these interlocking oppressive forces. The TWWA members appearing in *Black Woman's Manifesto* (Gayle Lynch, Eleanor Homes Norton, Maxine Williams, Frances Beal, and Linda La Rue) proceed from a similar starting place. Much of their focus across the pieces published in the *Black Woman's Manifesto* centers on the limitations of both the civil rights movement and the women's movement to accurately name the complex oppressive forces that shape their lives as women of color. It is because their unique lived experience is never articulated or addressed by these other progressive groups that the TWWA first formed (Burnham 2001).

The women of color who made up Combahee and TWWA were even more complexly situated than Luxemburg, and as such, they named a much more complicated system of oppression. At the beginning of their statement, Combahee explicitly calls out "racist, sexual, heterosexual, and class oppression" as the "interlocking" systems of oppression that they aim to dismantle (Combahee 1983, 210). Later, they name the "political-economic systems of capitalism and imperialism, as well as patriarchy" (213). Driving their treatment of imperialism, racism, sexism, and heterosexism, they imply here, is an appreciation of these systems as both political and economic. Capitalism, it would seem, is interconnected throughout. Indeed, they assert that they are "socialists," that this is their starting place, but they also insist that a "socialist revolution that is not also a feminist and antiracist revolution" will fail to guarantee true liberation (213). The oppressions they experience in their lives are not individual; as they assert, they are "interlocking" (210). As such, they are committed to working to dismantle all of them simultaneously.

The TWWA's newsletter, *Triple Jeopardy*, similarly names capitalism, racism, and sexism in one of its iconic covers with a picture of militant women of color and the phrase "Smash! Capitalism, Racism & Sexism." These same systems of oppression are repeatedly named across the articles and essays appearing in its *Black Woman's Manifesto*. As Lynch notes in the introduction to the manifesto, sexism is a kind of slavery, a "form of bondage," she asserts, that "is an integral part of the racist and capitalist system which black women and black men must work to oppose and overthrow" (Lynch 1970–75). Lynch's claim is typical of those of other contributors: while they name multiple, distinct systems of oppression—sexism, capitalism, and racism—they also insist that these forces are interconnected and mutually reinforcing. In her piece "For Sadie and Maude," Norton notes that the multiple and "complex" systems of oppression that shape the lived experience of women of color demand new ways of thinking and new ways of dismantling oppression (Norton 1970–75, 1). While she insists that there is something unique to these different oppressive structures, especially to racism (2), she is also attuned to the ways in which both capitalism and racism, for instance, condition sexist norms (7). Williams similarly notes the triple oppression of Black women wherein the "brutal exploitation of capitalism" is compounded for her by the brutal forces of racism and sexism (Williams 1970–75, 13).

In "Double Jeopardy: To Be Black and Female," Frances Beal is similarly attuned to the interconnection of racism, capitalism, and sexism. Though she uses the language of "double," which might incline us to assume she names only two oppressive forces in society—racism and sexism—her discussion of these forces is framed around the prominent role that capitalism plays in shaping both. As she puts it, "racism" might be thought of as the "after birth" of capitalism (Beal 1970–75, 19). As she immediately notes, even if racism is capitalism's afterbirth, it cannot truly be understood without appreciating the relationship between racism and sexism—the experience of the Black woman under racist capitalism, she insists, is not the same as that of the Black man (19). In this sense, perhaps we might say that capitalism births twins: racism and sexism. As she argues, the "capitalist system found it expedient" to not only enslave and oppress Black people (22), but it found it equally "expedient" to "reduce women to a state of enslavement" insofar as they "represent a surplus labor supply," "the control of which is absolutely necessary to the profitable functioning of capitalism" (24). If capitalism finds it expedient to oppress both Black people and women, we can immediately anticipate the compounded (double) effect this might have on Black women. Thus, when Beal uses the language of "double jeopardy," she is speaking to the unique precariousness of Black women insofar as they suffer under the compounded effects of *both* racist capitalism *and* sexist capitalism. While Beal does not focus explicitly on the relationship between sexist racism (or racist sexism), the other contributors do (see Norton 1970–75, Williams 1970–75, and La Rue 1970–75), calling out Black civil rights movements and leaders to reject white sexist stereotypes and familial structures.

The TWWA and Combahee come together once more in their appeal to coalition politics committed to tackling interlocking systems of oppression simultaneously. As Bohrer notes, the notion of solidarity that becomes central to intersectionality is a "coalitional" one wherein alliances are formed based on "shared enemies" (Bohrer 2019, 60, 94). As I will develop in chapter 2, the shared enemy here is best thought of not as an individual or even a group of individuals but rather as an interlocking *system* of oppression. Such an approach to group politics, they make unequivocally clear, is not politically "indeterminate" as it is for Laclau and Mouffe. In the same way that Luxemburg easily named the political goals and directions of coalescing wage struggles, these Women of Color feminists are explicit in their commitment to tackling interlocking systems of oppression simultaneously (see Combahee 1983, 210, 213, 218).

In addition to resisting political indeterminacy, Williams is equally suspicious of the notion that the white women's movement can or should shape Black women's political consciousness when white women lack any clear understanding of the interlocking forms of oppression that women of color live under (Williams 1970–75, 16–17). This is similar to Luxemburg's challenge to Lenin's claim that the workers must be brought to a proper political consciousness "from without"—that is, from the party leaders. Building on Luxemburg's claim that the political consciousness of the workers will emerge within the fight itself, within the living school of experience, we might similarly see Williams as rejecting the notion that the women's liberation movement can effectively shape the political consciousness of Black women from without, instead asserting that their political consciousness forms from within their lived experience of interlocking oppressions (17).

As they develop this complex consciousness, they will be positioned to enter into coalitions with all "revolutionary forces" mutually committed to the "complete destruction of this racist, capitalist, male-dominated" system (18). Beal speaks to a similar notion of revolutionary coalition politics, stating: "If the white groups do not realize that they are in fact, fighting capitalism and racism, we do not have common bonds. If they do not realize that the reasons for their condition lie in a debilitating economic and social system, and not simply that men get a vicarious pleasure out of 'consuming their bodies for exploitative reasons' . . . then we cannot unite with them around common grievances" (1970–75, 30–31). Like Williams, Beal is equally firm in the political vision that will guide her politics: it must be an intersectional one. Instead of relying on the women's movement or the civil rights movement to teach them about sexism and racism, they have learned through their own lived experiences the intricacies of this multifaceted and interconnected oppressive structure. With this in mind, they assert that they must enter into alliances with other groups, but they are also uncompromising on their intersectional commitments—that is, their political commitment to dismantling an interlocking system of oppression. Combahee makes a similar declaration in its statement, wherein the group traces its own origin story, explaining that while it began as more of a consciousness-raising group for Black, lesbian women, the group soon moved in the direction of working with other groups to tackle issues affecting their lives (Combahee 1983, 216–17). In these alliances, Combahee is equally uncompromising on its commitment to tackle interlocking oppressions from a self-reflexive perspective wherein the group interrogates potentially oppressive relationships that might emerge within the space of coalition itself (218).

With these dogged commitments to dismantling interlocking systems of oppression, we might say that, on this point, the Women of Color coalition feminists engaged here share something in common with Lenin's dogged commitment to Communist principles. The major difference here is that these Women of Color feminists want to dismantle an interlocking system of oppression, rather than a simple class binary. Thus, both TWWA's and Combahee's understandings of oppression are notably more complex than Lenin's insofar as they break up the ontological rigidity, specifically the rigid class binary, of Lenin's version of Marxism. With this also comes a movement away from scientific socialism and toward an epistemology rooted in the idea that political consciousness emerges out of one's experience of interlocking oppressions. Rigidity then enters back into the equation insofar as both Combahee's and the TWWA's political commitments *are* rigid; they are rigidly focused on an intersectional oppressive system. Anyone who is not committed to tackling all these interlocking systems of oppression simultaneously will not be invited into struggle with Combahee or the TWWA. Thus, whereas Laclau and Mouffe deemed it necessary to reject the ontological, epistemological, *and* political rigidity of Marxism-Leninism, Combahee and TWWA follow Luxemburg in resisting ontological and epistemological rigidity without sacrificing clear and uncompromising political goals and directions.

A careful reader of Luxemburg will pick up on comments that seem to challenge her intersectional commitments when she suggests that despite the presence of multiple interlocking oppressive forces, class oppression is fundamentally generative of all others (Luxemburg 2004b, 240–42, 244). On this point, it is worth noting Luxemburg's proximity to Women of Color coalition feminist thinkers and activists. Despite their strong endorsement of intersectionality (before *intersectionality* was coined by Kimberlé Crenshaw over a decade later), Combahee founders also note that their anticapitalist commitments were pivotal, foundational even, to their intersectional platform that opposed racism, sexism, heterosexism, capitalism, and imperialism. Similarly, Beal and the other contributors to the TWWA manifesto name capitalism as a kind of generative force—recall that for Beal racism and sexism are positioned as the twin "after birth[s]" of capitalism. As Bohrer notes, what was unique to the work of many Women of Color feminists was precisely this emphasis on what I would like to call *intersectional Marxism*, that is, an attention to the intersectional material conditions that shape interlocking systems of oppression wherein capitalism is understood as one such system but is thought to be interconnected with others that are all mutually reinforcing. As such, for the US Women of Color feminists engaged here, there was no "crisis" or contradiction inherent in their simultaneous intersectional and Marxist commitments.

Furthermore, while the political goal of dismantling interlocking oppressive forces may *seem* to resonate with the Enlightenment ideals of equality and liberty that were advocated for by Laclau and Mouffe, they are different in important ways. First, a commitment to fighting interlocking oppressive forces parts ways with the Enlightenment discourse of equality and liberty and its embarrassing track record on contesting *all* forms of oppression. More importantly, it is plainly clear at this point that, for both Luxemburg and the women of color engaged here, the political consciousness and goals of workers and women of color are not imparted to them *from without*, whether this "without" is represented by Communist Party propaganda (pace Lenin), a more amorphous notion of Enlightenment discourse (pace Laclau and Mouffe), or by the white women's movement. Indeed, as my analysis has shown, political awakening is not the result of a discursive exterior at all but rather is internal to the lived struggle of all workers under capitalism, patriarchy, and racism. If these intolerable conditions oppress subjects on multiple intersecting planes, then one's political consciousness will also come to name intersecting oppressive forces that warrant a careful and multidimensional response. It is precisely such a response that Luxemburg began to articulate in "Women's Suffrage and Class Struggle" and that US Women of Color feminists have been advocating since before

Luxemburg. While I cannot say that Luxemburg's own political conscious-ness was truly "intersectional" in the way that the Combahee cofounders' or the TWWA members' were, her version of Marxism adopts a much more fluid ontology of multiple and intersecting oppressive forces than what we saw in Lenin and, in so doing, opens an intersectional wedge in Marxist think-ing that maneuvers around the philosophical entanglements encountered by the contemporary political theorists who are at pains to get around the "crisis" of Marxism. On this point, one might think of Luxemburg's Marxism as one that parallels, at least methodologically, the intersectional Marxist trajectory of Stewart, Truth, and many other Women of Color feminists.

Conclusion

In this chapter, I have critically interrogated the perceived crisis of Marx-ism that contemporary scholars, namely, Laclau and Mouffe, misleadingly position as the backdrop to contemporary theories of progressive coalition politics. I say "misleadingly" because the central claim that the rigidity of Marxist ontology, epistemology, and politics necessarily sits in tension with progressive commitments to intersectional social justice group politics relies on one very narrow interpretation of the Marxist dialectic, exemplified in Lenin's version of scientific socialism. While it is certainly true that the party coalition politics on offer by Lenin leave little room for tackling multiple and mobile systems of oppression, my analysis suggests that Luxemburg's theory of spontaneity opens an intersectional wedge in Marxist thinking that lends itself to a theory of coalition politics capable of encapsulating the multidimensional response to interlocking oppressive forces suited to our contemporary moment.

Luxemburg's theory of spontaneity not only offers an alternative to Len-in's rigid scientific socialism, but it also offers a way around the philosophical tensions and entanglements of coalition in the form of Left hegemony. By theorizing out of lived experience, in the place of both rigid scientific socialism or discursive unfixity, I show that Luxemburg reconceives social oppression as a fluid site of multiple and mobile systems of oppression, political awakening or consciousness as internal to an experience of lived oppression, and coali-tion politics as equally contingent and shifting as they are inevitable. While Laclau and Mouffe seem to follow Luxemburg on these points of inevitability and unpredictability, they ignore the most sophisticated component of her theory of coalescing wage struggles: which is, of course, that such coali-tions emerge out of *internal* lived struggle and must therefore be theorized from the ground up. Once theorized from the ground up—that is, in the living political school of struggle—multiple, fluid, and mobile systems of oppression come immediately into view.

It is precisely such intersectional structures that come to occupy the attention of US Women of Color feminist activist-theorists such as Stewart, Wells-Barnett, Truth, Thompson, Jones, Combahee, and the TWWA. Rather than get caught up in assuming that multiplicity and the proliferation of differences bring "crisis" for progressive group politics, we might do better to sit with Women of Color feminism long enough to discern how they maneuvered so effortlessly around these so-called crises. With this starting point in mind, we are now in a position to proceed from the reality of the *challenge*, not the crisis, of intersectional progressive group politics. Seeing it only as a challenge—and one that Women of Color feminists have been effectively grappling with since at least the first half of the nineteenth century—helps us to avoid being confounded by the philosophical crisis of discursive unfixity and the tension it generates when attempting to articulate a politically determinate Left-oriented group politics. Articulating just such a politics is where I turn in chapter 2.

2

Women of Color Feminism and Politico-Ethical Coalition Politics

Recentering the Politics of Coalition with Reagon, Smith, Combahee, and Lorde

Early US Women of Color coalition feminists know better than anyone else that coalition politics across diverse subjugated groups, each invested in fighting different forms of oppression, is absolutely *necessary*. As Shirley Chisholm emphasized when she became the first African American and woman to seek the presidential nomination of the Democratic Party in 1972, Black Americans ought to see their struggle as linked to other groups treated as second-class citizens, whose discrimination is based on other difference markers (such as religion, sex, creed, or sexual orientation) and thereby "join in the struggle to end *all* forms of discrimination in America" through progressive coalition politics (Chisholm 1972, 32). The turn to coalition for Chisholm was rooted in necessity and urgency, not in naive aspirations of broad-based ethical, or sisterly, community. These are not natural or easy alliances; they are chosen coalitions. In such coalitions, Women of Color feminists have something to teach others in their ability to "move . . . readily around anti-racism and the politics of the oppressed" without viewing "these politics as standing in contradiction to the issues of women's rights" (31). Instead, they express "the issues of women as part and parcel of a broader program and coalition of the oppressed" (32). Because women of color "face discrimination based on both racism and sexism," including racism at the hands of white feminists or sexism at the hands of Black civil rights leaders, they must fight both of these oppressions at once (32). As Pat Parker put it the following decade, women of color "cannot afford not to" form coalitions with other oppressed groups (Parker 1983, 238). Coalition thus emerges in this context not as an optimistic solution but as an urgent and necessary strategy for dismantling interlocking oppressive forces.

Contrast this understanding of coalition with Reverend Jesse Jackson's optimistic calls a decade later to "make room" for "the White, the Hispanic, the Black, the Arab, the Jew, the woman, the Native American, the small farmer, the businessperson, the environmentalist, the peace activist, the young, the old, the lesbian, the gay and the disabled" in an expansive "rainbow" "coalition of conscience" (Jackson 1984). First coined by Fred Hampton (one of the leaders of the Black Panther Party) in 1969 to describe the class-conscious, multiracial alliance and nonaggression pact between Chicago's most powerful street gangs, Jackson appropriated the notion of "rainbow coalition" to describe a progressive, multiracial, multiethnic, and multireligious coalition meant to unite diverse subjugated people all suffering under the first four years of Reaganomics. Known as "the Great Unifier," Jackson invoked a sense of coalition characterized by optimistic aspirations of uniting all progressives dedicated to making the United States more inclusive. Jackson's optimism about the possibility of a broad-based coalition resonates with Judith Butler's much more recent, though slightly different, formulation of what I call "coalition as ethical community," wherein she, too, envisions a progressive stance against the uneven precarity of the most vulnerable but, in this instance, initiated by our universally shared condition of primary vulnerability (I return to this shortly).

Unlike Jackson and Butler, as a Black woman, Chisholm was soberly aware of the unique challenge of coalition politics across diverse subjugated groups. While Jackson's call to rainbow coalition politics centers on optimistic aspirations of unity across difference and "making room" for all minorities and while Butler's call for an ethical community centers again on optimistic aspirations toward coming together for the sake of aiding the most vulnerable, Chisholm's language of coalition continuously circles back to the idea of "struggle" (Chisholm 1972, 30–32). The sense of urgency Chisholm invokes here therefore better aligns with Hampton's original sense of "rainbow coalition" as a multiracial alliance and nonaggression pact between powerful and dangerous street gangs than with either Jackson's or Butler's optimistic sense of coming together. Nowhere is this emphasis on struggle more vividly depicted than in Bernice Johnson Reagon's now famous coalition speech, "Coalition Politics: Turning the Century," delivered three years before Jackson's rainbow coalition speech.

In her address to the West Coast Women's Music Festival in Yosemite, California, in 1981, Reagon, a woman of color singer-songwriter, activist, and scholar, vividly captures the challenge of engaging in coalition politics with diverse subjugated groups. Speaking to a women-only crowd, Reagon movingly outlines the ways in which this warm and comforting site of celebration and music is instead a site of coalition politics, with all of the hope and discomfort this brings with it. Such sites—sites that pretend to be "homes" or "communities" but are really coalitions—she notes, are disorienting for women who don't fit the prescribed definition of "woman" that shapes such events. Employing the geographically apt metaphor of altitude sickness, Reagon says that being in such unfamiliar spaces, spaces for which she lacks the appropriate "environmental conditioning" as a heterosexual woman of color, leaves her and others "staggering around," unable to think straight. This experience of confusion, panic, and disorientation is exactly what the workshop in Yosemite is all about. This is the experience of "*really* doing coalition work," an experience marked by the immanent feeling that you may "keel over any minute and die." "Most of the time, you feel threatened to the core and if you don't, you're not really doing no coalescing" (Reagon 1983, 343).

Echoing Chisholm and Hampton, sites of coalition, Reagon maintains throughout the speech, are not safe spaces; they are not homes that bring warmth and comfort. One does not go into coalition politics because she "just *like[s]* it"; "the only reason," she continues, "you would consider trying to team up with somebody who could possibly kill you, is because that's the only way you can figure you can stay alive" (343–44). This is the double-edged sword of coalition work: while coalescing with other subjugated groups fighting for social justice is indeed the only way for oppressed peoples to survive in a post-Marxist landscape, entering into coalitions with these other groups may be life threatening. Not only does this throw into question the ease with which Ernesto Laclau and Chantal Mouffe believe that "chains of equivalence" will form, but it similarly challenges both Jackson's aspiration to rainbow coalition and Butler's optimistic vision of coalition in the form of ethical community.

While it is unlikely that the women's music festival would have erupted in violent fights resulting in fatalities, Reagon's appeal to the visceral danger of coalition work no doubt struck a chord with at least some of the women listening. The real danger in women of color attempting to form coalitions with white women or Black men are well documented in US Women of Color feminist scholarship from this period (Hull, Scott, and Smith 1982; Moraga and Anzaldúa 1983a; and B. Smith 1983a). For women of color in particular, teaming up with either Black men to fight racism or white women to fight sexism could very well prove to be dangerous. It is worth recalling that Reagon's political consciousness formed during the civil rights era in which sit-ins, freedom riding, and other potentially dangerous forms of protest were a regular part of her activist experience. Furthermore, violence at the hands of Black men was a very real possibility for women of color feminists working in coalition with other civil rights groups. When she says that her awareness of doing coalition work is made clear when she feels like she could die any minute it is not just hyperbole; she is speaking from an authentic experience of fear of personal physical, emotional, and psychological harm within the space of coalition. In addition to the fear of working with others who may be invested in your continued subjugation, working in coalition can also be a dangerous affair for fear of such coalitions failing. As Reagon makes clear throughout the speech, the survival of poor, or lower income, women of color very much depends on forming successful coalitions to fight all forms of oppression and domination simultaneously.

Sorely needed at a time when women of color, Third World women, and their allies were feeling marginalized from the festival's activities, especially in light of the disappointingly small showing of white participants at the planned "solidarity day" organized to raise awareness about the political struggles that women face in Latin America (Gagliardi 1981, 3, 22), Reagon's compelling account of the reality of attempting to team up with people who might be invested in your continued marginalization not only made waves in 1981 but its impact has persisted across the decades following its first publication in Barbara Smith's edited anthology, *Home Girls: A Black Feminist Anthology* (see Honig 2001; Zivi 2004).

I turn to the speech here to introduce what I call Reagon's *challenge*, or the fact that even progressive coalition politics is a vexed affair, characterized by contentious disagreement and potentially life-threatening alliances across hostile differences of race, class, gender, sexuality, and other divides. It is this challenge (not crisis) that shapes progressive group politics outside of class-only, race-only, gender-only, and other single-identity categories. While Reagon's depiction highlights the inescapable discomfort that coalition work brings with it, there is no reason to believe that this will land us in full-blown "crisis" in the way that Laclau and Mouffe anticipated. Building from the arguments made in chapter 1, in turning to Reagon's coalition speech, this chapter soberly confronts precisely those challenges that face such an endeavor. In so doing and guided by a close engagement with Reagon's words, it also charts a way around these trials through locating a notion of politico-ethical coalition politics at the very heart of Reagon's speech. As I will demonstrate, politico-ethical coalition politics embodies three distinguishing characteristics, each referenced at some point in her speech: an emphasis on coalition as a dangerous and even life-threatening *struggle*; an understanding that coalition is generated out of a shared *self-reflexive political commitment* to undermining oppression; and an emphasis on *existential transformation* as inherent to the very process of coalescing.

Taken together, these characteristics recenter the politics of coalition. I say "recenter" because of a disconcerting trend in dominant strands of contemporary political theory, one most prominently seen within two incongruous accounts of coalition politics found in Butler's work. As I will argue in the first section of the chapter, attempts by Butler to relieve the tension between a philosophical commitment to the ontological unfixity of all categories and oppressive forces, on the one hand, and a practical commitment to a fixed Left-oriented collective politics, on the other, have succeeded only by obscuring the concrete politics of coalitional activism. In what I call *coalition as spectacle*, the politics of coalitional activism takes the form of unplanned collective performances of ontological defiance, anchored in notions of political indeterminacy. Parting ways with her commitment to notions of ontological unfixity and political indeterminacy, in *coalition as ethical community*, an incongruous form of ontological *fixity* curiously emerges, wherein all progressively minded people come together in a broad ethical community committed to fighting the precarity engendered by global market capitalism. Though in different ways, I will show that both formulations obscure the politics—that is, the arrangements of power that both demand and situate coalitional encounters—of coalitional activism. A better place to look for imagining collective politics in light of intersecting social justice struggles, I will argue, would be in the politico-ethical coalition politics of early US Women of Color coalitional feminism vividly on display in Reagon's 1981 coalition speech.

I then turn to a close reading of Reagon's speech, situated against Romand Coles's 1996 reading of Reagon. One of the few contemporary political theorists to seriously engage Reagon's 1981 speech, Coles uses Reagon's critical insights on the difficulty of coalition politics in a moment characterized by difference and diversity to challenge Laclau and

Mouffe's theorization of coalition politics as rooted in a shared commitment to equality and liberty.[1] Presenting a thoroughgoing challenge to naively optimistic calls to post-Marxist Left-oriented collective politics, Coles demonstrates the value in Reagon's work to contemporary discussions on activist coalition politics, placing his work on the cutting edge of where these conversations are and ought to be going. However, in his next move, Coles attempts to chart a possible way out of Reagon's challenge by reading into Reagon a neo-Nietzschean interpretation of coalition as *ethical* encounter. I examine that move, showing that for Reagon the glue that holds coalitions together is rooted in a self-reflexive political commitment. The nascent theory of politico-ethical coalition politics on display in Reagon's speech, I go on to show, is echoed across other prominent US Women of Color coalition feminist texts emerging in the 1970s and 1980s, specifically within works by Barbara Smith, the other cofounders of Combahee, and Audre Lorde. Demonstrating the continued relevance of politico-ethical coalition politics to contemporary discussions around intersectional group politics, I engage empirical accounts of coalitional activism from the 1960s through the turn of the century.

Across the chapter, I flesh out a notion of coalition *as politico-ethical encounter*. These authors maintain that coalition politics is best thought of as a potentially hostile and dangerous *encounter* with difference—for some it wouldn't be a stretch to call it a sort of collision of differences. As such, coalition politics is shaped most prominently by *struggle*. For this reason, these authors maintain that such encounters are best theorized as *political*. By this I mean to emphasize that they are actively chosen for the sake of a political commitment to undermining oppression in all its forms and acutely attentive to the arrangements of power that situate such encounters, thus differentiating what I am calling politico-ethical coalition politics from approaches to coalition that emphasize either ethics or antifoundational philosophical commitments as the articulatory core of coalitional activism. However, not only are these authors unique in their unabashed appeal to the *politics* that grounds coalitional efforts, but they are equally exceptional in their insistence that this political commitment necessarily engenders a particular *ethical comportment*—or way of treating one another within the space of coalition. It is the *self-reflexive* nature of their political commitment, I will show, that accounts for the *ethical* side of politico-ethical coalition politics insofar as it encourages an ethical sensibility characterized by love and existential transformation. Such a commitment, however, remains distinct from ethical accounts offered by Coles or Butler insofar as Reagon,

Smith, Combahee, and Lorde refuse to let their ethical orientation eclipse the political commitments that ground all coalitional activism.

At the end of the chapter, I contrast the notion of politico-ethical coalition politics located in early US Women of Color coalitional feminism and informing Chandra Mohanty with Butler's most recent formulation of coalition that continues to obscure political commitment in favor of antifoundational or ethical orientations. In thinking with Mohanty, alongside contemporary feminist theorists such as the authors appearing in *New Political Science*'s 2018 symposium issue on feminism and coalition (Zein Murib, Liza Taylor, Nana Osei-Kofi, Adela Licona, Karma Chávez, Shireen Roshanravan, and Cricket Keating), about Butler, I hope to encourage a critical rethinking of the tendency in contemporary scholarship to look toward Butler and others wedded to discursive unfixity and political indeterminacy as our guides in current coalition efforts.

The Obfuscation of Politics in Contemporary Accounts of Coalition

Among contemporary political theorists interested in coalition politics, Butler's work has been oddly influential. I say "oddly" because the concept of coalition is far from central in Butler's corpus—it often emerges briefly alongside other theoretical discussions and is rarely given thorough attention. Nevertheless, contemporary scholars position Butler as one of their guides in this area (see Puar 2007; Schram 2013; and Manning 2012). Indeed, despite Butler's openly critical stance toward assuming the role of coalition "theorist" (Butler 1990, 20), a careful engagement with a handful of her texts reveals at least two different accounts of progressive coalition politics. I excavate two of these accounts here, not with an eye toward settling whether they amount to full-blown "theories" of coalition politics but rather in an effort to reveal a disconcerting trend that persists across both of them: Butler's willingness to obscure the politics of coalitional activism. By "politics" I mean the arrangements of power that both demand coalitional activism in the first place and situate tensions and struggles within coalitional spaces. While both accounts might be read as attempts to relieve the fundamental tension that emerges for contemporary theorists who wed themselves to both a philosophical commitment to the ontological unfixity of all categories and structures of oppression and a practical political commitment to designating a progressive and therefore "fixed" form of collective group action, the obfuscation of politics that results should concern us.

In one such formulation, coalition emerges *as spectacle* wherein sexual minorities or precarious bodies find themselves performing collectively unplanned disruptive acts of gender, sexuality, or other forms of ontological defiance. This theory of *coalition as spectacle* is shaped most prominently by Butler's critique of gender categories in her groundbreaking work, *Gender Trouble*. As "ongoing discursive practices" that require repetitive signifying performances in order to *appear* stable—such as wearing a dress to signify being a woman—Butler argues that categories such as "man" or "woman" are forever "open to intervention and resignification" (Butler 1990, 45). Because gender requires "a constant repetition of [its] logic" to appear stable does not imply, according to Butler, that the goal should be to stop this repetition; as she attests, to do so would be impossible (44). Instead, Butler seeks to "make gender trouble" by repeating gender differently, subversively (44). Dressing in drag, as she has famously argued, is a defiant and highly subversive form of *political* engagement precisely because politics has been reoriented toward ontological disruption, its goal being to expose identity (in this case stable notions of what it means to be a "man" or a "woman") as illusory (187–88).

Butler states that her hope for *Gender Trouble* is that it would inspire coalitions "of sexual minorities that will transcend the simple categories of identity" (Butler 1990, xxvii–xxviii). In this account, coalition emerges as spectacle. The very purpose of the coalition reveals itself in a spectacular performance of collective gender and sexuality parody. My use of "spectacle" shares something with Guy Debord's use of this concept in *The Society of the Spectacle* (1994) insofar as it speaks to an instance of turning what is thought to be real (sex) into "mere representation" (Debord 1994, 12).[2] In so doing, it accomplishes a kind of "inversion of life" wherein "what has been passed off as authentic life turns out to be merely a life more *authentically spectacular*" (12). For Butler, the mere presence of a coalition of sexual minorities will challenge ontological certainties about sex, gender, and sexuality precisely by eluding the dividing line between what is real and what is fabricated, between the original and the copy, thereby "turning the material life" of what it means to be a man or woman "into a universe of speculation" (Debord 1994, 17).

In Butler's later work, coalition as spectacle takes the form of defiant bodies in alliance in the street. As she argued in 2011, echoing arguments she presented in *Precarious Life* (2004) and *Frames of War* (2009), a shared sense of precarity will eventually compel diverse groups to come together to name and contest this vulnerability, as was the case during the mass demonstrations marking the Arab Spring and the Occupy movement. The "politics" in Butler's understanding of coalition—what makes these "bodies in alliance" *political* coalitions—is rooted again in spectacle. By occupying public space, these bodies disrupt a social, political, economic, legal, and cultural imaginary that refuses their presence. By coalescing in public, they demand a recalibration of public space and who has a right to it. "Simply put, the bodies on the street redeploy the space of appearance in order to contest and negate the existing forms of political legitimacy.... These are subjugated and empowered actors who seek to wrest legitimacy from an existing state apparatus that depends upon the public space of appearance for its theatrical self-constitution. In wresting that power, a new space is created, a new 'between' of bodies, as it were, that lays claim to existing space through the action of a new alliance" (Butler 2011, 6). In the same way that a woman dressing as a man disrupts the signifying process that produces sex and gender, Occupy participants are behaving as bodies that "count" in a "distribution of the sensible" wherein they have not yet been recognized or permitted to exist, thereby calling into question the entire signifying process that partitions bodies as the counted and uncounted (Rancière 2004). By taking over public spaces such as town squares and streets and existing, literally living and sleeping, in these spaces, these bodies—taken as a collective—not only parody an already existing ontology of which bodies count, they also disrupt notions of "public" space. As Sanford Schram puts it, Occupy participants "occupy precarity" by "spitting back their marginalization in the face of those who have marginalized them" (2013). It is not, Butler asserts, simply about "entry of the excluded into an established ontology, but an insurrection at the level of ontology" itself that allows for "a critical opening up of questions" such as "What is real? Whose lives are real? How might reality be remade?" (Butler 2004, 33).

This form of what Butler has called "antifoundational" coalition politics mirrors the unfixity of the social through its emphasis on *political indeterminacy*, or the idea that while social justice struggles may emerge on their own in the form of collective spectacle, they cannot be planned, predicted, or even advocated for in advance (Butler 1990, 20). She uses the formulation "assemblage of positions" to resist any conflation with identity or representative politics (20). Rather, Butler envisions a notion of coalition politics wherein the coalition is treated as an "open assemblage that permits of multiple convergences and divergences without obedience to a normative telos of definitional closure" (22). Neither the identities of coalition members nor the "shape or meaning of a coalitional assemblage," Butler maintains, can be known "prior to its achievement" (21). The goal of a coalition, when understood as spectacle, is simply to form, because by forming it is already engaging in performative disruption. The question of what brings a coalition together is not the interesting one for Butler; these groups simply will form. What is interesting for Butler is what kind of trouble their unpredictable presence may cause. In the case of coalitions of sexual minorities, the spectacle consists in the gender trouble it performs through unified acts of parodic repetition. In the case of "bodies in alliance," the spectacle consists in their very presence within public spaces from which they have been barred. According to Butler, in both instances, the coalitions cannot be predicted, programmed, or planned. Such coalitions cannot even have concrete goals or directions. They are ontological inevitabilities, not political constructions. Because ontology—what exists in the world—for Butler is understood as a discursive and therefore political *process*, disruptive forms of parodic repetition (drag) or defiant presence (precariat bodies in alliance in the street) are also political acts. Politics here gets reduced to ontological disruption.

In a second formulation, Butler curiously reconceives the social as now marked by a *fixed* ontology of universal precariousness against the forces of global market capitalism, which is thought to engender a shared Left-oriented progressive agenda (Butler 2004, 27–29; 2009, 14, 25). In the preface to *Precarious Life*, Butler proposes that the fact of our heightened vulnerability to "the whim of another" (2004, xii), alongside the feelings of grief, set in motion by the catastrophic event of September 11, 2001, might together offer an opportunity for allowing the fact of our shared interdependency and precariousness to provide the basis for a "global political community" (xiii). Instead of outlining a Left coalition politics built around the experience of a particular social group, such as the proletariat, "coalition as ethical community" expands the very notion of class to include *all* people (2004, 28–29; 2009, 25).

While our shared vulnerability, as US residents, to the possibility of another large-scale terrorist attack speaks most directly to the sense of precariousness invoked here, for Butler, precariousness is an ontological condition that *all* humans share as social creatures whose lives are always in the hands of the "other" (Butler 2009, 14; 2004, 27). The events of 9/11 simply foregrounded this universally shared condition. Invoking Emmanuel Levinas, she insists: "It is not that we are born and then later become precarious, but rather that precariousness is coextensive with birth itself" (2004, 14). Building from Levinas's notion of "the face as the extreme precariousness of the other" (Levinas quoted in Butler 2004, 134), Butler maintains that we are born into this world as precarious beings; this is the "condition of primary vulnerability" that all newborns face insofar as an infant's survival is literally in the hands of other people (Butler 2004, 31–32). An orientation toward this primary vulnerability, she suggests, alerts us to the precariousness of all life. Particularly palpable when experiencing the grief associated with the loss of a loved one, a feeling of being "undone" by another situates us in relation to our dependency on others (23, 28), thus providing a conduit to our shared condition of primary vulnerability (24). As such, it provides a possible basis for the formation of an ethical community.

Whereas all beings are equally precarious (rooted in our shared condition of primary vulnerability), Butler acknowledges that beings experience different levels of *precarity*—whereas "precariousness" denotes a universally shared condition, "precarity" seems to denote the unevenly distributed levels of heightened precariousness that differently situated people face (Butler 2009, 3, 25). While for Butler the fact of uneven exposure to precarity *ought to* concern us ethically (or politically), what enables us to *actually* care enough to enter into collective progressive struggle against uneven precarity, according to Butler, is the fact of universal precariousness. "From where might a principle emerge by which we vow to protect others from the kinds of violence we have suffered," she asks in *Precarious Life*, "if not from an apprehension of a common human vulnerability?" (Butler 2004, 30). While nothing can be done about universal precariousness in relation to a shared condition of alterity (we all share this condition in equal amounts), this shared sense of vulnerability, it would seem for Butler, will compel us to condemn the uneven precarity of the most vulnerable. Indeed, it is "on this basis," on the "generalizability" of the condition of precariousness of all, she tells us, that one may "object to the differential allocation of precariousness and grievability" (precarity) for some (Butler 2009, 22).

In this formulation of what I am calling "coalition as ethical community," the politics of progressive collective action gets reconfigured in strictly *ethical* terms. Uneven precarity is the problem coalitions will form to contest; what ensures their emergence is a "recognition of [the] shared precariousness" of all (28). The concept of "class" is replaced here by that of global community rooted not in a political understanding of the uneven forces of global market capitalism but rather in an ethical understanding of the undiscriminating precariousness of *all* lives in relation to the fact of alterity. Politics as ontological disruption is replaced here by politics in the form of *ethical orienta-tion*. In this formulation, politics is eclipsed by a shared ethical commitment that is curiously rooted in a universally shared ontological condition.

This turn toward developing an all-inclusive ethical community seems particularly odd given Butler's strong "aversion to the collective" and to "proposing a universal theory of oppression" in earlier works such as *Gender Trouble* (Watson 2012). I am reading it here as a second attempt, though incongruous with Butler's first, to relieve the tension between ontological unfixity and political fixity. Whereas coalition as spectacle evades the tension between ontological unfixity and political fixity by resisting a fixed (Left-oriented) political direction, coalition as ethical community works on this tension from the other end: it firms up an ontology of shared vulnerability (ontological fixity) that makes possible a Left-oriented ethics (political fix-ity). The problem I have with Butler's formulations is that they both, each in a different way, manage to obscure the concrete politics of coalitional activism. Reducing the scope of coalition politics only to unpredictable mo-ments of ontological disturbance in the first instance severely overestimates the role of strictly discursive arrangements of power in situating variously positioned subjugated peoples, thereby concealing institutional and mate-rial arrangements of power that may not be troubled by such performative acts. In the second instance, a shared ethical condition of caring for others threatens to eclipse considerations of the arrangements of power that situ-ate and necessarily frustrate most coalitional efforts.

A better place to look for imagining collective politics in light of inter-sectional social justice struggles would be to the politico-ethical coalition politics located in Reagon's 1981 coalition speech and elaborated across contemporaneous US Women of Color coalitional feminism. This literature recenters the politics of coalition in a variety of ways that address the major shortcoming of Butler's incongruous approaches. By foregrounding the very real challenge of *struggling* to coalesce across hostile race, class, gender, sexuality, ethnicity, and other divides and for the sake of a *shared political commitment* to fighting interlocking oppressive forces, early US Women of Color coalition feminists such as Reagon, Smith, Combahee, and Lorde not only avoid naive aspirations to universal ethical community, but they also circumvent Butler's antifoundational leanings. Additionally, by insisting that the political commitment to fighting interlocking oppressions that ground coalition efforts be *self-reflexive*, these same authors attest to the importance of ethical comportment within the space of coalition without letting ethical commitments eclipse political ones.

Reagon's Politico-Ethical Alternative

Through a careful engagement with Reagon's speech, situated against Coles's reading of it, I locate a politico-ethical understanding of coalition at the heart of Reagon's speech that offers an alternative to the obfuscation of politics inherent to both of Butler's accounts of coalition politics. Taking issue with Coles's understanding of Reagon's "principles of coalition" as ethical principles, rooted in what he calls "receptive generosity," I argue instead that these principles must be understood as explicitly political. I will show this by analyzing two moves in particular: the distinction Reagon draws between homes and coalition, and the way in which Reagon conceives of giving within the space of coalition.

Coles first locates an ethic of generosity in Reagon's remarks on "turning the century with our principles intact" and particularly in the importance she places on our principles "surviving" (Coles 1996, 377; see also Reagon 1983, 349, 353). Coles interprets Reagon's appeal to survival as an "ethical survival" that somehow "exceeds mere survival" (1996, 377). From the passages he references here, it is not at all clear why Reagon would be speaking of an ethical, as opposed to a political, survival. In fact, given the context of her speech, her own commitments, and what she actually says in the text, it would be more correct to interpret these principles as explicitly political. The fact that she wants these principles to "survive" does not, in itself, give them an ethical form. A few pages later, Coles points to Reagon's comments on "giving" as further indication of her preference for generosity as the "highest virtue" with which we must turn the century (1996, 380; Reagon 1983, 346, 348, 352). However, if we return to these and other comments and put them in their proper context within Reagon's speech as a whole, we find that while developing a particular ethical comportment may indeed be valuable within the space of coalition, coalition politics requires more than an ethic of generosity. While these principles take on an ethical guise when self-reflexively applied to the coalition itself, they are unequivocally political insofar as they are fundamentally rooted in a political commitment to stand against oppression.

HOMES VERSUS COALITIONS: COALITION AS POLITICAL ENCOUNTER

Reagon makes a case for both the danger and the dire necessity of coalition work. The site of the music festival, she argues, is itself a site of coalition, which is why it is, in many ways, uncomfortable. Despite the fact that persisting in such a "coalitional" site provokes feelings of terror, nausea, and impending death (Reagon 1983, 343), Reagon is adamant that coalition work is absolutely essential. Because "We've ... come to the end of a time when you can have ... barred rooms" reserved for "X's-only"—"yours only" spaces for you and your people—Reagon argues that women must find themselves in uncomfortable sites of coalition (344–46, 349). Confronting difference, she implies, is inevitable. Despite the disorientation and anxiety that coalition politics between diverse subordinated groups engenders, Reagon believes that she and the other women at the music festival are "positioned to have the opportunity to have something to do with what makes it into the next century" and that "the principles of coalition are directly related to that" (343).

So, what, you may ask, are the "principles of coalition"? Coles interprets the principles to be a constellation of equality, liberty, and receptive generosity with generosity as the "slightly brighter star" (Coles 1996, 386). I want to offer an alternative reading in which we interpret the "principles" of coalition as a political commitment to undermining oppression and the corresponding ethical comportment that this political commitment self-reflexively generates. It is this principle of coalition—directed toward the vision of a world without oppression—that Reagon hopes will survive; it is also this very same commitment that will make possible this future and the coalitional work necessary to reach it.

Reagon writes: "You don't go into coalition because you just *like* it. The only reason you would consider trying to team up with somebody who could possibly kill you, is because that's the only way you can figure you can stay alive" (1983, 343–44). The principles of coalition, it would seem, are related to the fact that one does not "like" coalition work because it is an inherently dangerous affair. This danger lies in the fact that such spaces are no longer "X-only" spaces (344). While identity politics—in the form of safe spaces where groups may come together to define who they are and "shoulder up all of [their] energies so that [they] and [their] kind can survive" (345)—still has a place in the political landscape, the principles that govern these spaces are not, argues Reagon, the ones that will usher us into the next century; they are not the principles of coalition. These "little barred rooms"—wherein we are all alike, untouched by difference—are "nurturing spaces" (345). These are the "communities" that we may retreat to when we can't handle any more coalescing. These are the "homes" where we "take [our] bottle" in preparation to go back and coalesce some more (346). These are the places where we all share common experiences. These are sites marked by sameness. These are not, she asserts, spaces for coalescing. "You don't do no coalition building in a womb" (346).

Coalition work, she asserts, is always dangerous: "you shouldn't look for comfort," nurturing, or even food in a coalition (346). What you seek in coalitions is survival. But you don't seek it through nurturing; you seek it through mutual struggle to topple an oppressive system that is out to kill you (346). In this sense, coalitions are not "refuge place[s]" (347), even if they may succeed in saving one's life (344). When you enter them, you know you are in trouble. Reagon insists that we must not confuse homes with coalitions (347). An ethic of love, respect, and generosity *may* operate in communities and homes; a political commitment to a self-reflexive politics of undermining oppression, on the other hand, operates in coalitions. While this political commitment has certain ethical implications for how one ought to treat others within the space of coalition—one must try to uphold a commitment to undermining and challenging oppressive relationships with other coalition members—it is at its core a political commitment, meaning it is both something we strive and struggle for, and something that alerts us to the arrangements of power that situate coalitional encounters and at times prevent feelings of love and mutual respect. It is this commitment to both understanding and attempting to undermine oppression that compels us to join with others who may kill us, that compels us to leave our safe homes for the hard and dangerous work of coalition. In addition to the reasons outlined above, Reagon also implies that coalitions were potentially dangerous because one might lose a sense of oneself through coalitional work. The most successful activists, she tells us, were those who were open to self-transformation through the process of coalescing (350). I take up this concept more centrally in chapter 3.

Both spaces are crucial for feminist politics; the contribution Reagon makes is in her refusal to conflate them. A feminist coalition must not be mistaken for a warm, safe, and nurturing women-only space. Whereas one *may* be able to count on feelings of warmth and comfort being present within her home, there is certainly no guarantee of safety, comfort, love, generosity, or mutual respect emerging within the space of coalition. It is for precisely this reason that I am reluctant to accept Coles's interpretation of Reagon's principles as *ethical* principles. Rather, Reagon wants to distinguish spaces in which we may be able to count on an ethic of love and generosity from spaces in which we cannot count on ethics to guide our actions. The only force capable of generating and sustaining these more dangerous and tumultuous spaces, she implies, is a *political* commitment to undermining oppression.

The fact of difference, disagreement, and decisive action are therefore written into Reagon's understanding of coalition from the outset. Feelings of fear and disorientation coupled with the danger that is inherent to coalition politics profoundly shape Reagon's understanding of coalition as a uniquely *political* space. Because coalitions are made up of multiple and differently subjugated groups, these are inherently political spaces characterized both by decisive action—a political commitment to undermining oppression compels one to *choose* to be a part of the coalition—and by conflict and disagreement regarding the best course of action for the coalition. While it may be the case that all subjugated groups share a common existence as oppressed people, this commonality alone does not bring them together in the way Butler suggests around a shared sense of vulnerability. What brings them together in a coalition is a chosen political commitment, and even with this shared political commitment, such encounters are fraught. Therefore, also unlike Butler's antifoundational coalition politics, the political direction and purpose of the coalitions Reagon speaks of were made explicitly clear from the moment of their formation: they moved unequivocally in the direction of undermining interlocking oppressions.

GIVING IN COALITION: A SELF-REFLEXIVE
POLITICAL COMMITMENT

Unlike articulations of progressive coalition politics that remain optimistic regarding the ease with which subjugated groups will naturally form into a broad coalition (think of Jackson's rainbow coalition or Butler's ethical community), Reagon follows Chisholm in anticipating the power struggles, fears, and challenges of social justice coalition politics across unequal power differentials and at times hostile race, class, gender, and sexuality divides. For this reason Reagon insists that we do not conflate "home" spaces with "coalition" spaces. Key to this distinction is her assertion that while one may receive the love, generosity, and nurturing that one needs in home spaces, one is almost certain *not* to receive these things in coalition spaces. Attention to the absence of love, generosity, and nurturing within coalition spaces also shapes her understanding of the role of giving in coalition.

While Reagon concedes that we must give in coalitions without expecting anything in return (Reagon 1982, 346, 348), I remain unconvinced that such statements point toward an ethic of "generosity born in our efforts to receive the other as *other*" or "animated by a desire for the others' otherness" (Coles 1996, 380). Instead, this generosity, if we can call it that, is born of a survival instinct. Reagon does not speak in terms of giving to individual others; instead, she speaks in terms of giving to the coalition itself, and she conceives of the coalition as a "monster."

> You have to give it all. It is not to feed you; you have to feed it. And it's a monster. It never gets enough. It always wants more. So you better be sure you got your home someplace for you to go to so that you will not become a martyr to the coalition. Coalition *can* kill people; however, it is not by nature fatal. You do not have to die because you are committed to coalition.... But you do have to know how to pull back, and you do have to have an old-age perspective. You have to be beyond the womb stage. (Reagon 1983, 348)

The fact that Reagon speaks of giving to the coalition, as opposed to one another within the space of coalition, calls into question Coles's reading of her conception of giving as "receptive generosity." By giving to the coalition, one gives to a cause, not to an "other as other" (Coles 1996, 380). While it may very well prove to be wise to embrace the "other as other" within the space of coalition, an ethic of receptive generosity is not what animates giving for Reagon. According to Reagon, one doesn't give to an "other" that she is ready to receive in a generous way; one gives to a monster, and she does so because she has to, not because she wants to or likes to. In contrast to both Coles and Butler, Reagon shows us that it is highly unlikely that coalition spaces will be marked either by feelings of "receptive generosity" or an ethical orientation toward giving to the most vulnerable members.

She writes, "The reason we are stumbling is that we are at the point where in order to take the next step we've got to do it with some folks we don't care too much about" (Reagon 1983, 355). According to Reagon, we don't "care" about one another in coalition; we care about toppling oppression, including oppressive relationships in our encounters with others. "I am talking about turning the century with some principles intact. Today wherever women gather together it is not necessarily nurturing. It is coalition building. And if you feel the strain, you may be doing some good work" (349). While one *may* lovingly and generously give to the people in her home, one does not give to coalition members in the same way. One does not give to these others necessarily at all. One gives to the cause, and in order to effectively do so, one must know when to pull back from the coalition and get the nurturing, loving, giving, and receiving she needs from her home. Coalition work is hard, Reagon maintains, precisely because it is guided by a politics born out of necessity and not an ethics born out of a "desire for the others' otherness" (Coles 1996, 380).

The principle she has been alluding to is clearly outlined in the final pages of the speech. She speaks of the civil rights movement and how it eventually became bigger than a Black cause and then bigger than even a race cause. As people found themselves fighting for causes outside of their "identity" categories, they were clearing the way for coalition. Eventually, one realizes that she "cannot be fighting one oppression and be oppressed [herself] and not feel it" (Reagon 1983, 350). In these moments, a *self-reflexive* commitment to undermining oppression requires one to identify oppressive acts she may commit against others as well as those forms of oppressive behavior that she may be forced to bear by her own fellow travelers. Those who truly "hold the key to turning the century with [their] principles and ideals intact," she finally tells us, are those people who showed up at all of the different struggles, and who kept up with many issues at once. These people are very rare, she attests, but they must be studied and protected because they can "teach you how to cross cultures and not kill yourself" (350). They are the ones who are truly committed to toppling oppression. They are the ones who have learned how to recognize it in all of its forms and how to align with others in order to fight this expansive force without succumbing to it. In this sense, it is not other-oriented in the way in which Coles interprets Reagon's notion of coalition. The "other" that most interests Reagon is not an individual "other" person; it is a political cause. For this, she will risk her life, and she implores others to do the same.

For Reagon, it is about taking a political stand, about putting yourself and your "shit" out there so that others may either learn from it or call you on it and force you to change (Reagon 1983, 350). In this way, Reagon allows for mistakes. A commitment to a political cause does not guarantee a foolproof program of action for Reagon, but it does orient our coalition efforts. As such, it requires careful analysis of the situation of oppression; it requires seeing the way in which multiple forms of domination may be interlocking; and it requires giving one's commitment to fighting domination in the unique form in which one experiences it to a bigger cause and seeing how these causes are one and the same (352–53). The principle that must survive is a *political* principle of social justice generally and a commitment to undermining intersectional oppressions in particular. It is a "political" principle because it is *chosen* and it is *struggled* for. Reagon even calls it "biased" and "bigoted" insofar as it reflects a firm and unwavering belief in the rightness of a position against oppression (353).

There is ample evidence to suggest that Reagon's principles of coalition are political at their core. While a political commitment to undermining oppression necessarily guides a certain type of comportment characterized by a commitment to undermining or opposing oppressive interpersonal relationships within coalitional spaces, this ethics is rooted in a self-reflexive political commitment. It is for this reason that I am challenging Coles's picture of coalition as an *ethico*-political encounter: that is, an encounter in which the political ideals of liberty and equality must be second to receptive generosity.[3] What we instead find in Reagon, and what warrants further consideration, is a picture of coalition as a *politico*-ethical encounter: an encounter in which the political ideal of undermining oppression in fact generates a corresponding ethical comportment as a guide to encounters between coalition members.

Kitchen Table Dialogues: Fleshing Out Coalition as Politico-Ethical Encounter

Reagon was not alone in advocating a notion of politico-ethical coalition politics. Such an understanding of coalition was characteristic of US Women of Color coalition feminism across the 1970s and 1980s and emerges within empirical work on activist coalition politics from the 1960s through the turn of the century. Reagon's thoughts on coalition politics thus both reflected and profoundly shaped conversations among Women of Color coalition feminists during this generative period as they sought to unpack the difficult questions related to feminist, anti-racist, and anticapitalist political activism.

BARBARA SMITH: REAFFIRMING THE POLITICS OF COALITION

In exploring pieces by Smith published across three important Black and Women of Color feminist anthologies completed during this period (1977–83), I aim to make two broad points. By first examining the Combahee River Collective's "Black Feminist Statement" and Smith's coauthored piece with her sister, Beverly Smith, I demonstrate that Chisholm was not the only Women of Color feminist to have moved in this direction in the 1970s. Indeed, by the time of Reagon's speech, Chisholm, Combahee, the TWWA, Smith, and others had already acknowledged the absolute necessity in turning to coalition, the challenge of entering into coalitions with white women, and the crucial role that a self-reflexive political commitment to undermining oppression plays in guiding these encounters. Reagon's coalition speech therefore aligns with many dominant themes from Women of Color feminist scholarship of this period. By then putting Reagon's 1981 speech in conversation with Smith's (1983b) introduction to *Home Girls*, I further examine the rigid distinction Reagon draws between homes and coalitions, suggesting that for Reagon this distinction was rhetorical rather than analytical.

In line with Reagon's distinction between homes and coalitions, Combahee makes an important distinction between consciousness-raising groups and coalitions. While consciousness-raising groups may be governed by an ethical orientation to receive the other's otherness just for the sake of the interaction itself (in the sense that Coles advocates), a coalition is governed first and foremost by a shared political commitment. While some of their initial organizing occurred in consciousness-raising groups, once they were ready to "move beyond consciousness-raising and serving exclusively as an *emotional* support group"—ready to leave the comfort of their home—Combahee turned toward more explicitly "political work" involving analyzing oppression more holistically and in coalition with other groups (Combahee 1983, 272; my emphasis). As they turned to this more explicitly political work, Barbara Smith tells us in a dialogue with Beverly Smith, any kind of "separatism" became a "dead end" politically (Smith and Smith 1983, 126). While separating into "Black women–only" groups, or (in the context of the dialogue) into "lesbian-only groups," may prove useful for "forging identity and gathering strength" in the same way that Reagon believes "X-only spaces" provide a necessary kind of nurturing for coalition activists, Smith states that the "strongest politics are coalition politics that cover a broad base of issues" (126). Developing *politically* involves understanding the simultaneity of oppression, or the way in which a position against sexism must also be a position against racism, heterosexism, and economic oppression. What opened Combahee up to this position—what encouraged the group's "politics" to "evolve"—was a political commitment to combatting at least two forms of oppression at once (Combahee 1983, 267).

Due to its understanding of the simultaneity of oppression, Combahee, also like Reagon, is explicit in its commitment to a self-reflexive politics. The ability to work with others who are different, argues Smith and the other cofounders, is dependent on the coalition's ability to continually examine its politics to ensure that its internal structure reflects this core political commitment to undermining oppression in all its forms. As the cofounders of Combahee put it: "We are committed to a continual examination of our politics as they develop through criticism and self-criticism as an essential aspect of our practice" (Combahee 1983, 273). Instead of pursuing "correct" political goals that would justify merely "strategic" coalitions (273), doing anything required to achieve the goal, Combahee pursues "prefigurative politics" (Rowbotham 1979, 132–44) wherein the group enacts the very ideals it seeks to install in society. I characterize such encounters as *politico*-ethical to emphasize the importance of a shared political commitment, rather than a shared ethical orientation, as that which brings coalition members to the space of coalition in the first place. For these Women of Color coalition feminists, a shared political commitment is absolutely foundational to coalition work.[4] However, this political commitment also informs the internal functioning of the coalition itself— the *ethical* component—to ensure that it follows a "collective" process with a "nonhierarchical distribution of power" (Combahee 1983, 273). With their emphasis on continually examining their own politics through "criticism and self-criticism" (273), Combahee demonstrates the self-reflexivity that makes these coalitions "principled" in the way Reagon describes.

Despite these clear affinities with Reagon's speech, Smith is reluctant to give up on the metaphor of "home." Indeed, she begins the *Home Girls* introduction with an unapologetic appeal to home: "There is nothing more important to me than home" (B. Smith 1983b, xxi). For a Black feminist activist who is clearly committed to coalition politics, it is perplexing that she starts with this line and ultimately decides on the title, *Home Girls*. Did Reagon not tell us that we must give up on the idea of a coalition feeling like a home? If Smith subscribes to the same notion of coalition politics as Reagon, which I believe she does, then why this emphasis on home?

The simple answer is that like Reagon, Smith believes that for many young Black women their feminism is born and nurtured there. "There," for Smith, is the house where she grew up with her twin sister, mother, grandmother, and aunt. Smith's experience of "home" echoes the particular and distinctly positive, nurturing, and loving picture of home that Reagon uses to contrast with coalition. It is also in these spaces that one finds the kind of giving that Coles speaks of. As Assata Shakur puts it in "Women in Prison: How We Are," "The women in my grandmother's generation made giving an art form. 'Here, gal, take this pot of collards to Sister Sue'; 'Take this bag of pecans to school for the teacher'; 'Stay here while I go tend Mister Johnson's leg.' Every child in the neighborhood ate in their kitchens. They called each other sister because of a feeling rather than as a result of a movement. They supported each other through the lean times, sharing the little they had" (Shakur in B. Smith 1983b, xxiii). As indicated in this passage—which Smith takes as representative of the Black women that "filled her childhood" (xxiii)—no commitment to a political "movement" was needed to inspire the sort of giving that occurred in the home. As Shakur states, "They called each other sister because of [a] feeling," not because of a common political cause. For Smith, these were Black women–only spaces, safe spaces, exactly the kind of spaces out of which one's politics may be born and nurtured. It was at home, Smith tells us, that she "learned the rudiments of Black feminism" (B. Smith 1983b, xxii).

In the pages of this anthology Smith hopes to create a similar kind of home for other Black feminists (xxxiii). She hopes to counter the sense of loss of home that often accompanies Black women's choice to pursue feminism as a political and analytical project (xxiv). Smith holds onto the language of "home" because she believes many of the contributors to this anthology also learned their varied politics at home (xxiv). She also holds onto the language of "home" because she believes a crucial aspect of Black feminism includes "home-based concerns" or "home truths" related to the private sphere of the home and household and touching the "basic core of our community's survival" (xxix, xxxiii, xxxvii). For Smith, a focus on home includes both a celebration of this space as warm, loving, and nurturing alongside a critical awareness that compels one to simultaneously examine practices that take place there while protecting this space from external pressures. Indeed, the purpose of *Home Girls* is to create and protect this home space for other Black women so that they may begin to develop their own critical understanding of the way in which race, gender, sexuality, and other differences interact in oppressive practices—in short, to prepare them for politico-ethical coalition politics.

AUDRE LORDE: COALITIONAL SPACES AS ANGRY BUT NEVER HATEFUL

What is perhaps most remarkable about early US Women of Color coalitional feminism is the way in which, despite an unequivocal emphasis on a shared political commitment, many of these scholars and activists also emphasize the importance of something that comes to sound like a kind of ethics.[5] Nowhere is the symbiotic relationship between ethics and politics more eloquently depicted than in Lorde's work on the notion of difference, particularly present in *Sister Outsider* (1984f). While she raises the implications of difference for the possibility of "coalition" politics in only a few instances across this text, it is quite clear that much of her discussion on difference is in the service of opening up possibilities for coalition politics marked by the hostile divides and disagreements vividly outlined by Reagon. Her attention to the theme of coalition is most explicit in "The

Uses of Anger: Women Responding to Racism" (1981) and "Learning from the 60s" (1982).

In line with Reagon's *challenge*, Lorde depicts coalitional spaces as inherently uncomfortable and often characterized by feelings of anger and hostility as individuals attempt to work across difference.

> As Black people, if there is one thing we can learn from the 60s, it is how infinitely complex any move for liberation must be. For we must move against not only those forces which dehumanize us from the *outside*, but also against those oppressive values which we have been forced to take *into ourselves*. Through examining the combination of our triumphs and errors, we can examine the dangers of an *incomplete vision*. Not to condemn that vision but to alter it, construct templates for possible futures, and focus our rage for change upon our enemies rather than upon each other. (Lorde 1984b, 135; my emphasis)

A "complete" vision of coalition politics, while rooted in a *political* commitment to undermining oppression within society (on the outside) demands also that we root out (internal) oppressive inclinations within ourselves and against our potential allies—this is the *ethical* component. Maintaining a complete vision of coalitional efforts enables us to make important distinctions between enemies and allies as well as between hatred and anger. Anger "expressed and translated into action in the service of our vision and our future," Lorde states, "is a liberating and strengthening act of clarification" (1984g, 127). Though a "painful" process, facilitating this translation between the political and the ethical enables us to harness our anger, which is "loaded with information and energy" (128), to distinguish between our "allies" and our "genuine enemies" (127).

Lorde therefore helps to clarify Reagon's picture of coalition spaces. While such spaces may be dangerous and are often marked by hostile disagreement, ideally they would not be filled with feelings of hatred. According to Lorde, hatred has no place in effective coalition building. Hatred persists between enemies or those who do not share the same political commitment; anger, on the other hand, persists between peers and allies. Coalitions, we learn, are made up of the latter. "So we are working in a context of opposition and threat, the cause of which is certainly not the angers which lie between us, but rather that virulent *hatred* leveled against all women, people of color, lesbians and gay men, poor people—against all of us who are seeking to examine the particulars of our lives as we resist our oppressions, moving toward coalition and effective action" (128; my emphasis).

While one may hate those who support oppression, one does not, or at least should not, hate her potential allies or those also committed to fighting oppression. The object of hatred is "death and destruction." Anger, on the other hand, is "a grief of distortions between peers" whose "object is change." Anger, she continues, "implies peers meeting upon a common basis to examine difference, and to alter those distortions which history has created around our difference" (129). An ethic of anger therefore enables women to come together across difference in order to use their differences as a creative force for change. This is the potential of coalition when led by a complete politico-ethical vision.

This distinction is particularly apt for contemporary progressive struggles. Former US president Donald Trump's rhetoric, policy recommendations, and executive orders reflected a politics rooted in "hatred." The interlocking forces of hatred and oppression buoying Trump's platform, however, were not unique to him; they were present across large portions of the US population and persistently on display in the excessively violent police force unleashed on Black and Brown people.[6] The views of those who believe that most Mexicans are rapists and murderers (Trump 2015); that most Black men killed at the hands of police had it coming; that our country is being "invaded" by asylum seekers, migrant laborers, and women fleeing domestic violence;[7] and that African countries are "shithole" countries[8] reflect attitudes rooted in hatred, not anger. As Lorde clarifies, anger exists between potential allies—that is, between groups of people that might have been subject to the varying forms of oppressive and damaging rhetoric and policies shaping Trump's platform. At least these groups of people *might* find common cause in undermining the interlocking oppressive forces under which they all suffer. Between the Trump supporter who hates Mexicans and the Deferred Action for Childhood Arrivals (DACA) student who wants to organize with other marginalized communities in an effort to try to make her life a little less precarious, there may be no room for coalescing. Lorde helps us to be okay with this reality. Instead, our young DACA student should consider what coalitional possibilities might exist between DACA students and LGBTQ activists, feminist activists, Black Lives Matter activists, and environmental justice activists, to name only a few potential allies. Between these allies there may still exist anger, something Lorde again teaches us to accept. Consider, for instance, the variety of controversies that arose between white and nonwhite women surrounding the 2017 Women's March, something I will attend to in chapter 5. What we hope exists between the women caught up in such controversies is "anger," not "hatred." When the tension is rooted in anger, there is still hope for building alliances and doing the challenging work of politico-ethical coalition politics. When the tension is rooted in "hatred," Lorde helps us to see the value in simply walking away and looking for allies elsewhere.

Understood this way, the goal of coalition work is about "unity" and not "unanimity" (Lorde 1984b, 135–37). A political commitment to undermine oppression encourages an ethical commitment that is antithetical to unanimity. Lorde defines coalition as the "coming together of elements which are, to begin with, varied and diverse in their particular natures" (135).[9] For Lorde, coalitions are explicitly political, not ontological, spaces. As such, they are as complex and expansive as the oppressive system they form to contest. One must move against oppression in a self-reflexive manner. She must focus her actions against both external and internal oppression simultaneously. "We cannot," Lorde attests, "afford to do our enemies' work by destroying each other" (142). Instead, we must learn how to "make common cause with those others identified as outside the structures" and how to "take our differences and make them strengths" (Lorde 1984c, 112). Perhaps one of the most often-cited lines of Lorde's work, "the master's tools will never dismantle the master's house" (112), speaks directly to the self-reflexivity that is inherent to politico-ethical coalition politics. One cannot use oppressive means to undermine oppression. The master's tools are soaked in oppression; to dismantle the entire interlocking system, we must use tools that are not tainted by oppression. In this sense, a "complete" vision for radical coalition politics is needed: a vision that severs all oppressive ties and stands firmly against oppression in all its manifestations—in short, a politico-ethical vision.

EMPIRICAL ACCOUNTS: FORGING POLITICO-ETHICAL COALITIONS

The notion of politico-ethical coalition politics sketched by Reagon and supported by many of her contemporaries is also the dominant notion of activist coalition politics supported by much of the empirical research coming out of sociology, women's studies, and political science. This commonality is evident in the findings of one edited collection in particular (though I will cite similar findings across other journal articles and edited collections); *Forging Radical Alliances across Difference: Coalition Politics for the New Millennium* (Bystydzienski and Schlacht 2001a) is a collection of empirical case studies of activist coalition politics from the 1960s through the 1990s, which is clearly indebted to the theorizations of coalition coming out of early US

Women of Color feminism. As editors Jill M. Bystydzienski and Steven P. Schacht make clear in the introduction, echoing Luxemburg, this book is an attempt to theorize coalition from the ground up (from case studies) and in so doing to follow Women of Color feminist activists and theorists to develop a "critical social theory of coalition politics" (Bystydzienski and Schacht 2001b, 2, 3), an idea they borrow from Patricia Hill Collins (6). Influenced by the work of Collins, Nira Yuval-Davis, Lorde, and others, the editors seek to add "empirically grounded theory" to the growing body of knowledge coming out of Women of Color feminism (6). Much of the collection reiterates and empirically grounds the notion of politico-ethical coalition developed here.

Most centrally, these empirical findings further support the claim that activist coalition politics is fundamentally rooted in a political commitment to undermining oppression. Bystydzienski and Schacht are unequivocal on this point (see 2001b, 7). Any suggestion that social justice coalitions form for a reason other than an explicitly political one is simply not supported by their findings. While the editors and many contributors go on to discuss the importance of feelings and emotions such as empathy, mutual understanding, and a willingness to cross over into another's world, they all proceed from the starting point of the inherent political nature of coalitional relationships.[10] What is required for disparate groups to come together are "shared issues that engage members of two or more groups ... in such a manner that the given issue becomes more important than existing differences" (8–9). Some of the issues addressed in the collection include rape (Bevacqua 2001), violence against women (Schacht and Ewing 2001), and environmental protection (Grossman 2001). These scholars find, and this becomes one of the main contributions of the collection, that when committed to a common issue, difference may be "negotiated in such a way that it becomes a strength in the pursuit of the given social justice goal" instead of a weakness (Bystydzienski and Schacht 2001b, 9), thus recalling one of Lorde's central claims.

Much like Reagon and Lorde, they argue that forging alliances at the "interpersonal" level is absolutely essential to successful coalition politics. This process of negotiating difference at the interpersonal level consists of three stages, and closely mirrors what I am calling a "self-reflexive" political commitment to undermining oppression. First, coalition members must accept the discomfort that comes with leaving one's place of safety and comfort (Reagon's "home") "in order to reach out to one another" (Bystydzienski and Schacht 2001b, 9). Next, members must conduct "an honest appraisal of how privilege based on gender, race, class, sexuality, age, or other factors is played out in the specific relationship or alliance"—that is, within the coalition itself (10). In the final stage they must reaffirm a "common ground by accepting and honoring those perspectives, experiences, and insights that are shared between them" and thereby allow a "shared commitment to social justice" to "become more important than potentially divisive identities" (10). Rooted in a self-reflexive political commitment, by interacting with others within the space of coalitions committed to undermining oppression, members learn shared knowledge and mutual respect.

One particularly helpful example from the case studies is Christopher Bickel's account of the student coalition that formed at Indiana University in 1997. Bickel's findings reveal that early US Women of Color coalition feminists were hardly the only social justice activists approaching coalition politics as politico-ethical encounter. Additionally and unlike the emphasis placed on political indeterminacy within contemporary political theory, Bickel provides a full account of the motivation behind the coalition's formation and its internal functioning. As Bickel narrates it, having been an active participant himself, the students had a clear understanding of the interlocking nature of oppressive forces both on campus and in wider society. Echoing Reagon and Smith, Bickel recounts: "From past experience, we knew that if we organized separately, and around single-issue platforms, our ability to restructure radically oppressive power relations at IU [Indiana University] would remain limited at best and counterproductive at worst. The institution that we were fighting against was far too powerful and complex for any one organization to confront.... We decided that the way to contest the university was to develop a broad-based coalition, grounded in *democratic*, grassroots organizing that simultaneously confronted multiple forms of oppression at the university" (Bickel 2001, 212). Their understanding of the interlocking nature of the oppressive systems at work required them to break out of single-issue platforms in favor of a more broad-based political commitment to social justice. Additionally, he notes that the student coalition was organized around what Paulo Freire calls "dialogics" (Bickel also cites Lorde [1984f] and Anzaldúa [1990] when outlining this idea), or a "nonhierarchical method of praxis where people come together to speak *with* rather than *for* each other" (Bickel 2001, 213). In this way, the political commitment of the coalition was turned in on the coalition itself. "The dialogical method of organizing illuminated not only how we were oppressed, but also how we were in complicity with oppressive systems of power" (213). Their political commitment to social justice and democratic equality guided the formation, direction, and internal dynamics of the coalition. It therefore opened up possibilities for individual coalition members to engage in the emotional labor and transformation that is crucial to politico-*ethical* visions of coalition politics.

As Bickel reports, they started to "develop bonds that transcended boundaries of race, class, gender and sexuality," which compelled them to attend one another's events (215). Drawing from his experience in this student coalition, Bickel captures the essence of a politico-ethical vision of coalition building: "If our goal is to have a democratic university that involves everybody in the decision-making process, then it is necessary to *form coalitions that reflect this objective*. In other words, *the means we use must always coincide with the ends we want to accomplish*. By creating a coalition that embodied the goals of the movement in its day-to-day activities, we were trying to provide an example of a radically democratic organization that crossed social identity lines" (215; my emphasis). Like Combahee, the student coalition acted as a prefigurative political space in which the political goals it formed to achieve were enacted in the space of the coalition itself. It thus enacted politico-ethical coalition politics.

Resisting the Pull of Indeterminacy: Choosing Politico-Ethical Coalition Politics

First theorized in the late 1970s and early 1980s, a politico-ethical vision of coalition politics continues to inform certain contemporary feminist articulations of coalition politics, most notably those offered by Mohanty in the decades immediately following the 1980s.[11] As Angela Davis made explicitly clear in her lecture at University of Chicago's Rockefeller Chapel only weeks after Trump's 2016 election, in order to combat the varied hatred politics ignited by Trump's offensive campaign rhetoric, progressives are going to have to take lessons from Women of Color coalition feminists who have been engaging in effective coalitional activism since the 1970s. With this in mind, I want to close my discussion by contrasting what I perceive as Butler's third, and most recent, formulation of coalition politics (presented in fragments across *Frames of War* [2009] and recent lectures on the topic) with the conception of politico-ethical coalition politics forged by early US Women of Color coalition feminists and present within later work by Mohanty and others in the decades since the 1980s. In thinking with Mohanty and putting her in conversation with Bohrer (2019) and the *New Political Science* "Feminism in Coalition" symposium authors (2018), I invite contemporary feminists to resist the pull of indeterminacy and instead *choose* politico-ethical coalition politics.

In theorizing coalition as spectacle, Butler struggled to square her commitments to ontological unfixity and epistemological undecidability with her political commitment to progressive politics, and she thus arrived at a form of coalition rooted in unpredictable spectacle. Butler maneuvers around this tension between unfixity and fixity in theorizing coalition as ethical community insofar as she embraces ontological certainty and uniformity (we are all universally precarious) as the basis for an equally knowable and certain form of progressive politics. Unlike her other two formulations of coalition, in what appears to be a third formulation, Butler pivots entirely away from identity categories and ontology. By shifting the focus from the discursive production of infinitely unstable categories (what we saw in *Gender Trouble*) to the "interlocking networks of power and position" (Butler 2009, 31), Butler's understanding of the challenge of Marxism is now anchored in the movement of power, rather than the production of ontological categories. The form of collective group politics best suited to a world characterized by interlocking power structures, she argues, would be one that pivots away from identity politics and toward "coalition" politics rooted in a shared commitment to understanding and challenging "precarity and its differential distributions" (32).

With this emphasis on examining systems of power that position individuals and groups rather than the identity categories themselves, Butler moves in a direction that appears to resonate with politico-ethical coalition politics. With her insistence that the political commitment generating such alliances shapes an internally antagonistic coalitional space (32), Butler even moves in a direction that seems attentive to the ethical considerations raised by Reagon, Lorde, and others. Indeed, she cites Reagon on this point (Butler 2015, 151). Interestingly, however, Butler does not align this newer formulation of coalition with Women of Color coalitional feminism beyond mentioning Reagon's treatment of the danger inherent to coalition work. Furthermore, while she is certainly aware of the hostile relations that mark coalitional encounters, her attempt to articulate a possible way around or through these antagonisms runs into inconsistencies that resonate with her earlier formulations and effectively obscure political commitment. Specifically, in an attempt to clarify what it is that remains open or "mobile" in such alliances (Butler 2009, 149), Butler sketches the ethical orientation she deems appropriate to coalition politics. In so doing, she clarifies that the anchor for ethical considerations within the space of coalition centers on the "provisional" quality of the coalition's aims and goals (147).

Resuscitating the "antifoundational" component of coalition as spectacle, Butler's most recent formulation of coalition therefore mirrors what has now become a dominant trend among certain contemporary feminist theory scholars. This trend is particularly visible in Jasbir Puar's appropriation of Gayatri Spivak's notion of a "politics of the open end" (Spivak and Harasym 1990, 111) in her groundbreaking 2007 text, *Terrorist Assemblages* (Puar 2007, xx). Puar insists on the "political impossibility" of "being on one side or the other" (2007, 209), and in fact critically interrogates intersectionality theorists for their willingness to embrace stable notions of identity and political commitment (see Puar 2007, 216; 2012). In their stead, Puar follows Butler and others in embracing a project centered on enticing "unknowable political futures into our wake" (Puar 2007, xx).

This persistent appeal to political indeterminacy also reverberates across a special issue of *Theory and Event* on Quebec's Maple Spring in the spring of 2012,[12] specifically in the issue's treatment of the Coalition large de l'Association pour une solidarité syndicale étudiante (CLASSE) that formed in response to rising tuition fees and other neoliberal policies. Taking Butler and others similarly inclined toward political indeterminacy as their guides,[13] the articles highlight the undecidability, unpredictability, and indeterminacy of this coalition event (Lynes 2012; Al-Saji 2012; Manning 2012), instead of focusing on the concrete, knowable, and decidable political demands of CLASSE itself (centering on a more participatory democratic order) (CLASSE 2012). Krista Geneviève Lynes, for instance, puts Jacques Derrida in conversation with Spivak to argue that the classroom may act as a "preview of the formation of collectivities" typical of coalition building due to the "undecidability of the classroom as a space for solidarity" (Lynes 2012). Similarly, Alia Al-Saji and Erin Manning underscore the unexpected diversity of participants working in solidarity within the space of the demonstration. Echoing Puar's penchant for a politics of the "open," this leads them to emphasize the "unimaginability" or "unpredictability" of the event itself, in addition to its equally unknowable future course, thereby emphasizing a nonlinear opening of time and what Al-Saji calls a "politics of the future" that "in its unpredictability and newness, holds the promise of reconfiguring the present" (Al-Saji 2012). Evoking Butler and echoing Schram, Manning argues that the very presence of the Maple Spring protestors caused a kind of ontological trouble (Manning 2012). Other authors similarly read the strike as a rupture or disruptive moment that underscored the necessity of acts of civil disobedience wherein the uncounted or invisible (following Rancière 1999, 2004) unexpectedly make themselves visible (see Baillargeon and Barney 2012; Manning 2012), using the language of unpredictable "emergent collectives" (Manning 2012) and "assemblages" (Al-Saji 2012) to describe such collective efforts.

This reoccurring emphasis on undecidability, unimaginability, and unpredictability, however, seems odd given the fact that the CLASSE strike, much like the student coalition that Bickel reported on at Indiana University, was planned and organized by specific student groups on campus. For instance, while Al-Saji points out the remarkable diversity of protestors walking alongside her, it doesn't seem that she, nor many of the other scholars published here, takes the time to consider what it is *politically* that has brought such a diverse set of actors to the street. Instead, she is struck by the surprising, indeed "unimaginable," comfort she finds in walking alongside such a diverse array of people. CLASSE itself, on the other hand, was quite explicit in its demands. As I discussed in the introduction, it called for a social strike to unite students and nonstudents alike in contesting a social order that guarantees unequal access to public services, resulting in increasing wealth for a small number of people and corporations.

Recall also that while politico-ethical coalition politics is rooted in notions of flexibility, what is "provisional" or "unknowable" in such spaces are the methods for achieving the goal of undermining interlocking oppressions alongside one's sense of self within the space of coalition. As I have shown, because Reagon's, Lorde's, and Combahee's political commitment is self-reflexive, it shapes the internal dynamics of the coalition such that individual members are willing to critically examine their relations with one another within the coalition and embrace existential transformation as part and parcel to the process of coalescing. This is the ethical component of politico-*ethical* coalition politics: to reexamine one's behavior and methods within the space of coalition to ensure that one's political commitment to undermining interlocking oppressive forces is also reflected in her encounters with coalition members. Thus, the provisional quality is not centered on the political commitment or goals of the coalition; it is instead centered on the methods for achieving the shared goal and each member's sense of self when walking into the space. Butler, on the other hand, joins Puar and others in her willingness to sacrifice political commitment as the stable and cementing force of coalition politics. What becomes provisional for Butler, much like what we have seen with Laclau and Mouffe and with Butler's antifoundational formulation of coalition politics, are the goals and aims that bring us to the coalitional space in the first place. If this is so, we might then ask what it is that actually cements coalition efforts in this third formulation. To answer this, we must examine Butler's more recent lectures on the topic.

As she puts it in "Bodily Vulnerability, Coalition Politics" (2015), coalitional solidarity is generated out of the unpredictability of ethical encounter: the fact that coalition members never know with whom they will find themselves in the space of coalition. Think here of Lynes's comparison of the unpredictability of the classroom to spaces of coalitional activism. In this formulation, Butler has found a way to bring together components of her ethical formulation of coalition with her antifoundational formulation by naming the unpredictability of ethical encounter as the foundation of coalition politics. She arrives at this conclusion by way of Reagon's comments on the danger inherent to coalition politics and her assertion that we often find ourselves in coalition with people we may not like (see Butler 2015, 151–52). One never knows exactly, according to Butler, which bodies one will find oneself in alliance with on the street, "which means we accept a kind of unchosen dimension to our solidarity work with others." Butler asserts that this uncertainty provides the basis for solidarity, not any "deliberate agreements we enter knowingly" (152). Curiously invoking Reagon, Butler argues that in place of a shared political commitment, the glue that holds coalition members together is the mutual unknowability and precarity that results from the danger inherent to coalition work. Thus, while in this new formulation of coalition Butler has at least accounted for Reagon's *challenge*, she has eschewed political commitment as the cementing force and misread the most compelling component of Reagon's argument.

Yes, Reagon is well aware of the danger inherent in politico-ethical coalition politics: teaming up with people invested in your continued subordination. Rather than being rooted in an "unknowability," instead this danger is rooted in the life experiences of women of color who have been marginalized and mistreated within coalitional spaces by both white women and Black men. What they *knew* back in the 1970s and 1980s, and what Reagon is speaking to in her speech, is that there was a very *real* possibility that white women would not be self-reflexive in their commitment to undermining oppression and would likely practice oppressive behaviors in relation to other people within coalitional spaces. Think here of Lorde's account of working with white feminist academics that she shares in "The Master's Tools Will Never Dismantle the Master's House" (1984c) or her exchange with Mary Daly (1984d), both of which demonstrate a clear unwillingness on the part of white women to encounter women of color as equals. Knowing the reality of the dismissiveness (at its best) and outright hostility (at its worst) that persisted among white women toward nonwhite women made coalitions dangerous spaces for women of color. It is precisely this *knowledge* that led Reagon, Lorde, Smith, and others to argue that the cementing force behind coalition efforts must be political.

The ethical component, I have argued here, is generated out of the political commitment. It is their commitment to undermining oppression that might incline white women and Black men to turn this commitment in on themselves and examine their own behavior within the space of coalition. The cementing force is not the unpredictability of ethical encounter; rather, it is one's political commitment to undermining oppression that might compel her to wager predictability for the sake of a greater cause. Thus, the notion of politico-ethical coalition politics located in Reagon's speech and echoed across the work of contemporaneous US Women of Color coalition feminists sits in stark contrast to the latest articulation of coalition politics on offer by Butler as well as visions of assemblage theory made popular by Puar and dominant across recent treatments of coalitional activism within political theory and on display in the *Theory and Event* special issue.

Encouragingly, the pull of political indeterminacy has not enticed all contemporary scholars. Indeed, certain feminist theorists, most notably Mohanty, remain impervious to such seductions. Developed in the latter half of the 1980s and in the decades following Reagon's speech, Mohanty's work charts a vision of transnational feminist solidarity outside of hegemonic notions of white, Western feminism. In this undertaking, she is explicit both in her indebtedness to the work of early US Women of Color feminism (Mohanty 2003, 5, 49, 28) and in her wariness toward postmodern feminist approaches typical of Butler and others (6, 53, 81, 87–88, 107, 225). We see these influences (and avoidances) especially in her critique of sisterhood, her preference for solidarity rooted in struggle and political commitment, and her nuanced treatment of home and community. In these discussions, we find visible traces of politico-ethical coalition politics.

In "Feminist Encounters: Locating the Politics of Experience," Mohanty revisits the important distinction Reagon draws between homes and coalitions to critically interrogate models of cross-cultural feminist solidarity rooted in notions of "sisterhood" (Mohanty 1995). By contrasting Reagon's speech with Robin Morgan's (1984) introduction to *Sisterhood Is Global: The International Women's Movement Anthology*, Mohanty captures the danger in longing for feminist notions of home or community. Such notions are at work in visions of "global sisterhood" wherein women are unified by the sameness of their oppression, the sameness of their struggles, and a shared *good will* between them. Much like Butler's notion of ethical community, by presuming both a false sense of commonality between all women on these fronts and a shared ethic of good will, such visions, she argues, flatten conflicts between women and necessarily conceal the *politics* of feminist solidarity. Instead of encouraging an engagement with difference and conflict, notions of global sisterhood require that women "transcend" these differences so that they can work together in an international women's movement (Mohanty [1995] 2003, 114). Instead of collective action being defined on the basis of political choices made through collective interpretative analytical work—the hard work of coalescing—collective feminist action in a global sisterhood model becomes "defined on the basis of personal intentions, attitudes, or desires" wherein women may be conceived as "well-intentioned" but never as *political* actors (114). As I argued was the case with the ethical vision of coalition on offer by Coles and Butler, Mohanty similarly demonstrates the ways in which visions of global sisterhood obscure the politics of collective action in favor of unexamined and naively optimistic notions of ethical sisterhood.

In its stead, Mohanty points toward an understanding of feminist solidarity as political coalition. The "unity of women" must not be given "on the basis of a natural/psychological [or even emotional] commonality" but is something "that has to be worked for, struggled toward—in history" (2003, 116). Like Reagon and parting from Butler, Mohanty interprets feminist coalition politics as characterized by common struggle and shared political commitments. Elsewhere, Mohanty suggests that feminist solidarity ought to be rearticulated as "an 'imagined *community*' of Third World oppositional struggles—'imagined' not because it is not 'real' but because it suggests potential alliances and collaborations across divisive boundaries" (Mohanty [1991] 2003, 46; my emphasis). Like coalition, an imagined community provides a welcome alternative to visions of collective action that center on biological (commonality on the basis of being female) or cultural (commonality on the basis of a shared experience of oppression) bases for alliance (46). Instead, again like politico-ethical coalition politics, imagined communities propose a shared political commitment (rooted in the processes of dialectical materialism) as the basis for alliance. "It is not color or sex that constructs the ground for these struggles"—meaning, these are not barred rooms of Black men or white feminists (46). "Rather," she tells us, "it is the way we think about race, class, and gender—the political links we choose to make among and between struggles" that forms the basis of feminist solidarity (46).

As she put it a decade later in the introduction to *Feminism without Borders*:

> I define solidarity in terms of mutuality, accountability, and the recognition of *common interests* as the basis for relationships among *diverse* communities. Rather than assuming an enforced commonality of oppression, the *practice of solidarity* foregrounds communities of people who have *chosen* to work and fight together. *Diversity and difference are central* values here—to be acknowledged and respected, not erased in the building of alliances.... solidarity is always an achievement, the *result of active struggle* to *construct the universal* on the basis of particulars/differences. It is the praxis-oriented, active political struggle embodied in this notion of solidarity that is important to my thinking—and the reason I prefer to focus attention on solidarity rather than on the concept of "sisterhood." ... I believe feminist solidarity as defined here constitutes the *most principled* way to cross borders. (Mohanty 2003, 7; my emphasis)

Numerous key aspects of politico-ethical coalition politics emerge here. Like Reagon and challenging both Butler's starting place in ontological sameness in coalition as ethical community and her repudiation of political goals and directions in both coalition as spectacle and in her third formulation, Mohanty implies that the starting place for solidarity in the form of coalition must be in seeing and utilizing "differences." Such a starting place, however, is not shaped by naively optimistic calls to unite across difference. Instead, and again like Reagon, Mohanty is soberly aware of the fact not only that coalition politics must be "struggled" for but also that it must be shaped by a shared and actively "chosen" "political" commitment to undermine interlocking oppressive forces. As she attests, assuming such a political commitment is the "most *principled*" way to go about solidarity work. This approach, she clarifies, is one shaped by a "political as well as [an] ethical goal" (2003, 3; my emphasis).

Mohanty's politico-ethical approach to solidarity work remains consistent across all chapters of *Feminism without Borders*. What fluctuates is the language Mohanty uses to describe this version of feminist solidarity; *community, political alliance, coalition, collective*, and *network* are all used to describe enactments of feminist solidarity. Of these slippages, the one that concerns me the most is her use of *community*, especially when juxtaposed with her endorsement of Reagon's distinction between home and coalition (Mohanty 2003, 114). For Mohanty, the connection between home and community is explicit. She feels a sense of "home" and "community" with other "women of color" (128).[14] As was the case for Smith, Mohanty's feminist political consciousness emerges out of this space. Recall also that while Reagon's speech was very much in the service of drawing a sharp distinction between these spaces, she, too, sees the value in home spaces. Distinguishing these spaces is not tantamount to privileging one over the other.

For Smith, Mohanty, Lorde, and Reagon, "home" or "community" is a crucial training ground for politico-ethical coalition politics. They are each getting at the idea that politico-ethical coalition politics very much depends on a personal and individual journey that takes place in the most intimate of spaces. As Reagon argues, this is a journey that takes place both within one's self, as she transforms from "Mary" to "Maria" (Reagon 1983, 350) and within one's community (as she chooses to join up with other communities) (345). Similarly, Mohanty (2003) draws attention to the role that a politics of location (see Rich 1986)—or attention to the multiple and fluid sites in which individual people and selves are *positioned*—plays in discussions of feminist political solidarity. "But location, for feminists, necessarily implies self- as well as collective definition, since meanings of the self are inextricably bound up with our understanding of collectives as social agents.... Experience of the self, which is often discontinuous and fragmented, must be historicized before it can be generalized into a collective vision. In other words, experience must be historically interpreted and theorized if it is to become the basis of feminist solidarity and struggle, and it is at this moment that an understanding of the politics of location proves crucial" (Mohanty 2003, 122). Attention to the plurality that is characteristic of our own individual selves—our multiple and fluid identities—Mohanty suggests, may productively guide our thinking on feminist solidarity. In the same way that defining feminist solidarity in terms of "sisterhood" proves exclusionary because of its inattention to the many differences between women, defining our own individual identities as one-dimensional proves equally exclusionary precisely because the self, like a coalition, is equally "discontinuous and fragmented." In this sense, for Mohanty, Reagon, and many others, despite the potential nurturing found in homes, these spaces are also sites of struggle. As such, they provide fertile ground for engendering politico-ethical commitments.

Promisingly, Mohanty is not alone in her willingness to resist the pull of indeterminacy. Heeding Angela Davis's call, the March 2018 *New Political Science* symposium issue on "feminism in coalition" explicitly takes up questions related to possibilities for progressive coalitional activism in the age of Trump. In so doing, the authors self-consciously resist the pull of political indeterminacy in favor of taking early US Women of Color coalition feminists as well as contemporary fellow travelers indebted to this literature as their guides "to effectively navigating the political, ethical, emotional, psychic, and esthetic space of coalitional activism" (Murib and Taylor 2018a, 114n2).[15] Many of the authors included in this symposium offer accounts of coalitional activism that resonate strongly with key components of politico-ethical coalition politics, presented in a significantly abridged version in my contributing article to the symposium (L. Taylor 2018).

For instance, Zein Murib's (2018) critical discussion of the construction of GLBT and Queer coalitions during the National Policy Roundtables that convened "self-identified" lesbian, gay, bisexual, transgender, and Queer activists and political actors during the late 1990s and early 2000s exposes the danger in letting goals of unity erase Indigenous voices. Like Reagon, Lorde, and many others, Murib advocates for a form of coalitional solidarity that foregrounds difference, rather than aiming for unity (sameness or what Lorde called "unanimity" [Lorde 1984b, 135–37]). Both Shireen Roshanravan and Cricket Keating also speak to the dire necessity of bringing together political commitment and ethical orientation in the space of coalition. In her brilliant account of what she calls the "coalitional praxis of (dis)integration," Roshanravan warns against situating the "'getting shit done' of progressive coalition politics above the intersubjective transformative, and therefore emotional and psychic process of disintegrating (or decentering) the self" (Murib and Taylor 2018a, 115; see also Roshanravan 2018). Roshanravan's argument thereby integrates both Combahee's insistence on avoiding doing whatever one must do to reach their political goals—that is, letting the "getting shit done" take precedence over how one treats coalitional allies—in favor of a continuous examination of the internal dynamics of their group, alongside Reagon's suggestion that effective coalitional work requires self-transformation. Taking her lead from María Lugones (to whom I turn in chapter 3) and building on her own sophisticated rendering of coalitional consciousness-building (Keating 2005), Keating (2018) similarly emphasizes the importance of developing a set of interpersonal skills in order to achieve the critical self-understanding necessary for contesting intricate and interlocking oppressive forces. For Keating, we might then understand the development of the interpersonal skills necessary for engaging in collective mapping exercises geared toward becoming "interdependently resistant" as the generative force behind everyday coalition building (178).

Recent historical and conceptual accounts of intersectionality similarly attest that the politics of intersectional feminism manifests in coalitions rooted in difference, internal and external struggle, political commitment, and ethical orientation (see, e.g., Carastathis 2016). Building from such accounts and as already addressed in chapter 1, Bohrer similarly takes a genealogy of US Women of Color feminist as her guides in resisting both class-reductionist Marxism—insisting instead that multiple, diffuse, and interlocking forms of oppression intersect with capitalism to create the precarious conditions of our lives—and poststructuralist incommensurability that denies the possibility of naming and collectively contesting interlocking oppressive systems. Like Reagon, Lorde, and Mohanty, Bohrer's concept of solidarity under contemporary capitalism is grounded in the "incommensurable differences of social location" (2019, 234). This starting place in difference, she asserts, will generate possibilities for coalitional activism centered not on natural affinities, ontological sameness, or ethical orientation but rather on shared political commitments (254–56). "Coalitions," Bohrer asserts, "must thus be rethought, not as the natural coalescence of groups who have a natural affinity, but rather as an important, strategic investment of time, energy, resources, learning, and reflection" (256). For Bohrer and the many US Women of Color coalition feminist authors I have engaged here, the political and ethical dimensions of coalitional activism are indissoluble.

Note the contrast between the prominence of politico-ethical commitment shaping these works and Butler's, Puar's, and the *Theory and Event* contributors' persistent disavowal of political goals and directions. Choosing and committing to a direction, an end, or a political course, was not a problem for Reagon, Smith, or Lorde; nor is it a problem for Mohanty, Bohrer, and the NPS contributors. Along the way, one's actions will need to be updated and adjusted to fit this principle. But the principle itself, according to Reagon in her speech and unequivocally endorsed by the contemporary voices referenced here, is unwavering; it is, to use language from Laclau and Mouffe, "fixed." It is these activist-theorists who, I contend, and recalling Reagon's words, "hold the key" to successful progressive coalition politics in our contemporary moment.

By situating Reagon's renowned coalition speech in relation to her Women of Color feminist contemporaries and to contemporary fellow travelers, I have located a theory of coalition politics that may attend to the practical problems confronting political theorists such as Coles, Laclau and Mouffe, and Butler without obscuring politics in favor of either ethics or unpredictable spectacle. In addition to supporting the idea that Left-oriented activist politics is rooted fundamentally in a self-reflexive political commitment to undermining oppression, this literature expands on an idea only hinted at by Reagon; that is, despite the rhetorical advantage in distinguishing homes from coalitions, homes serve as an important training ground for politico-ethical coalition politics. As suggested by Reagon, Smith, Lorde, and Mohanty, the symbiotic movement between the ethics and politics of coalition is best understood when the concept of coalition is infused at the level of "home" and "identity"—in short, at the level of ontology. It is therefore to questions of identity and consciousness that I now turn.

3

Coalition from the Inside Out

Struggling toward Coalitional Identity and Developing a Coalitional Consciousness with Lorde, Anzaldúa, Sandoval, and Pratt

There were people who came south to work in the movement who were not Black. Most of them were white when they came. Before it was over, that category broke up—you know, some of them were Jewish, not simply white, and some others even changed their names. Say if it was Mary when they came South, by the time they were finished it was Maria, right? It's called finding yourself.

—BERNICE JOHNSON REAGON, "Coalition Politics: Turning the Century"

In her "Coalition Politics" speech, Bernice Johnson Reagon (1983) recounts her experiences working in coalition with multiple subjugated groups and white supporters during the civil rights movement, making a compelling case for engaging in the hard and, at times, dangerous work of progressive coalition politics. As I argued in chapter 2, this "danger" for Reagon inheres primarily in the fact of working as a Black woman in coalition with people who may be invested in her continued subjugation—Black men on account of her gender and white women on account of her race. Additionally, particularly for those who occupy relatively privileged positions within society (for instance, white, college-educated men and women who came to the South to work in the civil rights movement), Reagon suggests here, this danger also inheres in the likelihood of losing oneself (or at least one's sense of oneself) to the cause—that is, losing "Mary" to "Maria." While such a transformation certainly poses a certain existential threat to "Mary," Reagon depicts this existential transformation as a positive thing: "It's called finding yourself." This willingness to shift from one self to another is a crucial component—a prerequisite even—to successful politico-ethical coalition politics.

In this brief passage, then, Reagon points us in the direction of the third important aspect of successful politico-ethical coalition politics: the ability to cultivate, even the necessity of cultivating, a multiple and shifting *coalitional identity* and, in this sense, the engagement in politico-ethical coalition politics from the *inside out*. Reagon, of course, is not the only US Woman of Color coalition feminist we have seen who points us in this direction. As I addressed in the previous chapter, Barbara Smith, Reagon, and Mohanty all argue that coalition politics actually begins in the more intimate and familiar space of the "home." While this "home" space may refer to women of color–only spaces wherein women gain the strength and critical consciousness to understand and contest multiple and fluid systems of power, this "home" space may also refer to an even more intimate space *within* oneself. This is why I suggested that the distinction Reagon draws between homes and coalitions was rhetorical and not actual. She uses it as a metaphor to make the case for moving from identity politics to coalition politics. And yet, early US Women of Color coalition feminists were well aware of both the love and the danger present in home spaces. Reagon picks up on this dual quality in her brief mention of Mary. Home spaces are crucial training grounds for coalition precisely because they, too, are marked by struggle, mirroring the intimate struggle experienced in the transformation from "Mary" to "Maria." As María Lugones (2003) similarly argues in *Pilgrimages/Peregrinajes: Theorizing Coalition against Multiple Oppressions*, published two decades after Reagon's speech, but building on concepts she had been working through since the early 1980s (see Lugones and Spelman 1983; Lugones 1987, 1990a, 1990b, 1991, 1994, 1995), coalition work depends on a "metamorphosis of self" (Lugones 2003, ix).

We therefore find, embedded in Reagon's 1981 coalition speech, the beginning of an answer to the *perceived* crisis of Marxism in at least three of its permutations. Putting Rosa Luxemburg's version of Marxism in conversation with Black intersectional feminists, I showed in chapter 1, dissolved the first of these crises: the perceived incompatibility between intersectional social justice concerns and Marxist collective organizing (what I called the intersectionality crisis). Embedded within Reagon's coalition speech, we find a potential answer to the other three layers of the so-called crisis. As I argued in chapter 2, politically we find in Reagon a powerful call to action in the form of politico-ethical coalition politics that dispenses finally with class-only, race-only, or women-only politics and takes seriously the challenge of collective action among diverse subjugated groups. What has thus far been left unaddressed is how exactly we can be so sure that subjugated peoples are capable of entering into and working successfully within these coalitions. If the multiple, fluid, and "undecidable" structures of power leave subjugated groups permanently unstable or "unfixed," why are we to believe that they are capable of stabilizing long enough for purposeful political action? Indeed, if all subjects are understood as forever in the process of discursive becoming—as thinkers such as Judith Butler, Ernesto Laclau and Chantal Mouffe, and Moya Lloyd lead us to believe— how are they capable of decisive and directed political action? Does not the tension between the unfixity of being and knowing and the fixity of Left-oriented social justice politics again rear its head, leaving us with the unsatisfactory options of either coalition in the form of unplanned group spectacle or coalition in the form of ethical community?

Reagon points the way toward a possible answer to these ontological and epistemological challenges. Specifically, Reagon and other early US Women of Color coalition feminists (Anzaldúa, Lorde, Combahee, Sandoval, and Pratt), especially when put into conversation with works by Kimberlé Crenshaw, Linda Alcoff, Mohanty, Lugones, Edwina Barvosa-Carter, Anna Carastathis, and Shireen Roshanravan, will help us to locate *politics within ontology*, that is, *within identity*. However, the way in which they go about doing this profoundly reconfigures the notion of ontological unfixity on offer by thinkers such as Laclau and Mouffe, Butler, and other similarly inclined feminist theorists. By reconceiving ontological complexity and fluidity outside of notions of discursive unfixity, indeterminacy, or undecidability, this rich body of work offers a vision of coalition politics that stretches well beyond Butler's notion of *coalition as spectacle* (see chapter 2) or Lloyd's notion of *inessential coalitions* (Lloyd 2005, 151). Refocusing on identity need not confine us to notions of politics that center only on the possibility of unpredictable ontological disturbance. While such disruptions are certainly welcome and are unequivocally political, the politics of ontology centers on a decisive political struggle toward self-definition, unity, and coherence.

Reconfiguring identity and consciousness *coalitionally* thus offers a valuable alternative to theorizations of identity that conflate multiple identity or fluid identity with notions of permanent ontological unfixity, leading to notions of political indeterminacy. Learning to struggle toward unity also shapes their understanding (their epistemology) of the complicated and interconnected world in which they are situated. The *coalitional consciousness* they acquire through this process prepares them to confront the challenges inherent to politico-ethical coalition politics. Politico-ethical coalition politics thus both depends on and mirrors an internal (and psychological) journey that takes one through and across her multiple and shifting selves.

The chapter begins with a brief sketch of a twofold problem in contemporary poststructuralist theorizations of the feminist subject: the prominence of ontological unfixity and epistemological undecidability in such accounts, which leads to the complete disavowal of identity-based group politics, and the conspicuous dismissal of Women of Color coalition feminists as cotheorists in this endeavor. While I will use the label "poststructuralist" to designate a handful of contemporary feminist theorists (including most prominently Butler and Lloyd, as well as Diane Elam, Diana Coole, Joan Scott, Elizabeth Grosz, and Diana Fuss), I am less interested in placing feminists into camps (poststructuralist or not) and more interested in identifying certain theoretical and political orientations and probing their usefulness. The theoretical orientations I take to task here are those focused on ontological unfixity and epistemological undecidability, which often lead to notions of political indeterminacy. Differentiating poststructuralist feminists from US Women of Color coalition feminists might puzzle some readers. There are, for instance, several striking resonances between Gloria Anzaldúa's, Chela Sandoval's, and Lugones's arguments for a multiple and fluid sense of self and poststructuralist theoretical orientations toward ontological unfixity. The reason I have nevertheless purposefully avoided a project that aligns the Women of Color coalition feminists engaged here with "poststructuralist theory" is because doing so would undercut the sophistication of US Women of Color coalition feminists by overlooking some of their most important contributions to these discussions. My project rests on the claim that the immense value in the genealogy of US Women of Color coalitional feminism presented here resides in its divergences from poststructuralist theoretical commitments to ontological unfixity, epistemological undecidability, and political indeterminacy.[1] Thinking with US Women of Color coalition feminists to reconfigure identity and consciousness *coalitionally*, I will demonstrate later in this chapter, allows us to attend to multiplicity, ambiguity, fluidity, and even mobility outside of poststructuralist commitments to ontological unfixity and epistemological undecidability. After developing notions of coalitional identity and coalitional consciousness, I end by turning to an example of how this struggle unfolds for a white woman using Minnie Bruce Pratt's autobiography of her coming to consciousness. Like Reagon's "Mary," Pratt opens herself to self-transformation and in this way engages in politico-ethical coalition politics from the inside out.

Ontological Unfixity, Epistemological Undecidability, and the Dismissal of Women of Color Feminism

So the question arises in my mind, Mary, do you ever really read the work of Black women? Did you ever read my words, or did you merely finger through them for quotations which you thought might valuably support an already conceived idea concerning some old and distorted connection between us? . . .

Mary, I ask that you re-member what is dark and ancient and divine within yourself that aids your speaking. As outsiders, we need each other for support and connection and all the other necessities of living on the borders. But in order to come together we must recognize each other.
—AUDRE LORDE, "An Open Letter to Mary Daly"

Poststructuralist feminist engagements with the question of identity tend to move in troubling directions. These are troubling for a number of reasons. First, such accounts rarely engage the work of early US Women of Color coalition feminists, which is odd given the extensive treatment of multiple identity and intersecting and mobile forms of oppression found in their scholarship prior to the publication of many poststructuralist feminist texts. Second, when accounts do engage this literature, they tend either to dismiss it outright or to use it to advance their own theoretical claims, often resulting in a misreading of crucial concepts. Whether a nonreading, a dismissal, or a misreading, the pattern is worrisome not only because it fails to "recognize," in Audre Lorde's sense, the writing of women of color, but because in doing so such accounts forgo the theoretical richness and nuance of US Women of Color feminist accounts of identity and political consciousness, remaining trapped in the philosophical straitjacket of ontological unfixity and epistemological undecidability.

Before turning to accounts of these forms of dismissal, let me briefly sketch the tendency toward ontological unfixity and epistemological undecidability. This position takes its roots for many, and certainly for Butler, in a critique, following Nietzsche, of the "metaphysics of substance" (Butler 1990, 28). A clear presentation of this critique appears in Nietzsche's *On the Genealogy of Morality* where he tells us that "there is no 'being' behind doing, effecting, becoming; 'the doer' is merely a fiction added to the deed—the deed is everything" (1998, 25). According to Nietzsche, there is no ontological core—there is no "being" behind the acts that one carries out; the acts themselves are everything. It is only the seduction of language, specifically the grammatical formulation of the subject-predicate relationship wherein all actions must be performed by a subject, Nietzsche maintains, that fools us into thinking that there is a stable core (a subject) behind one's actions (the verb). Most philosophical ontologies, Nietzsche argues, are trapped within the illusion of "being" or "substance" created by the metaphysics of substance.

Butler famously uses this insight to argue, much in the same way, that there is also "no gender identity behind the expressions of gender" (1990, 34). She explains that a corollary humanist feminist iteration of the metaphysics of substance might understand "gender as an *attribute* of a person who is characterized essentially as a pregendered substance or 'core,' called the person, denoting a universal capacity for reason, moral deliberation, or language" (14). In the same way that Nietzsche argues that there is no subject (no doer) behind one's actions (one's deeds), Butler proposes that we similarly understand gender outside the metaphysics of substance. To do so, we must accept that there is no gender identity (no core or substance) behind the expressions (the deeds or actions) of gender. Instead, she maintains, "identity" is itself "performatively constituted" by "the very 'expressions that are said to be its results.'" In this sense, she asserts that gender is "always a doing, though not a doing by a subject who might be said to preexist the deed" (34). In what comes the closest to an actual definition of "gender" by a theorist who is openly hostile to definitions, Butler asserts that "gender is the repeated stylization of the body, a set of repeated acts within a highly rigid regulatory frame that congeal over time to produce the appearance of substance, of a natural sort of being" (45). Gender, quite simply, is a set of repeated acts that cohere (in a specific historical and social context) to produce the subject *effect* of man or woman.

Butler therefore joins other poststructuralist feminists such as Diane Elam (1994), Diana Coole (1993), Joan Scott (1997), Diana Fuss (1989), Elizabeth Grosz (1994), and Moya Lloyd (2005) in maintaining that rather than communicating a pregiven reality, language actually *constructs*, not reflects, meaning. The subject does not *enter* the polis but is *produced by* and within it, making the subject always a political subject and forever unfixed (Elam 1994, 70). As Lloyd has put it, these "subject[s]-in-process" *resist* the "fixity," "stability," or "closure" of identity (Lloyd 2005, 15, 17, 20, 22, 26), favoring instead *permanent open endedness* as a state of being (16, 17). This ontological state of *existing in process* (19, 22), Lloyd contends, embraces such qualities as fluidity (20), indeterminacy (21), and undecidability (22). For this reason, these feminists remain wary of a feminist project that requires a stable subject on which to ground its politics, favoring instead a "politics of displacement" of all stable categories (see Squires 1999, 132–36; Grosz 1994, 29–32; Elam 1994, 32, 74; Butler 1990, 406).

In the same way that identity categories are forever in flux and permanently unfixed, so, too, are all social forces. According to this understanding, and echoing Laclau and Mouffe, oppressions are undecidable; that is, they are incapable of being fully identified and pinned down. This lack of a clear grasp of oppressive forces, this inability to identify them with certainty—to capture their movements—reflects the tendency toward epistemological undecidability typical of many of these authors. Elam calls this moment of recognition (of both ontological unfixity and epistemological undecidability) the "necessity of indeterminacy" and argues that embracing this indeterminacy is the only thing, ironically, capable of holding feminists together (1994, 31).

In the excerpt from Lorde's "An Open Letter to Mary Daly" that began this section, Lorde invites Daly into a conversation about the distortion of Black female voices in Daly's 1978 text, *Gyn/Ecology: The Metaethics of Radical Feminism*. I say "invite" because Lorde speaks to Daly here as an "ally," not an "enemy" (Lorde 1984d). As "outsiders," Lorde attests, they need one another. They need dialogue so that they can learn to recognize each other's perspectives and experiences of oppression, even, in this instance, when one's experience of erasure or distortion is at the hands of a supposed feminist ally. By asking Daly to "re-member what is dark and ancient and divine" (69) in herself, Lorde invites her also on a journey of self-transformation. Through this process, Daly is likely to encounter dimensions of herself that she would rather not see: not only the self that erased the perspectives of Lorde and other Black women but, even worse, the self that appropriated their words to make her own point. Blocking identification with that self, refusing to look in the "faithful mirror" (Lugones 2003, 72) that Lorde places before her through the letter, Daly refuses any true connection to Lorde as a feminist ally and therefore also any true connection to her own plural self.

Daly refuses, that is, to follow Reagon's hypothetical Mary in transforming from "Mary" to "Maria."

Lorde's forceful calling out of Daly thus reveals a prescient lesson for contemporary scholars. If running into the political cul-de-sac of permanent ontological unfixity and epistemological undecidability were not bad enough, poststructuralist feminist accounts run into a second major problem: they dismiss highly relevant and alternative theoretical accounts of multiple identity and mobile and intersecting oppressions coming out of US Women of Color coalitional feminism. They do this in a few different ways: by naming but quickly dismissing such accounts as caught in the trap of essentialist identity politics; by ignoring such accounts altogether in a classic nonreading of Women of Color feminism while nevertheless appropriating their lived experience to substantiate their preformed theories; and by engaging with Women of Color feminist texts but misreading crucial conceptual moves.

Both Fuss's and Lloyd's treatment of Combahee and Barbara Smith are typical of the first form of outright dismissal. In Fuss's 1989 book, *Essentially Speaking: Feminism, Nature and Difference*, the only real engagement with US Women of Color feminism published in the decades preceding the publication of her book (the 1970s and 1980s) occurs in the form of a critical comment on the essentialist identity politics of the cofounders of Combahee, a position, Fuss implies, that was typical of Women of Color feminists of the time (Fuss 1989, 99–100). Citing Fuss's treatment of Combahee and Smith decades later in *Beyond Identity Politics*, Lloyd follows in step with Fuss, mentioning and swiftly rejecting Smith for embracing an "identitarian logic" wherein "unity" is sought beneath difference (Lloyd 2005, 36). In such instances, the experiences of Women of Color feminists are referenced but quickly dismissed as an example of precisely the form of problematic conceptualizations of identity that they aim to move beyond. (I will offer an alternative reading of Combahee shortly.)

Jasbir Puar's treatment of women of color in "'I Would Rather Be a Cyborg Than a Goddess': Becoming-Intersectional in Assemblage Theory" (2012) offers another incisive instance of this form of outright dismissal. Puar argues that Women of Color feminist accounts of intersectionality are incapable of "apprehending ontological becomings," remaining forever "trapped within the logic of identity" (Puar 2012, 50, 60). Of the category itself (women of color) Puar's misgivings are unambiguous; not only does she insist that the term *women of color* has become "emptied of specific meaning in its ubiquitous application and yet overdetermined in its deployment," she curiously asserts that it is guilty of "Othering" Black women and even colluding with white liberal feminism (52, 54). Due to its lack of philosophical sophistication, Puar insists that "intersectionality as an intellectual rubric and a tool for political intervention must be supplemented—if not complicated and reconceptualized—by a notion of assemblage" (50). In these instances, the experiences of women of color emerge as the counterexample, swiftly dismissed as unsophisticated treatments of a deeply complicated philosophical problem.

In the second type of dismissal, this time in the form of nonreading and disingenuous appropriation, the experiences of women of color are used to substantiate a preformed theoretical claim. Think here of the number of pages Butler has devoted to questions concerning multiple, fluid, or unstable identity and the conspicuous absence of Women of Color feminist voices in these engagements, even when these scholars theorized at length on this very topic long before Butler. To make matters worse, while one finds brief instances in *Gender Trouble* wherein Butler *implies* (without citing) that her theoretical argument dovetails with intersectional concerns about the interplay among "racial, class, ethnic, sexual, and regional modalities of discursively constituted identities" and the marginalization of women of color that often results from this (Butler 1990, 4–5), when juxtaposed against Lorde's "Letter to Mary Daly," Butler appears disturbingly caught in the trap of appropriating the experiences of women of color to support her own theoretical argument while refusing to engage these authors as serious and rigorous *cotheorists* of identity.

Similarly, while chapter 1 of Lloyd's *Beyond Identity Politics* begins with a passage from Lugones and continuously references Anzaldúa's notion of mestiza identity throughout her thematic summary of depictions of what Lloyd theorizes as the "subject-in-process," it never engages either Lugones or Anzaldúa as *theorists* of identity. In a move that seems surprisingly similar to Lorde's dismissal of Daly, Lloyd uses the experiences of women of color as a way to justify both the depth and breadth of her concept of the "subject-in-process." Indeed, she notes that the dissenting voices of "black feminists and women of color" ultimately compelled white feminists to move in the direction of destabilizing the category of women (Lloyd 2005, 13). While the notion of the mestiza figures prominently in her discussion of the "multiple subject" that results from this, in the following discussion Anzaldúa's words are absent (15–17). While Lloyd takes up Anzaldúa's work later in the book, her treatment distorts crucial aspects of Anzaldúa's unique theorization of multiple (or what I will call coalitional) identity, thereby ushering in a final form of dismissal.[2]

In the third form of dismissal, while the work of Women of Color feminists is genuinely engaged, a fundamental misreading occurs wherein the author selectively reads only those components of the work that validate her preformed theory. Puar's positioning of "assemblage" as an alternative both to "intersectional identities" and to poststructuralist accounts that remain ironically fixated on identity (even if in its "unfixed" form) is indicative of this (Puar 2012, 50). Like the poststructuralist accounts addressed above, Puar is equally critical of what she sees as a collapse back into identity categories (representational politics) typical of Women of Color feminism. Such gestures, she argues, unsuccessfully attempt to "quell the perpetual motion of assemblages, to capture and reduce them, to harness their threatening mobility" (Puar 2007, 213). In its stead, she offers Gilles Deleuze and Félix Guattari's notion of "assemblage" (or, *agencement*, in its original French equivalent), "a term that means design, layout, organization, arrangement, and relations—the focus being not on content but on relations, relations of patterns" (Puar 2012, 57). Puar insists that intersectionality must be supplemented by assemblage theory in order to become truly useful both politically and intellectually.

While Puar spends ample time (at least a third of the article) engaging with Women of Color feminist texts, she nevertheless insists that the value in accounts informed by assemblage theory (in place of intersectionality) rests in their unique ability to shift the focus to "the patterns of relations— not the entities themselves, but the patterns within which they are arranged with each other" (Puar 2012, 60–61). The implication here is that only assemblage theory, not intersectional feminism, is capable of shifting in this direction. To make such an assertion leads us to believe that despite Puar's discussion of certain Women of Color feminist texts, she has clearly not engaged carefully with the latent account of positionality present in Combahee's "Black Feminist Statement," to which I will turn shortly. As she similarly argues, the value in assemblage theory inheres in its ability to attend to the molecular level, whereas intersectionality, she insists, is equipped only to make sense of the "molar" level. Such an assertion leads us to believe that in addition to overlooking Combahee's more complicated appeal to identity politics, Puar's engagement with Women of Color feminism also overlooks the ubiquitous tendency across US Women of Color coalitional feminism to theorize from lived experience; that is, to theorize precisely from the granular or molecular level. Both Chela Sandoval's and Lugones's accounts of pedestrian theorizing (which I will turn to shortly) are particularly sophisticated treatments of this.

Lloyd's discussion of Anzaldúa offers another example of this final form of dismissal. Her choice to present mestiza identity as a metaphor is the first indication of this. Lloyd opts for "metaphor" because of what she sees as the impossibility of "prefiguring" "analytically how class, race and gender combine in any general sense to fashion specific subjectivities or to position those subjectivities upon the terrain of power" (Lloyd 2005, 46). The mestiza, she believes, reflects this impossibility and is therefore best deployed as "a metaphor for female subjectivity understood as processual" or "blended" (47). I see two problems with her choice of metaphor here. First, the presumption of impossibility seems unfounded, especially when much of Anzaldúa's account in *Borderlands/La Frontera* is devoted precisely to figuring how her multiple subjectivities combine and are positioned on the terrain of power. As I will show later, one's ability to make sense of one's multiplicity, despite the ambiguity, contradiction, and even trauma that one may encounter along the way, is precisely what it means to be a mestiza. As such, there is no need to treat mestiza only as metaphor; instead, it is the very real lived experience of Anzaldúa and other "border" women who straddle multiple identities and positionalities simultaneously. While I can appreciate the impulse for a white woman such as Lloyd to treat mestiza as a metaphor to make it accessible to other white women (under the presumption that many white women may not be "border" women), the richness of Anzaldúa's work lies precisely in the coalitional subjectivity inherent to mestiza identity—an identity that Pratt shows can be explicitly embraced by white women. For these reasons, limiting mestiza's explanatory power to only that of metaphor is both inaccurate and unnecessary.

The second misreading occurs in Lloyd's positioning of Anzaldúa's mestiza identity alongside poststructuralist accounts of the subject-in-process. As Lloyd's "cartography of the subject-of-process" reveals, what is unique across the variety of poststructuralist feminist approaches to identity she surveys—including Butler's theory of performative identity—is the prominent role of ontological unfixity. In the case of the multiple subject, where she places the mestiza, she attests that they "are never fixed," remaining instead in a "continual state of flux" (Lloyd 2005, 15). For Lloyd, what marks these subjects is their *refusal* of the stableness of a steady, fixed identity (17). Similarly, when Lloyd finally engages with Anzaldúa, her selective reading reconfirms the presence of ontological unfixity. We see this in a variety of interpretive moments when she suggests that mestiza identity emerges as an identity "that is always shifting and incomplete" (48); when she makes the assumption that Anzaldúa's depiction of the mestiza is always in the process of becoming and "never of being" (49); and when she comments that while Anzaldúa might have a "desire for identity," her experience reveals the "impossibility" of identity (50). Mestiza identity thus emerges for Lloyd as a metaphor for ontological *unfixity*.

My problem with this interpretive claim is that it seems to overlook another important thread in Anzaldúa's account of mestiza identity, which Lloyd references but fails to rigorously engage. For instance, while Lloyd is aware of Anzaldúa's inclination to both "deconstruct" *and* "construct" identity (Lloyd 2005, 48) and even cites an instructive passage on this point where Anzaldúa speaks of "keeping intact one's shifting and multiple identity and integrity" (Anzaldúa in Lloyd 2005, 48), she selectively ignores the implication of such an assertion. As I will demonstrate, rather than depicting ontological *unfixity*, Anzaldúa's border woman emerges as fixed in her multiplicity. As such, she actively seeks a stable, whole, and coherent center: this center is one of *fixed multiplicity*. It is therefore inaccurate to place the mestiza alongside other depictions of Lloyd's subject-in-process, amounting, yet again, to another instance of dismissal brought on by prior philosophical commitments to ontological unfixity.

Part of Lloyd's project in *Beyond Identity Politics* is to show that accounts of "mobile subjectivity" (what she seems to be using interchangeably here for the subject-in-process) have emerged from within feminism "*without recourse to poststructuralism*" (Lloyd 2005, 6). Clearly, disentangling the subject-in-process from the baggage of the political cul-de-sac that accompanies many poststructuralist feminist accounts of identity and aligning it instead with Women of Color feminist literature, Lloyd believes, will help her make the case for embracing visions of mobile subjectivity. While I can certainly appreciate her willingness to seek out diverse feminist literatures on this topic, without a careful reading of early US Women of Color coalitional feminism, some of the most insightful and certainly most nuanced aspects of their treatments of identity and oppression are lost. Most centrally, she misses the point (that I will develop shortly) that Lorde's and Anzaldúa's accounts of coalitional identity embrace ontological multiplicity and fluidity while ultimately resisting unfixity. Similarly, in her turn toward Deleuze and Guattari, Puar misses the equally valuable point that shifting attention to the context in which an individual finds herself positioned might be done without eschewing epistemological decidability and tactical political determinacy. Thus, besides the obvious charge of misappropriation that Lorde so eloquently reveals in her "Letter to Mary Daly," the issue I have with this oversight centers precisely on the theoretical richness lost through these various dismissals. With this in mind, I turn to US Women of Color coalition feminists to retrieve some of these insights.

Coalitional Identity: Rethinking Ontological Unfixity

As a Black lesbian feminist comfortable with the many different ingredients of my identity, and a woman committed to racial and sexual freedom from oppression, I find I am constantly being encouraged to pluck out some one aspect of myself and present this as the meaningful whole, eclipsing or denying the other parts of self. But this is a destructive and fragmenting way to live. My fullest concentration of energy is available to me only when I integrate all the parts of who I am, openly, allowing power from particular sources of my living to flow back and forth freely through all my different selves, without the restrictions of externally imposed definition. Only then can I bring myself and my energies as a whole to the service of those struggles which I embrace as part of my living.

—AUDRE LORDE, "Age, Race, Class, and Sex: Women Redefining Difference"

You say my name is ambivalence? Think of me as Shiva, a many-armed and legged body with one foot on brown soil, one on white, one in straight society, one in the gay world, the man's world, the women's, one limb in the literary world, another in the working class, the socialist, and the occult worlds. A sort of spider woman hanging by one thin strand of web.

Who, me confused? Ambivalent? Not so. Only your labels split me.

—GLORIA ANZALDÚA, "La Prieta"

Here, I develop a notion of feminist *coalitional identity* that, I argue, is particularly exemplified in the work of early US Women of Color coalitional feminism and those influenced by this scholarship. While this conception of identity shares some things in common with the ontology of multiplicity and complexity characteristic of contemporary theorizations of coalition by Laclau and Mouffe, Butler, and Lloyd, I will argue that a coalitional identity remains distinct from such theorizations of ontological pluralism in its refusal to take on the characteristic of unfixity. Such a refusal informs a corresponding resistance to epistemological undecidability.

Though I am certainly not the first to understand identity "coalitionally," I assert that the theory of coalitional identity on offer by US Women of Color coalitional feminism is a necessary component of politico-ethical coalition politics.[3] While it may strike one as odd to use the word *coalition* as an adjective—to describe identity or consciousness as "coalitional"—I believe something rather valuable is gained by holding onto the concept of coalition here. I take *coalition* to mean the intentional coming together of diverse or heterogeneous parts for the purpose of struggling toward a shared political commitment. Three crucial components of this process include the notions of *struggle*, shared *self-reflexive political commitment*, and the fact of profound *existential transformation* through such a process. Other contemporary articulations of the relationships among identity, political consciousness, and collective politics lose this emphasis on wholeness and focused or directed action. *Coalition*, by contrast, attends to multiplicity and ambiguity without foreclosing ontological wholeness (fixity), epistemological decidability, and political determinacy (directionality).

At first glance, it might seem that the accounts of multiple and plural identity that are ubiquitous across early US Women of Color coalitional feminism share poststructuralist feminists' commitment to disavowing identity, especially the category of woman. As discussed in chapters 1 and 2, a defining feature of US Women of Color feminists' work was to interrogate the notion of woman used by women's liberation activists on the ground and implicit in current feminist theory within the academy. Groups such as the TWWA were born out of the hypocrisy that nonwhite women confronted both within the civil rights movement that relegated Black women and women of color to subordinate positions, as well as within the women's liberation movement that claimed to fight for the liberation of all women and yet refused to listen to their nonwhite sisters. As mentioned, for some white feminists, the experiences of women of color in the 1970s and 1980s in fact offered the concrete empirical evidence needed to substantiate the poststructuralist feminist argument that all identities must ultimately be abandoned. However, while poststructuralist feminists writing within the American context in the 1980s and 1990s and Women of Color feminists writing in the same context as early as the late 1960s both emphasize the importance of examining the category of woman, they come at this project from two very different directions. As we have seen, for poststructuralist feminists such as Butler and Lloyd, the impetus to deconstruct "woman" comes from the notion that "woman" simply cannot exist within the realm of being at all. Indeed, no subject exists within this realm for Butler and Lloyd because of the ontological unfixity of all identities. Alternatively, for US Women of Color coalition feminists, their impetus in interrogating the category of woman was unhinged from philosophical commitments to discursive unfixity.

As Crenshaw's careful parsing of postmodern antiessentialism (typical of Butler) and Women of Color feminist critiques of monolithic and white renderings of the category of woman the following decade reveals, many Women of Color feminists were never interested in abandoning the category for merely "linguistic" reasons; for them, it was always "specifically political" (Crenshaw 1991, 1296, 1298). The problem for these authors is not the mere existence of categories or the simple fact of ontological closure; the problem for Crenshaw and the early US Women of Color coalition feminists she is in conversation with was related to the politically motivated values attached to such instances of closure, or, to put it another way, the way in which social hierarchies were inscribed on such categorizations (1297). It is for this reason that Crenshaw is forthright in her defense of the usefulness of identity categories for oppressed groups. "Identity-based politics," she asserts, "has been a source of strength, community, and intellectual development" for marginalized voices, thus casting the social power exercised in delineating, indeed naming, differences as a "source of empowerment and reconstruction" rather than solely as the "power to dominate" (1242).

Combahee similarly invoked an explicit call to "identity politics" over a decade before Crenshaw. In reading Combahee's "Black Feminist Statement" as a quintessential example of all that is wrong with essential identity politics, Fuss and Lloyd miss something rather valuable in Combahee's unique appeal to what they call "identity politics," something clearly not lost on Crenshaw. The passage used to justify its "identity politics" credentials reads as follows:

> Above all else, our politics initially sprang from the shared belief that Black women are inherently valuable, that our liberation is a necessity not as an adjunct to somebody else's but because of our need as human persons for autonomy.... We realize that the only people who care enough about us to work consistently for our liberation is us. Our politics evolve from a healthy love for ourselves, our sisters and our community which allows us to continue our struggle and work.
>
> This focusing upon our own oppression is embodied in the concept of identity politics. We believe that the most profound and potentially the most radical politics come directly out of our own identity, as opposed to working to end somebody else's oppression. (Combahee 1983, 266–67)

Combahee advocates a notion of a Black women's community very similar to Reagon's notion of "home." For Combahee, a community of Black women provides the nurturing that Reagon argued is characteristic of homes. However, Combahee's politics—what members are doing in their collective—we learn, arises not just from members' "identity" as Black women but from a particular "analytic" of Black feminism. This analytic—or way of perceiving their world, particularly their oppression—and not an essential notion of identity, grounds their politics. The reason they feel that they must root their politics in "identity," they tell us, is not simply because their politics will be defined by their identity as Black women, but because history has proven that the only people willing to focus on their particular type of oppression are Black feminists such as themselves.

Furthermore, while the collective uses the word *identity*, I believe what Combahee is really getting at is a notion of positionality—or, one's particular *position* vis-à-vis oppression. All Black *women*, Combahee tells us at different moments throughout the document, are positioned at the intersection of multiple and "interlocking" forms of oppression. Only Black *feminists*, however, have committed to exposing and struggling against this multifaceted oppressive system.

> The most general statement of our politics at the present time would be that we are actively committed to struggling against racial, sexual, heterosexual, and class oppression, and see as our particular task the development of integrated analysis and practice based upon the fact that the major systems of oppression are interlocking. The synthesis of these oppressions creates the conditions of our lives [as Black women]. As Black women we see Black feminism as the logical political movement to combat the manifold and simultaneous oppressions that all women of color face. (Combahee 1983, 264)

Like other Women of Color feminists, Combahee's position at the intersection of multiple forms of oppression enables a certain analytical frame that shapes the group's political project. Feminism is both a "political analysis" and a "political practice" (266). Feminism is not simply an ontological affinity group. Thus, Combahee's Black feminism is not simply rooted in members' identities as Black women; it is rooted in the *understanding* of the interlocking systems of oppression that members' *position* at the intersection of multiple, overlapping, and mobile systems of oppression affords them. I therefore contend that, even though Combahee advocated something called "identity politics," the value in focusing on identity had more to do with its ability to draw attention to this context of oppression, rather than its ability to define correctly woman or even Black lesbian woman.

While clearly ignored by contemporary scholars such as Puar, the latent conception of positionality hinted at by Combahee is developed to much fuller effect by Mohanty and Alcoff, both of whom were writing alongside Crenshaw on this topic in the 1990s. Unlike the notion of subject positions invoked by poststructuralist feminists such as Fuss (1989), the notion of positionality invoked by Mohanty shifts attention away from the subject and toward the context in which the subject is *positioned*. Unlike previous feminists who may have fixed their attention on one level of oppression—such as gender—Mohanty (1991, 13) follows Smith and others in characterizing the system of oppression by "multiple, fluid structures of domination." Therefore, it is "at the intersections of these relations of ruling that third world feminist struggles are positioned" (13). Building from Dorothy Smith's (1987, 3) formulation of the concept of "relations of ruling." Mohanty (1991, 14) argues that shifting focus to the intersectionality of oppression and domination emphasizes the "*process* or *form* of ruling" opposed to the "frozen embodiment of it." While this may seem to mirror Butler's shift toward focusing on systems of power in her third formulation of coalition presented in chapter 2 or Puar's use of assemblage sketched above, such an orientation does not lead Mohanty (as it did for both Butler and Puar) to the complete disavowal of identity-based politics, nor does it preclude political directionality. As Mohanty later frames it, her view is "a materialist and 'realist' one and is antithetical to that of postmodernist relativism" (2003, 231). Instead, aligning with Bohrer's (2019) argument in *Marxism and Intersectionality*, Mohanty (2003, 232) clarifies that, methodologically, her analytical perspective is "grounded in historical materialism." As such, it is attentive to the material conditions that situate poor Indigenous, Third World/Global South women's lives. The reason she turns to the stories of these women is because within a tightly integrated capitalist system, their perspectives offer the "most inclusive viewing of systemic power." As she attests, "It is precisely their critical reflections on their everyday lives as poor women of color that allow the kind of analysis of the power structure that has led to the many victories in environmental racism struggles" (232). As she implies here, attending to their unique experiences aids in political struggle insofar as it renders legible complex and mobile forces of oppression.

Like Mohanty, Alcoff (1997, 335) similarly attests that "one does not have to be influenced by French poststructuralism to disagree with essentialism." Feminism, she asserts, needs to find a way to challenge categories without relying on linguistic analysis or discursive unfixity. We find just such a way through Women of Color feminist treatments of positionality. As she puts it:

> When the concept "woman" is defined not by a particular set of attributes but by a particular position, the internal characteristics of the person

thus identified are not denoted so much as the external context within which that person is situated. The external situation determines the person's relative positions, just as the position of a pawn on a chessboard is considered safe or dangerous, powerful or weak, according to its relation to the other chess pieces. The essentialist definition of woman makes her identity independent of her external situation.... The positional definition, on the other hand, makes her identity relative to a constantly shifting context, to a situation that includes a network of elements involving others, the objective economic conditions, cultural and political institutions and ideologies, and so on. (Alcoff 1997, 349)

This shift away from the individual and toward the context around the individual is crucially important. For Women of Color feminists such as Combahee, Smith, Reagon, and many others, coalition politics is anchored in this particular analytical frame, what I call *coalitional consciousness*. I mention this only to demonstrate a clear shift away from identity politics and toward a form of politics based on rendering visible interlocking oppressive systems. Unlike both Butler's and Puar's attempt at this, for Alcoff, Mohanty, and the many US Women of Color coalition feminists I reference throughout the chapter, political goals and directions do not get sidelined from these discussions. Rather, as the Combahee members make explicitly clear, their freedom would "necessitate the destruction of all the systems of oppression" (Combahee 1983, 270). Their advantage, if you will, as Black women is that they are able to *see* these connections and fight against all forms of oppression simultaneously.

Particularly remarkable about treatments of ontology coming out of US Women of Color coalitional feminism is how these visions of multiple, discontinuous, decentered, and plural selves are understood as simultaneously multiple *and* whole. Early US Women of Color coalition feminists such as Lorde and Anzaldúa became *fixed* in their multiplicity, ambiguity, and contradiction *as coalitional selves*.[4] In this sense, the notion of coalitional identity initially circulated by Lorde and Anzaldúa not only breaks the tension between unfixity and fixity characteristic of contemporary articulations of coalition politics but also offers an alternative to the ontological unfixity and epistemological undecidability that often accompanies poststructuralist feminist engagements with identity.[5] Such a notion is characterized by ontologies of (1) embodied multiplicity, or the notion that coalitional selves are whole, complete, and coherent *in their* multiplicity, and (2) ongoing *struggle* toward self-definition.

As Lorde puts it in "Age, Race, Class, and Sex," women of color experience a multiple identity comprising many different selves. Despite attempts to "pluck out" different aspects of herself and have them stand in for the whole, the many different "ingredients" or "parts" of her identity, she tells us, must and can be integrated into a "meaningful," even if somewhat uneasy, "whole" (Lorde 1984a, 120–21). By bringing together her many different selves and allowing movement across these different "sources of her living," she attests, she is able to present herself as whole so that she may work in the service of political struggle (121). Doing this, however, is never easy. Though learning how to "hold onto all parts of [her] . . . in spite of the pressure to express only one to the exclusion of others" has been a struggle for Lorde, the challenge does not seem to rest in the trauma of existing as internally heterogeneous (143). Indeed, Lorde is "comfortable" with the many different "ingredients" of her "identity" (120). The challenge for Lorde inheres in resisting "externally imposed" definition and fragmentation (120). In this sense, it is not ontological fixity (in the form of wholeness, coherence, or definition) that poses a problem for her; it is only resisting *externally imposed* definition and struggling toward her own self-definition that proves challenging.

The kind of multiple identity Lorde is describing here bears a striking resemblance to the notion of border or mestiza identity developed by Anzaldúa also in the early 1980s. We can make out the first strokes of Anzaldúa's (1983e) theory of mestiza identity in "La Prieta." As reflected in the epigraph to this section and the passage below, many of the key aspects of coalitional identity first emerge in this early rendition of mestiza consciousness:

> I am a wind-swayed bridge, a crossroads inhabited by whirlwinds. Gloria, the facilitator, Gloria the mediator, straddling the walls between abysses. "Your allegiance is to La Raza, the Chicano movement," say the members of my race. "Your allegiance is to the Third World," say my Black and Asian friends. "Your allegiance is to your gender, to women," say the feminists. Then there's my allegiance to the Gay movement, to the socialist revolution, to the New Age, to magic and the occult. And there's my affinity to literature, to the world of the artist. What am I? *A third world lesbian feminist with Marxist and mystic leanings.* They would chop me up into little fragments and tag each piece with a label.
>
> You say my name is ambivalence? Think of me as Shiva, a many-armed and legged body with one foot on brown soil, one on white, one

in straight society, one in the gay world, the man's world, the women's, one limb in the literary world, another in the working class, the socialist, and the occult worlds. A sort of spider woman hanging by one thin strand of web.

Who, me confused? Ambivalent? Not so. Only your labels split me. (Anzaldúa 1983e, 205)

Anzaldúa is many-armed and many-legged, just as the spider woman metaphor demands. Border dwellers such as herself have "multiple" or "dual" identities (Anzaldúa 1987, 16, 63, 79).

Her face, like the reality in which she lives, contains a multiplicitous character: "*Y mi cara, como la realidad, tenía un character multiplice*" (44). Anzaldúa sees the world from multiple perspectives simultaneously, and often these multiple identities seem to be at war with one another: her multiple allegiances seem to want to fragment her. However, like Lorde, Anzaldúa resists the external pressure to split or fragment the many pieces of herself. While she fears externally imposed fragmentation for the sake of definition, her refusal to accept external definition, she is quite adamant, does not leave her ambivalent or confused. Ambivalence and confusion, she clarifies, emerge for her only in moments of *externally imposed* definition, moments that refuse her embodied multiplicity.

As the spider woman metaphor suggests, despite the multiplicity inherent in her identity, Anzaldúa is an embodied whole, gravitating toward a center. The spider with many legs and many arms, each resting in a different reality, represents this embodied multiplicity. There is a center or whole (a "self") and an acting agent. In contradistinction to both Nietzsche and Butler, there is a "doer" behind the deed. Inherent to being a "border woman," we learn in *Borderlands/La Frontera*, is the ability to keep "*intact* one's shifting and multiple identity and integrity" (Anzaldúa 1987, preface; my emphasis). Anzaldúa spends much of *Borderlands* recounting this very process of locating her center—of finding her "own intrinsic nature buried under the personality that has been imposed on [her]" as a mestiza or border woman, straddling the Téjas-Mexico border and two, sometimes three, cultures at once (16). While living within and embracing her multiplicity, Anzaldúa works toward a more whole perspective (79). Through the process of crossing over into the different parts of herself and accepting her multiplicity, Anzaldúa "suddenly ... feel[s] everything rushing to a center, a nucleus. All the lost pieces of myself come flying from the deserts and the mountains and the valleys, magnetized toward that center. *Completa*" (51).

What makes Anzaldúa "whole" or "complete," it seems, is her embodied multiplicity. Once she accepts this multiplicity and learns to move tactically within this space, she becomes whole. In this sense, her existence is not one of "unfixity"; rather, it is one of *fixed multiplicity*.

While many Women of Color feminists have become comfortable with coalescing toward multiple and shifting centers, they also recount this process as challenging, taxing, and at times traumatic.[6] For Anzaldúa, her very existence as a border woman is characterized by this "inner struggle" of herself toward a center, toward self-definition (Anzaldúa 1987, preface, 87). As such, her life is "plagued by psychic restlessness" (78).

> To live in the Borderlands means you
> are neither *hispana india negra española*
> *ni gabacha, eres mestiza, mulata,* half-breed
> caught in the crossfire between camps
> while carrying all five races on your back
> not knowing which side to turn to, run from;
>
> To live in the Borderlands means knowing
> that the *india* in you, betrayed for 500 years,
> is no longer speaking to you,
> that the *mexicans* call you *rajetas,*
> that denying the Anglo inside you
> is as bad as having denied the Indian or Black; . . .
>
> In the Borderlands
> you are the battleground
> where enemies are kin to each other;
> you are at home, a stranger. (Anzaldúa 1987, 194–95)

As we can see here, living in the Borderlands is a traumatic experience because one is constantly caught in the crossfire between competing allegiances and competing logics. Such a place is an uncomfortable territory to live in because it is a place of contradiction, hatred, anger, and exploitation (16). To live as Anzaldúa does—as a *"mita' y mita'"* (a "half and half," what queer women were called in south Texas)—she says, is to embody contradiction, to live as "two in one body," representing the coming together of opposites, which produces an ontological state of being "neither one nor the other but a strange doubling, a deviation of nature that horrifies, a work of nature inverted" (19). Embodying the contradictions of opposites, her existence is one of ontological struggle toward self-definition and wholeness despite internal heterogeneity and contradiction. This struggle, we learn above, is in fact a "home" struggle; even at "home," she tells us, she feels like a "stranger."

This is the same struggle that Lorde speaks of when she urges women of color to "sharpen self-definition" despite how painful and difficult this process may be (Lorde 1984a, 122–23). For, she tells us, it is only through the "coming together of *self-actualized* individuals ... that any real advances can be made" (1984e, 46; my emphasis). Struggling toward self-definition is very much part of, even a prerequisite for, social justice activism. Lorde and Anzaldúa live in a kind of battlefield, thus forcing them to develop the necessary coping skills to survive such an ontological state. The knowledge gained here informs a coalitional consciousness that not only helps one to struggle toward a center but also helps one to struggle in coalitions with others toward social justice.

It is in the process of preserving the integrity of a center, despite how traumatic this process may be, that Anzaldúa's multiple selves emerge as a *coalitional* identity. For something to be "coalitional" in the way I am using it, it must embody a political struggle of multiple, heterogeneous, and even discontinuous parts toward a center, or a shared political goal or commitment. The shared goal for women of color is self-definition (internal coherence or completeness); as Cynthia Burack has put it, it is to move toward "wholeness" through an "act of will and creativity" (2004, 147).

The discontinuous parts of one's coalitional self, however, do not just find themselves together; one must work and struggle toward a shared center, toward unity. Thus, these actions are chosen and directed. This ontological picture of multiplicity in unity therefore challenges ontological pictures handed down by Nietzsche and Laclau and Mouffe. It also parts ways with feminist articulations of "antifoundationalist" (Butler 1990, 21) and "inessential" (Lloyd 2005, 151) coalition politics informed by similar theoretical commitments. While Lloyd, for instance, acknowledges that Reagon's work "prefigures" some of the major concerns motivating the notion of "the subject-in-process" that she develops, she refuses the sense of political direction embedded in Reagon's, and other Women of Color feminists', notions of multiple or *coalitional* identity (see Lloyd 2005, 153). Instead, Lloyd proceeds from what she calls a "loss of ontological certainty" that she believes is entailed in the notion of a "subject-in-process" (154). I seek to challenge this notion through the concept of coalitional identity. Though Lloyd engages Women of Color feminism through the work of Chela Sandoval, Lloyd fails to appreciate the nuanced conception of coalitional identity on offer by Women of Color coalitional feminism by insisting that such a conception resists "completeness" or "wholeness" (155). On the contrary, this body of work is remarkable in its ability to hold onto completeness and reimagine this wholeness in its multiplicity.

Similarly, though my reading of Anzaldúa's notion of a mestiza or coalitional identity accords, to an extent, with Cristina Beltrán's (2004) account of Anzaldúa in "Patrolling Borders: Hybrids, Hierarchies and the Challenge of *Mestizaje*" insofar as I concur that Anzaldúa seeks ontological wholeness through her conceptualization of the mestiza woman, I part ways with Beltrán in her insistence that this is something to be condemned. As Beltrán (2004, 600) puts it, for Anzaldúa, "hybridity becomes a kind of foundational or 'fixed' identity that forecloses more creative and productively defiant approaches to identity and subjectivity." Beltrán is referring to instances such as those cited here wherein Anzaldúa insists that despite her multiplicity, she is whole, complete, or fixed. Beltrán argues that such invocations to a "fixed" identity present a whole or complete identity that is at odds with an equally fixed Western identity (600). This tendency toward "essentialism" and the "reification of categories" (603, 604), Beltrán warns, leads Anzaldúa to "construct," problematically, a "more-evolved hybrid" or "*mestiza*" identity "whose experience gives her privileged insight and knowledge" (604).

While Beltrán (2004) is reluctant to concede that a mestiza woman might have a "*special* role to play in the politics of democracy and multiculturalism" rooted in the unique "standpoint" of her position as a border woman (605), I am arguing that it is precisely her unique ontological existence as a *coalitional self*, and the corresponding coalitional consciousness that it engenders, that is the greatest strength of this reconceptualization of identity. As Carastathis puts it: "To the extent that our identities are constructed by oppression and by resistance, members of multiply oppressed groups face the existential challenge of constructing internal as well as external bridges. Bringing together the aspects of one's identity that have been falsely separated (both in the institutions of dominant society and in single-issue political movements) amounts to forming a *coalition of one*, in which one is aligned with all parts of oneself, especially those we are taught to deny, repress, or even annihilate" (2013, 960; my emphasis). By bringing together the multiple and at times contradictory and even hostile components of one's identity (of her competing and shifting selves), Carastathis argues, one enters into a coalition with oneself. This is something that "outsiders," especially those suffering from multiple oppressions, have learned to do by necessity as a kind of survival strategy (960). Such outsiders must fight against an imposed fragmentation of their multiple selves and instead struggle toward a sense of wholeness or merging—that is, toward coalition—*within* themselves. Doing so not only enables someone like Anzaldúa to dispense finally with ontological unfixity, engaging in the painful and challenging process of forming what Carastathis calls a coalition of one (960) also equips border women to coalesce with others in progressive struggle. As Carastathis, Anzaldúa, and Lorde all imply or explicitly state, the alliance formed within and through this process mirrors the political alliance one will form with others in the context of progressive coalition politics. I return to this point shortly.

Like Butler's understanding of *woman* as a verb and Lloyd's "subject-in-process," a coalitional self is indeed a *doing* as opposed to a *being*. But unlike Butler's emphasis on an *external* discursive field being responsible for the doing and both Butler's and Lloyd's insistence that we (feminists) must resist definitions and foundations outright, a coalitional self is born out of a conscious internal struggle *toward self-definition*. If we move away from Butler, Lloyd, and others in understanding identity as permanently unfixed and instead reconceive it coalitionally, an ontology of multiplicity makes possible both complete and fixed selves as well as directed group politics. This path, Anzaldúa tells us, is a two-way movement that involves "going deep into the self" *and* "expanding out into the world, a simultaneous recreation of the self and a reconstruction of society" (Anzaldúa 1983e, 208). Such a path shapes a corresponding shifting, tactical, self-conscious, and purposeful *coalitional consciousness*.

Coalitional Consciousness: Rethinking Epistemological Undecidability

U.S. third world feminists must recognize that our learned sensitivity to the mobile webs of power is a skill that, once developed, can become a sophisticated form of oppositional consciousness. This is a form of oppositional consciousness which creates the opportunity for flexible, dynamic and tactical responses, it is another critical theory for political action which allows us no *single* conceptualization of our position in society. Rather, it focuses us instead upon the process of the circulation of power, on the skill of reading its moves, and on the recognition that a new morality and effective opposition resides in a self-conscious flexibility of identity and of political action which is capable, above all else, of tactically intervening in the moves of power in the name of egalitarian social relations.

—CHELA SANDOVAL, "Feminism and Racism: A Report on the 1981 National Women's Studies Association Conference"

As I have argued, early US Women of Color coalition feminists such as Anzaldúa and Lorde describe an ontology of both multiplicity and contradiction *and* continuous struggle toward coherence and self-definition. In attempting this "synthesis" of one's multiple selves, a unique epistemology—or way of understanding oneself, the world, and one's place in the world—is born (Anzaldúa 1987, 79). This consciousness emerges from ontological struggle; it is one's creative response to one's inherent multiplicity and internal contradiction. This "*mestiza* consciousness," as Anzaldúa calls it, works to break down binaries and rigid ways of understanding that fail to incorporate the multiplicity, ambiguity, and discontinuity that marks a person's existence as a coalitional self (77). This particular epistemology, I will demonstrate, parts ways with the epistemology of undecidability characteristic of poststructuralist accounts of coalition politics.

While this way of understanding and interpreting one's place in the world demands that one "develop a tolerance for contradictions, a tolerance for ambiguity" (Anzaldúa 1987, 79), it also guides one toward concrete self-understanding and decisive action. "The new *mestiza* . . . learns to be an Indian in Mexican culture, to be a Mexican from an Anglo point of view. She learns to juggle cultures. She has a plural personality, she operates in a pluralistic mode. . . . Not only does she sustain contradictions, she turns the ambivalence into something else" (79). A mestiza consciousness actually creates something out of contradiction and ambivalence. A mestiza learns to be different selves in different contexts. She learns to shift between her selves. She sits with contradiction but only long enough to learn how to move creatively within, through, and outside of it. While women of color such as Anzaldúa emphasize acquiring tolerance for ambiguity and contradiction, they do not advocate an epistemology of undecidability—that is, an epistemology that subscribes to the notion that the discursive unfixity of the social world necessarily prevents one from identifying concrete forms of oppression. Just because the self is understood here as decentered does not mean that it cannot and will not recenter itself. The mestiza does this by "remaining flexible" and shifting in and out of different "habitual formations" and different ways of thinking (79). Through such acts of "kneading," "uniting and joining," Anzaldúa emerges as "both a creature of darkness and a creature of light, but also a creature that questions the definitions of light and dark and gives them new meanings" (81). The flexibility of coalitional selves, therefore, inheres not in the selves' ability to permanently resist definition but rather in their ability to move between multiple selves and to assume different mobile and tactical subjectivities depending on the demands of the situation. In short, this flexibility inheres in an acquired coalitional consciousness that enables the selves to *decide* within a context of multiplicity, ambiguity, and contradiction. This emphasis on decisive action distinguishes a coalitional consciousness from an epistemology of undecidability.

US Women of Color coalition feminist theorists such as Anzaldúa and Lugones have variously described this epistemological process as one of "crossing" (Anzaldúa 1987, 48), weaving, and "'world'-traveling" (Lugones 2003, 7). "It is only when she is on the other side," Anzaldúa tells us, "and the shell cracks open and the lid from her eyes lifts, that she sees things in a different perspective.... It is only then that her consciousness expands a tiny notch" (1987, 49). In order for one to assume a coalitional conscious- ness, one must be willing to "cross over" or travel between the different components of oneself, but also across the divides that separate her from others (49). Women of color, Lugones, Anzaldúa, Lorde, and Sandoval all argue, are particularly adept at such forms of traveling. The multiple con- sciousness that women of color develop due to their embodied multiplicity prepare them to embrace flexibility as a creative strength (see Lugones 2003, 17–18, 77; Sandoval 2000, 5; Anzaldúa 1987, 38–39; 2009, 144; Lorde 1984h, 55; 1984a, 115, 116; 1984g, 128, 131; and Burack 2004, 147).

This capacity to see the "deep structure [of oppression] below the surface" (Anzaldúa 1987, 38) first emerges out of necessity when one finds herself "up against a wall" with "all sorts of oppressions coming at [her]" (38), help- ing her to discern "when the next person is going to slap [her] or lock [her] away" (39). It helps them, for instance, to know when to tone down or play up different aspects of their identity depending on the situation. In this sense, we can understand it as a "kind of survival tactic that people, caught between worlds, unknowingly cultivate" (39). While this faculty is required of the outsider by the logic of oppression, when such traveling becomes purposeful and tactical instead of a subconscious coping mechanism for surviving the conditions of one's situation (see Lugones [1987] 2003, 77, 88), it takes on a uniquely *coalitional* form. As Anzaldúa argues, women of color can and must "turn this fusion or confusion of the individual/collectivity around and use it as a tool for collective strength" (Anzaldúa 2009, 144). This unique understanding (consciousness) emerges as an ontological core or center; in this sense, a coalitional identity is fixed simultaneously in its multiplicity and complexity and its ability to move creatively and tactically across this multiplicity—that is, in its coalitional consciousness.

In the epigraph from "Feminism and Racism," Sandoval writes that US Third World feminists' "learned sensitivity to the mobile webs of power" may be understood as a "skill that, once developed, can become a sophisticated form of oppositional consciousness" (Sandoval 1990, 66). In this passage, Sandoval outlines what I understand to be the three primary components of a uniquely *coalitional* consciousness.[7] Sandoval writes there as the secretary to the Third World feminist consciousness-raising group, a group of women of color who attended the 1981 NWSA conference and felt that a report documenting the work they had done within their allocated "'Third World' women only" consciousness-raising group was necessary (Sandoval 1990, 60). Despite the conference theme on women responding to racism, its hegemonic white structure left women of color marginalized into one homogeneous category, "Third World women." In her report, Sandoval both documents and analyzes their experience working in this group.

Sandoval's main arguments may therefore be understood as reflecting wider sentiments across 1970s and 1980s US Women of Color feminism, certainly those across the US Third World feminists attending the 1981 NWSA conference. Sandoval hopes to develop a theory or, as she will later call it, a methodology, of US Third World feminism (Sandoval 2000). Absolutely central to this methodology, we learn here, is the *epistemological* "common ground" discovered through the Third World meeting groups that took place there (Sandoval 1990 63, 60). Theorizing from their lived experience at the conference—the same year as Reagon's coalition speech—a consensus emerged that moved unequivocally in the direction of politico-ethical coalition politics and the coalitional consciousness on which it depends. Like Anzaldúa, Sandoval's epigraph recognizes that the particular way of understanding and interpreting the world (as well as the operation of power within the world) that is forced upon subjugated peoples (such as women of color) may be retooled for something else. Echoing Luxemburg, this "learned *sensitivity*" to the movement of power is the first component of coalitional consciousness (66; my emphasis). Directly rooted in an ontological experience of multiplicity and contradiction, this component, Anzaldúa and Lorde show us, is often experienced in a traumatic register.

Transforming this sensitivity into a learned *skill* of reading and mapping the "circulation of power" is the second component of coalitional consciousness, what Sandoval calls here a "sophisticated form of oppositional consciousness" (Sandoval 1990, 66). This particular epistemology, she argues later in *Methodology of the Oppressed*, is a "mobile, flexible, diasporic force that migrates between contending ideological systems" (Sandoval 2000, 30). It is this acuity that would tell Anzaldúa, for instance, how to balance her multiple "allegiances"—to her "Raza," to the Third World, to women, to lesbians, and so on—in different contexts (Anzaldúa 1983e, 205). Ulti-mately, it guides Anazaldúa toward resisting any one of these allegiances and embracing, instead, a shifting mestiza consciousness. In this sense, this knowledge "operates as does a technology—a weapon of consciousness that functions like a compass" allowing us "to chart out the positions available and the directions to move in a large social totality" (Sandoval 2000, 30).

This insight enabled women of color activists in Somos Hermanas (We Are Sisters) in the 1980s to bring together the falsely (and externally) frag-mented components of their multiple identities into a "coalition of one" (Carastathis 2013, 960).[8] As Carmen Vázquez, one of the members of the coalition, puts it: "I believe in coalitions because my survival is dependent on my ability to close the gaps between the different worlds that converge in me, and on my ability to cross over from my queer world or my Puerto Rican world or my women's world and build alliances. It is only on the strength of those alliances that I can be whole—a Puerto Rican lesbian living in a straight, sexist, and racist world" (quoted in Carastathis 2013, 960). In line with Chisholm, Reagon, and many others, Vázquez believes in coalition work because her very survival depends on it. As she recounts elsewhere, mirroring accounts given by Anzaldúa, the experience of work-ing in Somos Hermanas helped her to integrate "all of [her identities] in a living, joyful, experience" (quoted in Carastathis 2013, 957). Her commit-ment to this process of forming a coalitional identity therefore enabled Vázquez to remain committed to the hard work of coalescing within the space of Somos Hermanas. The knowledge gained through this ontological experience—of integration across stark internal divides—both prepared and motivated her activist work.

The notion that a special knowledge might be gained through this map-ping exercise—which took Vázquez across both her own multiple, fluid, and contradictory selves and across difference within the space of Somos Hermanas—resonates strongly with accounts given above by Anzaldúa and Lorde. Lugones is similarly attentive to the role of mapping multiple and "in-termeshing" oppressions in her work across the 1980s (Lugones and Spelman 1983; Lugones 1987), 1990s (Lugones 1990a, 1990b, 1991,1994, 1995), and into the early 2000s with the publication of her book, *Pilgrimages/Peregrinajes* (Lugones 2003). In addition to multiple levels of internal mapping—wherein one maps where one sits relative to a variety of mobile and intermeshing oppressive forces in a variety of different contexts (oppressions move and change in different contexts) (Lugones 2003, 17–20)—Lugones insists that people must travel to others' worlds (Lugones and Spelman 1983; Lugones

1987; 2003). Doing so will afford a different view on oppression. The best way to make sense of oppression, she argues, is by following it on this granular level—that is, to "tantear [feel] for meaning" in the dark and to "move with people" (Lugones 2003, 1, 6). It is only on this "pedestrian level," wherein one moves with others in the dark, that one gains a true grasp of both oppression and resistance (5). The example of following her mother as she worked in the kitchen is helpful here. Lugones tells us: *"You'll have to follow her through her path in the chaotic production, you'll have to know her comings and goings, her fluidity through the production. You'll have to, that is, if you want to use any of it"* (Lugones [1994] 2003, 124). Because her mother never used names for the various "things" she needed, the only way to make sense of which "thing" she was referring to was to be in the kitchen with her, tracing her movements in order to keep up with where she was and what her commands might have meant at any given time. When she followed her movements on this intimate level, Lugones recounts, she knew *"just what she mean[t]"* (124). It is here, on this granular level, Lugones maintains, that one might achieve the "closeness of understanding" to grasp the "levels of motility" that reveal not only if someone is moving, but *how* they are moving—the subtle, almost undetectable, movements that indicate levels of resistance (Lugones 2003, 2).

With the emphasis here placed on mapping, the connection to Deleuze and Guattari is immediately apparent. Like Women of Color feminist depictions of intersectionality, Deleuze and Guattari offer a vision of the social world that is simultaneously attentive to rigid oppressive binaries as well as multiple, diffuse, and supple forms of what Lugones calls "intermeshing" oppressions (see Lugones 2003, 223; Deleuze and Guattari 1987, 352–53). Attentive to both the multiplicity and motility of the social world, Deleuze and Guattari advance a similarly mobile epistemology, "mobile" in the sense that it demands movement and following. Offering a variety of words to capture this quality of movement—*nomadic* and *ambulant*—Deleuze and Guattari (1987, 362, 374) resist "royal" or "theorematic" science that prizes implementing theorems and proceeding from axioms. In its stead, they offer a "nomad" science that is "problematic" rather than axiomatic, meaning it starts with a problem, not a theorem, developing "eccentrically" as it follows the problem to possible solutions (372–74). As an "ambulant" science, it is a moving science, a science attentive to movement, willing to move with that which it traces.

Politics for Deleuze and Guattari is therefore fundamentally about "diagramming" both striated and smooth social formations (Deleuze and Guattari 1987, 140–41, 161, 352–53). Sandoval similarly tells us that oppositional consciousness offers a "new cartography" or "*topography* of consciousness in opposition" that charts "psychic and material realities that occupy a particular cultural region" (Sandoval 2000, 54). Such diagramming processes, Deleuze and Guattari have argued, might reveal potential "lines of flight" wherein "micropolitical" disturbances by various minority groups have occurred (Deleuze and Guattari 1987, 161, 469). Sandoval similarly tells us that this "*cultural topography* delineates a set of critical points within which individuals and groups seeking to transform dominant and oppressive powers can constitute themselves as resistant and oppositional citizen-subjects" (Sandoval 2000, 54). Perhaps once constituted, we may imagine that these oppositional citizen subjects will cause the kinds of "disturbances" that Deleuze and Guattari have in mind.

However, an important difference between Lugones's and Sandoval's and Deleuze and Guattari's epistemologies remains. While the diagramming process may reveal lines of flight, Deleuze and Guattari are quite explicit that it cannot predict or prescribe these disturbances; instead, it traces them after their occurrence. While the "abstract machine" responsible for the diagramming function plays a "piloting" role, they do not mean to suggest that it steers or directs potential lines of flight. They are quite insistent that lines of flight can move in radically Left-oriented or Right-oriented directions. Rather, the "abstract machine" provides a canvass on which to "test" potential lines of flight (Deleuze and Guattari 1987, 141–43). Mapping striated and smooth social formations might reveal where potential lines of flight *could* form, but it does not *prescribe* them.[9] This is why I find it particularly unfortunate that contemporary feminist scholars such as Puar opt for turning away from US Women of Color coalitional feminism in favor of Deleuzian and Guattarian accounts. In refusing directed (i.e., Left-oriented) political action, the epistemology of Deleuze and Guattari (and its contemporary formulation by Puar) drastically differs from the one on offer by Sandoval and Lugones. It is on this point that the third component of coalitional consciousness emerges.

For Sandoval, the particular consciousness of US Third World feminists is not only flexible, mobile, and dynamic; it is also self-conscious, tactical, and *directed*. These latter three interrelated characteristics distinguish a coalitional consciousness from an epistemology of undecidability. As Sandoval states, an oppositional (or coalitional) consciousness, typical of US Third World feminism, focuses us on the "recognition that a new morality and effective opposition resides in a *self-conscious* flexibility of identity and of political action which is capable, above all else, of *tactically intervening in the moves of power in the name of egalitarian social relations*" (Sandoval 1990, 66; my emphasis). The act of reading and mapping the circulation of power, we find, is a *political* act. But not because mapping power is intrinsically political in the sense that thinkers such as Laclau and Mouffe, Deleuze and Guattari, Butler, and Puar may argue; it is political because it moves in a self-conscious and purposeful direction toward undermining oppression (see Burack 2004, 147).

According to Sandoval, this form of mobile consciousness is not "nomadic" in the sense that Deleuze and Guattari speak of (Deleuze and Guattari 1986, 52); it is instead "cinematographic" (Sandoval 2000, 44). Understood by Sandoval as an art form—as a creative process—coalitional consciousness acquires a sense of direction that is absent from an understanding of nomadic or simply mobile consciousness. It is, as Sandoval puts it, "a kinetic motion that *maneuvers*, poetically *transfigures*, and *orchestrates*" (44; my emphasis). In this sense, it is purposeful, clever, and creative. A coalitional consciousness is not *just* a sensitivity to the circulation of power, even if this sensitivity proves to be hugely instructive; it is also fundamentally preoccupied with turning this sensitivity into the skill of knowing when and how to disrupt current power structures and reconfigure the social world in the name of egalitarian social justice.

The distinction Lugones later draws between "bird's-eye view" theorizing and "pedestrian" theorizing is instructive for teasing this out. Whereas "bird's-eye view" theorizing "disengages" from the concrete (Lugones 2003, 207) in order to plan from "up high" the takeover of the town (5)—think here of Lenin's Marxism discussed in chapter 1—pedestrian theorizing theorizes from "inside the midst of people, from inside the layers of relations and institutions and practices" (5). Pedestrian theory is therefore produced at a more granular and intimate level, from "within the concreteness of body-to-body engagement" (207). It is Deleuze and Guattari's sincere commitment to avoiding the dogmatic and programmatic politics that follows from bird's-eye view theorizing and leads to Lenin's dogmatic socialism that I believe compels them to insist that politics is diagrammatic, not prescriptive. Their abstract machine maps the movements of power and resistance, but it does so from a distance and after the fact. While their diagram accounts for the existence of minorities and the potential for "minoritarian becomings," they do not map from the perspective of such minorities (Deleuze and Guattari 1987, 469–70). Women of Color coalition feminists, on the other hand, step inside the map and theorize from this granular, intimate, pedestrian level (Lugones 2003, 15). This is why I find untenable Puar's claim that intersectionality is attentive only to the molar level. It is precisely because they theorize from *within* the space of lived struggle that they part ways with Puar in being unabashed in their appeal to *prescriptive* coalition politics.

Sandoval writes that a "coalitional consciousness" emerges when one self-consciously decides which tactical subjectivity to assume in order to bring about egalitarian social relations (2000, 71). The ability to read the movement and flow of power that subjugated people acquire out of necessity guides them in reading the "current situation of power" and then creatively and "self-consciously" "choosing" the best ideological stance to push back against it (60). To use this skill tactically and effectively, Sandoval tells us, one must have grace, flexibility, and strength (60). The strength to commit to different temporary identities and the flexibility to change these identities depending on what the situation demands are both skills women of color learned out of necessity by way of their embodied multiplicity. It is here that grace becomes important: the grace to recognize when to form alliances with others who are also committed to egalitarian social relations (60) and to distinguish between what Lorde calls our "peers" or "allies" and our true "enemies" (Lorde 1984g, 127; 1984b, 137). A person's ability to understand and harness their own shifting selves enables them to form coalitions with others (Sandoval 2000, 45). Such coalitional selves, I am arguing, resist an epistemology of undecidability (17) and offer instead a decidable and directed epistemology of political movement, a *coalitional consciousness*.

In "Purity, Impurity, and Separation," Lugones captures this tactical movement toward a center in the metaphor of "curdle-separation." As she reminds us, the process of curdling is not just the act of ingredients separating (such as in mayonnaise when the oil and water separate); instead, the ingredients "coalesce toward oil or toward water" (Lugones 2003, 121). In this sense, curdling is "a matter of different degrees of co-alescence," not simply separation (122). Curdle-separation in the form of coalition thus offers an alternative to essential identity politics, which follows what Lugones calls the pure logic of "split-separation," wherein two isolated identities are separated from one another (separating the egg white from the yolk). Curdle-separation, on the other hand, is a process of coming together and separating simultaneously, an exercise, she tells us, in both purity and impurity. This process of coalescence or "multiplic-ity," as opposed to "fragmentation," follows the logic of curdling in which the "social world" is understood as "complex and heterogeneous" and each person as "multiple, nonfragmented, embodied" (126–27). Like Lorde and Anzaldúa a decade earlier, Lugones resists all metaphors of fragmentation or split-separation to describe her mestiza identity because they conjure up notions of distinct and separate parts. The language of coalescing and the metaphor of curdling, on the other hand, allow for tactical coming together across multiplicity and heterogeneity. For Lugones, individuals are best thought of as multiple flowing particles that can and will tactically coalesce, or curdle, into different and shifting formations (of self) (2003, 133). However, this "against the grain" coming together is always a tactical response to externally imposed fragmentation or "domination" (133). This is why it can be described as an exercise in both purity (assuming a label that appears as if it is fragmented, distinct) and impurity (appreciating the way in which that which is subsumed beneath the label is always multiple, ambiguous, and plural).

Barvosa-Carter's discussion of the tactical deployment of the label "Latino/a" by a group of Mexicans and Puerto Ricans living in Chicago in the 1970s is instructive here. In keeping with Lugones's notion of multiple identity, Barvosa-Carter states, "cultural intermixture generates multiple identity when displaced peoples (their new neighbors) respond to changing life conditions by learning new identities (e.g., gender, ethnic, national, and subcultural) while maintaining their preexisting identities. ... Inhabitants of these 'borderlands' [citing Anzaldúa 1987] often learn and retain several identities in order to thrive in the diverse social contexts that comprise the places where they reside" (Barvosa-Carter 2001, 22). In the case of Mexicans and Puerto Ricans living in Chicago at the time, in reaction to externally imposed fragmentation that lumped all Spanish speaking populations under one label, "Latino/a," they chose to curdle-separate—that is, to tactically assume the label "Latino/a" in order to render visible diverse Latino/a identified communities for the sake of garnering rights and privileges that were currently unavailable to them, while knowing full well that what existed beneath this label was multiple and fluid (21, 24). The tactical label resulting from this form of curdle-separation, Barvosa-Carter clarifies, was a *political* identity, not an ontological identity, rooted in the "shared social justice values and goals that derived from common experiences of ethnic/racial discrimination, economic marginalization, and persistent social barriers to upward mobility" (24).

Such political appeals to tactically useful subject positions signal those "creative and productively defiant approaches to identity and subjectivity" that Beltrán so longs for (Beltrán 2004, 596). Beltrán's inability to see the value in the coalitional self that is articulated across Anzaldúa's text is rooted in her equivocation of standpoint theory with *epistemic privilege* (604–6). Rather than taking our lead from Nancy Hartsock (1985) on standpoint theory, we would do better in this context to take a lesson from Lugones and Elizabeth Spelman. As they argued in "Have We Got a Theory for You!" (Lugones and Spelman, 1983), the value in learning from the experiences of a border woman inheres not in claims she might make to epistemic privilege—that is, to a right or more accurate understanding of systems of oppression, even if she will gain precisely this through the process of "traveling"—but rather in the tactical know-how she has been forced to acquire as a coalitional self. Treated as perennial outsiders across multiple contexts, mestiza women have been forced to "travel" to worlds not fully their own and to gain cultural fluency in such contexts (575–76). Doing so, Lugones and Spelman have argued, affords them a critical insight into how to engage in difficult democratic and reciprocal dialogues (577).

Crucial to the process of democratic discussion *within* the space of coalition is not deferring to the "right knowledge" or epistemic authority of "more-evolved" coalitional or "hybrid" subjects in the way that Beltrán (2004, 604) fears but, rather, engaging with—that is, speaking to not for—coalitional selves and "developing ideas together" (Lugones and Spelman 1983, 579), which will form the basis of a more effective coalition politics. The skills Women of Color feminists have gained on this front make them invaluable "democratic interlocutors," to put it in Beltrán's (2004, 595) own words, and sophisticated coalitional theorists and practitioners. I purposefully use *coalition theorist* here to differentiate my project from Butler's articulation of coalition as spectacle wherein she is explicit in her resistance to embracing the notion of a coalition theorist (Butler 1990, 20). When Women of Color feminists theorize coalition politics, they do so not from the abstract or privileged bird's-eye view. This bird's-eye view is precisely what these activists and scholars set out to contest through theorizing from within lived experience. In so doing, they eschew both abstract scientific principles and either poststructuralist theoretical commitments to antifoundationalism or Puar's more recent appeal to assemblage as the basis of their "theory." While they are comfortable embracing a theoretical base or foundation, this foundation is rooted in the shifting lived experiences of subjugated people. Like Puar's notion of assemblage, it is therefore attentive to the contexts in which people are positioned; unlike Puar's alternative, these theorists theorize *prescriptive* coalition politics from the granular level.

As Sandoval argues in her 2000 book, building on arguments she made in her 1982 article, this form of coalitional consciousness is particularly exemplified in US Third World feminism. US Third World feminists have used this consciousness, she argues, to tactically shift between different feminist ideological positions, such as between "equal rights" feminism (women are the same as men), "revolutionary" feminism (women are different from men and so society must be completely restructured in their likeness), "supremacist" feminism (women are superior to men), and "socialist" feminism (women are a racially divided *class*) (Sandoval 2000, 44–52). Sandoval argues that US Third World feminism (also referred to as US Women of Color feminism) is unlike other kinds of feminism in its ability to advocate all four of these positions at different times and different contexts, without committing permanently to any one firm ideological framework other than that of "differential" or coalitional consciousness. She understands this fifth mode of resistance as one which has "kaleidoscoped" the other four ideological positions into "an original, eccentric, and queer sight," which can then be used as a "theoretical and methodological device" for discerning which of the four tactical positions to assume in any given context (44).

Sandoval argues that US Third World feminism, though often overlooked by white feminists, comprises a history of differential oppositional consciousness wherein US Third World feminists often enact one of the four other modes of oppositional consciousness but rarely for long and without the "kind of fervid belief systems and identity politics that tend to accompany their construction" (Sandoval 2000, 58). In this sense, they treat each ideological oppositional stance "not as overriding strategies, but as *tactics* for intervening in and transforming social relations" (62). This differential or coalitional "praxis," Sandoval argues,

> understands, wields, and deploys each mode of resistant ideology as if it represents only another potential *technology of power*. The cruising mobilities required in this effort demand of the differential practitioner commitment to the process of metamorphosis itself: this is the activity of the trickster who practices subjectivity as masquerade, the oppositional agent who accesses differing identity, ideological, aesthetic, and political positions. This nomadic "morphing" is not performed only for survival's sake, as in earlier, modernist times. It is a set of *principled conversions* that requires (guided) movement, a directed but also diasporic migration in both consciousness and politics, performed to ensure that ethical commitment to egalitarian social relations be enacted in the everyday, political sphere of culture. (Sandoval 2000, 62)

Coalitional consciousness requires the kind of "cruising mobilities" that are no doubt made possible by US Third World feminists' coalitional selves and resonant with Lugones's notion of pedestrian theorizing. A "commitment to the process of metamorphosis" of self is something that women of color learn first as a survival tactic (think here of Vázquez from Somos Hermanas). This process of metamorphosis enables them to hold on to a center (self-definition) in the midst of their multiple, shifting, and contradictory selves. Recall that existential transformation is one of the three key characteristics of politico-ethical coalition politics. This ontological state provides a kind of training ground for women of color to later "practice subjectivity as masquerade." These "trickster" activities, first developed as coping skills to survive the shifting currents of their being, have since been utilized as tactics for collective resistance (think here of the tactical deployment of *Latino/a*). Once developed into a sophisticated and tactical form of coalitional consciousness, these "tricks" and "metamorphoses" take on a new register. They become self-consciously "principled," "guided," or "directed" toward a politics of resistance and intervention in the name of egalitarian social relations. It is precisely on this latter point, then, that a coalitional consciousness describes a unique epistemology not of undecidability but of concerted and directed political action.[10]

In this discussion, Sandoval cites a wide literature, including works by Anzaldúa, Smith, Bonnie Thorton Dill, bell hooks, Lugones, Patricia Hill Collins, Barbara Christian, and Alice Walker, as well as Black feminist anthologies such as *This Bridge Called My Back* (Moraga and Anzaldúa 1983a) and *But Some of Us Are Brave* (Hull, Scott, and Smith 1982). I am engaging a similar literature here. While the differences among these authors are important, I believe, like Sandoval, that attention must be paid to the similarities, particularly to these authors' tendency toward coalition: as a preferred mode of political engagement; as a sophisticated concept to aid us in rethinking identity, subjectivity, and consciousness; and as I will argue in the subsequent chapter, toward coalition as a methodological commitment that reshapes how Women of Color coalition feminists do political theory. Their resistance to any one mode of opposition created the conditions for a strained affiliation between US Third World feminism and the women's movement, as their behavior was often misinterpreted as "disloyalty, betrayal, absence, or lack" (Sandoval 2000, 58). The nuance of Third World feminism's shifting and tactical coalitional consciousness, it would seem, has gone unnoticed and unappreciated by many white feminists. It is not surprising that it has also gone unnoticed by many contemporary political theorists.

In an effort to demonstrate the potential reach these notions of coalitional identity and coalitional consciousness may have for social justice coalition politics, I want to end by examining an autobiographical account of a white woman's journey toward coalitional consciousness. Such an exercise brings us back to where this chapter began by giving a narrative account of the kind of personal journey that white women such as Reagon's hypothetical "Mary" must undergo when attempting to coalesce with diverse subjugated groups committed to undermining oppression. While a coalitional identity—along with its corresponding coalition consciousness—emerges as a survival strategy for many Women of Color feminists, this ontology (and its corresponding epistemology) may also emerge for white women and men if they self-consciously and self-reflexively examine their own positionality vis-à-vis oppression.

Confronting One's Complicity in Oppression: A White Woman's Struggle toward Coalitional Consciousness

In "Identity: Skin Blood Heart," Minnie Bruce Pratt (1984) recounts her coming to consciousness as a white, middle-class, rural, Southern, Christian, lesbian woman committed to fighting interlocking oppressions. To do this, Pratt walks us through different periods in her life: her adult life living in a predominantly Black neighborhood with her lesbian lover in Washington, DC, in the 1980s; moments from her early childhood in Alabama; moments from the time she spent with her husband and children in an eastern North Carolina town; and moments from the time she spent both alone and with other women in North Carolina after her husband took the kids and left her. Rather than unfolding in chronological order, Pratt's autobiographical narrative recounts different and discontinuous moments of her coming to consciousness, of her "trying to figure out [her own] responsibility and [her] need in struggles against injustice" (Pratt 1984, 15).

I choose to end this chapter with Pratt's story because it shows how even white women may struggle toward coalitional identity and develop coalitional consciousness. One does not have to be nonwhite to engage in politico-ethical coalition politics. As we saw with Reagon's emphasis on "Mary" changing to "Maria," in such cases, self-reflexivity becomes hugely important. For Pratt, this journey depended on her ability to discover and confront her "negative identity" (Pratt 1983, 46), that is, to accept the various invitations of women and people of color, poor women, Jewish women, and others to act as her "faithful mirrors" (Lugones 2003, 72), rendering visible not only her multiple selves but also those selves that might have been, or are still, implicated in racism, sexism, heterosexism, and ethnocentrism, among other oppressive structures. Once her sense of self is self-reflexively decentered or "(dis)integrated" (Roshanravan 2018), she is able to begin to reconstruct a positive and, I argue, truly coalitional identity.[11] By traveling, in Lugones's sense of the word, to the other side of her family history, Pratt discovers the many facets of her multiple and contradictory self. Despite the devastation of arriving at the other side, Pratt uses this self-discovery to redefine her identity in coalitional terms, which necessarily prepares her to engage in social justice coalitions with other women. In this sense, Pratt's autobiography leads us across the three levels of politico-ethical coalition politics—across the ontological level, the epistemological level, and the political level. As I argue in chapter 5, it therefore also provides an instructive example for contemporary white feminists as they attempt large-scale multiracial alliances such as those that occurred in the 2017 Women's March on Washington and the various Black Lives Matter protests erupting in late spring and early summer of 2020.

Moments leading Pratt to coalitional consciousness occurred in those instances in which she felt threatened or unsafe, in which her privilege could no longer protect her. Just as Reagon insisted, if you do not feel threatened to your core, then you are probably not doing any real coalescing. One of these dangerous moments occurred for Pratt when living in an unfamiliar eastern North Carolina town in which her family ties carried no weight or protection against misogynist sexual violence against women. It was here, she recounts, that for the "first time in [her] life, [she] was living in a place where [she] was afraid because [she] was a *woman*," and where she first thought of herself as "belonging to an *oppressed* group" (Pratt 1984, 22).

A second and profound moment in which "the shell of [her] privilege was [again] broken" occurred when Pratt's husband discovered her lesbianism and took custody of their children. In her grief she "became obsessed with justice" and active in women's liberation (27). In these years she experienced her "expanding consciousness of oppression as painful but ultimately *positive*" (35; my emphasis). It was not yet traumatic for her. She was "breaking through to an understanding of [her] life as a woman." This was a process toward her own liberation, a process of "freeing [her]self." From the experience of being hated and punished for being who she was as a lesbian, Pratt developed a heightened and urgent political consciousness toward "justice" and setting things "right." It was not until her understanding of injustice extended beyond her own "narrow circle of being" and toward all subjugated peoples, however, that her consciousness took on a truly coalitional form (35).

In her initial work with other women in women's liberation action, Pratt kept her lesbianism a secret. She recounts that in these years she was "in fact, not seeking liberation as [her] particular, *complex* self" (33; my emphasis); on the contrary, she was "denying publicly a basic part of [her]self, while not seeing the subtle and overt pressures on other women to also deny their different aspects, in order to exist in the outside world, and in order to come to our place" (33). At this moment, Pratt began a concerted *struggle* toward a *coalitional self*. She began to appreciate herself as multiple, internally discontinuous, and even contradictory. As she puts it, she learned to see herself and the world as a series of "overlapping circles." This gave her a more "accurate, complex, multi-layered, multi-dimensioned," and "more truthful" understanding of the world (17). Pratt's coalitional identity and coalitional consciousness emerge together in this moment. Part of a coalitional *consciousness* involves becoming acquainted with one's coalitional self, that is, to begin to appreciate one's internal contradictions and to struggle toward coherent and positive self-definition despite this multiplicity and contradiction. She expanded her "constricted eye" (17) or her "circle of self" (18) by "jumping" from her "edge and outside herself, into radical change" (19). In this sense, Pratt begins the painful journey of "'world'-traveling" (Lugones 2003).

For Pratt, this journey entailed setting out to "find out what had been done or was being done in [her] name" as a white, middle-class, Southern, Christian woman (Pratt 1984, 34). This painful process of self-discovery included learning that both sides of her family owned slaves and that much of her family's wealth was "stolen from the lives of others" (34). In these difficult moments, Pratt's identity takes on a self-reflexive form as she considers the ways in which she and "her people" are implicated in the oppression of others.[12] For this, she held herself and her people responsible, projecting her into a long and difficult "struggle with" and "against [her]self" (35–36). It is in this process of struggling with and against herself toward a positive and whole vision of who she is that a coalitional self emerges.

This "breaking through," she states, "did not feel like liberation but like destruction" (36). In this sense, it shares much with the "psychic restlessness" and shock experienced by Anzaldúa as she recounts her struggle toward mestiza identity (Anzaldúa 1987, 78). "During the time that I was first feeling all of this information," Pratt recounts, "I lived in a kind of vertigo: a sensation of my body having no fixed place to be: the earth having opened, I was falling through space" (1984, 35). In this moment of self-reflection, staring in the faithful mirror of women and people of color, Pratt's self became multiple, fluid, contradictory; in Roshanravan's words, quoting Lugones, it began the painful process of "disintegrating and rewiring 'expectations desires, and beliefs that fit one for a life in allegiance with oppression'" (Roshanravan 2018, 152). Pratt narrates a similar process of becoming decentered. Through this process of "expanding" her "limited being," an "upheaval" took place but one less like a "catastrophe" and more like a "shedding" of one's skin or outer layers in order to make room for an "expansion" or "growth" (Pratt 1984, 39) toward coalitional identity and its corresponding coalitional consciousness.

Coalitional selves do not remain in this space of unfixity or undecidability for long. Instead, they learn to move between their multiple and contradictory selves, thus creating a new and positive coalitional self. Pratt "re-creates" this "positive" and whole self by learning to travel among her multiple selves, among the multiple facets of her past and upbringing (Pratt 1984, 35, 41, 42–44). This is the next step. By exploring the positive components of what she has "carried with [her] from [her white, Southern] culture," she discovers that there are alternative ways of being a white, Southern woman. Drawing inspiration from white women such as Sarah and Angelina Grimké of South Carolina who organized both for the abolition of slavery and for women's rights, Jessie Daniel Ames of Texas who led an antilynching campaign, and Lillian Smith of Georgia who was a novelist, essayist, and antisegregationist speaker, Pratt learns to tactically take on different components of her multiple identity for the sake of progressive struggle against multiple, fluid, and intersecting oppressions.

The new understanding or "consciousness" opened up by way of this decentering and directed recentering is one wherein she understands that she is "entrapped *as* a woman, not just by the sexual fear of the men of [her] group, but also by their racial and religious terrors" (Pratt 1984, 38). This helps her to understand the deep connection between her oppression as a lesbian and as a woman and that of others. She learns that when white men of her culture condemn her "as a lesbian and a free woman for being 'dirty,' 'unholy,' 'perverted,' 'immoral,'" this is "a judgment that has been called down on people of color and Jews throughout history by the men of [her] culture, as they have shifted their justification for hatred according to their desires of the moment" (38). Such an understanding makes a coalitional self possible: one who can not only navigate tactically among her contradictory and multiple selves in an effort to strive toward a coherent center but who can navigate tactically among ideological positions in an effort to strive toward coalition with other "justice-seeking" coalitional identities (Caraway 1991, 111). In this sense, one is thought to be "coalitional" both on the inside, as a "coalition of one" (Carastathis 2013, 960), and on the outside, as one working with others in coalitions to fight social injustice (see Pratt 1984, 46, 47, 48). For Pratt and for the other US Women of Color coalition feminists addressed throughout this chapter, the connection between the inside and outside is indissoluble: when she "passively witnesses the repetition of the old ways of doing things" and does "nothing," she confesses, she feels her "rigid circle close around [her], tightening, painful" (Pratt 1984, 52). Her coalitional self is very much tied to her coalitional work for social justice. They feed each other. She is the fullest and widest sense of herself when her actions are directed toward social justice in coalition with other subjugated people.

Before closing and in an attempt to further emphasize the role of political commitment within politico-ethical coalition politics, I want to address the place of love in Pratt's struggle toward coalitional identity and coalitional consciousness. She began the process of internal change and political commitment to fighting for social justice when, she recounts, "I jumped from my edge and outside myself, into radical change, for love: simply love: for myself and for other women. I acted on that love by becoming a lesbian, falling in love with and becoming sexual with a particular woman; and this love led me directly, but by a complicated way, to work against racism and anti-Semitism" (19). She goes on to clarify that she did not arrive at this position of political commitment because she knew it was the "right" thing to do or even out of a sense of "justice" or "general principles" (19–20). Instead, she learned to work against racism, sexism, and anti-Semitism by loving and becoming sexually intimate with a woman.

This prompts the question: how are we to interpret the emphasis Pratt places on love here? One could interpret this as a challenge to the *politico-*ethical conception of coalition politics I developed in chapter 2. There, I argued that it was not an ethical commitment, rooted in feelings of love and respect for others, that brought women such as Reagon, Smith, Lorde, and others to social justice struggles. It was rather a self-reflexive political commitment to undermining oppression and to upholding egalitarian social justice. In the passage above, one might argue that Pratt suggests that it was not in fact a political commitment to justice that brought her to change; it was, instead, love for other women, thereby implying that for her an ethical commitment ultimately drives her politics. I would, however, like to offer an alternative reading.

While it is certain that love plays a pivotal role in Pratt's journey toward self-discovery and political commitment, we must be careful to understand what about her love propelled her in this direction. Though it seems fair to suggest that her intimate or romantic love for other women helped Pratt to be more generous, giving, and accepting with women in coalitional spaces (lesbian Women of Color feminists such as Lorde, Anzaldúa, Moraga, and others have similarly attributed their ability to work effectively in coalition at least in part to their love for other women), to suggest that Pratt's self-discovery and political commitment to fighting social injustice is fundamentally rooted in her sexual or romantic love for women is to miss an important nuance in this autobiographical account of her coming to consciousness.

Pratt, in fact, says that it was not *that* she loved women that brought her to consciousness (extending feelings of love to all women regardless of race, religious orientation, or other differences) but rather *how* she was *perceived by others* for loving women that brought her to change (Pratt 1984, 20). It was in reflecting on the ways in which she was reviled for being a lesbian that she became aware of the multilayered and interconnected workings of power. Because of how she loved she learned what it was to "lose a position of safety" and to be "despised for *who* [she was]" (20). This journey inside herself therefore aided Pratt in mapping intermeshing oppressions, thus expanding her understanding of social injustice and oppression. It was this breaking through that allowed Pratt to understand how her struggle was connected to the struggles of other oppressed groups (20). In this sense, it was in fact a self-reflexive *political* commitment that propelled her to action. Her lesbian love is highly political due to the marginalization it has brought with it. So, yes, her lesbianism did bring her to political commitment, but not because an ethics of love motivates her political actions; rather, the fact that she was condemned and oppressed for how she chose to love alerted her to the interconnected and sophisticated maneuvering of power. In this sense, her coming to consciousness shares much with accounts given by the other Women of Color coalition feminists engaged here and provides an excellent example of how white allies might also discover their coalitional selves so that they might join Vázquez and others in coalitional solidarity.

Conclusion

By infusing the concept of coalition into philosophical discussions related to reimagining multiple and fluid identity and better understanding shifting power structures, we are able to avoid the unworkable tensions that have emerged for other contemporary coalition scholars as they try to hold in play two untenable positions: ontological unfixity and epistemological undecidability, on the one hand, and a Left-oriented coalition politics, or political fixity, on the other. By reconceiving identity coalitionally, I have offered an alternative way of theorizing identity that attends to multiplicity and fluidity without subscribing to permanent unfixity. Coalitional selves are fundamentally preoccupied with struggling toward a coherent and definable whole, or center. This center is fixed both in its multiplicity and in the coalitional consciousness that emerges to guide one in navigating this multiplicity.

Parting ways with thinkers such as Laclau and Mouffe, Butler, Lloyd, and others, I have located politics in the very heart of ontology, but *not* because the discursive production of all ontological categories must be thought of as a political process. Rather, for the Women of Color feminists I have engaged here, ontology (or existence) has always been a political struggle toward fixity and wholeness and against externally imposed definition and erasure. It is precisely for this reason that they are willing to hold onto a notion of ontological fixity as a sophisticated consciousness that emerges through this internal struggle and helps them to move creatively and tactically across their own multiplicity and contradiction. This ontology of coalitional identity and its corresponding coalitional consciousness helps women of color, and anyone else willing to engage in this internal and self-reflexive journey, to develop the skills necessary to become comfortable with ambiguity even as they move in purposeful directions. It helps them to tactically assume different subjectivities and ideological positions depending on what the current structure of power demands. In short, it prepares them for the hard work of politico-ethical coalition politics.

As such, politico-ethical coalition politics dissolves the perceived crises of Marxism through its ability to address its interconnected components: ontologically, it allows us to retain a sense of multiplicity and complexity while refusing permanent unfixity; epistemologically, it allows us to appreciate the complicated, interconnected, and mobile systems of power that subjugate variously positioned individuals, while refusing undecidability; and politically, it allows us to think more rigorously about how to engage in directed progressive coalition politics across diverse subjugated groups. By thinking with the concept of coalition within the context of ontological and epistemological discussions about multiple identity and political consciousness, I have acquainted readers with some of the levels on which politico-ethical coalition politics unfolds. In chapter 4, I turn to one final way in which early US Women of Color coalition feminists think with and, in this case, *through* coalition. I turn to a fourth level of coalition by examining how early US Women of Color coalition feminists *do political theory*. In turning my attention to this methodological level, I seek to uncover a unique mode of feminist *coalitional scholarship*.

4

Writing Feminist Theory, Doing Feminist Politics

Rethinking Collective Feminist Authorship
with *This Bridge Called My Back*

The reparativeness of black feminist thought is most plainly revealed precisely in the dimension that is so often celebrated by scholars and commentators of black feminism: coalition-building and coalition politics. It would be easy to assume that coalitions are, for black feminist theory and practice, merely an indispensable instrumental tool of minority politics. But close examination suggests another plot behind the instrumental necessities of politics. Black feminist theory is a coalitional discourse, not only because it insists upon the political expediency of coalitions, but because it constitutes itself in and through a persistent discussion of the ubiquity of difference and the necessity of intellectual, political, and emotional work across difference.

—CYNTHIA BURACK, *Healing Identities: Black Feminist Thought and the Politics of Groups*

At the end of *Healing Identities: Black Feminist Thought and the Politics of Groups*, Cynthia Burack (2004) astutely identifies the unique political and theoretical contributions of Black feminist thought to political and social theory invested in theorizing activist group politics. I am in agreement with Burack that this contribution resides in the thinking Black and Women of Color feminists from Bernice Johnson Reagon to Chela Sandoval have done around the theory and practice of coalition politics, best captured in the notion of politico-ethical coalition politics present across Reagon's 1981 coalition speech. Like Burack, I also maintain that both the sophistication and promise of their concept of coalition lie in its multidimensionality. As I have demonstrated, this multidimensionality helps us rethink several important political, ontological, and epistemological questions about theorizing a post-Marxist notion of Left-oriented collective politics outside of unitary categories such as "class" or "women." In this chapter, I continue to think *with* these scholars in an effort to orient us to thinking *through* coalition by exploring one final component of this multidimensionality. In addition to alerting us to the "instrumental necessities" of coalition politics, this literature points us in the direction of developing a unique "coalitional discourse" (Burack 2004, 159) that not only arrives at coalition as the answer to the politics question provoked by the perceived crisis of Marxism but also enacts a form of politico-ethical *coalitional scholarship*.

In an article examining US Women of Color feminist writing from the 1970s and 1980s, Erica Townsend-Bell (2012) challenges conventional knowledge that Women of Color feminists only turned to coalition in the 1980s. She shows that the theme of coalition politics has been central to their writing since the 1970s (think here of Shirley Chisholm). Nevertheless, Townsend-Bell finds that there was something unique to 1980s US Women of Color feminism. Not only did writing in this decade focus "even greater attention" on the question of coalitions and on challenging the basis for assumed feminist unity, Townsend-Bell argues that this writing resembled a "literal written coalition of women of color among authors and readers" (2012, 130).

With the emergence of women of color–only presses such as Kitchen Table: Women of Color Press, this period saw a shift in control over writing spaces that brought with it a number of Women of Color feminist anthologies that were written, compiled, edited, and published by women of color. These include *All the Women Are White, All the Blacks Are Men, But Some of Us Are Brave* by Gloria T. Hull, Patricia Bell Scott, and Barbara Smith (1982), *Home Girls: A Black Anthology* by Barbara Smith (1983a), and *This Bridge Called My Back: Writings by Radical Women of Color* by Cherríe Moraga and Gloria Anzaldúa (1983a). "Activist collections" such as these, Townsend-Bell argues, both sought to and succeeded at creating "*text-based coalitions* that mapped activism on the ground and encouraged further reflection and activity around the possibilities and the difficulties of coalitions" (Townsend-Bell 2012, 144; my emphasis). As I will show, the feminist collective authorship practices on display in *This Bridge Called My Back* ushered in radically different approaches to feminist scholarship. "Beyond their writing about alliance," I follow Townsend-Bell in appreciating the way in which, the "collective orientation of the edited texts created a *written coalition* in and of itself" (145; my emphasis).

While it might seem odd to describe a material object such as a book *as* a coalition, to pass such references off as careless or less than rigorous would be to miss an important and defining feature of early US Women of Color coalitional feminism. I believe that the fact that this notion seemed appropriate to Townsend-Bell in 2012 speaks to both the prevalence and multidimensionality of the notion of politico-ethical coalition politics emerging out of this period. As I have argued, for Women of Color feminists, coalition is understood as the merging or coming together of different *parts*—not necessarily people, political parties, or groups—for the sake of a shared, self-reflexive politico-ethical commitment to undermining oppression. While these "parts" refer to different individuals or groups of people in the case of coalition politics on the ground, these "parts" may refer to the shifting and contradictory components of one's own psyche (through the notion of coalitional identity). In the case of a "textual coalition," these parts refer to the different authors and their respective writings that come together in the pages of a single text.

With this in mind and elaborating on Townsend-Bell's casual references to "textual" or "written" coalition, this chapter argues that Cherríe Moraga and Gloria Anzaldúa's (1983a) coedited anthology, *This Bridge Called My Back: Writings by Radical Women of Color* (hereafter referred to as *Bridge*), is an indispensable resource for theorizing progressive coalition politics insofar as it comes to function as a textual coalition, offering an exemplary enactment of the coalitional scholarship unique to US Women of Color feminism of this period. For a text to take on a truly "coalitional" character, it must represent a coming together of diverse voices in the service of a shared politico-ethical commitment to undermining oppression. The manifestation of this merging is the anthology itself. Not only is *Bridge* unambiguously political through its activist publishing location in Kitchen Table and its explicit content-driven focus on coalition politics, but the text itself takes on a politico-ethical coalitional form in its overt self-reflexivity and its firm commitment to stand collectively against all forms of oppression. In addition to entering into difficult and self-reflexive conversations with other women of color about their own differences within the pages of the book, *Bridge* adopts a self-reflexive and radically transparent editing process that prefigures the anthology itself as an egalitarian and coalitional space. In this sense, the text becomes a living coalitional conversation that not only arrives at politico-ethical coalition as the best way of carrying out collective politics but also depicts, enacts, and encourages a collective struggle toward coalitional consciousness.

To make this argument, I contrast *Bridge* with two other feminist anthologies, one appearing the decade before *Bridge* (Robin Morgan's [1970] *Sisterhood Is Powerful: An Anthology of Writings from the Women's Liberation Movement*, hereafter referred to as *Sisterhood*) and one appearing the decade after it (Rebecca Walker's [1995] *To Be Real: Telling the Truth and Changing the Face of Feminism*, hereafter referred to as *Real*). I have chosen to focus on the progression from early 1970s feminist anthologies to 1990s feminist anthologies to isolate what is unique to the coalitional scholarship of early US Women of Color coalitional feminism. I am in agreement with Brian Norman (2006, 39) that feminist anthologies tend to "enact the collectivity for which they call." For this reason, I closely examine what kind of feminist collectivity each anthology summons. This enables me to reveal the danger in relying on either ethical notions of what I call "textual sisterhood" (in one instance) or ontological visions of lifestyle feminism in the form of what I call "textual mosaic" (in the other instance) as the cementing force behind progressive coalition politics. While textual sisterhood takes an additive approach to difference that unself-reflexively advocates for naively optimistic notions of universal sisterhood, textual mosaic ushers in a dangerously apolitical and unself-reflexive form of feminist collective authorship that celebrates privileged, highly individualistic and defiant "choice" feminism. Only *Bridge*, I argue, emerges as a true textual coalition, making it an indispensable resource for contemporary feminist theorists interested in either theorizing coalition or attempting collective, activist, and certainly coalitional, modes of scholarship.

By turning to even more recent experiments with coalitional modes of engaging in collective scholarship, such as that undertaken by the Sangtin Writers and Richa Nagar (2006) in *Playing with Fire: Feminist Thought and Activism through Seven Lives in India*, the chapter ends by demonstrating the continued relevance of the scholarly practices of early US Women of Color coalitional feminism. While the decade immediately following the publication of *Bridge* brought with it a disturbing trend away from feminist collective authorship in the form of politico-ethical textual coalition, more recent scholarly practices suggest a promising resurgence of the radical coalitional scholarship gifted to us in *Bridge*. Insofar as feminist activism is moving unequivocally in the direction of coalition politics, this chapter thus invites feminist scholars to learn from the radical US Women of Color coalition feminists who brought us *Bridge* in embracing coalitional ways of thinking and writing that not only emphasize collective authorship—a common scholarly practice within feminist studies—but that succeed in forming politico-ethical textual coalitions.

Sisterhood Is Powerful: *On the Limitations of Textual Sisterhood*

In order to appreciate what was unique to politico-ethical coalitional scholarship, I situate it in relation to the collective feminist authorship practices typical of late 1960s and early 1970s feminism. Works such as Shulamith Firestone's (1968; 1970) *Notes from the First Year* and *Notes from the Second Year*, Morgan's (1970) *Sisterhood*, and Leslie Tanner's (1971) *Voices from Women's Liberation* reflected common sentiments, concepts, and demands of the burgeoning women's liberation movement. Invested in both reflecting and building a women's liberation community, these anthologies were most definitely activist feminist texts. Morgan's *Sisterhood* is indicative of this, insofar as it is unapologetically political in both its form and content.

As Morgan asserts, the book itself is an "action" (1970b, xv). "Conceived, written, edited, copy-edited, proofread, designed, and illustrated by women" (xv), *Sisterhood* is the outcome of what Morgan understands as a "collective" feminist project centered on resisting sexist oppression (Morgan 1970a, acknowledgments). In addition to donating all monies from the book's sales to cover a variety of costs of the women's movement (abortion, day care, bail, and defense funds), Morgan self-consciously resists nonegalitarian editing practices by inviting the contributors to write their own short biographies in the "Notes on Sister Contributors," being transparent about the selection process, and by using "we" instead of "I" as she recounts various editorial decisions (Morgan 1970b, xix, xxi–xxii, xxx). In terms of writing style and method, the pieces across the anthology reject a "certain kind of linear, tight, dry, boring, male super-consistency," in favor of multiple forms of writing—articles, poems, graphics, and sundry papers—combining "well-documented, statistically solid pieces" alongside "intensely personal experiences" (xx). As such, *Sisterhood* offers a specifically feminist mode of doing theory that theorizes out of human experience and feeling and not out of "textbook rhetoric," which is made conspicuously present in the anthology's introduction wherein Morgan recounts the various personal and material sacrifices and "reprisals" that the women made in the service of pulling this anthology together (the intimate relationships ended, the pregnancies, the miscarriages, the abortions, the lost jobs) (xx, xv–xvi). Morgan thus stages these personal events as part and parcel to the anthology itself, thereby further dissolving the public-private distinction and helping us to understand feminist scholarship itself as an intensely personal and material struggle. This is most certainly a collective, activist text.

Sisterhood enacts a feminism that is committed to identifying and undermining sexist oppression and it even goes so far as to acknowledge the ways in which sexism exists in constellation with other forms of oppression, such as racism and classism (xxxi, xxxv–xxxvi). Paying attention to these divisions, Morgan argues, has opened the women's movement to new ways of understanding the multiple forms of oppression suffered by women (xxix). Morgan believes that this anthology is engaged in a similar process of analyzing race, class, age, and sexuality divisions in the women's movement. *Sisterhood*, she contends, depicts and enacts a new "revolutionary feminism" that attempts to avoid the trap of bourgeois feminism, which refused any real analysis of race and class (xxvi). Instead, Morgan seeks to bring together many different female voices—young women, middle-aged women, older women, white women, Black women, Chicana women, college-educated women, working-class women, professional women—in a united sisterhood committed to fighting oppression.

Across fifty-seven entries, besides her own introduction, and fourteen historical documents from the women's liberation movement, far more than one hundred different women's voices find a platform in this anthology. The anthology is organized thematically in five broad sections, in addition to the introductory material by Morgan, Connie Brown, and Jane Seitz.[1] In this sense, *Sisterhood* succeeds in bringing together multiple voices. The first section, for instance, includes a number of pieces on the conditions of living under sexism, with special attention to experiences across different job sectors. By including pieces by women working within diverse professions (medicine, publishing, television, military, journalism, secretarial, academia, factory, pastoral, legal), including one essay by a Black professional woman, the anthology seeks to speak across, at least some, class and race divisions within the women's movement. By adding the voices of lesbian women in another section, the anthology continues to expand this diversity. The section that most explicitly aims to address difference within the movement is the third, which includes three articles by Black women, three articles by high school–age women, and two articles by Chicana women. Discussions of redefining feminism in light of such interventions continue in the fourth section, which includes another article by a Black woman.

While it is certain that *Sisterhood* is motivated by a clear political purpose, I want to examine the extent to which this political purpose might be construed as a politico-*ethical* one. As we will soon see, attempts at creating a print-based textual "sisterhood" ran into a variety of now familiar problems.[2] As bell hooks has argued, the goal of "sisterhood" underpinning many women's liberation projects risked seeking universal community around the "common oppression" of all women at the expense of attending to the race and class differences that warrant a fundamental rethinking of feminist goals and projects. hooks writes: "Bonding as 'victims,' white women liberationists were not required to assume responsibility for confronting the complexity of their own experience.... Identifying as 'victims,' they could abdicate the responsibility for their role in the maintenance and perpetuation of sexism, racism, and classism, which they did by insisting that only men were the enemy. They did not acknowledge and confront the enemy within" (hooks [1984] 2000, 46). This reluctance to "confront the enemy within" reverberates across 1970s anthologies such as Morgan's. While *Sisterhood* enacts a feminism committed to identifying and undermining sexist oppression, attending to the ways in which sexism exists in constellation with other forms of oppression, and committed to bringing together a diverse range of women's voices, scholars of the time noted that it seemed more interested in celebrating common ground through the universal notion of "sisterhood" than confronting conflict and differences *between* women (Simons 1979). As I will demonstrate, despite the presence of some diversity, both Morgan's introduction and the rest of the anthology fail to engage diversity and difference from a truly politico-ethical perspective that demands turning one's political commitment to undermining oppression in on oneself—that is, to self-reflexively (and therefore also self-critically) commit oneself to a feminist project of undermining *all* forms of oppression. While Morgan and the other authors display sensitivity to the existence of multiple oppressions, there is no sense that they are interested in *self-reflexively* addressing the challenge this poses to "sisterhood."

Thus, though *Sisterhood* certainly engages difference, it does so additively, as opposed to intersectionally.[3] By this, I mean to suggest that while the anthology may speak to multiple forms of oppression and even attempt to put other forms of oppression—racism, classism, heterosexism—in conversation with sexism, it does so only to the extent that it reveals the ways in which a poor, Black, lesbian woman may be oppressed by four oppressions at once: corporate capitalism, racism, heterosexism, and sexism. These analyses do not attempt to consider the ways in which these oppressions may interact with one another. Instead, *Sisterhood* sees other forms of oppression only as symptoms of one root or primary oppression, which is sexism (Morgan 1970b, xxxix–xl). As Morgan argues, all women essentially play the same role in patriarchal society but with different "sets and costumes" (xx). While these sets and costumes may *add* new dimensions to their oppression, they do not, it would seem, fundamentally alter their experience of sexism.

This additive approach to understanding multiple oppressions lends itself to analogies such as the race-sex analogy (King 1988, 43–46). At the time, such analogies proved useful for women's rights activists when confronted with blatant gender inequities. As Laura Furman argues in her article on gender inequities in the publishing world, while the justification that "women simply don't make that much money" still seemed acceptable to many men in the profession, the equivalent raced statement would never have been acceptable: "If I were a black man," she recounts one woman saying, "you wouldn't dare say that to me" (Furman 1970, 72). As Morgan states in her introduction, the women's movement was born at least partially out of the civil rights movement. "There's something contagious," she asserts, "about demanding freedom" (Morgan 1970b, xxiii). Experiencing one form of oppression (such as racism) she implies, will incline one toward understanding and contesting other forms of oppression (such as sexism). However, while this inclination may occur, there is no guarantee that it will occur, especially if one refuses to see the differences between forms of oppression or the ways in which multiple forms of oppression interact with one another. An understanding of this more complicated picture may in fact make liberation struggles much more challenging (recall Reagon's challenge). By assuming that the oppression endured by enslaved Black women under slavery parallels the oppression that white women experience within a patriarchal society dangerously obscures the particular experience of Black women. In this additive approach to multiple oppressions, the experience of Black women is thought to be synonymous either with that of Black men or that of white women (King 1988, 47–49). Such an approach thus fails to consider the ways in which racism and sexism interact with one another.

All the articles written by white women that address race in the anthology do so in this additive sense. While they may, for instance, point to statistics, facts, and figures on race or class differences between women, it is not clear that these authors understand or address the implications of the interaction of multiple forms of oppression at once. For instance, while Joreen acknowledges that the highest unemployment rate exists among nonwhite women between the ages of eighteen and twenty, she does not spend time addressing how multiple oppressive forces interact to create a particularly difficult situation for women of color besides stating that they are victims of two forms of oppression simultaneously (Joreen 1970, 40). She does not, for instance, consider what workplace justice may mean to poor, nonwhite women and whether their experience of work or un- and underemployment may challenge or reshape other priorities within the feminist movement. Similarly, in Lucina Cisler's celebration of sterilization as another liberating form of birth control, she resists emphasizing the extent to which Puerto Rican women were forcefully or coercively sterilized (Cisler 1970, 285–87).

In her discussion of women and the welfare system, Carol Glassman acknowledges the difference in attitudes toward being on welfare between white women and Black women, but she does not consider how these differing attitudes and experience may challenge and reshape feminist political solidarity (Glassman 1970, 122–23). In Beverly Jones's article on marriage and motherhood, she presumes that all married women share a common identity—they all, she says, carry the same "little bundle of secrets" with them regarding their particular situation as a married woman (Jones 1970, 65). While she states that there is some diversity within the "married women" group, she does not consider how the needs and demands of married women may shift depending on one's race and socioeconomic status. In Roxanne Dunbar's discussion of whether we can hope for solidarity between white and Black women, she states that Black women will "continue to fight as blacks alongside black men ... in order for him to gain his 'due' masculine status according to the prevailing masculine ideology" (Dunbar 1970, 549–50). Dunbar seems completely unaware of the ways in which the racism of the women's movement may also account for why Black women would choose to fight for Black liberation over women's liberation.

Across the fifty-eight contributions to the anthology (including Morgan's introduction and excluding the historical documents), seven are written by women of color (five by Black women and two by Chicana women). In this sense, the representation of race difference across the pages of this book is rather underwhelming. While some representation is better than no representation, and while the need to speak to race, class, and other differences was clearly on Morgan's radar as she set out to compile this anthology, it seems fair to say that the anthology itself, even if we approach it from a strictly additive sense, falls short. This failure, however, is not simply one of lack of sufficient representation of women of color among the contributors to the anthology. If we look closely at the articles that were published by women of color, other disturbing trends emerge.

In a section titled "Women in the Professions," Morgan includes an article by Sheila Smith Hobson, a Black woman working in television. As Hobson recounts her experiences, she, too, deals with the multiple oppressions she experienced on account of her race and sex in an additive way. She shows us the ways in which the television world was both racist and sexist, emphasizing the ways in which even Black-controlled television programs were equally sexist (Hobson 1970, 78–79). The focus here is on sexism in the television world, and while it may be compounded by racism for Black women in the profession, the focus of her critique is the television industry itself. Her critical eye is not on feminism or women's liberation; it is on sexism and on racism within the television industry. While articles such as this one do reveal multiple layers of oppression, they do not yet address how feminism may be affected by a truly intersectional analysis. A similar kind of externally focused critique emerges across the section titled "Women in the Black Liberation Movement: Three Views." While this section is devoted to the views of Black women, it is not focused on the ways in which interconnected oppressions may incline Black women to challenge or critique aspects of women's liberation. Instead, Morgan selected articles by Black women in which they only take to task Black men on account of their sexism. In its most explicit form, the Black Women's Liberation Group's "Statement on Birth Control" is addressed directly to Black men ("Dear Brothers") (Morgan 1970a, 404).

With the exception of Frances Beal's "Double Jeopardy," none of the pieces that Morgan selected for this section demands a contentious dialogue between white and nonwhite women. And even though Beal does turn her critical eye on feminism in her piece, it is not clear that the other women in *Sisterhood*, or even Morgan herself, have adequately heard Beal's critique. For example, Beal's discussion of forced sterilization of women in Puerto Rico (Beal 1970a, 389–93) has clearly done little to sway Cisler's enthusiastic endorsement of sterilization as another liberating form of birth control for women. While Morgan attempts to make up for this oversight by adding an editorial note in Cisler's piece directing the reader's attention to Beal's article for "an analysis of the racism in many birth-control programs"

(Morgan 1970a, 287; editorial note), it is not yet clear that either Morgan or Cisler are aware of the ways in which women's liberation would need to alter its stance on reproductive rights to adequately accommodate an intersectional analysis of the ways in which racism, capitalism, and sexism intersect to control the reproductive capacity of women of color.[4]

As Elizabeth Sutherland states: "Let Anglo women listen for her [the Chicana's, Enriqueta Vasquez's] voice, not merely for echoes of their own" (Sutherland 1970, 426). Similar to Beal, Sutherland challenges white women to listen and to finally hear the Chicana's voice and to allow it to trouble their own understandings of patriarchy and feminism. While this is a clear invitation to enter into a kind of coalitional conversation, it does not seem Morgan has fully accepted it. Despite Vasquez's clear call to rethink the ways in which the family is an absolutely essential component to liberation struggles for Mexican American men and women, Morgan insists that the one thing she knows with absolute certainty is that the nuclear family is oppressive to women (Vasquez 1970, 432; Morgan 1970b, xxxvi).[5] Which women does she have in mind here? The point of an intersectional, as opposed to an additive, approach to multiple oppressions is precisely its ability to trouble both our understanding of oppression and our approach to dismantling it. By taking firm stances on things such as dissolving the family and advocating sterilization as a form of birth control, Morgan and other white contributors are closing down rather than opening up fruitful coalitional conversations.

As was the case with notions of coalition as ethical community, what gets obscured in a project centered on "sisterhood" are the arrangements of power that situate encounters between "sisters." Relying on a shared ontological experience of sexist oppression coupled with a shared ethics of good will and care toward one's "sisters," Morgan believes she can additively and unself-reflexively struggle toward feminist unity across profound race, class, ethnicity, and sexuality differences.[6] Morgan is self-reflexive enough to acknowledge the ways in which she has in the past identified herself with the oppressor by "nurtur[ing] a secret contempt for other women who weren't as strong, free, and respected (by men) as [she] thought [she] was" (Morgan 1970b, xvii). Moving away from this oppressor subject position entailed learning to understand the ways in which she was not above other women but actually needed other women. This process gave Morgan a more complete understanding of oppression (xviii). With this more complete understanding, she believes that the women's movement, unlike other movements toward social justice, has the potential of "cutting across all class, race, age, economic, and geographical barriers" (xx).

However, while Morgan and even *Sisterhood* is self-reflexive up to a point, neither Morgan nor the anthology exhibits the level of self-reflexivity that would be required of truly coalitional scholarship. The anthology seems uninterested in beginning a conversation about how to change feminism or, more specifically, about troubling the notion of "sisterhood." *Sisterhood* is interested in diversity in the service of challenging multiple systems of oppression, but it is not interested in turning this critical eye against the internal oppressive forces *within* feminism. The struggle these women are collectively engaged in is a struggle against an external threat that Morgan misidentifies as a single primary oppression—sexism. What this accounting of sexism necessarily prevents, unfortunately, is the kind of intersectional feminist struggle that is required of politico-ethical coalition politics. Thus, while it is clear that *Sisterhood* is motivated by a clear political purpose, it seems to lack the ethical dimension that marks politico-ethical coalition politics. While *Sisterhood* is unlike some anthologies of the time wherein the experiences of minority women remained completely invisible (such as in Firestone 1970), it nevertheless suffers from a common problem of the time insofar as the insights presented in the notable contributions by women of color are seldomly taken up by the white contributors in a way that might compel them to rethink their feminist goals and priorities (see Townsend-Bell 2012, 134–41; Simons 1979, 388–91). Absent this more self-reflexive orientation, *Sisterhood* remains a project in the service of (unsuccessfully) attempting textual "sisterhood" and in so doing necessarily foreclosing possibilities for textual coalition.

This Bridge Called My Back: *Enacting Politico-Ethical Textual Coalition*

Where 1970s anthologies such as *Sisterhood* fail in enacting politico-ethical coalitional scholarship, 1980s anthologies such as *Bridge* succeed emphatically. While coalition politics was already a central theme among US Women of Color feminists writing in the 1970s (think here of Chisholm and the many speeches and essays written and delivered by Women of Color feminists in the 1970s), the 1980s brought with it a profound shift both within the broader political climate and within the publishing world that refocused even more attention on coalitional work. To begin with, intersectional coalition politics was simply on a lot of people's minds during this period. Many Left-oriented movements entered a period of decline in the 1980s as the Reagan administration set out to dismantle the progressive gains of the 1960s and 1970s. The movements that survived were those willing to confront diversity and form coalitions across multiple subjugated groups (see Townsend-Bell 2012, 142; Chisholm 1983). In the publishing world, not only had the book-length anthology format become very popular, but autonomous Women of Color feminist presses were becoming the new norm for women of color authors looking to publish their work—as opposed to the minority (Black) controlled or white-feminist controlled presses that they had turned to in the 1970s (Townsend-Bell 2012, 142).

Gaining editorial control over publications in the 1980s allowed women of color authors the freedom to honestly address the challenges of difference *within* the women's movement, on account of its racism, and *within* the civil rights movement, on account of its sexism. In their original description of Kitchen Table, Smith, Audre Lorde, and the other Women of Color feminists who were involved at its inception in 1981, wrote: "Kitchen Table: Women of Color Press is the only publisher in North America committed to publishing and distributing the writing of Third World women of all racial/cultural heritages, sexualities, and classes." Echoing the activist tone of *Sisterhood*, in 1984 they added: "Our work is both cultural and political, connected to the struggles for freedom of all of our peoples. We hope to serve as a communication network for women of color in the U.S. and around the world." "We publish work," Smith continues, "not simply because it is by a woman of color, but because it consciously examines, from a positive and original perspective, the specific situations and issues that women of color face" (B. Smith 1989, 12). Kitchen Table is clearly invested in the kind of activist-oriented scholarship that motivated 1970s anthologies such as *Sisterhood*.

Bridge thus continues in the spirit of *Sisterhood* by being unapologetically political in its intentions, by bringing the personal and material conditions of women's lives to their writing, by challenging masculine styles of scholarship, and by engaging in a transparent, nonhierarchical, and truly collaborative editing process. However, this commitment to activist publishing took on a new form in the 1980s as women of color–controlled presses more honestly and self-reflexively confronted the challenge of working together across divides of race, class, and sexuality. In addition to entering into difficult and self-reflexive conversations with other women of color about their own differences within the pages of the book, *Bridge* adopts a self-reflexive and radically transparent editing process that prefigures the anthology as an egalitarian and coalitional space. The book itself can be understood as a journey toward coalitional consciousness, both through the individual journeys chronicled there and through the form of the anthology itself.

The first thing to note about *Bridge* is its unapologetic politico-ethical purpose. As Moraga and Anzaldúa state in the introduction, the anthology seeks to make connections across women (Moraga and Anzaldúa 1983b, xxiii–xxvi). While it was originally meant to be an invitation to white women to begin a difficult conversation about feminism's internal racism, classism, and heterosexism, the project quickly became a "positive affirmation of the commitment of women of color to [their] *own* feminism" (xxiii). The "uncompromised definition of feminism" that guides this text is borrowed from Smith and resonates strongly with the political commitment grounding politico-ethical coalition politics (xxiii). It reads: "Feminism is the political theory and practice to free *all* women: women of color, working-class women, poor women, physically challenged women, lesbians, old women, as well as white economically privileged heterosexual women" (Smith in Moraga 1983g, 61). The political commitment in this understanding of feminism is explicit—as Smith states, it is to free all women from oppression. The ethical dimension is elaborated by Moraga when she emphasizes the "love" that "feminists" (not necessarily women) have for one another (Moraga 1983g, 62).

As Moraga implies below, echoing the sentiments behind Lorde's invitation to Mary Daly, the point of convergence between the women of color writing in *Bridge* and the white women reading it resides in this shared politico-ethical commitment *as feminists*.

> The women writing here are committed feminists. We are challenging white feminists to be accountable for their racism because at the base we still *want* to believe that they really *want* freedom for *all* of us. The letter from Audre Lorde to Mary Daly appearing in this section is an example to all of us of how we as feminists can criticize each other. It is an act of love to take someone at her word, to expect the most out of a woman who calls herself a feminist—to challenge her as you yourself wish to be challenged.
>
> As women, on some level we all know oppression. We must use this knowledge, as Rosario Morales suggests, to "identify, understand, and feel with the oppressed as a way out of the morass of racism and guilt." . . .
>
> For "We are all in the same boat."
>
> And it is sinking fast. (Moraga 1983g, 62)

After many failed attempts to connect to white women and despite the anger and rage that such failures have generated, Moraga acknowledges that the one possible point of connection between them is not around a shared identity as *women*—amounting to forging a sisterhood—but rather a shared political commitment as *feminists* to free all women through collectively mapping and fighting oppression in its many forms. Contrary to accounts of ethical feminism (Morgan 1970a) or ethical community (Butler 2004; 2009), this attempt at connection, this invitation to white women, is not one born out of naive aspirations of communal or sisterly love. Whereas feelings of love, empathy, and compassion appear across the other sections of the anthology wherein women of color talk to and about one another, these feelings all but vanish when they talk about and to white women. The dominant sentiments expressed across this section of the anthology are those of anger, rage, frustration, and disappointment. The type of connection that becomes possible in this context, Moraga implies, is a *feminist* (not a sisterly) one—and, for these authors, a feminist one must also be a coalitional one insofar as it embraces self-reflexively tackling interlocking oppressions.

While Moraga notes that the book was originally conceived out of a dream for a "unified Third World feminist movement," she immediately self-consciously examines the challenges that such a project poses, even for women of color.

> Third World feminism does not provide the kind of easy political framework that women of color are running to in droves. We are not so much a "natural" affinity group, as women who have come together out of political necessity. The *idea* of Third World feminism has proved to be much easier between the covers of a book than between real live women. There *are* many issues that divide us; and, recognizing that fact can make that dream at times seem quite remote. Still, the need for a broad-based U.S. women of color movement capable of spanning the borders of nation and ethnicity has never been so strong.
>
> If we are interested in building a movement that will not constantly be subverted by internal differences, then we must build from the insideout, not the other way around. Coming to terms with the suffering of others has never meant looking away from our own.
>
> And we must look deeply. We must acknowledge that to change the world, we have to change ourselves—even sometimes our most cherished block-hard convictions. As *This Bridge Called My Back* is not written in stone, neither is our political vision. (Moraga 1983a)

Moraga and Anzaldúa's commitment to Third World feminism is not built on ontological or "natural" affinity but is instead born out of the necessity of shared *political* commitment. This shared political commitment, however, is not one that is easily nurtured. It is one that is struggled for and continuously reaffirmed. There are issues, Moraga explains, that continue to divide even Women of Color feminists. The challenge of shared political commitment, however, does not deter her or other contributors from continuing to struggle toward it. In order to struggle successfully, this political commitment must take on a politico-*ethical* character: it must be consciously self-reflexive. They must, Moraga argues, build their movement from the "insideout." This journey starts on an internal level. As such, one must be willing to be fully self-reflexive: one must look deeply inside oneself and prepare for radical transformation, much in the way Lorde, Anzaldúa, and Pratt did in chapter 3.

It is telling that the first real mention of "coalition" politics emerges in the anthology's fourth section, "Between the Lines: On Culture, Class, and Homophobia," wherein the contributors turn their attention away from external relations with white women and toward internal relations between women of color. It is within this context of turning inward and examining their own politics with a spirit of *feminist* love and reflexivity that the contributors learn the most about collective feminist politics. It is no surprise that politico-ethical coalition emerges here as the best way forward. At the end of her dialogue with her sister, Beverly, Barbara Smith makes a strong appeal to "coalition politics that cover a broad base of issues" as the best form of politics for the feminist movement (Smith and Smith 1983, 126). Echoing arguments she and the other cofounders of Combahee made in the "Black Feminist Statement" (reprinted in the final section of *Bridge*), as well as arguments made by many of the other contributors to *Bridge* (Morales 1983b, 93; Anzaldúa 1983e, 208–9; 1983d, 196; Canaan 1983, 234–37), Smith argues that the reality of interlocking oppressions in fact necessitates coalition politics between different subjugated groups. "There is no way," Smith asserts, "that one oppressed group is going to topple a system by itself. Forming principled coalitions around specific issues is very important. You don't necessarily have to like or love the people you're in coalition with" (Smith and Smith 1983, 126). In the same way that coalitional selves struggle toward a center out of necessity, subjugated peoples must struggle toward coalitions with one another. While love *may* exist in these spaces between feminists, love is not a prerequisite. A political commitment to undermining oppression, however, is absolutely essential. Such a commitment, when adopted self-reflexively, will, as Moraga has argued, incline one toward loving acts with other *feminists* (not just women) in coalition.

In its overt self-reflexivity, I contend that the political commitment driving this anthology differs from the one driving *Sisterhood*. While originally centered on the promise of autonomy and community for women of color (a home space), necessarily in opposition to white women, through an intensely self-reflexive process, the focus of the anthology shifted. As Toni Cade Bambara puts it in the original foreword to the anthology, *Bridge* documents "particular rites of passage" and "coming to terms with community—race, group, class, gender, self—its expectations, supports, and lessons" (Bambara 1983, vii). This is a particularly apt way to describe the anthology. Indeed, I believe one could read the anthology itself as a sustained treatment of community, specifically the transition from community (home) or "sisterhood" to coalition. These authors call out white women for their desire to coalesce only on their own white feminist terms. Community, or "sisterhood," within this space proves unworkable. For this reason, women of color seek autonomous community with one another. It is through this process of seeking connection with one another that I believe the anthology takes on a coalitional form. As Women of Color feminists confront difference within this group, they learn the valuable lessons of politico-ethical coalition politics, which compel them to critically interrogate notions of community or sisterhood even among women of color. *Bridge*, as Bambara puts it, provides the planks for this crossing: it can, she argues, "coax us into the habit of listening to each other and learning each other's ways of seeing and being" (vii).

In addition to the explicit politico-ethical commitment grounding this text, it both chronicles individual journeys and *enacts* its own collective journey toward coalitional consciousness. As Moraga reveals, compiling the anthology has brought her on her "own journey of struggle, growing consciousness, and subsequent politicization and vision as a woman of color" (Moraga 1983b, xiii). This anthology and the women in and around it "have personally transformed [her] life, sometimes rather painfully but always with richness and meaning" (xiii). Moraga's journey has been one of confronting difference and contradiction and of longing for a feminist movement that can make sense of the complicated intersection of race, class, gender, and sexuality. It was "through" the passage of making this anthology, she recounts, that her growing consciousness emerged (xiv). She hopes that the book will lead those encountering it on a similar kind of journey of self-transformation (xv). It is precisely this kind of profound internal shift that Moraga and Anzaldúa hope their readers will experience while reading *Bridge*. For them, the anthology functions as a vehicle toward coalitional consciousness.

We are first introduced to the emerging coalitional selves that populate this book in "Children Passing in the Streets: The Roots of Our Radicalism." This section offers a collection of four poems and two stream-of-consciousness journal entries by six different women of color authors. Together, these pieces tell stories of the contradictions inherent in growing up non-white and female. Moraga begins the section with a quotation from Maxine Hong Kingston, illustrating the authors' shared experiences of confronting contradiction that shaped their lives as young girls: "I learned to make my mind large, as the universe is large, so that there is room for paradoxes" (Kingston in Moraga 1983c, 5). As we learned in chapter 3, experiencing paradoxes and contradictions is an important part of one's journey toward coalitional identity.

> We are women from all kinds of childhood streets: the farms of Puerto Rico, the downtown streets of Chinatown, the barrio, city-Bronx Streets, quiet suburban sidewalks, the plains, and the reservation.
>
> In this first section, you will find voices from our childhoods, our youth. What we learned about survival—trying to-pass-for-white, easy-to-pass-for-white, "she couldn't pass in a million years." Here, we intro-duce to you the "color problem" as it was first introduced to us" "not white enuf, not dark enuf," always up against a color chart that first got erected far outside our families and our neighborhoods, but which invaded them both with systematic determination.
>
> In speaking of color and class, Tillie Olsen once said: "There's no such thing as passing." Here are women of every shade of color and grade of class to prove that point. For although some of us traveled more easily from street corner to corner than the sister whose color or poverty made her an especially visible target to the violence on the street, *all* of us have been victims of the invisible violation which happens indoors and inside ourselves: the self-abnegation, the silence, the constant threat of cultural obliteration. . . .
>
> We were born into colored homes. We grew up with the inherent color contradictions in the color spectrum right inside those homes: the lighter sister, the mixed-blood cousin, being the darkest one in the family. It doesn't take many years to realize the privileges, or lack thereof, attached to a particular shade of skin or texture of hair. It is this experience that moves light-skinned or "passable" Third World women to put ourselves on the line for our darker sisters. We are all family. . . .
>
> We learned to live with these contradictions. This is the root of our radicalism. (Moraga 1983c, 5)

Moraga achieves several things here. First, she introduces the diverse range of voices appearing in this section of the anthology. This diversity, she makes clear, transcends shades of color, national boundaries, geographical location, and socioeconomic status. Second, she prepares her readers for the stories of struggle—stories of struggling for survival against the color line. In Nellie Wong's poem, "When I Was Growing Up," she confesses to her readers of her own longing to be white and of the ways she tried to scrub the darkness off her skin in the bathtub (Wong 1983, 7–8). Conversely, in "on not being," mary hope lee shares her desire to be darker (lee 1983, 9–11). This is the nature of a color contradiction that compels longing for lightness and darkness, depending on the context. Rosario Morales's stream-of-consciousness journal entry, "I Am What I Am," repeats this theme of contradiction as she grapples with the many aspects of her identity as Puerto Rican, US American, New York Manhattan, and New York Bronx (Morales 1983a, 14–15). Naomi Littlebear's stream-of-consciousness journal entry, "Dreams of Violence," details the violence attached to these contradictions. She recounts stories of getting beaten up by whites on the way home from school, simply for existing on the street as a Native American, only to arrive home to endure further beatings at the hands of her parents for getting into fights with white people in the first place (Littlebear 1983, 16–17). This emphasis on "survival" resembles the sense of survival found in Reagon, where a crucial component of the danger of coalition inhered in the likelihood of losing oneself in the process of coalescing. The "root of their radicalism," Moraga seems to be suggesting, rests in these accounts of internal struggle and existential threat and transformation. The anthology's first section is invested primarily in revealing the challenge of such a project, resonating strongly with the *struggle* inherent to politico-ethical coalition politics.

It is an experience of living these color contradictions, Moraga asserts above, that will enable these women to "put [them]selves on the line for [their] darker sisters." They do this because "they are all family." In a family—a space ideally defined by at least some component of love, compassion, and empathy—these women learned to live with these contradictions. This capacity, we are led to believe, gives these women the strength and love to connect to one another and to forge their own coherent centers across their internal contradictions. Highlighted across this section and accounting for why I refer to them only as *emerging* coalitional selves, however, is the inherent challenge in achieving internal coherence across the contradictions and paradoxes that define their plurality.

In "For the Color of My Mother," for instance, Moraga—a light-skinned girl who could pass for white—seeks a connection to her dark-skinned mother. "*I am a white girl gone brown to the blood color of my mother speaking for her*"

(Moraga 1983d, 12–13), Moraga repeats throughout the poem. There is a strong sense across this poem of the challenge in making such a connection. As a fair-skinned child, Moraga did not experience the same kind of pain and suffering as her mother. Nevertheless, she tries to connect to the pain her mother endured getting her lips caught in a seam as she sewed a child's linen by comparing this to her own experience of her upper lip splitting open at the age of two. Moraga desperately seeks a connection to her mother and struggles to accomplish this. Similarly, in Chrystos's poem, "He Saw," she attempts to connect to her Native American father who "cut off his hair / joined the government / to be safe" (Chrystos 1983, 18). Across this poem, Chrystos laments the loss of a connection to her father's Native American past. In his efforts to give her "all the whitest advantages" (18), she believes he has put into jeopardy a deeper connection to this past. Thus, despite the optimism Moraga expresses in the introduction, these poems instead reveal the difficulty in making connections across difference. Revealing the challenge of this internal struggle is an important component of coalitional scholarship.

In the second section, "Entering the Lives of Others: Theory in the Flesh," these multiplicitous selves begin to achieve connection and coherence across difference, discontinuity, and contradiction. Whereas the first section introduces *emerging* coalitional selves, the second section offers depictions of actual coalitional selves. In her introduction to the section, Moraga writes: "A theory in the flesh means one where the physical realities of our lives—our skin, the land or concrete we grew up on, our sexual longings—all fuse to create a politic born out of necessity. Here we attempt to bridge the contradictions in our experience. ... Daily, we feel the pull and tug of having to choose between which parts of our mothers' heritages we want to claim and wear and which parts have served to cloak us from the knowledge of ourselves" (Moraga 1983e, 23). Many of the themes I introduced in chapter 3 emerge here. Their "theory in the flesh," Moraga states, is one that will attempt to move across contradiction and difference and toward completeness or wholeness. Together, these authors will bring together—"fuse"—the many and discontinuous realities of their lives. This coming together, Moraga suggests, is one that forms the basis of "a politic born out of necessity." This "politic" is rooted in a coalitional consciousness that forms as these women share their stories of struggling toward knowing their complete selves and resisting the external pull of fragmentation.

Moraga's own essay, "La Güera," is exemplary here. Moraga begins with a quotation from Emma Goldman. The experience of an event alone, Goldman argues, is not enough to give us a "philosophy" or "point of view." "It is the quality of our response to the event," she continues, "and our capacity to enter into the lives of others that helps us make their lives and experiences our own" (Goldman in Moraga 1983f, 27). This section of the anthology is invested in facilitating this kind of crossing by going under the skin and into the flesh-world of another, mimicking the sense of "traveling" María Lugones gestures toward in her coauthored article with Spelman (Lugones and Spelman 1983) and develops more fully years later (Lugones 1987, 2003). The ability to travel to another's world and even across one's own discontinuous selves, I argued in chapter 3, is a crucial component to collectively mapping oppression and forging a coalitional consciousness. Moraga's essay maps her own crossing.

The title of the essay, "La Güera," refers to the name Moraga was given as the "fair-skinned: born with the features of [her] Chicana mother, but with the skin of [her] Anglo father." According to her mother, Moraga had it made as a fair-skinned girl, and her mother did what she could to further "bleach [her] of what color [she] did have." Moraga explains her mother's intentions: "It was through my mother's desire to protect her children from poverty and illiteracy that we became 'anglocized': the more effectively we could pass in the white world, the better guaranteed our future" (Moraga 1983f, 28). Through such a process, Moraga was differentiated from her dark-skinned mother. Nevertheless, the profound familial connection Moraga had with her mother enabled her to connect to her mother's experiences of poverty, racism, and oppression. "From all of this, I experience, daily, a huge disparity between what I was born into and what I was to grow up to become. Because (as Goldman suggests) these stories my mother told me crept under my 'güera' skin. I had no choice but to enter into the life of my mother. *I had no choice*. I took her life into my heart" (Moraga 1983f, 28). The love Moraga had for her mother made it impossible for her *not* to take her mother's life, and her mother's experiences of oppression, into her heart.

While this love for her mother began this crossing, Moraga reveals that the connection between herself and her mother was not complete until something else happened. "When I finally lifted the lid to my lesbianism, a profound connection with my mother reawakened in me. It wasn't until I acknowledged and confronted my own lesbianism in the flesh, that my heartfelt identification with and empathy for my mother's oppression—due to being poor, uneducated, and Chicana—was realized. My lesbianism is the avenue through which I have learned the most about silence and oppression, and it continues to be the most tactile reminder to me that we are not free human beings" (Moraga 1983f, 28–29). As is evidenced here, it was not only love that allowed Moraga to enter into the life of her mother.

As a young child, the love Moraga had for her mother and proximity to her world through repeated stories helped Moraga to empathize with her up to a point. However, it was not until Moraga was old enough to comprehend the one marker of difference that her mother was not able to wash away—that of being a lesbian—that Moraga was truly able to connect to her. It was her "love of women," Moraga states in the preface, that "drew [her] to politics" (Moraga 1983b, xiv). Similar to Minnie Bruce Pratt's recounting, it was not just the fact of her love for other women that compelled Moraga to enter into coalitions with them; rather, Moraga's lesbianism acted as a marker of difference and oppression that enabled her to connect to the oppressions endured by other women.

Traveling for Moraga therefore happened on two planes. While she traveled to her mother's world through the stories her mother told her, she was never fully able to grasp what her mother was attempting to share with her (what she was attempting to map with her) until she also traveled across her own selves. Like Pratt, uncovering this additional layer of her own plurality helped Moraga to collectively map oppression and connect to her mother. Doing so allowed Moraga to work on what Lorde refers to as the horizontal axis of oppression in alliance with others as they together contest multiple, diffuse and interlocking forms of vertical power (Lorde 1984e, 47–48). It was thus the *politics* of her lesbianism that compelled her to turn inward and to begin to negotiate across her multiple and contradictory selves. It was the flesh and blood experience of being a lesbian—of knowing she could be "beaten on the street for being a dyke" (Moraga 1983f, 29)—that helped her to connect to her mother's experiences of oppression. Through this self-reflexive process—through her journey "under the skin," both her mother's and her own (30)—her coalitional consciousness is born:

> In this country, lesbianism is a poverty—as is being brown, as is being a woman, as is being just plain poor. The danger lies in ranking the oppressions. *The danger lies in failing to acknowledge the specificity of the oppression.* The danger lies in attempting to deal with oppression purely from a theoretical base. Without an emotional, heartfelt grappling with the source of our own oppression, without naming the enemy within ourselves and outside of us, no authentic, non-hierarchical connection among oppressed groups can take place. (Moraga 1983f, 29)

Despite the privileges she may have experienced because of her lighter skin and educational attainment, Moraga was unable to avoid the oppressions attached to being a lesbian. It was this component of her identity that, like

Pratt, cracked "the shell of [her] privilege" and thus compelled her to turn inward (Pratt 1984, 27). This enabled her to connect to other women by reconciling her own multiple and shifting selves and thus discovering her coalitional identity and coming to appreciate the ways in which all oppressions are interlocking. This mapping exercise gave her knowledge of how oppression operates, the "specificity" of its movements in different contexts.

Moraga arrives at this political consciousness, however, neither through love nor through abstract theoretical analysis. Like Pratt and many Women of Color feminists, Moraga's *lived self-reflexive struggle* as a lesbian brought her to it. As she says when reflecting on this experience, "the real battle with ... oppression, for all of us, begins under the skin" wherein we ask ourselves how we may have internalized our oppression and even oppressed others (Moraga 1983f, 30, 32). At this point, Moraga's discussion about her mother quickly transforms into a discussion about the feminist movement. As I argued in chapter 3, it is by turning inward and focusing on one's own contradictions that she learns how to deal with the contradictions and challenges that emerge as she tries to coalesce with other women. Moraga tells this story about her mother in an effort to negotiate her own contradictory selves and to reflect on how these discontinuous parts have kept her from connecting to her mother. She does this, however, in the service of collective struggle with others.

This theme of struggling toward a coherent self despite the contradictions that make up one's multiple selves reverberates throughout *Bridge*. This seems to be the very purpose of the anthology. This act of writing—this act of pulling the anthology together—Anzaldúa argues, "is the act of making soul, alchemy. It is the quest for the self, for the center of the self, which we women of color have come to think as 'other'—the dark, the feminine. Didn't we start writing to reconcile this other within us?" (1983c, 169). Anzaldúa and the many other Women of Color feminists contributing to this anthology write precisely in order to undo the fragmentation that society attempts to impose on them. They write in order to "discover" their coherent selves, to "preserve" these selves, and to "achieve self-autonomy" (169). The insistence on struggling toward a coherent self or center is a crucial component to coalitional identity for Women of Color feminists writing in this period.[7] The Women of Color feminists appearing in this book embark on a "trip back into the self, travel to the deep core of [their] roots to discover and reclaim [their] colored souls," rituals, and religions (165). As I argued in chapter 3, it was on this journey, in her essay "La Prieta," that Anzaldúa first introduced us to her coalitional self, a self that refused to fragment her multiplicity and instead struggled toward a coherent center (Anzaldúa 1983e, 205).

In addition to tracing individual journeys and a collective journey toward coalitional consciousness, *Bridge* adopts a self-reflexive and radically transparent editing process that prefigures the anthology itself as an egalitarian and coalitional space. Almost everything about this text reinforces a self-reflexive conversational character. In "Refugees of a World on Fire," Moraga begins in a spirit of collective conversation by turning to the words of Alma Ayala, a nineteen-year-old Puerto Rican woman, in a letter Ayala wrote to Anzaldúa about the impact *Bridge* had on her life. "Your introduction or even reintroduction," Moraga tells her readers, "should come from the voices of women of color who first discovered the book" (Moraga 1983a). Breaking the audience-author barrier, Anzaldúa positions the text as a collaborative exercise in the service of feminist struggle. Unlike what occurred in *Sisterhood*, here both the editors and contributors quote one another. This dialogue helps to remind us that the text itself offers a kind of written record—a "living entity," as Moraga and Anzaldúa call it (1983b, xxiii)—of this ongoing collaboration. As their new home at Kitchen Table makes even more vivid, this anthology is the product of collaboration and struggle both between the women of color contributors and between them and their white and nonwhite readership.

Moraga and Anzaldúa also go out of their way to challenge the traditional editorial hierarchy within anthologies. As Townsend-Bell notes when surveying texts from this period, one of the most striking things about Women of Color feminist anthologies such as *Bridge* is their "candor about selection processes, the difficulty with submissions, and the number of first-time and nonprofessional writers" (Townsend-Bell 2012, 130). In the spirit of the original mission of Kitchen Table, Moraga and Anzaldúa are thoroughly self-reflexive regarding the production of the anthology. In addition to including their own work in the main body of the anthology—a notable divergence from *Sisterhood* and *Real*—they present lengthy introductory material (including three forewords, a preface, a poem, and an introduction) in which they include the voices of the other women of color involved in the anthology and the voices of their readership. By including their own biographies in the contributors' section, instead of in a separate section "on the editors," Moraga and Anzaldúa further resist the hierarchical demarcation between editor and contributor in favor of a more egalitarian relationship among the women involved in the book's production.

Their investment in a more collaborative process, however, does not preclude them from taking ownership over the structure of the text, another notable divergence from third-wave feminist anthologies such as *Real*. As Moraga and Anzaldúa explain, Moraga was primarily responsible for the "thematic structure and organization of the book as a whole" (1983b, xxiv), writing the introductions for the first four sections of the book (Anzaldúa wrote the introductions for the final two sections of the book). Challenging the notion of "editor as leader" does not necessarily entail giving up on an organizational structure: quite the opposite, actually. Refusing the "hands-off" approach that comes to define feminist anthologies in the 1990s, Moraga and Anzaldúa were heavily involved in conceptualizing the book's structure and direction. They did this planning in conversation with the other contributors. This collaboration inclined them to come to know the other contributors quite well, to puzzle over the major themes and messages of their collective works, and to map the evolving political consciousness emerging out of the textual and actual discussions at the beginning of each section. The exercise in mapping occurs on multiple levels for the editors. In addition to offering their stories of mapping their own individual consciousnesses, they were, like Sandoval in her role as secretary to the US Third World feminist consciousness-raising group at the 1981 NWSA conference, the secretaries tasked with capturing the evolving collective consciousness of the radical women of color appearing in *Bridge*. Any anthology requires organization, structure, editing, proofreading, a variety of other administrative tasks, and emotional and spiritual support, but Moraga and Anzaldúa show us that these tasks can be performed in a spirit of collaborative social justice. In this sense, the very format of the text itself takes on a politico-ethical coalitional character insofar as they succeed in "enacting the collectivity for which they call" (Norman 2006, 39).

The politico-ethical mission of this text is further emphasized through the content and style of their writing. The women of color writing in *Bridge* bring "flesh and blood experiences" to their writing by writing about the *material* conditions and struggles of their lives and through a corresponding linguistic style that, as Moraga and Anzaldúa put it, "is intended to reflect [their] color loud and clear, not tone it down" (Moraga 1983e, 23; Moraga and Anzaldúa 1983b, xxiv). Whether writing in a combination of English and Spanish (Anzaldúa 1983c, 1983e), insisting on lowercase names (lee 1983; davenport 1983; and gosset 1983), spelling *women* in the colloquial form *wimmin* (davenport 1983), or refusing to punctuate their writing (Chrystos 1983), the women of color writing across *Bridge* bring flesh to their writing as poor and working-class women and lesbians of color, thereby concret-izing the contradictory and paradoxical experiences of *both* the interlocking oppressions *and* strength that mark their lives.

As Anzaldúa aptly puts it:

> Forget the room of one's own—write in the kitchen, lock yourself up in the bathroom. Write on the bus or the welfare line, on the job or during meals, between sleeping or waking. I write while sitting on the john. No long stretches at the typewriter unless you're wealthy or have a patron— you may not even own a typewriter. While you wash the floors or clothes listen to the words chanting in your body. When you're depressed, angry, hurt, when compassion and love possess you. When you cannot help but write. (Anzaldúa 1983c, 170)

Anzaldúa offers here a vivid example of what I mean by the *materiality of writing* present across this text: it emphasizes both the material cir-cumstances and sacrifices that one makes in order to bring pen to paper (sacrifices that are complexly shaped by interlocking class, race, and gender considerations) and sees the defiance in such acts of writing from within oppression and resistance. Anzaldúa and Moraga further foreground this materiality by including a brief section on "Time and Money" in the in-troduction. "*How do you concentrate on a project when you're worried about paying the rent?*" they ask (Moraga and Anzaldúa 1983b, xxv). The women writing here are not privileged academics; on the contrary, they are (mostly) "first-generation writers" and poor and working-class women of color. The form their writing takes reflects these material conditions, ranging from "extemporaneous stream of consciousness journal entries to well thought-out theoretical statements; from intimate letters to friends to full-scale public addresses ... poems and transcripts, personal conversations and interviews" (xxiv). When editing the anthology, Moraga and Anzaldúa state that their "primary commitment" was to "retaining this diversity, as well as each writer's especial voice and style" (xxiv). This is an activist-edited collection that is meant to reflect the materiality of their lives as struggling activist writers. Instead of trying to fit within the academy, they aimed to disrupt it; instead of suppressing the material conditions that mark their lives, they sought to enliven them.

Their overt transparency regarding this process of writing from within resistance is one of the many striking ways in which this text enacts politico-ethical coalition politics. This form of "resistant writing," Lugones has since argued, not only helps us to "rethink the task of political philosophy" but also enables the contributors to "write within resistance," as opposed to only about it, by "playfully" putting on display both their multiplicity and their materiality as poor and working-class women of color (Lugones 2003, ix, 30, 41). Unlike bird's-eye view theorists (whether a dogmatic strategist, such as Lenin, or more hands-off, descriptive cartographers, such as Deleuze and Guattari), the *Bridge* authors map from so deep within the map that the very nature of their writing reflects the materiality of their lived experiences of oppression and resistance (Lugones 2003, 53–62, 208). It was precisely this granular or pedestrian level mapping that led Moraga and Anzaldúa to unproblematically assume the task of puzzling over the format of the book, the canvas, if you will, of their collective mapping. This puzzling took place from deep *within* the map, in collaboration and discussion with the other authors. This commitment to an egalitarian editorial process and self-reflexive resistant writing all but vanished only a decade later.

To Be Real: *On the Limitations of Textual Mosaic*

The textual coalition on display in *Bridge* clearly diverges from the textual sisterhood attempted in *Sisterhood*. Here, I want to take the time to contrast *Bridge*'s alternative to sisterhood with another alternative emerging in the 1990s, during what is known as "third-wave" feminism. Though difficult to define, third-wave feminism is often explicitly anti-intellectual, favoring highly individualized first-person accounts of defiant feminist lifestyle choices (Snyder 2008; Snyder-Hall 2010). While attention to difference continues to be central here, the spirit of politico-ethical coalition politics has all but vanished. Instead, we find a dangerous push away from feminist politics rooted in self-reflexively working to undermine oppression and toward a highly individualized lifestyle feminism that resonates strongly with the political indeterminacy grounding Butler's notion of what I call "coalition as spectacle."

As members from the Third Wave Direct Action Corporation stated in April 1996, "third wave practice seeks to create what Angela Davis calls 'unpredicted coalitions'" (Siegel 1997, 58). Building on this definition, Deborah Siegel argues that third-wave feminist anthologies actually function *as* unpredicted coalitions (58). The collective politics of "third-wave feminism," argues Claire Snyder, replaces exclusionary "attempts at unity" (on display in *Sisterhood*) with a "dynamic and welcoming politics of coalition" by indiscriminately celebrating all women's individual lifestyle choices (Snyder 2008, 176). An infinitely "welcoming" politics of coalition is clearly evident, scholars such as Siegel have noted, in the numerous third-wave anthologies

(Findlen 1995; Karp and Stoller 1999; Johnson 2002) that were published in the years following Rebecca Walker's coining of the phrase.

For instance, the voices appearing in Walker's *Real*, Siegel argues, "coalesce in the space between differences" (Siegel 1997, 58). What is unique and helpful about third-wave anthologies, Siegel attests, is the way in which they replace traditional notions of unity—the "organized chorus" of earlier anthologies such as *Sisterhood* (Gallop 1992, 8)—with an understanding of anthology as an "unpredicted" textual coalition now united in the goal of "postfeminist feminist defiance" and an indiscriminately welcoming politics of coalition (Siegel 1997, 58). These texts, she argues, are rightly understood "as feminist anthologies *without* the fixity of one feminist agenda in view" (53; my emphasis). It is precisely this political indeterminacy, Siegel believes, that allows these anthologies to be understood as unpredicted coalitions.

While in attempting to move away from notions of feminist unity it would seem that third-wave anthologies certainly seek to avoid problematic versions of "textual sisterhood," I would like to challenge the notion that they share much in common with the politico-ethical textual coalition on display in *Bridge* or even with Davis's notion of "unpredicted coalitions," a phrase that emerges in an interview with Lisa Lowe in July 1995 (Davis 1997, 322). Following Reagon's lead, Davis calls on progressive activists to continue the hard work of coalition politics and to remain wary of coalitions centering on identity. Davis spends much of this interview thoughtfully reflecting on the important difference between coalition politics rooted in essentialist notions of identity and coalition politics rooted in a shared political commitment. When Davis emphasizes the need for "unpredictable" coalitions, she means to emphasize the necessity of unlikely allies gaining a critical coalitional consciousness that would help them to understand the ways in which multiple and interlocking oppressive forces act on all of them simultaneously as well as the necessary steps for contesting such structures (322). The sense of coalition politics she advocates here therefore closely resembles politico-ethical coalition politics.

With this understanding of "unpredictable coalition" in mind, I seek to challenge Siegel's interpretation of *Real* as an unpredictable *textual coalition*. I conjecture that the sense of unpredictability Siegel has in mind here takes its roots in poststructuralist critiques of stable notions of identity, power, and the social world and results in a textual version of Butler's antifoundational theorization of coalition as spectacle. Though Davis wrote the afterword to *Real*, nowhere in it does she refer to an "unpredicted" or "unpredictable" coalition to describe what is taking place within the pages of the book. Instead, she appeals to the metaphor of a mosaic (Davis 1995, 280). Although *Real* offers an excellent example of coalition as spectacle in the form of *textual mosaic*, in so doing it forecloses possibilities for politico-ethical coalition politics and therefore also coalitional scholarship.

Walker believes that the type of feminism presented in *Real* moves beyond previous generations of feminism in its open embrace of difference, diversity, complexity, contradiction, and ambiguity (Walker 1995b). To illustrate this emphasis on difference, she is careful (herself the mixed-race daughter of an African American mother and a white Jewish American father) to include work by white women, women of color, men, bisexual women, lesbian women, and women with disabilities. With this show of diversity, *Real* appears to differ from *Sisterhood* by resembling a colorful mosaic of feminists, rather than a homogenous picture of sisterhood. However, closer examination reveals a rather narrow depiction of difference once we factor in other identity markers such as class and age. As Walker makes clear, *Real* is unapologetically meant to represent the voices of "young" feminists who grew up within feminism (Walker 1995b, xxxii–xxxiii).[8] In addition to narrowing the voices engaged across these texts by age, Walker narrows her pool of contributors by class, educational attainment, and geographical location. A quick look at the contributor biographies confirms this pattern. Not only did almost all of the contributors attend elite colleges (many also receiving postgraduate degrees), they reside primarily in major urban centers such as New York, Boston, Los Angeles, San Francisco, and Washington, DC. One gets the sense that this anthology is comprised of essays by Walker's Ivy League (herself a Yale graduate) peers—all multiply privileged in terms of socioeconomic status, the educational privileges this status often bestows, and exposure to feminism.

Though seemingly committed to offering a diverse range of voices, what we find instead is a rather narrow brand of *privileged feminism*. It is precisely this sense of entitlement that would lead Walker in the first line of her introduction to describe her life as a kind of "feminist ghetto" (Walker 1995b, xxix). Walker appears to be disturbingly unaware of the privileges her upbringing in a "feminist ghetto"—where she was raised by feminist celebrities such as her own mother, Alice Walker, as well as Gloria Steinem and Angela Davis (both appearing in her edited collection)—have bestowed on her. Feeling that she is already well versed in the workings of power, the importance of incessant critique, and the intersection of racism, classism, sexism, and other structures of oppression, Walker seeks to escape the old-style, boring, and uninteresting feminism of her mother's generation (Walker 1995b, xxxix–xl).

Instead of interrogating systemic interlocking oppressions in the way that the *Bridge* authors did, Walker uses the anthology to justify as "feminist" her individual choices. Toward this end, Walker sought out young men and women who felt similarly stifled by a feminism wherein everything one did had to "measure up to an image [one] had in [her] mind of what was morally and politically right according to [her] vision of female empowerment" (xxix). Walker rejects this exacting vision of feminism by offering alternative ways of living as feminists. This brand of individualistic lifestyle feminism is reflected across the various contributions to *Real*, wherein the authors focus on recounting their own individual struggles *against* feminist dogma that tells them: they shouldn't be "girly" (DeLombard 1995); they shouldn't wear lipstick (Senna 1995); they shouldn't get excited about planning a wedding (Wolf 1995); they shouldn't embrace violence (Cabreros-Sud 1995); they shouldn't get turned on by rape and torture (Minkowitz 1995); they—men in this case—shouldn't plan bachelor parties that include strippers (Schultz 1995); they shouldn't listen to misogynistic rappers like Snoop Dogg (E. Davis 1995); they shouldn't take their husband's last name in marriage (Allyn and Allyn 1995); they shouldn't be upper middle class (Bondoc 1995); they shouldn't be supermodels (Webb 1995) or strippers (Taylor 1995); they must be full-time activists (Bondoc 1995); they must be permanently angry (Bondoc 1995); and they must continue to work after becoming mothers (Abner 1995). The men and women across this anthology all choose their own unique lifestyle and assert that this kind of self-determination and defiance defines feminist empowerment. Also known as "choice" feminism (Snyder-Hall 2010), for this generation of feminists, feminism is about choosing to live however they want to live.

It is for this reason that the "mosaic" metaphor is an apt one, sharing something in common with Butler's notion of coalition as spectacle. The purpose of the anthology, much like the purpose of coalition when understood as spectacle, is none other than to exist in a spectacular performance of ontological defiance. As the full title suggests, *To Be Real: Telling the Truth and Changing the Face of Feminism*, the anthology is invested in "feminism as ontology"—feminism, that is, as a way of *being*, feminism as an identity or face that can be worn or put on display. Lisa Jones's article offers an example of what this spectacle may look like in practice. Recounting her experience in the "Rodeo Caldonia High-Fidelity Performance Theater" traveling conceptual art piece on Black female representation, Jones emphasizes the ways in which this group worked to challenge stereotypical *images* of Black women (Jones 1995, 255). "There was this assumption that being black and a woman carries with it a responsibility to be dire and remorseful" (257). Her group worked to challenge these assumptions by performing contradictory images of Black women having fun and being happy, playful, and unabashedly sexual: "We are smart-ass girls with a sense of entitlement, who avail ourselves of the goods of two continents, delight in our sexual bravura, and live womanism as pleasure, not academic mandate" (255). In performing spectacles of unexpected Black womanism, Jones and the other members of the group challenged stereotypical images of Black femininity. In so doing, Jones embraces a form of performative feminist empowerment that is explicitly anti-intellectual and infinitely open to redefinition. Given Jones's insistence on this kind of feminism being nonacademic, it is at least noteworthy that Jones herself attended Yale University in addition to the New York University's Graduate School of Film and Television.

Just like the "Rodeo Caldonia High-Fidelity Performance Theater," I contend that *Real*, understood as unexpected or unpredictable *mosaic*, attempts a similar kind of ontological trouble by disrupting traditional notions of what feminists are supposed to look like. In this sense, it enables its reader to "behold a mosaic of vastly different ways" to wear feminist consciousness (Davis 1995, 280). In it we find a "gathering of 'introspective' voices" (281) and an "ever-expanding" picture of the multiple ways to live as feminists (Walker 1995b, xxxv). However, neither a "mosaic" nor a "gathering" is equivalent to a textual *coalition* in the way I understand it. A mosaic does not act; it simply is. While the anthology certainly achieves a kind of ontology of limited (by class, age, education, and ideology) multiplicity and in so doing influences our conceptions of what feminists *look like*, it does not achieve any sense of coalition outside of group spectacle.

"It is not surprising," bell hooks argued back in the early 1980s, "that the vast majority of women who equate feminism with alternative lifestyle are from middle-class backgrounds, unmarried, college-educated, often students who are without many of the social and economic responsibilities that working-class and poor women who are laborers, parents, homemakers, and wives confront daily" (hooks [1984] 2000, 29). Though hooks wrote these words a decade before third-wave feminist anthologies first appeared and the women she speaks of here are second-wave white feminists, her critique is disturbingly appropriate when applied to Walker's anthology. Instead of unpacking where narrow images of feminism may have come from, including structural or institutional forces that work to reproduce them,[9] Walker seeks to collect essays by men and women who struggle *against feminism*.[10] Instead of interrogating the emergence of lifestyle feminism, Walker and the other contributors seek only to expand the range of possible feminist lifestyle choices on offer.[11] In this sense, like the privileged white feminism decades before, the third-wave feminism of Walker and her contributors fails to see the ways in which treating "feminist" as a "pre-packaged role women can now select as they search for identity," even when these roles are infinitely more diverse than what they were in the 1970s, nevertheless reinforces feminism as ontology in the place of feminism as political commitment (hooks 2000, 29). In so doing, it also effectively replaces coalition as politico-ethical encounter with coalition as spectacle.

Instead of sincerely confronting difference in the way that authors from *Bridge* have done, Walker simply puts limited and additive difference *on display*. Unlike the living coalitional conversation enacted across *Bridge*, *Real* does not seem to be conversational at all. The pieces do not explicitly engage, let alone reference, one another, and Walker does very little in the introduction to encourage this kind of exchange. As such, she resists her role as cartographer. Perhaps aware of the bird's-eye view that accompanies her refusal to engage, see, or map intersectional oppressions, she remains at a safe distance from the contributors and topics explored. In so doing, a clear hierarchy emerges between herself, as the editor, and the rest of the contributors who are there to echo the vision of feminism that Walker sets out to defend. Instead of allowing each contributor to write their own biography, as seen in *Bridge* wherein all entries are written in the first person, we are left to assume that Walker writes these herself (all entries are written in the third person here). What is more, she positions her own short biography in a separate section titled, "About the Editor," thereby preserving a clear demarcation between herself and the other contributors. Despite assuming a gatekeeper role, Walker departs even further from earlier anthologies by refusing to organize the anthology into categories or sections. Instead, all twenty-three contributions (including Steinem's foreword, Walker's introduction, and Davis's afterword) appear one after the other with no demarcations whatsoever—just one list of authors and titles.[12] Thus, while assuming the role as gatekeeper, she refuses the responsibility of mapping that comes with this. Or, perhaps, because she is aware of her role as gatekeeper, she feels uncomfortable taking control of the format of the book. Unlike Moraga and Anzaldúa, Walker offers no guidance on how to read the text or what kind of purpose the text may serve beyond putting additive and indiscriminating difference on display. This resistance to categorizing and structuring the text is reminiscent of the epistemological undecidability and political indeterminacy that grounds coalition as spectacle and effectively refuses foundational claims to identity, categorization, and shared political goals and directions—a notable and troubling divergence from the coalitional scholarship of *Bridge*. As we learned in chapter 3, foundational claims, naming oppressions, naming resistance, asserting political commitments, and employing political tactics can all be done without worry, as long as they are done collectively and from the pedestrian level. What Walker seems to be resisting, then, is theorizing from the streets, and perhaps this is because she is self-aware enough to know that she has already adopted a bird's-eye view in her role as gatekeeper.

Relatedly, the anthology as a whole fails to achieve a truly self-reflective feminist critique. In Walker's one moment of self-reflexivity, she pauses to ask herself: "Am I a bad feminist by making a book that isn't about welfare reform, environmental racism, and RU486? What about the politics? What about the activism that people need to hear about?" (Walker 1995b, xxxix). Walker immediately brushes off these important and potentially self-critical questions, and instead defends the type of book that she wanted to create for herself.

> This question came up early on when I found myself feeling internal pressure to make a book I really wasn't all that desperate to read. That book was filled with incisive critique of the patriarchy, plenty of young women from every background fighting against all manner of oppression, and inspirational rhetorical prose meant to uplift, empower, and motivate. It would be a great book to buy one day … but would it pull me along a journey that captivated and intrigued me, would it get at what was most relevant in my life and the lives of others I talked to, forcing us to face and embrace, confront and understand? Would it help me to learn more about myself, and thus help me to learn more about the nature of female empowerment? Doubtful. (Walker 1995b, xxxix–xl)

While Walker enters into a moment of acknowledging her own internal pressures and contradictions, she does not sit with these uncomfortable feelings for long, nor does she challenge herself to confront components of her privileged feminism. Instead, she goes on to defend the type of feminist book that she wants to make by turning it into an individualistic and perhaps even self-indulgent project. Why is it that a book about intersectional oppressions did not "intrigue" her? Was it that the stories of oppression that would have filled that book were perhaps too familiar, too boring even, to captivate her, given the many facets of her privileged feminism?[13] There is absolutely no sense here that Walker is engaged in a collective project with other feminists on a journey toward a more self-reflexive feminism aimed at undermining oppression and interrogating her own privilege. Instead, we get a strong sense from Walker's introduction that the book is there to serve her—that is, to justify a type of feminism she feels she has been forced to hide due to the ways in which it fails to resemble the structural analyses of interlocking systems of power that earlier forms of feminism have been built on.

In the foreword, Steinem begins by painting a picture of ten different people in a room, taking the time to give her reader what may seem to be superfluous detail on what each person in the room *looks* like. There is a "white married couple, both lawyers in their twenties, wearing jeans and carrying briefcases" (Steinem 1995, xiii). There is a "tall black man in a suit who runs an urban antipoverty organization" (xiii). There is an Irish-looking "round ladylike executive in a print dress" and pearls; a "rounder black woman editor in a tunic"; three "youngish women," one with a lesbian slogan on her T-shirt, another wearing a sexy transparent blouse; a "white writer with long hair and a short skirt"; and an "energetic, thirtyish black woman in a maid's uniform complete with frilly apron" (xiii–xiv). The question she poses her reader: "*who is the feminist*" (xiv)? The answer she gives us: "*all of them*" (xiv).

This question and answer, I believe, are particularly appropriate for *Real*. As Steinem goes on to argue, feminists have often defied our expectations of what they ought to look like (xiv). The room Steinem was describing, we learn, was an actual room in which she found herself (as the writer in the short skirt) twenty-two years ago. The woman in the maid's uniform (Carolyn Reed), it turns out, organized the gathering of friends and activists in an attempt to break down stereotypes surrounding what feminists or activists committed to working on household worker's rights or even household workers themselves were supposed to look like. As Steinem puts it, Reed used the diversity of the people in that room to "instruct [them] in the tyranny of expectation" (xiv).

For some, it may seem Walker was interested in a similar kind of project. However, the point for Reed went beyond expanding our conceptions of what household workers or activists working on household workers' rights *look like*. More so, the meeting was the beginning of the creation of a household workers' campaign that eventually grew into a coalition that successfully fought for various household workers' rights. Hearkening back to the origin of that coalition, then, Steinem invites us to consider whether *Real* may be engaged in a similar kind of project. At first glance, the book seems to resemble Steinem's room. However, unlike the coalitional possibilities that emerged out of that room of household workers' rights and feminist activists, I contend that the essays in this anthology are locked into a static, though colorful, mosaic of limited, additive, and individualistic difference. They succeed at ontological disruption in the way that one might expect coalition as spectacle to play out. They do not, however, succeed in enacting or even encouraging politico-ethical coalition politics.

Coalitional Scholarship Today: On the Promise of Becoming Sangtin

As I have shown here, *Bridge* is an indispensable resource for contemporary feminist theorists interested in theorizing intersectional coalition politics. It embodies key components of politico-ethical coalition politics and offers an instructive guide for contemporary scholars interested in either theorizing coalition or attempting collective, activist, and certainly coalitional modes of feminist scholarship. I am in agreement with Burack that the great theoretical insights of early US Women of Color coalitional feminism comes to us in the unconventional approach to feminist theory vividly captured across texts such as *Bridge*. In it, we not only find a sustained treatment of the value of coalition politics, but we bear witness to how this mode of feminist solidarity may be put into practice between the pages of a single text. This value becomes even more apparent, I have shown, when *Bridge* is juxtaposed with *Sisterhood* and *Real*.

Sisterhood embodies many components of "activist" feminist scholarship. By being unapologetically political in its purpose, by actively challenging traditional objective and rational modes of doing theory, by exploding single master narratives with a cacophony of voices employing a range of writing styles, and by challenging traditional hierarchical editing practices, Morgan takes important steps toward compiling a truly activist text. However, it ultimately fails to resemble a politico-ethical textual coalition on account of both the unself-reflexive notion of "sisterhood" on which it rests and its additive approach to difference. While one could claim that this text attempts a kind of textual community (not coalition) in the form of sisterhood, it ultimately fails to achieve any form of feminist solidarity that is not in some way exclusionary.

In addition to doing those things that mark an activist feminist text such as *Sisterhood*, *Bridge*, by contrast, overtly and self-reflexively confronts the challenge of difference. Not only do the many pieces in this anthology ultimately arrive at the notion of coalition, the book itself resembles a struggle toward unity across the internal differences that divide, even, Women of Color feminists. This internal journey—which turns a critical eye on Women of Color feminism itself—resembles a journey toward coalitional consciousness. In both the content appearing in this anthology and the very form it takes, *Bridge* comes to resemble an exercise in politico-ethical textual coalition.

While an interest in attending to limited difference animates *Real*, the collective "we" of politico-ethical coalition is dangerously replaced here by a defiant and highly individualized lifestyle feminism, wherein juxtaposing an infinite number of individual lifestyle choices in the form of a "mosaic" comes to stand in for feminist collectivity. A collective feminist project centered on the metaphor of textual mosaic suffers from many of the same limitations as Butler's notion of coalition as spectacle by obscuring the concrete politics of feminist solidarity in favor of the ontological disruption staged by this unexpected depiction of "feminism" that eschews many key components of what feminism was thought to mean only a decade prior to its publication.

Insofar as contemporary feminism is defined by a turn to coalition, retrieving some of our most insightful texts on theorizing coalition politics is worthwhile. Not only does *Bridge* offer instructive lessons on how to coalesce across stark differences, it also provides an invaluable illustration of how to bring these commitments into our scholarly practices. A brief look at a handful of contemporary examples of experiments in collective feminist authorship suggests that the lessons from *Bridge* continue to be heeded. Anzaldúa and AnaLouise Keating's 2002 edited anthology, *This Bridge We Call Home: Radical Visions of Transformation*, for instance, explicitly continues in the spirit of coalitional scholarship. With Anzaldúa as one of the editors, it is unsurprising that this anthology recovers common themes from *Bridge*, including a commitment to the "activist" mission inherent in making anthologies (Anzaldúa 2002, 9), the importance of the process of "shifting consciousness" to any kind of "bridge" work, a commitment to working collaboratively and dialogically within the pages of the text, and a commitment to avoiding the seduction of comfort found in the goal of sameness in favor, instead, of "opening the gate to the stranger, within and without" (1, 2, 3). As she nicely captures it, "A bridge, such as this book, is ... about honoring people's otherness in ways that allow us to be changed by embracing that otherness rather than punishing others for having a different view, belief system, skin color, or spiritual practice. Diversity of perspectives expands and alters the dialogue, not in the add-on fashion but through a multiplicity that's transformational" (4). Mirroring the ethical dimension of coalitional scholarship originally presented in *Bridge*, Anzaldúa ensures us that *This Bridge We Call Home* has pivoted dramatically away from the troubling pattern of textual mosaic on offer the decade before. Anzaldúa's commitment to "diversity" parts ways with Walker's insofar as Anzaldúa names the self-reflexive and transformative process inherent to dialoging across difference. Instead of using others' accounts to echo her own, Anzaldúa reflects on the importance of allowing otherness to radically transform one's consciousness and sense of self. This kind of self-work is pivotal to the politico-ethical coalitional scholarship of *Bridge* and was conspicuously absent from both *Sisterhood* and *Real*.

In closing, I want to briefly reflect on a second contemporary example that provides an even more encouraging depiction of the positive influence of coalitional scholarship initiated by the *Bridge* authors. While we would expect to see the coalitional scholarship of *Bridge* continued in a text such as *This Bridge We Call Home*, explicitly framed as an extension of *Bridge*, the coalitional scholarship presented in *Playing with Fire* not only demonstrates the breadth of impact of the coalitional scholarly practices initiated by Moraga and Anzaldúa, it also moves politico-ethical textual coalition into new and promising terrain.

Breaking out of the "editor" format typical of collective authorship practices in the form of anthology, the Sangtin Writers in India and Richa Nagar take this a step further in their choice to *coauthor* their 2006 text. Richa Nagar (a teacher of women's studies at the University of Minnesota), seven village-level nongovernmental organization activists from diverse caste and religious backgrounds in India (Anupamlata, Ramsheela, Reshma Ansari, Shashibala, Shashi Vaish, Surbala, and Vibha Bajpayee), and Richa Singh (their coworker and district-level NGO activist in India) engage in a collectively written and spoken conversation with each other, captured in the text. In phase one of the collective authorship process, the seven autobiographers (the seven village-level activists) created written autobiographical narratives about their childhoods, adolescence, marriages, and involvement in women's NGOs. Meeting regularly with each other and Singh, they shared and discussed their accounts, reflected further on them, and continued to write. Nagar communicated with them by phone about their accounts after each group discussion. These collective discussions were revisited in phase two of the project wherein Nagar spent her sabbatical year with the Sangtin Writers in India. During this phase of the project, more focused discussions on the complexities of caste, gender, poverty, and sexuality emerged. Out of these discussions, these nine authors started planning and drafting chapters of their book (Nagar 2006).

Notice how this approach is both collaborative and deeply self-reflexive, thereby modeling key components of coalitional scholarship. What I find particularly remarkable about this experiment in collective feminist authorship, however, is the way in which these authors have managed to turn the self-reflexive component of politico-ethical coalitional scholarship into a *collective* exercise wherein the Sangtin Writers share and collectively reflect on their personal journal entries. After this group reflection, the writers reflected further on this experience in more individual journal entries. This process ensures multiple levels of both internal self-reflection and collective group reflection. Their goal in approaching it this way was to "use reflexive activism and collective analysis of the lives and work of the seven village-level activists to articulate the nuanced intersectionality of caste, class, gender, religion, and sociospatial location, on the one hand, and the multivalent and hierarchical characters of donor-driven women's empowerment, on the other" (Nagar 2006, xxii). As such, they sought to collectively tell their story as a "chorus in which nine travelers from varied sociopolitical locations self-reflexively merge their voices to seek answers to a set of shared concerns" (xxi). Throughout the book, this chorus does not remain constant; that is, one voice might surface and then get blended with many others, after which another, new, voice might also surface, thus creating what they call a "blended 'we'" (xxxiv). As they put it, "*Sangtin Yatra/ Playing with Fire* has emerged from a collectively produced methodology in which autobiographical writing and discussions of that writing became tools through which we built our analysis and critique of societal structures and processes, ranging from the very personal to the global" (xxviii). Moving decisively away from both the unified chorus of "sisterhood" and the textual "mosaic" of *Real*, *Playing with Fire* resuscitates and expands on *Bridge*'s commitment to textual solidarity (not sisterhood) in the form of politico-ethical textual coalition. This mode of collective and "reflexive" (xxix) analysis and critique mirrors the very features of coalitional scholarship that set *Bridge* apart from both *Sisterhood* and *Real*.

Notwithstanding the troubling trend of feminist collective authorship practices emerging in the 1990s, I am deeply encouraged by the innovative collective feminist authorship of Nagar and the Sangtin Writers. Aligning *Playing with Fire* with the political autobiographical work of 1970s and 1980s US Women of Color feminists such as Anzaldúa and June Jordan, Mohanty comments in her foreword that "the stories in this text enact this process of becoming *sangtin*—of a collective journey of the personal and political struggle of nine women toward solidarity, reciprocity, and friendship across class, caste, and religious differences in the profoundly hierarchical world of rural Uttar Pradesh" (Mohanty 2006, x). As Bambara knew when writing the foreword to *Bridge*, it was always the "Afterword" of *Bridge*—its ability to build "coalitions of women determined to be a danger to our enemies" (Bambara 1983, viii)—that would count most. *Playing with Fire* assures us that Bambara's faith in the ability of *Bridge* to provide the planks for this crossing, to "coax us into the habit of listening to each other and learning each other's ways of seeing and being" (vii), was not without merit. As Mohanty affirms here, the radical coalitional scholarship practices of *Bridge* have traversed oceans, showing us that such practices might by shepherded by new feminist voices and in new ways that remain true to the spirit of politico-ethical textual co-alitional possibilities but imagine them in new contexts and in new ways: at least one of these ways is becoming *sangtin*.

5

*The Women's March on Washington
and Politico-Ethical Coalitional
Opportunities in the Age of Trump*

The preceding four chapters have provided an account of the challenge facing
contemporary coalition theorists; rather than being located in a perceived
crisis of post-Marxist collective politics, this *challenge* centers on how to
accommodate the social complexity that results from multiple and at times
hostile differences while not subscribing to ontological unfixity and epistemological undecidability or the political indeterminacy that they together
engender. These chapters have also constructed a three-part response to
this challenge: to proceed from an assumption of the compatibility between
intersectionality and Marxism; to reconceive coalition as a politico-ethical
encounter with difference; and to reconceive identity, consciousness, and
the very practice of doing political theory in coalitional terms.

As I will demonstrate in this chapter, many of the ideas, tactics, and
concepts recovered here have shaped the most far-reaching call to action in
US history to date. The 2017 Women's March on Washington (wmw), with
corresponding sister marches in many cities across the globe, offers a helpful

case study of an attempt at large-scale intersectional group politics across diverse markers of difference. At a time when the widespread hatred politics of the former Trump administration demanded a united front to oppose a variety of oppressive policies and rhetoric, the post-Marxist challenge of re-envisioning progressive group politics outside of class-only, women-only, Black-only, and so on, identity politics seemed ever more pressing (see Davis and Taylor 2016; Gökariksel and Smith 2017). On this front, contemporary scholars and activists have much to learn from the savvy coalitional strategies of early US Women of Color coalitional feminism, many of which were utilized to shape the unity principles of the 2017 WMW. Rooted in a clear political commitment to undermining interlocking oppressions and driven by a critical self-awareness of the potentially oppressive and exclusionary internal dynamics that have haunted feminist organizing since the 1960s, the 2017 WMW national team succeeded in putting effective politico-ethical coalitional organizing into practice.

This chapter thus undertakes a practical application of the constellation of concepts developed by *thinking with* US Women of Color coalitional feminism in chapters 1 through 4 of the book. It does this in four steps. I begin by offering a brief overview of the march that highlights both its successes in staging a large-scale intersectional event and the various controversies that emerged. Rather than speaking to the impossibility of realizing intersectional political commitments on a mass scale, I look to the concepts developed in chapters 1 through 4 to guide us in a reading of the 2017 WMW *as* a politico-ethical coalitional event, even if an imperfect one. I suggest that the various controversies surrounding the march that erupted across news platforms in the weeks leading up to and in the months following the march might instead reflect the strength of a coalitional strategy rooted in struggle, self-reflexive political commitment, and existential transformation. In conceiving of the march as an *imperfect* politico-ethical coalitional event, in addition to defending features of the march that others have been critical of (the fact of controversy and political marginalization and the struggle surrounding critical self-transformation), such a reading will nevertheless expose those areas wherein the WMW seemed to falter. The choice to invoke an ontological basis for alliance through naming it a "women's" march led to confusion around two conflicting messages: the shared intersectional political commitment espoused in the unity principles and the commitment to unbounded inclusivity espoused in the name. Acknowledging this misstep does little to disqualify the event as "coalitional." As we have learned from early US Women of Color coalitional feminism, coalition work is always hard work. As María Lugones has put it, such work amounts to stumbling around with others in the dark. There are bound to be missteps, and if there are not, then it is likely that no real coalescing is occurring. With every misstep or stumble, an opportunity for growth arises, and such opportunities are sorely needed in our contemporary social justice struggles.

A Brief Overview of the March

Though originally initiated by a white grandmother's (Teresa Shook) Face-book event page calling for a march on Washington, DC, after Trump's elec-tion on November 8, 2016 (Agrawal 2017), this call to action quickly morphed into a broad coalition that would garner the visible support of five million people from all backgrounds and across all seven continents (TWM 2017a). This unprecedented success was matched by an intersectional platform on a scale not yet seen in collective feminist organizing history (Fisher, Dow, and Ray 2017). Conceptualized by a national board of four women made up of three women of color (Tamika D. Mallory, Carmen Perez, and Linda Sarsour) and one white woman (Bob Bland), the mission statement and unity principles guiding the WMW reflect a number of key components of politico-ethical coalition politics. As the single largest coordinated protest in US history and one of the largest in the world (TWM 2017a), this mo-ment of intersectional coalitional activism was an unprecedented success. Analyzing a data set collected from a random sampling of participants in the Washington, DC, march, Dana Fisher, Dawn Dow, and Rashawn Ray's research confirms that across this varied set of identity categories, partici-pants were "motivated by a diverse set of issues connected to intersectional concerns," indicating that the goals set forth in "the Women's March's unity principles and its organizational coalition were successful in mobilizing a crowd with diverse interests" (Fisher, Dow, and Ray 2017, 2). Such findings support previous research that has highlighted the success of coalitions informed by intersectional motivations (5). Desperately needed in the age of Trump, the WMW's commitment to intersectional feminist politics is unmistakable and indeed admirable (see Gökariksel and Smith 2017, 632–33; Presley and Presswood 2018, 61, 67).

For all its success in staging a truly intersectional coalitional event, however, the WMW has nevertheless been the subject of much controversy. Indeed, the origin story of the WMW has been both criticized as another instance of hegemonic white feminism effectively erasing the experiences of nonwhite and trans women (see Emejulu 2018; Boothroyd et al. 2017;

Brewer and Dundes 2018) and heralded as an example of self-reflexive feminism in action (Tambe 2017; Gökariksel and Smith 2017). With two white women (Shook and Bland) as the face of the movement at its inception, many women of color worried the movement would reproduce monolithic and exclusionary images of "women," effectively resulting in a feminist movement that would fail to speak to and advocate for their needs. Punctuated by the fact that 53 percent of white women voted for Trump, while 98 percent of Black women voted for Hillary Clinton, many Black women and other women of color had little patience for working with white women who had a proven track record of exclusionary feminist politics (Obie 2017).

To be fair, concerns about the marginalization of Black women and women of color were not unwarranted. While many of the most visible speakers at the 2017 WMW were women of color (America Ferrera, the Honduran American actress; Janet Mock, a US writer, television host, and transgender rights activist; and Angela Davis all spoke at the DC march, while celebrities such as Aishe Tyler and Jessica Williams spoke at the march in Utah), the crowds in attendance were predominantly white (Wortham 2017). As Angela Peoples, a Black activist and attendee of the Washington march, put it: "It definitely felt very white. The other black women that I talked to there, and even women in other marches around the country, felt like they were alone, like more of the same was happening. I know that a lot of the organizers, particularly of the DC march, did a lot of work to make sure that the speakers were diverse, that the issue points reflected black folks' experiences; but there's also this reality that when we talk about feminism in this country, the faces have been white" (quoted in Obie 2017). In addition to the troubling optics of the conspicuous absence of women of color in the sea of white women, others noted how certain white attendees seemed oblivious to what this absence meant. For instance, as Ijeoma Oluo, the editor at large of the feminist website the Establishment, noted, to "brag" about the absence of arrests and police violence at a march that is predominantly white seems blissfully ignorant of the reality of targeted police brutality against peaceful Black and Brown bodies. As Oluo put it, "The truth is, we are all fighting for very important things, but only certain people get to march down the street and not have to worry about violence from police officers" (quoted in Richardson 2017), a point made all the more salient in summer 2020.[1] As Alicia Garza, one of the cofounders of Black Lives Matter (BLM), similarly recounted: "Like many other black women, I was conflicted about participating. That a group of white women had drawn clear inspiration from the 1963 March on Washington for Jobs and Freedom, yet failed to acknowledge the historical precedent, rubbed me the wrong way. Here they go again, I thought, adopting the work of black people while erasing us.... Where were all of these white people while our people are being killed in the streets, jobless, homeless, over incarcerated, under educated? Are you committed to freedom for everyone, or just yourselves?" (Garza 2017). As Garza reveals, it proved challenging for women of color to believe that the WMW would be any different from the many other white feminist attempts to lead a feminist movement and sideline women of color in the process, and all the more so when white women rarely showed up at events fighting for the lives of people of color.

What is more, at some of the sister marches, it seemed that the absence of women of color might have been by design. While the core national team made the views and concerns of women of color central to the organizing platform, attempts at the local level to ensure the inclusion of the perspectives of women of color were at times met with hostility. Even though the WMW in Vancouver, for instance, attested that it sought to organize an "inclusive" and "intersectional" event, organizers failed to contact local activist groups representing marginalized voices, such as Black Lives Matter Vancouver (Boothroyd et al. 2017, 713). When local Indigenous women and women of color posted their concerns regarding this lack of collaboration, WMW Vancouver deleted posts from its website. Instead of reaching out to these potential allies and learning from their concerns, the group's organizers chose to silence them altogether.

In addition to the absence, at its best, and outright erasure, at its worst, of women of color that plagued the events, others have noted the marginalization of trans participants through iconic march symbols, such as the pink pussy hats. As Sydney Boothroyd and colleagues put it, in attempting to unite marchers around "womanhood," the PussyHat project "discursively equat[ed] womanhood with vulvae" (Boothroyd et al. 2017, 718). In addition to erasing and marginalizing bodies without vulvae, this form of sex erasure dovetailed with race erasure insofar as it further conflated "being" a woman with "having a *pink* vagina," effectively marginalizing those who do not have "pink" vaginas (Gökariskel and Smith 2017, 635). Insofar as the WMW provided a space for donning these exclusionary symbols, Boothroyd and colleagues concluded, "The WMW participates in and reinforces hegemonic notions of feminine bodies as pure bodies that are racialized as white, possessing specific (reproductive) body parts" (Boothroyd et al. 2017, 712). Charges of erasure and marginalization did not stop at forms of ontological exclusion—

that is, exclusion on account of one's identity. Another interesting site of controversy revolved around political marginalization based on one's political or ideological commitments and viewpoints. The most visible incident of this form of marginalization came when the WMW's core national team decided to remove anti-abortion groups from their list of partners (Fisher, Dow, and Ray 2017, 1; Bernstein 2017). Such a move, Destiny Herndon-De La Rosa, president and cofounder of the pro-life feminist group, New Wave Feminists, recounted, sent the message that the supposed "diversity" called for by WMW was limited (Bernstein 2017). As I will demonstrate in the rest of the chapter, such missteps should not, however, be read as indicative of failure; rather, they ought to be read as politico-ethical coalitional politics in action.

The Value in Dogged Political Commitment

To emphasize that engagement with feminist struggle as political commitment, we could avoid using the phrase "I am a feminist" (a linguistic structure designed to refer to some personal aspect of identity and self-definition) and could state, "I advocate feminism." . . . It implies that a choice has been made, that commitment to feminism is an act of will.
—BELL HOOKS, *Feminist Theory: From Margin to Center*

All sister marches signed on to the core Unity Principles that represent our movement . . . and shared in the common goals and messaging that emerged from the national organizing team. . . . *The core principles of solidarity, inclusivity, and intersectionality were nonnegotiable.*
—MRINALINA CHAKRABORTY, head of field operations
and strategy for the Women's March

While some might cite the uncompromising political platform that led the WMW to remove pro-life organizations from their list of partners as a misstep that resulted in problematic instances of marginalization, I read it instead as indicative of one of the greatest strengths of the WMW. If there is one thing that I hope to now be unequivocally clear from my journey with early US Women of Color coalition feminists, it is the role that dogged political commitment plays in their work. As I have shown, this feature distinguishes their approach to coalition from those on offer by contemporary feminist and political theorists influenced by poststructuralist theoretical orientations. Rather than resisting political "unity," in the way that Judith Butler or Moya Lloyd might do, Bernice Johnson Reagon, Barbara Smith, Audre Lorde, and others show us that unity centered on political commitment, rather than on ontology, is absolutely necessary for effective social change.

As hooks puts it in the epigraph, it is about *choosing* to advocate for a specific political program. That program for US Women of Color coalitional feminism in the 1970s and 1980s was geared toward dismantling interlocking oppressions. The ability to both see and contest what Combahee named "interlocking" systems of oppression (Combahee 1983, 264), to appreciate the fact of the "simultaneity of oppression," as Barbara Smith has put it, is the "crux of a Black feminist understanding of political reality" (B. Smith 1983b, xxxiv). This insight, Smith continues, shapes their political commitment to forming "principled coalitions" devoted to fighting multiple and interlocking systems of oppressions simultaneously (xxxv). The breadth of what such a platform might demand, we will see, is clearly on display in the unity principles shaping the WMW.

Indeed, one of the most remarkable things about the WMW's guiding principles is their explicitly political, rather than ontological (rooted in being and identity), focus. While the first short paragraph of the 2017 unity principles document references identity—"The Women's March on Washington is a *women-led* movement"—it quickly pivots away from identity politics and toward an inclusive commitment to "shared humanity," "resistance," and "self-determination" among "people of all genders, ages, races, cultures, political affiliations, disabilities and backgrounds" (TWM 2017b). While the second paragraph returns again to "identity," the sense of identity invoked here resists any notion of an "essential" or universal woman, emphasizing instead the fact that "women have intersecting identities and are therefore impacted by a multitude of social justice and human rights issues" (TWM 2017b). Similar to Combahee's "Black Feminist Statement" decades earlier and explicitly inspired by early US Women of Color coalition feminists and activists such as Shirley Chisholm, Davis, hooks, Lorde, and Smith, the national leadership team was forthright in making the concerns and experiences of women of color, Third World and Indigenous women central to the "Unity Principles" shaping the march. The goal for their movement, they assert, is "liberty and justice for *all*," which necessarily entails a commitment to work toward undermining the variety of interlocking oppressive forces that restrict liberty and justice for so many (TWM 2017b). This goal is reflected across the nineteen distinct "values and principles" listed in the remainder of the document.

The first of these principles and the original tenet for which they organized the march is that "Women's Rights are Human Rights and Human Rights are Women's Rights" (TWM 2017b). Though the focus here is on "women's" rights and therefore might signal a return to representative identity politics fighting for "women's" rights and "women's" issues, the point here is simply to include women under the banner of human rights. To avoid being exclusionary of LGBTQ people, women of color and Indigenous women, and women with disabilities, the eighth, fourteenth, and fifteenth principles make explicit reference to the inclusive sense of "women" that guides their efforts. Beyond these explicit references to something that might be labeled inclusive identity politics, the remainder of the principles are issue-specific and unabashedly political. Following in the footsteps of hooks's emphasis on "advocating" feminism versus "being" a feminist (hooks 2000), they outline the variety of issues and causes that the WMW supports rather than detailing what it means to be a "woman."

The issues listed here reflect the clear intersectional commitments guiding the mission. The second of the principles makes the link between gender, race, and class explicitly clear, stating that they believe that "Gender Justice is Racial Justice is Economic Justice" (TWM 2017b, 2). The third principle addresses violence against women, with an emphasis on the uniquely precarious position of Black, Indigenous, and transgender women and girls, and makes the explicit link between standing against violence against women and combating gun violence. The fourth and fifth principles address the criminal justice system, focusing both on combating police brutality and the racial profiling of communities of color and Indigenous peoples and on dismantling the racial and gender inequities within the criminal justice system more broadly. The remaining principles include a wide array of overlapping social justice issues: reproductive justice; gender justice and control over one's body; economic justice, including antidiscrimination commitments; caregiving and basic workplace protection, especially for women of color and Indigenous women; equal pay for equal work for *all* women, including trans women, again with special attention to the vulnerability of women of color; workers' rights, including sex workers' rights, and the right to form unions, especially for both documented and undocumented domestic and farmworkers; civil rights focused on voting rights, freedom to worship, free speech, protections for all citizens; passing an equal rights amendment to the US Constitution; immigrant and refugee rights rooted in the firm belief that migration is a human right and that no human is illegal; environmental justice; and, finally, ending war and living in peace.

The WMW was not only unabashed in centering the voices of the most marginalized, as Mrinalina Chakraborty put it, but it was completely uncompromising on its intersectional unity principles. Indeed, for sister marches to sign on, the WMW had to adopt the unity principles guiding the national team; as Chakraborty put it, this was simply "nonnegotiable" (quoted in Tambe 2017, 228), thereby drawing a direct link to early US Women of Color coalitional feminism. Drawing political lines in the sand was never a problem for Reagon, Smith, Combahee, Lorde, and many others. As Reagon put it, her political views in relation to dismantling interlocking oppressions were so steadfast that she called them "bigoted" and "biased" (Reagon 1983, 353). If potential allies were not mutually committed to undermining intersectional oppressions, then they were no longer treated as allies. As Lorde argued, learning to distinguish between allies and enemies was an important part of effective coalescing. Forming the "us" or the "we" was never at risk of essentializing because the category thus formed was rooted in political commitment, not shared identity or ontology. "By seeing who the *we* is," Lorde argues, "we learn to use our energies with greater precision against our enemies rather than against ourselves" (1984b, 137). Fierce political commitment is what helps us to differentiate these enemies and allies.

These dogged political commitments shaped the decision to remove pro-life supporters from the WMW's list of partners. The effect of devising the unity principles in the first place, the core team was well aware, was precisely to draw (political) lines in the sand. The team stated what the WMW stood for, and it was unafraid to embrace what this implied about what the group stood *against*. When the team responded to discontent registered by pro-life supporters at the decision to remove those supporters from WMW's list of partners, it was unabashed in the choice to "exclude" them and apologized for the "error" of having unwittingly included any "anti-abortion" groups among the WMW's partners, stating that the march's platform "is pro-choice and that has been [its] stance from day one" (quoted in Bernstein 2017). Such a response necessarily implies that, despite its name, the WMW was geared toward a pro-*feminist* stance, rooted in an intersectional feminist political platform, rather than simply a pro-*woman* one. Resonating with the distinction between woman and feminist drawn by Women of Color feminists such as Moraga and hooks, feminism in this instance is related to uncompromising political commitments, not shared identities.

The Necessity of Controversy for Growth

I feel as if I'm gonna keel over any minute and die. That is often what it feels like if you're *really* doing coalition work. Most of the time you feel threatened to the core and if you don't, you're not really doing no coalescing.
—BERNICE JOHNSON REAGON, "Coalition Politics: Turning the Century"

We [women of color] are noticed when you [white women] realize that we are mirrors in which you can see yourselves as no other mirror shows you.... What we reveal to you is that you are many—something that may in itself be frightening to you. But the self we reveal to you is also one that you are not eager to know.... You block identification with that self because it is not quite consistent with your image of yourself.... You block identification because remembering that self fractures you into more than one person. You know a self that is decent and good, and knowing your self in our mirror frightens you with losing your center, your integrity, your oneness.... In blocking identification with that self, you block identification with us and in blocking identification with us, you block identification with that self.
—MARÍA LUGONES, *Pilgrimages/Peregrinajes: Theorizing Coalition against Multiple Oppressions*

Coalition work is not easy, and these women have operated from a place of authentic love for all people. My work requires an operational unity that is sometimes extremely painful and uncomfortable, even for me. But I push forward even when I am personally conflicted because our people are more important.
—TAMIKA MALLORY, cochair of Women's March national team

Taking strong political stances, early US Women of Color coalitional feminism has shown us, will inevitably result in controversy. Indeed, perhaps the most unmistakable message from Reagon's famous 1981 "Coalition Politics" speech was that coalition work is not only hard work but bound to be uncomfortable. She equates it to the feeling of altitude sickness and suggests that if you are not feeling like you might keel over and die, you're not really doing any coalescing. As I have shown, this emphasis on discomfort is also prominent across the work of Lorde, Smith, and the many women of color authors appearing in *This Bridge Called My Back* (Moraga and Anzaldúa 1983a). The reason for this discomfort, they all agree, is because of the inevitable controversy that accompanies the kind of struggle typical of coalescing.

I suggest that the various controversies shaping the WMW were not simply the unfortunate and inevitable offshoot of dogged political commitment (though they were this too); rather, for the WMW core national team, echoing the Women of Color feminist texts engaged throughout this book, such controversy was *by design* and for the purpose of inciting the kind of existential transformation that is absolutely necessary for successful politico-ethical coalition politics. The emotion that accompanies controversy, early US Women of Color coalitional feminism has shown us, is a valuable resource for mapping both internal and external interlocking oppressions. While exposing the differences between coalition members might reveal the ways in which certain members are explicitly or implicitly invested in the continued subordination of others—for instance, white members reluctant to confront and actively refuse their privilege—this process of what Lugones has called "traveling" to others' worlds also can help us better map and track intermeshing oppressive forces (Lugones and Spelman 1983; Lugones 1987, 2003). When doing this mapping or traveling, controversy is inevitable; both controversy between coalition members and, as Gloria Anzaldúa, Carmen Vázquez, and Minnie Bruce Pratt have all demonstrated (see chapter 3), controversy between one's own multiple, shifting selves.

Both the controversy that emerges between potential coalition allies and between one's multiple selves, these authors show us, is a good thing. As Lorde (1984b, 1984g) and Lugones (2003) attest, the "anger" that likely accompanies controversy is a source of knowledge and growth. Without it, we would not become nimble and sophisticated cartographers of oppression. Lorde writes:

> Every woman has a well-stocked arsenal of anger potentially useful against those oppressions, personal and institutional, which brought that anger into being. Focused with precision it can become a powerful source of energy serving progress and change. . . . [A]nger expressed and translated into action in the service of our vision and our future is a liberating and strengthening act of clarification, for it is in the painful process of this translation that we identify who are our allies with whom we have grave differences, and who are our genuine enemies.
>
> Anger is loaded with information and energy. (Lorde 1984g, 127)

The anger that emerges from controversy, Lorde maintains, helps us identify our allies and enemies. It also helps us uncover oppression and better understand its subtle moves and repercussions. As she goes on to argue, being on the receiving end of an ally's anger might expose one to a source of oppression that one has unwittingly participated in. In such an instance, an ally's anger is therefore necessary because it helps reveal the subtle movements of power. It therefore helps us to become better coalitional allies, now equipped to use the anger between us to combat the "virulent hatred leveled against all women, people of Color, lesbians and gay men, poor people—against all of us who are seeking to examine the particulars of our lives as we resist our oppressions, moving toward coalition and effective action" (Lorde 1984g, 128). While "hatred is the fury of those who do *not* share our goals, and its object is death and destruction," Lorde clarifies that "anger" is only "a grief of distortions between peers, and its object is change" (128). While Lorde is okay with walking away from hatred, she insists that the presence of anger offers a unique opportunity for growth (131). When she suggests that anger might help us to "transform difference through insight into power" (131), Lorde speaks to what Lugones has referred to as traveling. For Lorde, difference is a resource that encourages one to descend "into the chaos of knowledge and return with true visions of our future" (Lorde 1984c, 111). With this "descent" might come anger, controversy, and discomfort. All of this is necessary for the sake of growth—growth toward understanding and positioning ourselves to dismantle intermeshing systems of oppression.

What will sustain this growth, these authors insist, is a shared political commitment to tackling interlocking oppressions. This commitment is the point of connection with white feminists who will no doubt become very uncomfortable when called out on their privilege. Specifically, it might help white women navigate processes of self-(dis)integration that Shireen Roshanravan (2010, 2014, 2018) shows proves absolutely essential to effective coalitional activism. Much like my elaboration of coalitional identity, Roshanravan follows early US Women of Color feminists in developing a "coalitional praxis of (dis)integration" wherein white women's perceptions of themselves as well-intentioned allies might be disrupted in tense exchanges with activists of color (Roshanravan 2018). In such instances, white allies would do well to learn to see themselves in polymorphous and fluid ways.

As Lugones attests in *Pilgrimages/Peregrinajes*, white women must be willing to look in the faithful mirrors held up by women of color, mirrors that might reveal facets of their privilege that prevent them from fighting effectively against oppression. Such encounters between white and nonwhite coalition allies are inevitably fraught. There are many reasons, for instance, why white women will "block identification" with the selves presented to them in the faithful mirrors of their women of color allies: on account of the multiplicity that threatens their unified sense of a stable and coherent self, on account of troubling the good-intentioned allied self that they believe themselves to be, or on account of revealing to them a logic of plurality that they are not equipped to make sense of. When asked to look into these faithful mirrors, something is bound to break, whether this be the white woman's sense of self that begins, in this moment, the painful process of what Pratt (1984) recounted as decentering, and what Roshanravan (2018) theorizes as "(dis)integrating" the self, or the breaking of a potential allied relationship when the invitation to disintegrate is blatantly refused.

The strength of the WMW rests in its ability to provide a space wherein contemporary feminists might follow Pratt, Lugones, and Roshanravan in beginning (or, for some, continuing) the painful process toward coalitional self-craft—that is, permitting one's self to disintegrate into unflattering plurality and then recenter on political commitment to dismantling intermeshing oppressions (see also Barvosa 2008 on self-craft). Such a process might help us critically interrogate the missteps of white women such as Jennifer Willis who canceled her trip to Washington due to feeling unwelcome by Black activists who asked of white women allies that they talk less and listen more. Rather than perceiving moments such as these as indicative of failure, I read them as opportunities for growth and struggle toward coalitional consciousness, especially when white women take cues from Pratt, Lorde, Lugones, and Roshanravan. Learning to check their privilege, discover their coalitional selves, develop a coalitional consciousness, and "self-(dis)integrate" in the face of hostile feedback from Black and Brown allies is exactly what is needed of white allies in progressive coalitional struggles against the intersectional hatred politics running rampant in Trump's United States (Roshanravan 2018).

Though I am not suggesting that the WMW was *fully* successful in crafting coalitional selves for all who attended, I am saying that it at least provided a canvas for existential transformation for feminist allies to embark on this journey of existential transformation. This process was aided, I contend, by the numerous callouts, or what we might rather understand as "invitations," to white women from their Women of Color feminist allies. As Amir Talai (a Persian American actor) put it in her sign for the march in Los Angeles, "I'll see you nice white ladies at the next #blacklivesmater march, right?" (quoted in Rose-Redwood and Rose-Redwood 2017, 647). Through her sign, Talai invites white allies to take the commitment to intersectional social justice that brought them to the march and turn it in on themselves to interrogate the extent to which it might compel them to get out and fight for other interrelated social justice causes, such as Black Lives Matter.

Or, as ShiShi Rose (a Black activist in Brooklyn) put it when interviewed about her controversial post to white allies in the weeks leading up to the march:

> [Writing in her post] Now is the time for you to be listening more, talking less.... You should be reading our books and understanding the roots of racism and white supremacy. Listening to our speeches. You should be drowning yourselves in our poetry.... You don't get to join because now you're scared too. I was born scared. (quoted in Stockman 2017; also quoted in Obie 2017)

> [Commenting on her post in an interview] I needed them to understand that they don't just get to join the march and not check their privilege constantly. (quoted in Stockman 2017)

Speaking to her anticipated white co-marchers, Rose invites them to consider talking less and listening more to their Black and Brown allies, who were "born scared." Like Talai and echoing Lorde in her critical exchange with Mary Daly, Rose invites white *feminists*—those who have clearly already chosen a feminist political commitment—to turn this commitment in on themselves and interrogate the extent to which they are ready to learn from women of color. Learning from their Black and Brown allies, Rose implies, will help them to better understand the many-headed monster of oppression that has been terrifying people of color for centuries.

Or, as Angela Peoples, another Black activist, put it when interviewed about the photo that went viral of her sign that read, "Don't Forget, White Women Voted for Trump," juxtaposed against three cheerful white women taking and posting selfies on their phones in front of the Capitol: "That's why the photo was such a great moment to capture, because it tells the story of white women in this moment wanting to just show up in a very superficial way and not wanting to do the hard work of making change, or challenging their own privilege.... We're only being seen when we're coming together behind you. When we're speaking about our pain, when we're asking you to show up, then it's divisive, then it's somehow detrimental to the broader cause" (quoted in Obie 2017). Here, Peoples invites white allies to consider, yet again, why they are only just now compelled to protest against an oppressive system that has been operating for centuries. She also implies that the attitude of at least some of the white women who did attend was one that registered as completely oblivious to just how dangerous interlocking oppressions can be. She thus invites them to listen as women of color speak to their pain, without feeling somehow threatened by their presence. Peoples's words thus strike me as an invitation to white women to begin the difficult self-work that marks the existential transformation that is part and parcel to politico-ethical coalition politics.

Offering the site of the march (the physical spaces of the march, the print spaces of the march, and the virtual spaces of the social media platforms related to the march) as a canvas for this kind of self-work was intentional on the part of the WMW core national team. Moving well beyond "celebrating" our differences, the WMW not only made "difference" *pivotal* to the organizational structure of the march (as demonstrated in the unity principles), it further embraced self-reflexivity and transformation as foundational to effective coalescing. As all versions of the story accurately recount, by the morning after Shook's Facebook post, the post had gone viral with thousands of people pledging to show up for a march on Washington. In the same short time frame spanning the evening of the election and the morning and day following, other people had started similar groups to march on Washington, including Bland, a white American female fashion designer who designed the "Nasty Woman" T-shirts during the presidential campaign (Tolentino 2017). Within this first twenty-four-hour time span, various groups started connecting online, including Bland and Shook, who had separately formed two of the larger event groups. Initial efforts across these different event groups were centered on forming state chapters to organize the march and ensure that participants from all fifty states would be in attendance (Tambe 2017, 225). It was also in this first twenty-four- to seventy-two-hour period that initial concerns over the potential for the formation of an exclusionary white feminist platform surfaced in reaction to the presence of two white women who seemed to be at the helm of a rapidly growing movement.

Sensitive to the posts coming in and the issues raised therein, Vanessa Wruble, a white woman who had worked in predominantly Black spaces and was involved in the early stages of planning the march, went to Shook and Bland and advised them to displace themselves as the "leaders" and to instead center the voices of women of color (Felsenthal 2017). In response, Bland immediately (within hours of these concerns surfacing) called on board three prominent women of color activists to form the majority of the core national team, co-chaired by Bland, Mallory (an African American activist working in New York City), Sarsour (a Palestinian American Muslim political activist), and Perez (a Latina woman working on issues of mass incarceration and gender equality). Shook chose to take a more supportive and less active role in the organizing of the march and was thus not included in the core national team (Tambe 2017).

Thus, not only did the original leaders welcome this site of controversy, they made it pivotal to their organizing platform. As Stockman found, the discord and controversy surrounding the march were therefore "by design" insofar as the new team of national organizers that emerged in response to this controversy "made a deliberate decision to highlight the plight of minority and undocumented immigrant women and provoke uncomfortable discussions about race" (Stockman 2017). As Sarsour put it, "This was an opportunity to take the conversation to the deep places," and when doing so, "you are going to upset people" (quoted in Stockman 2017). This message was also explicit on the group's Facebook page where hooks was quoted calling on feminist allies to "confront the ways women—through sex, class, and race—dominated and exploited other women" (quoted in Stockman 2017).

Once formed, the core team began organizing efforts, including brainstorming principles, values, and goals for the march. As Chakraborty recounts, a number of productive and difficult conversations began at this point, the first of which centered on the change of the original name of the march from Million Women's March, proposed by Shook in her original post, to the Women's March on Washington (Tambe 2017). As critics have noted, the original name co-opted the language of, and functioned to erase, the Million Man and Million Women Marches organized by the Nation of Islam in the 1990s and thus by and for African Americans (Emejulu 2018). Originally presented by Shook, prior to the formation of the multiracial core national team, the name ignited concerns that a white woman was appropriating the language of Black activists without making the issues of Black people central to the organizing platform. This was one of the concerns that led to the formation of the multiracial core national team in the first place (Gökariskel and Smith 2017, 632). With this team in place and with the concerns of people of color now central to the unity principles taking shape, the team selected a new name that still invoked Black activism but now under the banner of an explicitly intersectional feminist platform.

For those critical of the wmw, these events are read as indicative of a familiar brand of exclusionary white feminism (Emejulu 2018; Boothroyd et al. 2017; Brewer and Dundes 2018); for others, the sequence of events reflects encouraging efforts toward intersectional feminism (Tambe 2017; Presley and Presswood 2018). I read them as promising echoes of the self-reflexive feminism on display in Pratt's journey and advocated for by Women of Color coalition feminists such as Lorde, Lugones, and Roshanravan. Bland

and Shook responded quickly and effectively to concerns about the marginalization of Black and Brown women, ultimately displacing themselves as the leaders of the march and turning over decision-making power to the nonhierarchical core national team composed primarily of women of color. When invited to see themselves as potential oppressors, Bland and Shook thus embraced the invitation and then reacted effectively and promptly to what this new lens revealed. Resonating with the self-reflexive political commitment driving Combahee's prefigurative politics, Bland and the other co-organizers anchored their "decentralized leader-full structure" in the firm conviction that "[their] liberation is bound in each other's" (Tolentino 2017). Alongside self-consciously putting her perspective as a white woman in the minority position on the national team and noting the importance of centering the voices of "Asian and Pacific Islanders, Trans Women, Native Americans, disabled women, men, children, and many others ... in the evolving expression of this grassroots movement" in her official diversity statement, Bland invited other white women participants to "understand their privilege, and acknowledge the struggle that women of color face" (quoted in Tolentino 2017). As Rachel Presley and Alane Presswood have summarized: "The success of the Women's March became contingent on the organizers' ability to reorient the dominant script toward woman of color and those whose struggles are often ignored by the whitewashing of feminism" (Presley and Presswood 2018, 67). And reorient they did! Insofar as they were able to do this (at least at the national level), we might, as Presley and Presswood put it, understand the WMW as "the first large-scale movement that pushes beyond notions of allies to that of accomplices" (67) wherein participants and organizers become "complicit in a struggle toward liberation" and truly "accountable and responsible to each other" (67).

As Anne Valk, the author of *Radical Sisters: Second-Wave Feminism and Black Liberation in Washington, D.C.*, put it when asked about the controversies erupting in and around the march: "If your short-term goal is to get as many people as possible at the march, maybe you don't want to alienate people.... But if your longer-term goal is to use the march as a catalyst for progressive social and political change, then that has to include thinking about race and class privilege" (quoted in Stockman 2017). While embracing the controversy that will inevitably result from this will come with "bumps" along the road, UCLA women's studies scholar Grace Kyungwon Hong similarly attests that "discord" of this nature is good for feminism (Bates 2017). The point, Hong suggests, is to "*not* all agree," to opt instead to have the "tough conversations" (quoted in Bates 2017). Gloria Steinem agreed, stating that "even contentious conversations about race were a 'good thing'" (quoted in Stockman 2017). Echoing Lorde, other accounts of the march suggest that we might "find in these uncomfortable conversations and spaces the possibility of dismantling the structures of power, willful ignorance, and feigned innocence that brought us to our current historical moment" (Gökariksel and Smith 2017, 640). Every difficult conversation that involves attempting to travel to another's world, to another's perspective, offers an opportunity to attempt to make sense of a slightly different manifestation of the same many-headed monster of oppression. The better we understand its many incarnations, the better equipped we are to dismantle it.

What makes this process scary and intimidating—what, as Lugones has argued, inclines many potential white feminist allies to "block identification" with the selves they see reflected back in the faithful mirrors held up to them by women of color allies—is the invitation to self-disintegrate that comes along with this process. Feeling snubbed or angry at the national team's directive to check white privilege and center the voices of women of color, a number of white women expressed their discontent on social media platforms, complaining that the event "had turned from a march for all women into a march for black women" (Stockman 2017). This infuriated many, especially those who felt that white women, particularly those who were victims of sexual and other physical abuse, would be asked "to check their privilege" (Stockman 2017). Falling into the classic trap of uniting around shared victimhood (see hooks 2000, 46), many white women resented the suggestion that those who suffer from sexual and physical abuse could possibly occupy the position of "oppressor."

Perhaps the most talked about incident of outright refusal on the part of a white woman to an invitation of critical self-reflection came from Jennifer Willis, a fifty-year-old white wedding minister from South Carolina. In response to Rose's post wherein she asked of white allies that they talk less and listen more, Willis canceled her trip to DC. Notably less graceful than Bland's response to interrogate her privilege and shocked by what she perceived as Rose's hostile and uninviting tone, Willis refused this invitation of critical self-reflection, stating: "This is a women's march.... We're supposed to be allies in equal pay, marriage, adoption. Why is it now about, 'White women don't understand black women'?" Maintaining that such callouts would hurt the chances of solidarity, Willis continued, "How do you know that I'm not reading black poetry? ... The last thing that is going to make me endeared to you, to know you and love you more, is if you are sitting there wagging your finger at me" (quoted in Stockman 2017). Willis thus turned the callout back on Rose, suggesting that if there were a bad feminist in this scenario, it would be her insofar as Rose's actions prevented, rather than encouraged, feminist solidarity. Hearkening back to the very logic used during the women's liberation movement to refuse the invitations of Black women to embrace a more self-critical feminism, Willis made clear that she was not interested in traveling to Rose's world. Clearly willing to risk solidarity with the Willis's of the world in the event that they refuse her invitation, Rose boldly asserted when questioned about her post, "I needed them to understand that they don't just get to join the march and not check their privilege constantly" (quoted in Stockman 2017).

Clearly, Willis felt that this constant check on her privilege was unwarranted. Even if she was reading Black women's poetry, why, she thought, must she prove that to Rose and other Black attendees who might be questioning her intentions? What is particularly interesting about Willis's response is the way in which it presumes that to attend to interpersonal race issues *within* the movement is to take away from the more important work of fighting for the feminist platform (equal pay, marriage, adoption). Willis thus failed to see how managing her relationship to Rose and to her own plural self, including her oppressor selves, *was* part of the feminist platform espoused both in the unity principles and in statements by the core national team. Until Willis can see how her refusal of Rose's invitation not only hurts Rose and feminist alliance more generally but also hurts Willis herself, she is not yet equipped for successful coalition politics. When she blocks identification with the self mirrored back to her in Rose's post, she blocks identification with Rose, and when she blocks identification with Rose, she blocks identification with one of her plural selves.

For many, reactions such as those from Willis and other reluctant white women might be indicative of the many imperfections of the march rendering it more of a cautionary tale than an exemplar of politico-ethical coalition politics in practice. I resist this sense of "imperfect." Instead, I see these very imperfections as indicative of the great potential of the WMW on politico-ethical grounds. Having these difficult conversations— ones that force white women out of positions of privilege, leadership, and comfort—is precisely what is needed in our contemporary moment, and incidentally, it is precisely what Women of Color feminists called for decades ago. The simple fact of these controversies is indicative that we are in the midst of the hard work of coalescing. Those who chose to not attend the march—both white women and Black women who made this choice—have effectively opted out of this coalitional moment. Those who did attend, especially with the controversies, the callouts, the acts of erasure, and the refusals all in plain view on social media and captured in news coverage leading up the march, effectively said "yes" to a moment of discomfort and for the sake of an intersectional social justice platform. In my estimation, that is a noteworthy success for contemporary feminism and for progressive group politics more generally.

Consider, for instance, how one white woman depicted it when she looked around at the crowd and noticed a severe dearth of women of color in attendance:

> The crowd was largely White, there was no denying it. Protestors wore the undeniable privilege of being able to afford to travel to the March, find care for any young children who couldn't participate in the event, take time off from work if needed to make the journey. But the longer I stood in the crowd, ... the more I thought—good. These White women are EXACTLY the people who needed to be here. I watched as older women like the wine drinkers from the bus listened to America Ferrera demand "an end to the systemic murder and incarceration of our Black brothers and sisters" (Chan, 2017). ... Together, we witnessed. (Presley and Presswood 2018, 64)

Presswood nicely captures the unique opportunity that an overwhelming presence of white women at an intersectional social justice event organized and led by women of color offers for contemporary feminism. The presence of so many white women at an event that openly asked of white attendees that they listen more and talk less (ShiShi Rose), that they be open to checking their race privilege (Bob Bland), and that they prepare to be uncomfortable (Linda Sarsour) registers in my mind as an overwhelming success in attempting large-scale politico-*ethical* coalition politics.

What is more, for every Willis, there were other white women who did not resist invitations to interrogate their privilege and to opt for a self-critical feminism. As Bates noted when interviewing a white Boston writer and corporate executive in attendance, Julie Wittes Schlack, who was "neither rattled nor offended by criticism from women of color." ... "The benefits of our work so far around things like reproductive rights aren't conferred equally across all women. ... And that's what I think younger feminists, feminists of color, particularly, are trying to wake us up to." The issues, Bates (2017) comments, "are broader, messier, more intersectional: race, gender, class, nationality, immigration status, everything is connected." Yes, there were white women like Willis and others who refused to attend a march that unapologetically centered the voices and perspectives of women of color. But there were also many white women who, like Schlack, openly embraced the invitation to learn from women of color and to turn their feminist commitments into truly intersectional political commitments. Even for those white women who did not *self-consciously* attend the march to learn from women of color, the agenda of the march ensured that they came and listened to women of color speakers and, potentially, learned from the messages on the posters of women of color attendees. Peoples's poster, for instance, garnered attention and support from many women, initiating dialogue about why it matters that 53 percent of white women voted for Trump. As Peoples recounted: "Most were saying, 'Not this white woman,' or 'No one I know!' I'd say, '[Fifty-three percent] of white women voted for Trump. That means that someone you know, someone who is in close community with you, voted for Trump. You need to organize your people.' And some people said, 'Oh, I'm so ashamed.' Don't be ashamed; organize your people" (quoted in Obie 2017). Showing up and carrying her sign afforded Peoples the opportunity to begin these dialogues on a large scale. It allowed her to push white women to interrogate why their white peers voted for Trump. Peoples puts the onus back on white folks: "Organize your people." Categorizing white folks as a "people" is a powerful rhetorical gesture. It asks of white allies to venture into uncomfortable spaces with other white folks and start difficult conversations about race with them.

The fact that many white women may not have cared about the range of issues on the WMW agenda before Trump was elected is all the more reason to celebrate the event as an opportunity to move contemporary feminism in the direction of politico-ethical coalition politics. Before the WMW, certain white women might not have ever found themselves on the same feminist media platforms as women of color. Trump ignited passionate calls to collective action in the name of social justice, broadly conceived. The emergence of the WMW thus provided a site for a national conversation around what it might mean to engage in collective progressive group politics. We have seen the stumbling around that we might anticipate in an undertaking of this sort, but the great successes should not be discounted. For every white woman who left an uncomfortable encounter motivated to learn more about the blind spot in her social justice rearview mirror, the march provided a place for her to begin a journey toward coalitional consciousness.

What is more, the callouts were bold, resisting any catering to white fragility that we might have seen in years before. As Margo Jefferson, a Pulitzer Prize–winning Black feminist cultural critic for the *New York Times*, put it when advising white women on how to react to Rose's post: "'Sit back. You're associated with a history that has to do with being bossy and self-absorbed and bigoted in some ways. I can see how that would rattle, and even anger you,' she says gently. 'But I do not consider it reason enough to cancel an attendance at a march like this. Get over it'" (Bates 2017). The core national team set the stage, finally, for a truly politico-ethical coalitional event, one wherein white women were explicitly called on to decenter our voices and leadership roles and to listen to women of color. It also created a space wherein Black women and women of color were emboldened to give white women the straight talk so sorely needed, especially for those white women who are not already seeking it out by reading works by women of color. While this is certainly not to say that the burden falls on women of color to educate white women on the intersection of racism, patriarchy, and corporate capitalism, I do believe that the space of the march provided an opportunity to ignite conversations, to compel white women to go and do the self-work, the gut-wrenching soul searching that reveals our complicity in systems of domination but also, if we stick with it, shows us a path for reconstructing a coalitional self that is prepared to look tactically to our white sisters who have already fought intersectional battles and *choose* to align with them, to redefine our whiteness in a way that reveals our commitment to being true accomplices that actively "weaponize our privilege" and organize our people to confront our role in the systematic oppression and domination of Black and Brown people (*Indigenous Action* 2014).

On the question of how to interpret the instances of Black refusal to engage in the difficult work of coalescing, I find Garza's thoughts instructive. Unlike the majority of the African American women interviewed in Sierra Brewer and Lauren Dundes's (2018) article, "Concerned, Meet Terrified: Intersectional Feminism and the Women's March," who opted out of attending the march in reaction to what they feared would be another exclusionary white feminist event, Garza decided to attend, citing the necessity of "multi-racial" and "multi-class" "mass movement" in order to "transform power" in this country as well as the importance of organizing "beyond the choir"—or beyond those who are already on board with your intersectional platform. Garza thus opened herself to the notion that she could be "critical of white women and, at the same time, seek out and join with women, white and of color, who are awakening to the fact that all lives do, in fact, matter, without compromising [her] dignity, [her] safety and radical politics" (Garza 2017). She noted that even if many of the white women in attendance do not already fully get it—do not "grasp our black, queer, feminist, intersectional, anti-capitalist, anti-imperialist ideology"—joining with a bunch of people who at least "know that we deserve a better life and who are willing to fight for it and win" seemed worth the risk of encountering pushback from white attendees when called out on their privilege (Garza 2017).

Garza's reflections on her own journey toward her evolving coalitional consciousness are equally instructive. Noting that she did not have the same intersectional and self-reflexive consciousness at the beginning of her activist work that she had in 2017, she recalls:

> I remember who I was before I gave my life to the movement. Someone was patient with me. Someone saw that I had something to contribute. Someone stuck with me. Someone did the work to increase my commitment. Someone taught me how to be accountable. Someone opened my eyes to the root causes of the problems we face. Someone pushed me to call forward my vision for the future. Someone trained me to bring other people who are looking for a movement into one. . . .
>
> Building a movement requires reaching out beyond the people who agree with you. Simply said, we need each other, and we need leadership and strategy. (Garza 2017)

It was only after veteran activists took Garza under their wing that she slowly developed the kind of coalitional consciousness necessary to work effectively with others in progressive struggle. Acknowledging that her political awakening to intermeshing oppressions was not immediate and appreciating the urgency of intersectional progressive struggle, Garza chose to accept the invitation of politico-ethical encounter. As Women of Color coalition feminists have shown us, mapping oppression is something that must be done in concert with others. Without showing up to the difficult conversations, transformation will never happen.

I want to close this section by offering some thoughts on another highly visible and quite explosive controversy pivoting the WMW and recalling again concerns of erasure and marginalization. Despite Wruble's role in turning the nascent national team from a pair of white women into a team of predominantly women of color, she struggled with being called out by this very leadership team (specifically by Mallory and Perez) to interrogate the ways in which her Jewish heritage might be implicated in racism and the institution of slavery (Stockman 2018). Wruble's immediate response encouragingly echoed Pratt's, noting that after the calling out, she was "taken aback" and immediately dove into research on those things she didn't "know about

[her] own people" (quoted in Stockman 2018). When she came across Louis Farrakhan's 1991 book, *The Secret Relationship between Blacks and Jews*—the first thing that appeared in her Google search—she stopped digging. Given his known anti-Semitic remarks, Wruble concluded, the book was not credible and so her search was presumably over. However, given the number of Black leaders and activists that see validity in some brand of Farrakhan's message—Davis immediately springs to mind, especially given that she was one of the celebrity speakers at the WMW—and given that Wruble's own coalitional allies (Mallory and Perez) were the ones alerting her to what they saw as a potentially valid site of critical self-reflection, it is puzzling that Wruble chose to stop her searching there. While she set off on a journey similar to Pratt's, she seemed to have bailed rather quickly.

This is a shame, especially because Wruble had Jewish feminist foremothers to turn to as her guides in the difficult self-work that could have followed. In the coauthored text in which Pratt's essay appeared, *Yours in Struggle: Three Feminist Perspectives on Anti-Semitism and Racism*, one of her coauthors, Elly Bulkin (the third coauthor was Barbara Smith), wrote a lengthy personal narrative on this very struggle titled "Hard Ground: Jewish Identity, Racism, and Anti-Semitism." In addition to tracing the contours of the racism and anti-Semitism tension in the feminist movement—the fact that many white Jewish feminists in the 1970s seemed to pay little attention to racism, while many anti-racist Black feminists gave little attention to issues of anti-Semitism—she reflected on her own implication in these struggles. Her lengthy narrative thus comes to resemble Pratt's journey of decentering the self and directed recentering, as Bulkin finds a sense of self that could self-consciously assume the mantle of both struggles—she supports both the Palestinian and the Jewish national movements. Though she was always "taught that Jews played a positive role in the civil rights movement and that Jews, as oppressed people, had a 'special understanding' of Black people," Bullkin interrogated the site of her upbringing, within the "unique crucible of New York City," hosting the largest Jewish population of any city in the world, to uncover the "extent of the paternalism of whites in the civil rights and anti-racist struggles" and the "oppression of people of color by white Jews" (Bulkin 1984, 92). When reflecting on this journey, Bulkin notes:

> How much easier is it for someone to say simply that she is oppressed—as a woman, a Black, a lesbian, a low-income woman, a Native American, a Jew, an older woman, an Arab-American, a Latina—and not to examine the various forms of privilege which so often co-exist with an individual's

oppression. Essential as it is for women to explore our particular oppression, I feel keenly the limitations of stopping there, of not filling in the less comfortable contours of a more complete picture in which we might exist as oppressor, as well as oppressed. (99)

Bulkin shows someone like Wruble how she might accept the invitation to look deeply in the mirror of her Jewish heritage and to therefore trust Mallory and Perez as coalitional allies by not looking away from the uncomfortable sight they place before her. While Bulkin engages in instances of "criticizing non-Jewish women of color for specific acts of anti-Semitism" across her essay, she offers these as genuine invitations to her feminist allies to engage in "further thought, discussion, *and* disagreement" (100), and she weaves these criticisms with her own critical reflections on the policies of Israel. Engaging with Bulkin's, rather than Farrakhan's, text would have offered Wruble an opportunity to self-disintegrate along a path toward reintegration and for the cause of intersectional social justice.

The invitation offered to Wruble was not the only invitation presented in this controversy. In the days immediately following the 2017 march, an explosive argument unfolded at the national level, resulting in Wruble's departure from the national organizing team on account of what she understood as anti-Semitic leanings among the cochairs (Bland, Perez, Mallory, and Sarsour). Wruble's calling out of the cochairs gained considerable traction in the public eye the following year when cochair Mallory attended an event by Farrakhan, publicly praised him on social media, and refused to publicly denounce him (Yang 2019). While Mallory issued a statement denouncing Farrakhan's anti-Semitic, homophobic, and transphobic *remarks*, it stopped short of denouncing or cutting ties with *him*. As she has explained in interviews since then, she will not condemn Farrakhan the man because of the amount of good he has done for the Black community (Yang 2019). While the other members of the core national team stood with Mallory, Shook called on all of them to resign due to their connection to Farrakhan. By September 2019, Mallory, Sarsour, and Bland stepped down, leaving only Perez.

This controversy is notable for a couple of reasons. If the national cochairs are guilty of holding anti-Semitic leanings, then this certainly calls into question the intersectional platform that I have just praised as a beacon of politico-ethical coalition politics in action. Similarly, if the national cochairs responded poorly to such a calling out, this would equally call into question the *ethical* dimensions of what I have otherwise depicted as a potential space for self-transformation toward coalitional identity and coalitional consciousness. With Farrakhan at the center of this controversy, it also provokes questions of a slightly different sort. What might this moment of coalitional controversy share with previous instances of coalitional possibilities unrealized due to a Black leader's refusal to denounce Farrakhan? And why have so many important progressive Black activists refused to cut ties with Farrakhan?

To help me make sense of Mallory's refusal to denounce Farrakhan, I want to turn to some brief remarks made by Davis in 1986 when questioned on Reverend Jesse Jackson's similar choice to refuse to cut ties with Farrakhan during his 1984 bid for the democratic presidential nomination. This is a particularly interesting comparison because Jackson's 1984 campaign was the site of the Rainbow Coalition—his attempt to unite all subjugated people under a wide banner in an attempt to move the Democratic Party in a decidedly progressive direction. Thus, here we have two attempts at broad-based coalitional solidarity that were upended, to a certain extent, by controversial ties to Farrakhan. Like Mallory, Jackson condemned Farrakhan's *remarks* but stopped short of condemning him (Joyce 1984).

Davis's response to a question regarding what she thought of Farrakhan is instructive as we ponder why important Black activists have been reluctant to walk completely away from him:

> Well, Farrakhan—there's a lot of things he says that I agree with and a lot of things I *very vehemently* disagree with. He has made anti-Semitic remarks. I'm *totally* opposed to any expression of anti-Semitism. But at the same time, he makes some important points about Israel. I think that people tend to confuse those who are anti-Zionist or opposed to the policies of Israel with anti-Semitism. There's been a propagandistic effort to create the impression that the one is equivalent to the other. But there are Jews in Israel who demonstrate against the policies of their government, just as we demonstrate against the policies of the U.S. government in this country. (quoted in Woodson 1986)

As Davis suggests here, the difference between being anti-Semitic and anti-Zionist is an important distinction for making sense of the controversies surrounding Farrakhan. While she, like others, condemns his anti-Semitic remarks, she does not dismiss entirely his anti-Zionist remarks. The state of Israel, she acknowledges, has done things that run up against a fervent political commitment to dismantling all forms of oppression. With this in mind, she is not opposed to standing against this, and she suggests one can do this without being anti-Semitic.

As Bulkin has similarly attested, "The pitting of anti-Semitism and racism against each other, the pressure to see opposing them in either/or terms, arguments about the degrees of oppression, degrees of opposition—all are part of a cycle of competition which is oiled by the powers that be, and is often played into by those of us with relatively little power" (Bulkin 1984, 139). Coming out much more forcefully than Mallory, who has strategically dodged wading into the nuances of Farrakhan's criticisms of Israel, Davis and Bulkin help us to understand how one might differentiate between condemnable anti-Semitic sentiments and measured criticisms of the policies of Israel. With this in mind, we might read Mallory's, Bland's, and Sarsour's departure from the WMW as the messy fallout of uniting around political commitment. They are politically committed to condemning all acts of oppression and domination. This is why they are quick to denounce truly anti-Semitic and homophobic remarks; this is also why they are reluctant to fully denounce a figure who has not only done so much to help the Black community but who has also spotlighted oppressive policies in Israel. Davis, Mallory, Perez, and even BLM supporters have all expressed sympathies both with Farrakhan and with Palestinians under Israeli occupation. Instead of reading this as an act that precipitated the failure of the original core national team's vision of the WMW, I read this instead as a bold testament to the firm political commitment undergirding their activist work. No one said political commitment was easy or that it would come without controversy. Rather, early US Women of Color coalition feminists have been steadfast in their position that coalition politics is dangerous, difficult, and uncomfortable precisely because of the inevitable role that controversy plays when we hold tight to intersectional political commitment.

It is hard to know with certainty that the cochairs fared much better than Wruble in embarking on profound existential transformation in the face of Wruble's faithful mirror, which might have revealed to them oppressor selves implicated in anti-Semitic rhetoric, actions, or intentions. What we do know, however, is that the cochairs implicated in the heated conversation with Wruble (Mallory and Perez) have both attested that this controversy afforded them the opportunity to learn more about the hurt of their Jewish siblings and to grow into better coalitional allies. Mallory does this in her statement in response to the critical attention she received for attending the Nation of Islam's annual Saviour's Day event: "I have heard the pain and concerns of my LGBTQAI siblings, my Jewish friends and Black women (including those who do and those who don't check off either of those other boxes). I affirm the validity of those feelings, and as I continue to grow and learn as both an activist and as a woman, I will continue to grapple with the complicated nature of working across ideological lines and the question of how to do so without causing harm to vulnerable people" (Mallory 2018). Perez similarly attests in an interview with Emma Green: "I do not support racism or bigotry. I do not support anti-Semitism. As a Latina woman, we don't denounce people, but that does not mean that we cannot stand up and fight for our Jewish siblings and the Jewish community. The work that I feel is important is to make sure that we're building transformational relationships and also opportunities for reconciliation. That is my life's work. And so I listened to the Jewish community and their concerns, and they've also listened to me, and it's about us building stronger relationships" (quoted in Green 2020). Mallory and Perez have learned some tough lessons about their actions and allegiances. Specifically, they have learned how to hear the hurt feelings of coalitional allies and how to transform their approach in response to these feelings without sacrificing the firm political commitments that shape their activist work. Perhaps, more accurately, they have learned how these very political commitments actually demand that they engage in the critical self-work that would bring them to the table with their Jewish siblings in common struggle. As Mallory reminds us, in the closing lines in her response to the Farrakhan controversy, "Coalition work is not easy." Indeed, it can be "painful and uncomfortable," she attests, even for her (a seasoned activist). She nevertheless pushes forward in this risky and uncomfortable work for the sake of the political commitment that has brought her to this place of struggle in the first place.

The Danger in Centering "Women"

I believe that the Women's March is a space for all women.... The Women's March is a place for people who identify as women, whether you're trans or you're a person who has always been a woman.
—CARMEN PEREZ, cochair of Women's March national team

The danger of the WMW, I maintain, did not inhere in the forceful callouts that led to explosive controversy. I have instead read such invitations for white allies to look in the faithful mirror of self-disintegration as opportunities for growth toward politico-ethical coalition politics and perhaps even as indicative of politico-ethical coalition politics happening before our eyes. Neither did the danger inhere in the WMW's unwavering political commitment that resulted in the marginalization of certain women's voices, specifically those of pro-life women. As I have shown, taking a stance against pro-life positions is the expected outcome of the intersectional political commitment shaping the march. Rather, I conjecture that the biggest misstep of the WMW centered on the name chosen for the march, and by this I do not refer to the controversy surrounding the originally proposed name, the Million Women's March. The WMW's error was the centering of *women*. Earlier criticisms centered on the race insensitivity of appropriating *million* in the title, but what was completely overlooked in these initial discussions was the problematic legacy of appropriating a potentially exclusionary identity category, such as women.

I call this misstep an instance of *ontological entrapment*. By this I mean that the WMW became trapped within the language and therefore logic of identity politics in its choice to foreground women in the title. The only way out of the potential controversies that surround *identity* politics, especially when the identity label has not been deployed tactically, is to double down on some notion of "unbounded" inclusivity wherein the umbrella label claims to include an ever-expanding group of women. The choice to foreground identity therefore muddled the message of uniting around the political commitment shaping the unity principles and some of the group's most controversial decisions, such as removing pro-life women from its list of partners and refusing to condemn Farrakhan. In a number of heated exchanges, the subtlety and dexterity that come with uniting around political commitment, as opposed to identity, were therefore lost as the march emerged as a large umbrella movement *for women* rather than a politico-ethical coalition committed to undermining intersectional oppressions.

The effects of this misstep, I believe, shaped some of the most explosive controversies surrounding the event. For instance, when Willis lamented Rose's callout to white women that they speak less, listen more, and arrive at the march prepared to check their privilege, she appealed to the way in which Rose's comments seemed to run up against the spirit of a "women's" march. "This is a women's march," she declared, "Why is it now about, 'White women don't understand black women'?" (Stockman 2017). Other white women who reacted poorly to callouts and invitations to check their privilege similarly cited how such acts contradicted the inclusive spirit of "women" shaping the event, turning it from a march for all women to a march only for Black women (Stockman 2017). The criticisms surrounding the pink pussy hats similarly attested that what was problematic about the PussyHat symbol was that it narrowed the boundaries of the WMW's organizing trope, the identity category of women. It conflated *being* a woman with "having a pink vagina," thereby marginalizing women-identifying people who do not have vulvae (trans women) or who do not have a "pink" vagina (cisgender women of color). This same theme echoes across the comments made by Abby Johnson, a pro-life advocate responding to the WMW's decision to remove pro-life groups from their list of partners: "But to say, 'Your concern about women's rights is not valued here,' that is disappointing. It shows me that they're not actually interested in representing all women, but only a certain group of women" (quoted in Bernstein 2017). For many of the women who felt marginalized by the WMW, these feelings were profoundly shaped by the fact that the WMW advertised itself as a "women's" march. As a "women's" march, they contend, *all* women should be welcome. Such a stance, one can easily see, leaves absolutely no justifiable grounds on which to exclude any women. When trapped within the logic of identity politics, the only way to avoid its essentializing tendencies is to hold fast to a vision of "unbounded inclusivity" (Boothroyd et al. 2017, 718). While it seems likely that many women attending the march may not have read the unity principles, everyone knew the name of the march. From a branding perspective then, the message that landed was the name, not the carefully worded intersectional political commitments shaping the principles.

By trapping themselves within the logic of unbounded inclusivity, the WMW core national team effectively disarmed themselves of the very language they needed in heated exchanges about the pro-life and Farrakhan controversies. When examining interviews and statements in relation to these controversies, a confusing message surfaces as they wade back and forth between political commitment and unbounded inclusivity. When asked, as the only remaining original member of the core national team, whether she is willing to denounce Farrakhan, Perez begins her remarks sticking firmly to political commitment. She reminds her audience that the original unity principles were not anti-Trump but instead outlined the group's shared political commitments and goals; they were "for" something, and that something was an intersectional platform. She then positions her own commitments as very much in line with those original principles— she does not, for instance, support racism, bigotry, or anti-Semitism. This does not imply, however, that she is willing to "denounce" an individual person. While she will denounce political and ideological views, actions and remarks, "as a Latina woman," she attests, she will not "denounce people." Instead, she will "stand up and fight" for people, specifically for "our Jewish siblings and the Jewish community." She will engage them in dialogue and try to learn from their concerns and experiences in order to "build stronger relationships" (Green 2020). She will, as Lugones has advised, attempt to travel to their worlds and gain a better grasp on oppression from their unique perspective, all for the sake of advancing an intersectional vision of feminist political commitment. In many ways then, Perez's response mirrors what I perceive to be the most promising aspect of the WMW as a potential coalitional site—its foregrounding of self-reflexive political commitment. When pushed by her interviewer to state whether the WMW would be willing to make room for "Jewish women who identify as Zionists and supporters of the state of Israel," Perez remains firm in her appeal to political commitment: "Everyone that is aligned with our unity principles is welcome into the Women's March" (Green 2020). Eschewing the attempt at ontological entrapment staged by her interviewer—one that might incline her to respond with something like, "*all women* are welcome"—Perez deftly maneuvers back to political commitment.

Perez forgives this ground, however, and finds herself trapped within ontology when pushed a third time by her interviewer. "Does the Women's March have space for women who disagree with certain portions of the unity principles ... who disagree with expanding access to abortion?" Green asks. Notice how the question's phrasing pushes in the direction of ontological entrapment by questioning who the march may *not* have space for, thereby clearly summoning the spirit of unbounded inclusivity as the appropriate response. Perez replies:

> I believe that the Women's March is a space for all women. When women feel a desire to participate in the Women's March, they may not agree with every piece of ideology, they may not agree with the whole feminist platform, but I'm sure there's something that they do agree with. I believe that the Women's March is for you. The Women's March is a place for people who identify as women, whether you're trans or you're a person who has always been a woman. The unity principles were an entry point for people to get involved. (quoted in Green 2020)

With her first remark, naming the Women's March as a "space for all women," Perez places herself within the grasp of ontological entrapment. To avoid this, she could have instead said, "I believe the Women's March is a space for all *people who adopt our principles*." She reiterates the same message of unbounded inclusivity a few lines later by stating that the Women's March "is a place for people who identify as women, whether you're trans or you're a person who has always been a woman." Through these remarks, Perez retreats to unbounded inclusivity as the core message of the WMW. Trying to finesse her position, Perez clarifies that the women in attendance at the march would ideally agree with some of the unity principles, even if not all, and that the principles must be treated only as an "entry point" for involvement at the march. Perhaps Perez's intention here is to frame the WMW as a site for difficult, or what Bland will call "courageous," dialogues among women on what the intersectional feminist platform shaping the unity principles might entail (Bland in Yang 2019). She undoes this finessing, however, by stating unequivocally that the WMW is a place for people "who identify as women," rather than a place of committed intersectional feminists. If she could have expanded on what was meant by "entry point," she might have been able to retrieve the shared political commitment messaging from the dicey waters of unbounded inclusivity. Without this clarification, the message remains muddled and unclear.

Similarly, when Mallory and Bland are interviewed about the Farrakhan controversy in the months leading up to the 2019 WMW, Mallory begins her remarks appealing to the dexterity of political commitment (in place of ontological commitment) and how it has led her to denounce hateful remarks that are antithetical to her political commitments but nevertheless to stop short of condemning Farrakhan precisely because of how his actions (outside of his hateful remarks) have advanced lives in the Black community. She attests that she was able to separate her appreciation of Farrakhan's work in the Black community from some of the more hateful remarks he has made in relation to Jews, homosexuals, and trans people. The conversation, aired on *The View* (see Yang 2019), takes a heated turn when one of the interviewers, Meghan McCain, cites the Tablet report (see McSweeney and Siegel 2018) alleging that Mallory and Perez expressed anti-Semitic views in their meeting with Wruble. McCain then pushes Mallory on whether she would make space in the 2019 march for pro-life conservative women, reminding her that they were "not invited" to the 2017 march (referencing the removal of pro-life groups from the list of partners). After denying the allegations of anti-Semitism and clarifying that the women the Tablet journalist spoke to "did not tell the truth, period, full stop," Bland follows Mallory in condemning all statements of hate, bigotry and anti-Semitism, including those made by Farrakhan.

Mallory echoes Bland's sentiments of not agreeing with Farrakhan's statements but comes short of "condemning" them, stating that her record of activism speaks plainly to her political commitments, which are clearly opposed to those espoused by Farrakhan in the statements under scrutiny. Unsatisfied with this response, McCain retreats to the logic of unbounded inclusivity, noting that she does not want to be associated with an organization that is "speaking for all women" but associates with "extreme anti-Semitism." From there, she quickly moves to her next question of whether they would be willing to share a WMW *stage* with a pro-life or pro-Trump woman such as herself. By reinvoking the logic of identity and unbounded inclusivity, McCain thus pivots back to the notion that the march is a march for women, not a march for intersectional feminism. Now trapped within the logic of unbounded inclusivity rather than political commitment, Bland and Mallory must answer which women they are willing to include in the march events: not just which women are allowed to attend the march, but which women might be *included in the march program*. Ensnared within the logic of ontological commitment, Mallory's and Bland's responses become muddled and notably unsatisfying. They attest that they never "disinvited" pro-life women from attending the march, presumably distinguishing between removing them as partners from actually disinviting them from the march. Asserting that she has pro-life women in her family, Bland notes that the space of the march welcomes pro-life women so that they might engage in "courageous conversations" with other women, presumably on what it means to adopt an intersectional feminist platform. Under this pretext Bland closes by saying that the WMW is open to all women.

With Bland's suggestion that the goal of the march is at least in part to open up difficult or "courageous" conversations, one might read the WMW as an attempt at Lugones's notion of curdle-separation. As Lugones argued (see my discussion of this in chapter 3), curdle-separation is the creative redeployment of a label that has been forced on a marginalized group from the outside for the purpose of attaining rights that are only legible through the labels chosen by the state, all the while ensuring that what resides beneath the label remains fluid (impure) and open to contestation (Lugones 2003, 133, 144). In this instance, we might read the tension between the conflicting messages of political commitment and unbounded inclusivity as the WMW's creative attempt at curdle-separating around the category of women. Perhaps the core national team wanted an umbrella label that would be both legible to the state, especially to Trump, and expansive enough to bring an overwhelming number of women together so that they might then engage in difficult dialogues about what it means to be a woman in Trump's United States. For such an interpretation of the WMW's intentions to be convincing, however, the deployment of the label "women" would need to be a response to "external fragmentation" along these same lines (Lugones 2003, 133, 144). While Trump certainly targeted women in some of his hatred-filled vitriol, it is a bit of a stretch to suggest that the group under attack by Trump is effectively captured in the label of "women." Trump was rather undiscriminating in his hatred politics. The only group spared from his remarks was that of able-bodied, working-class, white, heterosexual, cisgender, Christian men. Pretty much everyone else was under "attack" at some point. With this in mind, it is hard to believe that the label chosen in response to this would have been "women." I therefore contend that the choice to use "women" in the title was a poor one, especially without strong and consistent messaging that would ensure its tactical deployment.

Does such a misstep lead us to believe that the WMW failed in achieving its intended purpose? I don't believe so. Instead, it shows us the danger in venturing away from political commitment and toward ontology, something early US Women of Color coalition feminists alerted us to long ago. Encouragingly, if we flash forward three years, we see the resurgence of dogged political commitment shaping the Women's March platform as it openly endorses both the wearing of masks (to prevent the spread of COVID-19) and the defunding of police (in response to the Black Lives Matter protests throughout the summer of 2020) on the main page of their website. Their statement in relation to defunding the police reads: "The Women's March is proud to support The Movement for Black Lives in their call to #DefundPolice. Defunding the police is a feminist issue because black, poor, immigrant and undocumented women are disproportionately targeted, abused and murdered by police. Women's Marchers across the country are sharing information with their networks as a means to contribute meaningful conversation. This is our small way to channel energy into sustained organizing to bring about the new world we so desperately need" (TWM 2020a). Directly beneath this statement, one finds their "Women's Response to COVID-19" statement, which states that their response, called #MaskUp, aims to: "EDUCATE the public about safe mask wearing; MAKE your own mask and connect to those in need; [and] BUILD COMMUNITY with 'Stitch and Bitch' sessions to encourage mask making and wearing" (TWM 2020b). In relation to these current and controversial topics, then, the Women's March continues to make its stance unequivocal. While this will not necessarily get the group out of potentially heated exchanges on whether the WMW will welcome people at its next march who do not support defunding the police or wearing masks, if it enters into such exchanges prepared to be more forthcoming about the tactical use of the category women to bring as many people to the table as possible so that they might then have difficult conversations about intersectional social justice in Trump's

United States, then perhaps it will succeed in squaring its uncompromising political commitments with the logic of inclusion implied in the name the Women's March.

Either way, it seems noteworthy that in July 2020, the WMW was far from alone in centering Black and Brown lives. We would of course expect the group to come out with such statements, given the unity principles. I want to therefore end by conjecturing that the wider national response we saw in summer 2020 to the continued violence and murder of Black and Brown people at the hands of police is encouraging on politico-ethical grounds. Not only did numerous white allies join people of color in protests and demonstrations across the country that continued for months throughout summer 2020,[2] the national conversation taking place on social media platforms,[3] in mainstream news coverage (Cuomo 2020), talk shows (Winfrey 2020), and radio programs (Deggans 2020; Shapiro 2020a, 2020b; King 2020), all directly took up questions centered on naming the various facets of systemic racism and white supremacy and on self-consciously resisting white privilege. The language of becoming "uncomfortable" and the call for white people to embrace discomfort as necessary for growth toward racial justice are now commonplace on mainstream news programs (Martin 2020; Chappet 2020). In addition to standing on the front lines with Black and Brown allies, making themselves vulnerable to the various forms of police violence unleashed on the peaceful protestors, white allies also flooded social media platforms with support and self-reflexive messages on discovering their privilege. White support for taking down Confederate statues, monuments, and memorials is now abundant (Klar 2020). Even NASCAR has banned the Confederate flag at its events (Mangan 2020).[4]

All this suggests that a different kind of national conversation is underway. To be sure, I certainly cannot claim that the WMW is responsible for this collective shift in consciousness. Numerous things have happened since January 2017: the continuation of harmful Trump policies and rhetoric that target Black and Brown people; increased visible incidents of police brutality (and most notably those of George Floyd, Breonna Taylor, and Ahmaud Arbery); and Senator Bernie Sanders's 2020 campaign, which was notably more focused on race and intersectional social justice issues, garnering the support of radical Black activists such as Cornel West, Senator Nina Turner, Angela Davis, Barbara Smith, and Reverend Jesse Jackson, to name only a few. While these and many other incidents have certainly shaped the national consciousness forming over the past few years, I nevertheless proclaim that the continuity in messaging surrounding the WMW and the current messaging of interrogating white privilege and systemic racism that has landed with several mainstream white audiences, leave me feeling optimistic. This is not to deny the very real and present danger to intersectional social justice staged by Trump's racist rhetoric (one of Trump's summer 2020 campaign ads played into the racist trope of urban Black violence supposedly seeping into white suburban neighborhoods) and his supporters' emboldened commitment to making the United States white again by protecting vestiges of white privilege.[5] Even still, in my estimation, the fact that key concepts orbiting early US Women of Color coalitional feminism are gaining traction in mainstream society gives me hope that we might just be stockpiling the kind of politico-ethical arsenal needed to stand up to the hatred politics of Trump's United States. Contemporary theorists and activists alike would be wise to follow the example set for us by the various authors engaged across this text. Disregarding some of our most rigorous coalition theorists moves us dangerously away from the discerning politics and activist scholarship that are required in a contemporary moment marked by proliferating hostilities as well as complex and shifting forms of social injustice.

Conclusion

Lessons for Contemporary and
Future Feminist Activists

As Angela Davis attests in an interview with Chandra Mohanty and Linda E. Carty on February 27, 2016, the early 1980s, especially 1981, were a "pivotal" time for her and for the coming together of what we now understand as intersectional feminism (Davis 2016). On the formation of this moment, Davis recalls the key role that Frances Beal's 1970 essay, "Double Jeopardy: To Be Black and Female," and the work of Third World Women's Alliance (TWWA), especially its *Triple Jeopardy* newspaper, played in developing a framework for an intersectional feminism that would confront sexism, racism, and imperialism (which embraced capitalism) simultaneously. While before the early 1980s Davis would not have been inclined to see her antiracist and anticapitalist activism as necessarily "feminist," in the early 1980s she had the good fortune to be in regular conversation with Women of Color feminists such as bell hooks, Cherríe Moraga, and Gloria Anzaldúa. While Beal and the other TWWA members named sexism as one of the interlocking oppressive structures they set out to contest, hooks, Moraga, and Anzaldúa helped Davis to see that the intersectional political commitment of TWWA was in fact a *feminist* one all along. It was these conversations, alongside the publication of seminal intersectional feminist texts (such as hooks's book, *Ain't I a Woman*; Moraga and Anzaldúa's edited anthology, *This Bridge Called My Back*; and Gloria Joseph and Jill Lewis's coauthored conversational text, *Common Differences: Conflicts in Black and White Feminist Perspectives*), and the amazing conferences that took place in the early 1980s (such as the 1981 NWSA conference), Davis recounts, that "set" the "scene" and the "framework" for this incredibly "productive, generative period," one that would gift us a version of feminism that was truly intersectional (Davis 2016).

In line with Davis's accounting of this exceptionally generative period, this book has argued that contemporary activist-theorists have much to learn from early US Women of Color coalitional feminism. Here, I would like to situate their innovative concepts and renderings of power, identity, collective politics, political consciousness, and activist scholarship in relation to our present-day struggles as well as to future and unimagined social justice struggles. As I do so, I intentionally texture my "takeaways" with the most recent thoughts, views, and reflections of some of our earliest US Women of Color coalition feminist theorists, alongside more contemporary theorists, as given to us in a handful of recent written and spoken spaces: María Lugones and Cricket Keating's coauthored forthcoming book, *Educating for Coalition*, alongside Keating's 2005 "Building Coalitional Consciousness" article; numerous interviews and op-ed pieces by Barbara Smith, Zillah Eisenstein, and Keeanga-Yamahtta Taylor; and the *Feminist Freedom Warriors* (FFW) video digital archive interviews conducted by Mohanty and Carty (beginning in 2015) and featuring Minnie Bruce Pratt, Linda Martín Alcoff, Eisenstein, Smith, Davis, and Moraga, among others. By *thinking with* these important Women of Color coalition feminists, I seek to get several things straight in relation to what feminism must mean in our contemporary moment and how we might best organize, both within and outside of the academy, for intersectional social justice.

Turning Back to Move Forward

Yes, my friends, this is called a coalition of conscience, but what it really is and what it really needs to be is a coalition of confrontation ... against the policies and the philosophies and the personalities of the Reagan Administration [and]

President Reagan's regulatory and fiscal karate chops.... We've got to once again ... become angry enough to rise up in righteous indignation and say we have to move in another kind of direction.
—SHIRLEY CHISHOLM, "A Coalition of Conscience"

When I came back to the Combahee Statement, in the aftermath of the Ferguson uprising, I saw that its politics had the potential to make a way out of what felt like no way. ... I read it as a powerful intervention for the left as a whole. In a political moment when futile arguments claimed to pit race against class, and identity politics against mass movements, the C.R.C. showed how to understand the relationship between race, class, and gender through the actual experiences of Black women.... Black women were at the helm of the growing Black Lives Matter movement, and they, too, were gravitating to the politics of the C.R.C. Smith told me, "Many of the people in the Movement for Black Lives absolutely acknowledge that they are inspired by the politics of the Combahee River Collective and by the feminism of women of color, not just Black women." She was thinking of Audre Lorde, June Jordan, and Cheryl Clarke, and of the pioneering Chicana activists Cherríe Moraga and Gloria Anzaldúa.... She added, "One of the signs to me that feminist-of-color politics are influencing this moment is the multiracial, multiethnic diversity—and not just racial and ethnic, but every kind of diversity—of the people who are in the streets now. That's right out of the Black feminist playbook."
—KEEANGA-YAMAHTTA TAYLOR, "Until Black Women Are Free, None of Us Will Be Free"

The connection between the impetus for Chisholm's "coalition of conscience" in 1983 and more recent calls for intersectional social justice movements—such as Black Lives Matter (BLM)—shaping our contemporary moment could not be clearer. As I argued in the introduction, the backlash to the progressive gains of the movements of the 1960s and 1970s embodied in President Ronald Reagan's candidacy and policy agenda in the 1980s bears a striking resemblance to the backlash we have witnessed since the election of President Barack Obama, culminating in the successful candidacy of President Donald Trump, an openly racist, misogynist, ableist, trans- and homophobic, ethnocentric, capitalist millionaire with a penchant for refusing to pay his workers. Trump's stinginess in relation to paying fair, or even any, wages to (mostly) working-class immigrants also shaped his policy agenda, wherein he enthusiastically cut programs that support working-class and poor Americans to benefit the richest among us, that is until a devastating global pandemic presented an opportunity to send relief checks with his name (brand) on it, no doubt a calculated campaign stunt in the months leading up to the 2020 presidential election. While Reagan's economic policies were forthright in their attack on the social safety net and welfare programs geared toward helping working-class and poor Americans, his racist and misogynist intentions were more covert. While Trump's brazen racism and misogyny might distinguish our contemporary moment from the 1980s, the synergies must not be overlooked. The wholesale attack on progressive change, both materially and culturally, ought to now, as Chisholm hoped it would in the 1980s, unite the Left not just against Trump, the person, but against the fiscal and cultural backlash to progressive change that his presidency symbolized and reinforced.

In the same way that Chisholm called for a coalition of "conscience," the Left today also needs progressive coalitional activism rooted in shared and unwavering *political* commitments. We need, as Taylor and Smith both attest in the above epigraph, movements such as BLM. We need a coalition of this kind not only because it is led by women of color who expressly name the politics of Combahee as a source of inspiration but also because this movement has never been a single-issue movement. What Taylor and Smith both see as hopeful in the politics of BLM is its intersectional diversity, its ability to summon "every kind of diversity" to the streets. Indeed, most of the activist-theorists engaged in these concluding remarks speak to the promise of BLM, and especially to their intersectional political commitments and how such commitments might shape collective organizing.

When asked by Carty in her *FFW* interview in 2015 what impact she believes her work has had, Pratt seems to regret the continued relevance of her 1984 essay, "Identity: Skin Blood Heart." She tells Carty and Mohanty: "I'm glad that it's still useful, and I also wish that it weren't still useful. I wish that it had fulfilled its historical task, and then we were able to go on to other tasks" (Pratt 2015). Pratt is aware that her work on how to be a white anti-racist intersectional feminist costruggler is still very relevant to activist work today. Indeed, she goes on to note how encouraged she is by BLM's presence, remarking that her essay might have something to offer contemporary BLM anti-racists and especially white anti-racist coconspirators (Pratt 2015). I'm purposefully avoiding the word "ally" in light of Eisenstein's astute observation that "ally" does not fully capture the extent of her own commitment. Instead, Eisenstein names herself an "anti-racist sister/comrade, freedom fighter" in "this struggle to finally up-end white supremacy's gendered racist abuse of all" (Eisenstein 2016). When speaking at a virtual event hosted at City University of New York's Brooklyn College on

April 9, 2021, Smith similarly resisted the language of ally, opting instead for that of "coconspirator." Coconspirator, costruggler, comrade in struggle, and co-freedom fighter all seem to capture the sense of "accomplice" brought forward by *Indigenous Action Media* and discussed in chapter 5 insofar as they all suggest that organizers must move beyond sympathizers to true participants who are "complicit in a struggle toward liberation" and "accountable" to each other (Presley and Presswood 2018, 67). I believe it is precisely this sense of accomplice, coconspirator, and comrade that Pratt is speaking to when noting the unfortunate relevance of her 1984 essay. For better or worse, the ideas presented there, forged in the late 1970s and early 1980s while in conversation with "women of color within feminism or Women's Liberation" (Pratt 2015), are still highly relevant to the "how-to" of contemporary intersectional coalitional activism, the very activism, Pratt and many others note, that BLM is attempting.

As Smith put it when speaking to one of the Women's March on Washington (WMW) organizers (Amy Sonnie) in July 2020, despite the fact that BLM was led by a group of queer women of color, their focus of organizing was never singularly focused on gender or sexuality issues; instead, they organized to contest mass incarceration, police brutality, and other issues, while also resisting the notion of a "charismatic" leader (Smith, Breedlove, and Sonnie 2020). BLM has thus avoided the ontological entrapment that beset the WMW by centering a *political commitment* rather than an identity. It is not just about defining the identity "Blackness"—although surely this is also part of the project—it is about adopting a political commitment to exposing and contesting intersectional oppressive forces and to naming at least one of these forces "white supremacy."

When asked by Amy Goodman in a *Democracy Now!* interview on February 12, 2020, what "advice" Smith has for "young activists" today, Smith's response is telling: "Work in coalition," she urges (Goodman 2020a). "Avoid being immersed in your own particular experiences," she implores them, so that you might see the "wider arc to work for social justice" (Goodman 2020a). As she attests in her FFW interview, young activists ought to return specifically to the politico-ethical coalition politics of Bernice Johnson Reagon (B. Smith 2016). Smith advises them to seek out savvy coconspirators who have learned how to see their social justice struggle as part of a bigger struggle and who have learned how to team up with others to dismantle the many-headed monster of oppression. She implores them to "take the risk" of joining in coalitions on the ground where they live, of "stretching" and working for social justice across the board, while also advising them to maintain a "home" somewhere so that they might get the nurturing they need to effectively engage in the dangerous work of coalition politics (Goodman 2020a).

When asked in the WMW interview months later what reading list she might offer to young feminist activists, she tells them that if there is one single text that contemporary feminist activists must all read it would be Reagon's 1981 coalition speech (Smith, Breedlove, and Sonnie 2020), intentionally placed at the very end of Smith's (1983a) edited anthology, *Home Girls*, due to its relevance not only to feminist organizing in the 1980s but also (clearly) to future and unimagined feminist struggles. And if we recall the key features of coalition politics espoused in that brilliant speech—the emphasis on centering political commitment or principles above all else, the emphasis on struggle, the emphasis on turning our political commitments in on ourselves to ensure that we are not unwittingly reinforcing oppressive structures within our activist spaces, the emphasis on the danger and riskiness of coalition politics, and the importance of existential transformation as part and parcel of coalitional activism—we find these very same features peppered across recent comments by the feminist theorists referenced here. I would like to end by highlighting just a few of these central messages and by reframing them as urgent recommendations for current and future activists.

While I draw on recent work by some of the primary coalition theorists referenced throughout this book to texture these concluding remarks (in this sense, I continue to *think with* this evolving conversation), and while I believe that at least some of these authors will likely agree with the forcefulness in my formulations (emphasizing what contemporary feminism *demands* and *must do*), these takeaways are ultimately my own and therefore not meant to outline a prescriptive agenda from US Women of Color coalitional feminism. Born of the experience of traveling with these texts over the pages of this book, I offer these suggestions in the spirit of politico-ethical encounter. While my political commitments will be unabashed in their presentation, I look forward to revisiting the specific suggestions and even radically rethinking them in generative conversation with feminist coconspirators.

Contemporary Feminism Must Be *Intersectional Feminism!*

The reason racism is a feminist issue is easily explained by the inherent definition of feminism. Feminism is the political theory and practice to free *all* women: women of color, working-class women, poor women, physically challenged women, lesbians, old women, as well as white economically privileged heterosexual women. Anything less than this is not feminism, but merely female self-aggrandizement.

—BARBARA SMITH, "Racism and Women's Studies"

Feminism is the struggle to end sexist oppression. Therefore, it is necessarily a struggle to eradicate the ideology of domination that permeates Western culture on various levels, as well as a commitment to reorganizing society so that the self-development of people can take precedence over imperialism, economic expansion, and material desires.

—BELL HOOKS, *Feminist Theory: From Margin to Center*

If the white [women's] groups do not realize that they are in fact, fighting capitalism and racism, we do not have common bonds. If they do not realize that the reasons for their condition lie in a debilitating economic and social system, and not simply that men get a vicarious pleasure out of "consuming their bodies for exploitative reasons" . . . then we cannot unite with them around common grievances.

—FRANCES BEAL, "Double Jeopardy: To Be Black and Female"

Perhaps *the* most valuable lesson from early US Women of Color coalitional feminism—valuable precisely because of how often this insight is overlooked, or blatantly refused, in contemporary feminist circles—is their unabashed willingness to draw *political* lines in the sand. As the epigraphs by Smith, hooks, and Beal help us see, contemporary feminism is, and *must be*, intersectional! Quite simply, feminism is a political commitment to eradicating the intersectional oppressive forces that thwart the liberation of *all* people, especially women. Borrowing from Flavia Dzodan, Sara Ahmed succinctly puts it in *Living a Feminist Life*, "Feminism will be intersectional 'or it will be bullshit'" (Ahmed 2017, 5). Its value, as Davis argued in her FFW interview, rests precisely in its ability to produce "broad" and "flexible" frameworks for capturing interlocking oppressions (Davis 2016). It "helps us to see," Smith asserts, "that we cannot address one roadblock to freedom without addressing all" (Goodman 2020b). Thus, and let me be quite clear here, advocating feminism necessarily implies a critical orientation not just toward hetero-patriarchy but also toward capitalism, toward white supremacy, toward neoliberalism, and toward imperialism.

As we learned in chapter 1, Combahee's political roots were always *socialist* at their core, and this firm anticapitalist commitment was fully compatible with and was the very basis for their intersectional feminist platform. No "crisis" of post-Marxist Left-oriented politics here! Smith has reasserted this point in numerous interviews since the publication of Taylor's 2017 book on the Combahee cofounders. Combahee's "Black Feminist Statement," Smith reminds her audience whenever asked to speak about her work with Combahee, was originally solicited by Eisenstein (1978) to be included in her anthology, *Capitalist Patriarchy and the Case for Socialist Feminism*. Its usefulness to activists today, Smith contends, rests precisely in its *anticapitalist* moorings and its *material understanding* of what is going on (Smith, Breedlove, and Sonnie 2020).

Similarly, in Taylor's (2020b) recent *New Yorker* piece on Alicia Garza's book *The Purpose of Power: How We Come Together When We Fall Apart*, it is hard not to read Taylor's commentary on the BLM cofounder's "sparing" treatment of capitalism as a potential weakness not only of Garza's book but also of contemporary social justice movements that remain divorced from anticapitalist political orientations. Taylor astutely notes that regardless of its absence in Garza's book, capitalism has clearly "helped to constitute much of the misery that [Garza] has spent her adult life organizing against" (Taylor 2020b). It is precisely the reality of interlocking oppressions, Taylor attests, that necessitates the very mass movement tactics that define BLM activism. What most troubles Taylor is Garza's suggestion that it is time for BLM to shift attention toward gaining political power through electoral victories rather than through mass movements in the streets. I therefore read Taylor's article as a cautionary one, imploring Garza and the many BLM activists and coconspirators out there to continue with mass movement struggle anchored in anticapitalist orientations.

Feminist Candidates Must Advocate for Intersectional Feminism!

You know one of the things that I . . . was reminded of, about how [for] white women, it's still single-issue feminism. . . . They wouldn't vote for Bernie because [Hillary's] a woman. Some feminists I very much respect, they still say I'll take her over Bernie. . . . And I would say that's a limitation of your feminism.
—CHERRÍE MORAGA, *Feminist Freedom Warriors* interview

And while I am at it: can we recognize that it is not enough for a Democratic candidate to be female; or Black or Brown—they must have policy commitments to END white supremacy and economic suffering and sexual violence. . . . Let us build movements to assist this process. Revolutionary acts are never simply individual.

—ZILLAH EISENSTEIN, "Why March?: Women's March/es till Trump Is Gone"

Learning that feminists she deeply respected supported Hillary Clinton over Bernie Sanders in 2016, simply because Clinton is a woman, revealed to Moraga the severe limitations of what she calls "single-issue feminism." What it further reveals to me and to Eisenstein, as reflected in the epigraph above, is that if and when feminists choose to engage in electoral politics, we must move beyond a politics of presence—the notion that adding minority and marginalized faces to political decision-making spaces will *necessarily* produce the progressive policy changes needed to alleviate the intersecting forms of oppression suffered by those who share one or more of the identities of the newly elected representatives. Instead, the focus needs to be on our candidate's political commitments (what they "advocate," in hooks's sense of the word), not the identities they wear, and these commitments must be to *intersectional* feminism. Thus, another lesson gleaned from recent comments by Eisenstein, Smith, Moraga, and Taylor is that for those who choose to participate in electoral politics, advocating intersectional feminism also means supporting intersectional feminist candidates. In other words, it means naming Sanders, not Clinton (or Joe Biden), as our "feminist" candidate. The message is clear: the critique of capitalism—which is instrumental to any intersectional feminist platform—must not be sacrificed when engaging in electoral politics.

As Smith put it in a *Guardian* op-ed piece on February 10, 2020, "I am supporting Bernie Sanders for president because I believe that his campaign and his understanding of politics compliments the priorities that women of color defined decades ago" (B. Smith 2020). Some of these priorities include his enduring (since the civil rights movement in the 1960s) commitment to fighting for racial justice and his appreciation of the importance of mass-based social justice movements, as captured in his promise to be "organizer-in-chief" if elected president. To those who have questioned Sanders's concern for "the specific ways that people with varying intersecting identities experience oppression," Smith replies, "As a black lesbian feminist who has been out since the mid-seventies, I believe that, among all the candidates, his leadership offers us the best chance to eradicate the unique injustices that marginalized groups in America endure" (B. Smith 2020). In addition to noting that Sanders's anti-racist commitments have been enduring since he was a young activist, and in response to those, including Angela Davis, who questioned Sanders's intersectional commitments back in 2016 (Davis and Taylor 2016), Smith points out that Sanders modified his

2020 campaign rhetoric and some aspects of his platform, inspiring Women of Color feminist surrogates such as Nina Turner, Alexandria Ocasio-Cortez, Ilhan Omar, Barbara Smith, and Keeanga-Yamahtta Taylor to help relay the deeply intersectional commitments at the heart of his platform. In one of many op-eds on Sanders, Taylor helps us see that those who attest that Sanders does not talk enough about racism have "underestimate[ed] the economic dimensions of racial oppression in the United States." She reminds us that when Sanders attacks the "oligarchs of the Walmart Empire, this is unmistakably confronting the overlapping issue of racism and class exploitation"—Walmart after all is the largest private employer of African Americans (K.-Y. Taylor 2019). In her *Hear the Bern* interview in 2020, Taylor further exposes the myth that socialism is a white person's thing. As she reminds us there, the Black Panther Party was an avowed socialist organization, and it was one of the largest political organizations of the twentieth century (K.-Y. Taylor 2020a).

Such forthright endorsements of Sanders by Smith and Taylor call into question "single-issue feminism" and recenter the interlocking nature of capitalism, white supremacy, and hetero-patriarchy. Political commitments matter! The identities worn by our candidates are less important than the political commitments they hold. Building intersectional social justice movements also matters. Revolutionary change, as Eisenstein reminds us, will never be individual. We are not looking for star politicians; we are looking for unwavering political commitments to radical and progressive change, because that is what is needed to dislodge the intermeshing forms of oppression that so many are suffering under.

Contemporary Feminism Must Center Political Commitment and Struggle!

We can't be afraid to establish a base that is larger than the people we feel comfortable with. . . . We have to reach beyond the choir and take seriously the task of organizing the unorganized.
—ALICIA GARZA, quoted in Keeanga-Yamahtta Taylor, "A Black Lives Matter Founder on Building Modern Movements"

Instead of working with people on the basis of shared victimization and oppression, we may instead work with people on the basis of shared resistance to oppression.
—MARÍA LUGONES AND CRICKET KEATING, *Educating for Coalition: Popular Education and Contemporary Political Praxis*

It is precisely the centering of political commitment—of "conscience," as Chisholm puts it—that is sorely needed in our contemporary moment, especially as misunderstandings about both identity politics and intersectionality circulate in the academy and among activists. Both Smith (2020) and Taylor (2020b) lament the distortion of Combahee's central insights in relation to these concepts. To get these concepts straight, they implore us to return to groundbreaking works by US Women of Color feminists writing in the 1970s and 1980s. As Smith has gone to great lengths to clarify in almost all of the interviews she has done in the past few years, when she and the other cofounders of Combahee originally conceived of it, labeling their politics "identity politics" simply meant that as Black women, they had a "right to determine their own political agenda" and that this agenda would come out of their identities. This was significant because at the time it was not accepted (either by Black male liberation activists or white women's liberation activists) that Black women had their own, valuable perspective (Goodman 2020a). The point for Smith and other early intersectional activists such as Pratt, Eisenstein, Alcoff, Lugones, and Mohanty and for contemporary coconspirators such as Taylor and Keating is that political consciousness is born out of one's position vis-à-vis oppression, especially when one engages in dialogic analysis with others. The "whole point of looking at the particularity of Black women's oppression," Taylor reminds us in her *Hear the Bern* interview, is to "gain insight into really the depths of oppression and exploitation in capitalist society and U.S. society" (K.-Y. Taylor 2020a).

Intersectionality is best thought of as an analytic for naming interlocking and mutually reinforcing systems of oppression. Identity is relevant in this endeavor only insofar as one's position vis-à-vis oppression will, and should, inform one's rendering of the system of interlocking oppressions and therefore also one's political agenda for contesting this multifaceted system. As Mohanty succinctly puts it in the *FFW* interview, "To me sometimes it doesn't even matter what the hell your identity is—what's the issue that we are organized around" (quoted in Alcoff, Mohanty, and Carty 2015). As Smith similarly attests in her *FFW* interview, it is about gaining a "deeper understanding of how power and oppression are connected so you know what you should be struggling for and who you should be aligned with. I always talk about how I connect with people whose politics I share, as opposed to people whose identities I share" (B. Smith 2016). Smith helps us see that while contemporary feminism must be *intersectional* feminism, such a feminism invites, indeed it welcomes, coconspirators who share our political commitments, even if such costrugglers arrive at these political commitments through unexpected pathways. Lori Marso's work on Simone de Beauvoir is exemplary here (see Marso 2006, 2017). When we come together based on shared principles or political commitments, and especially when these commitments are intersectional social justice commitments, we are truly poised to pose a danger to the status quo and the powers that be.

Indeed, in the same way that "working-class white women were down with the Black Panthers" in the heyday of civil and women's rights, and tenant farmer unions formed in the South between whites and Blacks, Smith urges contemporary feminist audiences to learn from the form of *intersectional* coalitional activism that *did* occur in the 1960s and 1970s, and to note the role that shared political commitment and collective struggle played in these alliances. She recalls these lessons by way of trying to dissuade young activists from eschewing coalitional opportunities with white women. "Simplistic anti-whiteness," she reminds them, "erases history.... I don't see that simplistic way about looking at things," she continues, "I'm about struggle" (quoted in Smith, Breedlove, and Sonnie 2020). As Taylor similarly recalls, the Black Panther Party argued for a politics of interracial solidarity: "We don't hate white people, we hate capitalism" (Taylor 2020b). When we make it about political commitment, when we, as Reagon urges, turn the century with our "principles intact" (Reagon 1983, 349), we have the chance of making real progressive change. It is precisely the very real possibility of such radical change that mobilizes the political establishment and the military state so mightily against it. "And what happened to them?" Taylor asks in reference to the Black Panther Party. "They were murdered. Or they were hectored into exile. And that wasn't just for the purpose of revenge, it was because it was necessary to bury the legacy of that particular kind of political radicalism" (Taylor 2020b). Taylor notes that we are now living with the consequences of this onslaught against the Left, specifically against the principles and savvy coalitional tactics of interracial collaboration.

We find ourselves today at a pivotal moment of heightened and overt forms of bigoted hatred politics (we can thank Donald Trump for this) and entrenched structural inequity (we can thank decades of bipartisan support for varying versions of Reaganomics for this), emboldened by a neoliberal philosophy and its corresponding capitalist structure that renders many folks even worse off now than they were in the height of 1960s radicalism. Though the intersectional oppressive forces may seem more powerful than ever, I find it encouraging that young activists today are in generative conversation with veteran comrades in struggle such as Smith, Pratt, Beal, Lugones,

Alcoff, Mohanty, Moraga, Eisenstein, Carty, Taylor, and Keating, among many others. They are inviting some of these coconspirators to come speak at events, they are running out and reading (for some, rereading) their written words, and they are referencing their concepts and tactics when articulating their own visions of intersectional coalitional activism (I think here of the WMW's unity principles, the references to Combahee among BLM activists, and the numerous references to Lugones and Audre Lorde that appear in manifestos written by students in my Feminism in Coalition class when asked to engage in a semester-long intersectional social justice coalition simulation).[1] As young activists struggle with the challenges of collective politics across intractable difference, they are encouragingly turning to and building on the politico-ethical basis of early US Women of Color coalitional feminism.

Contemporary Feminists Must Trust *in Dialectical Materialism,* Embrace *Dialogic Analysis, and* Prepare *for Existential Transformation!*

Lived experience of oppression does not, alone, constitute radical politics.... Experiencing oppression is not nearly the same as knowing what to do about it. That comes from history, politics, and, ultimately, organizing.
—KEEANGA-YAMAHTTA TAYLOR, "A Black Lives Matter Founder on Building Movements"

While sexual violence and intimidation have escalated under neoliberalism, the resistance to it has now been mobilized, nationally and internationally. Similarly, poverty and unequal wages now unites restaurant workers and teachers and most wage-earning women into a newly shared class-consciousness, often global. *Our lives continue to radicalize us.*
—ZILLAH EISENSTEIN, "The Making of a New Anti-racist Feminist Working Class"

And one of the things I understood as I was doing anti-racist work, was how profoundly my imagination has been distorted by white supremacy.... what does it mean to be a writer, and this is your tool, and it's contaminated. It's polluted. You know, your tool is damaged—by racism. And that certainly was true of my imagination. My language, my vocabulary, my images, my metaphors, my idea of what human beings were, everything, everything. And so for me, anti-racist work has been organizing and it's also been—being demanding of myself in relation to my writing that I not replicate that white supremacy in how I do my work. How I do my writing and the only way that has changed ...

is in collective work, in actual on the ground work, with people of color, women of color, anti-racist white people, with people who are opposed to capitalism, opposed to profiting off of other people's labor and bodies.... So it wasn't imagination that made it happen, individually. It was collective imagination. Collective hope, and also the springing from moment to moment of collective work.

—MINNIE BRUCE PRATT, *Feminist Freedom Warriors* interview

In such coalitions, the possibility of self and collective transformation is at the heart of why we form groups with one another. We come together not only to pool our collective resources in a mutual fight against oppression but also, and perhaps more powerfully in terms of long-lasting change, to transform ourselves and our relationships with each other, recognizing that our own understandings and potential enactments of our lives are deeply tied to one another and to the meanings that we create together.

—MARÍA LUGONES AND CRICKET KEATING, *Educating for Coalition: Popular Education and Contemporary Political Praxis*

The cotheorizing that Keating and Lugones have undertaken helps us to see that one of the most generative strategies coming out of US Women of Color coalitional feminism is its attention to *dialogic* analysis, something that is done collectively, wherein costrugglers come to know one another in their multiplicity as they collectively map diffuse, interconnected, and mobile powers and resistances.[2] Keating's 2005 article on coalitional consciousness-building and Keating and Lugones's forthcoming book on educating for coalition together offer critical insight on the practical "how-to" of dialogic analysis, which I and they both attest, is the very basis of *politico-ethical* coalitional activism.

As indicated in the name Keating gives to step one of dialogic analysis, "locating experience," intersectional coalitional activism is anchored in an epistemological project, not an ontological one (Keating 2005, 95). It thus resists facile appeals to experience as sacrosanct; the emphasis here is on dialogic analysis, not just existing. Keating concurs with Mohanty that "experience must be *historically interpreted and theorized* if is to become the basis of feminist solidarity and struggle" (quoted in Keating 2005, 95; my emphasis). As Taylor, Lugones, and Keating all indicate, as reflected in the epigraphs above, lived experience of oppression must be analyzed in conversation with others, both in history and in the present struggle, to constitute a radical politics. As Moraga similarly insists in her FFW interview, it must be done together, "it can't happen when you do it alone" (quoted in Moraga 2017). As Pratt's epigraph also recounts, the way she was ultimately able to reform her "contaminated" tool was *in conversation* with women of color, people of color, anti-racist white people, and people who were opposed to capitalism, who called her on her racist imaginary—her language, her vocabulary, her images, her metaphors, and her ideas were all polluted by racism. Heeding Eisenstein's (2017) advice and reflecting the ethical dimension of politico-ethical coalitional activism, Pratt uses these encounters as opportunities for growth, as invitations to embrace existential transformation, a transformation of her entire imaginary up until that point.

Utilizing experience in a coalitional project thus requires an "interrogative structure that could be usefully brought to bear on a particular experience articulated in a coalitional consciousness-building group" (Keating 2005, 95). Thus, step one involves collectively sharing experiences of confronting oppressive structures from our different situated localities *and* asking one another critical questions that might reveal multiple and complex systems of power at play in our shared stories. "How is your experience marked by your own and others' particular racial, sexual national, class, or other context?" and, "Whose interests are served and whose are not by the ways that you and others are/were racialized/gendered/classed/sexualized in the experience?" are two such questions that might aid in this process (Keating 2005, 95). As Eisenstein, Smith, Mohanty, and Pratt all attest in the FFW interviews, we ought to *trust in dialectical materialism*. Echoing the notion of dialectical materialism developed in chapter 1 by thinking with Rosa Luxemburg and a genealogy of US Women of Color feminism, we must have faith in the truth that our lived experiences of struggle can and will "radicalize us," especially if we engage in dialogical analysis of these experiences. It is this truth that keeps Smith (Smith, Breedlove, and Sonnie 2020), Alcoff (2015), Pratt (2015), and Eisenstein (2016) optimistic. Theirs, however, is not a naive optimism. As they and Lugones and Keating help us see, radicalization comes in and through dialogue and collective struggle.

As Keating outlines it, step two, "seeing resistance to multiple oppressions," is focused on using the experiences shared in step one, including the critical questions raised and answered, to collectively see both power and resistance to power. During this step, Keating draws on Lugones's concept of witnessing "faithfully" (Lugones 2003, 7). Mobilizing this concept, Keating argues that during this step, participants will "develop their capacity for faithful witnessing by looking for and analyzing resistance in their own and each other's experiences" (Keating 2005, 97). Thus, in this step, the group transitions from sharing experiences to collectively *analyzing* their experiences. However, rather than orienting their analysis toward searching for commonalities in their experiences (as was typical of the consciousness-raising groups in the women's liberation movement), they orient their analysis toward the important and valuable differences they bring to the group. Among other things, these differences can underscore the "multiplicity of relational hierarchies of power" that might situate them simultaneously as "oppressors" and the "oppressed" and might reveal subtle practices of resistance enacted by both "oppressors" and the "oppressed" (Keating 2005, 97). Such positionalities—those of the "oppressor" and the "oppressed"—however, would be treated as transient and layered insofar as the analysis undertaken here amounts to Lugones's concept of "'world'-traveling" or situating ourselves in the map of power by not only traveling across our own multiple selves and experiences but also by, as Pratt and others have done, traveling to others' worlds and others' complex webs of power and considering how our worlds overlap and interact (Lugones 2003, 16–20, 77–98). In such journeys, white women would be wise to follow Eisenstein in embracing voices of critique by women of color as opportunities for growth rather than as condemnations. This of course is the very essence of politico-*ethical* coalition politics. Such an exercise, Keating argues, would help us "to develop a keen eye for both the intersection of different relations of power and the way power moves through our lives to both enable and constrain resistance as well as to enforce or forbid particular interpretations of resistance" (Keating 2005, 97).

The final step, "coalitional risk-taking," involves collectively interrogating "the possibilities for coalitional action" by being willing to "risk" our ground (Keating 2005, 98; see also Lugones 2003, 96). Recalling Reagon's attention to the hard work of coalescing, Keating writes that this process asks us to be willing to enter into potentially uncomfortable spaces, uncomfortable for a woman of color because she might be entering into a space where she might experience betrayal from her coalitional coconspirators, uncomfortable for a white woman because of the challenge of being called on and learning how to consistently reject her privilege (Keating 2005, 99). Such uncomfortable and risky encounters, she insists, are necessary for the sake of the dialogic analysis undertaken in intersectional coalitional activism insofar as they might reveal complex power structures and potential sites of collective and individual resistance.

As Eisenstein puts it when reflecting on what advice Lorde and Luxemburg might give contemporary WMW activists, "Following Audre and Rosa 'we' need to imagine beyond what feels like possibility. We need to mobilize our different movements of so many differing voices into a risk-taking set of actions" (Eisenstein 2017). As Smith similarly attests, this work has never been, and never will be, easy. But, with an "open heart and an open mind," it might just lead to transformation (B. Smith 2016). Reflecting on the meaning and impact of intersectionality and identity politics, Smith helps us to see the fruition of such transformation. It was only after years of BLM organizing, she attests—years of raising collective consciousness, offering society the language, terminology, and analysis to make sense of what news pundits and politicians are now regularly referring to as "structural" or "systemic" racism and "white supremacy"—that we were ready in the late spring of 2020 to make sense of George Floyd's public lynching (Smith, Breedlove, and Sonnie 2020). It was no doubt in part because of the protests that continued for months in the wake of his execution that just shy of a year later, the police officer that murdered Floyd was found guilty of all three charges (second-degree murder, third-degree murder, and second-degree manslaughter). So, yes, I concur with Smith. The movement of BLM gave us the language, the terminology, and the analysis to make sense of what happened to Floyd; it also, importantly, created the kind of groundswell needed to finally affirm that, at least in this instance, a Black life mattered.

Contemporary Feminism Demands Coalitional Theory Making!

I always see it as a collective process. And even things that I've done, like the book that I wrote in 1981, *Women, Race, and Class*, a lot of those ideas came from my activism and came from my community.
—ANGELA DAVIS, *Feminist Freedom Warriors* interview

The dissolving of the systemic analyses of women of color and transnational feminist projects into purely discursive (representational) analyses of ruptures, fluidity, and discontinuities symptomatic of poststructural critique contributes to a threshold of disappearance of materialist antiracist feminist projects that target the state and other governing institutions ... this danger of the appropriation of radical women of color and transnational feminist projects ... should be of deep concern to us all.
—CHANDRA MOHANTY, "Transnational Feminist Crossings: On Neoliberalism and Radical Critique"

Feminism is at stake in how we generate knowledge; in how we write, in who we cite. I think of feminism as a building project: if our texts are worlds, they need to be made out of feminist materials.... Feminism goes wherever we go. If not, we are not. We thus enact feminism in how we relate to the academy....

Citation is feminist memory. Citation is how we acknowledge our debt to those who came before; those who helped us find our way when the way was obscured because we deviated from the paths we were told to follow.

—SARA AHMED, *Living a Feminist Life*

Knowledge is not something "given" from one person to another, instead it is something that people create together.

—MARÍA LUGONES AND CRICKET KEATING, *Educating for Coalition: Popular Education and Contemporary Political Praxis*

In line with the notion of *coalitional scholarship* gifted to us in *This Bridge Called My Back* and discussed in chapter 4, contemporary feminism must reassert its commitment to coalitional theory making. Doing so will help us to avoid the depoliticization of theory that Mohanty speaks to in the epigraph provided above. Building from the notion of coalitional scholarship and textured by recent comments by our primary theorists, coalitional theory making involves several things.

Think with activist-theorists. This necessarily means that we must trust in dialectical materialism. Theory making can and will happen in coalitional spaces, among those engaged in dialogic analysis; so, learn from these spaces, trust in these spaces, listen to what is emerging out of these spaces, and anchor theory in these spaces! In practical terms, this means to pass the theory mic to those engaged in active struggle, to those organizing for intersectional social justice. As Mohanty urges us to ponder when considering the danger in letting neoliberal ideology infiltrate the academy:

> What would it mean to be attentive to the politics of activist feminist communities in different sites in the global South and North as they imagine and create cross-border feminist solidarities anchored in struggles on the ground? How would academic feminist projects be changed if we were accountable to activist/academic communities[?] ... I believe we need to return to the radical feminist politics of the contextual as both local and structural and to the collectivity that is being defined out of existence by privatization projects. I think we need to recommit to insurgent knowledges and the complex politics of antiracist, anti-imperialist feminisms. (Mohanty 2013, 987)

I could not agree more. Let's recommit to "insurgent" knowledges and acknowledge that it is precisely these knowledges and within these spaces (spaces of struggle on the ground) that the most fruitful and sophisticated "theory" develops. Scholars within the "academy" ought to think with activists, ought to become activist-theorists themselves. We ought to, as Keating and Lugones are doing in their forthcoming book, generate theory collectively and out of spaces such as the popular education collective in northern New Mexico, La Escuela Popular Norteña (EPN), of which they were both participants. In those instances wherein you do not find yourself coalescing with activists on the ground and forging theory together there, you can still engage in coalitional theory making by elevating those voices on the ground, by being accountable to those voices (citing those voices!), by thinking with, rather than appropriating, their insights.

Engage in coalitional scholarship through anthology and other forms of coauthorship. Instead of writing about coalitional groups as researcher, write *with* coalitional actors; coauthor with them, cotheorize with them, much in the way that Richa Nagar did with the Sangtin Writers in *Playing with Fire* (discussed in chapter 4), or the way in which Keating and Lugones are doing with the members of EPN, and the way that Mohanty and Carty recently did in their *Feminist Freedom Warriors* digital video archive and 2019 book. While my journey with early US Women of Color feminists has certainly taught me that the best scholarship will be coalitional and, in this sense, will likely be coauthored, they and other fellow travelers have also helped me to see that coalitional theory making can occur in single-authored texts. I think here of Chela Sandoval adopting the role of "secretary" in her "report" on the 1981 NWSA conference; I think here of how Lugones (2003) situates *Pilgrimages* and how and Mohanty (2003) situates *Feminism without Borders* as collectively forged; I think also of how they indebt their insights to other Women of Color feminist activist-theorists. On this front, I'm deeply encouraged by the work of Ahmed (2017), who is unabashed in her politics of citation and in her choice to elevate Women of Color coconspirators. I have attempted to do the same here in my insistence that early US Women of Color coalitional feminism is an incredibly rich resource for contemporary political theory making. In *thinking with* them, I have intentionally positioned them as my cotheorists, as my theory guides. Like Sandoval, I see my role as cartographer, engaged in the practice of mapping the brilliant insights of my primary coalition cotheorists. Though perhaps not in the concrete flesh, I have nevertheless attempted to *travel* with them in my reading of their texts and in my listening to their words from recent speeches, recorded interviews, and presentations.

Don't be afraid to assume the label of coalition theorist, but know that you are assuming it collectively. Anyone engaging in coalitional activism *is* a coalition theorist, period! I urge us to therefore resist Judith Butler's warning call around assuming the label of "coalition theorist." If one were to assume this label from what Lugones calls a "bird's-eye view" perspective, then this would be highly problematic. But, if this label is assumed collectively and from within the space of lived struggle, from what Lugones calls the "pedestrian" level, then it seems quite appropriate. No one person is *the* coalition theorist, the authority on coalitional activism, but we can all be cotheorists. As Ahmed has put it, "Feminism as a collective movement is made out of how we are moved to become feminist in dialogue with others" (2017, 5). Collectively analyzing and politicizing lived experience of oppression and resistance and using this as the basis of our coalitional activism is something all of us can do. *Thinking with* (and even deferring to) those activist-theorists who are situated at a more granular level than oneself in relation to the issue at hand is something we can all do. When we do this, we can theorize together.

Know that the act of citation is always a political act! As Ahmed makes clear, and as is reflected in the epigraph that began this section, whom you cite matters. We make political choices when we decide whom to cite. We must therefore ask ourselves, which voices will we choose to elevate through our citation practices? If work becomes "theory" because it "refers to other work that is known as theory," then we ought to be much more intentional about how we construct our "citational chains" (Ahmed 2017, 8). Who are the "theorists" to whom we are indebted in the construction of our concepts and our arguments? I have intentionally tried to disrupt what we might understand as the *political theory* citational chain by naming a range of US Women of Color coalition feminists as my primary cotheorists. In so doing, I have named texts that various political theory mentors have explicitly told me are not "real" political theory texts. I have intentionally published this book as a work of "political theory" (with a political theory press) to encourage the discipline to move away from such forms of shortsighted epistemic policing. As I have argued throughout this book, political theory is *better for* the sophisticated conceptual formulations gifted to us by the Women of Color feminist activist-theorists I have traveled with in these pages. I urge contemporary political theorists who have not yet done so to turn toward them instead of away from them.

Don't depoliticize theory! How you cite matters. I think of Lorde's "An Open Letter to Mary Daly" here. We must ask ourselves: Are you citing people's stories and experiences to authenticate your preformed theory? Are you depoliticizing other theorists' contributions by writing out what was most radical in their arguments? As Mohanty notes, this is precisely what happened to her 1986 article, "Under Western Eyes," as it got absorbed within a hegemonic intellectual culture of postmodernism, primarily by rewriting the materialist basis of the discursive analysis of power and the call for attentiveness to specificity, historicity, and difference among women in marginalized communities into what was described, oddly enough, as support for a theoretical and methodological emphasis on "the local" and "the particular"—hence, against all forms of generalization." This particular misreading of my work ignored the materialist emphasis on a "common context of struggle" … and undermined the possibility of solidarity across differences. (Mohanty 2013, 976–77)

As Mohanty relays here, the material and therefore also the political message of her work got written out through such misinterpretations. This helps us to appreciate that it is not just about whom you cite, it is about *how* you cite them, which is really about how you read them or, as Lorde pointed out in relation to Daly, *if* you actually read them on their own terms. Or, if you instead impose your terms on their words and ideas, which can result in appropriation and misrepresentation. My attempt to avoid such patterns is captured in my emphasis on "thinking with" the coalition theorists referenced throughout this book. Rather than cherry-picking their ideas to prove my claims, I have tried to think and travel with the texts engaged here. Although I may not have gotten it right every time, I have put some effort into thinking carefully and deeply with the brilliant coalition theorists appearing across these pages. The best coalition theory, I contend, is coming out of Women of Color feminism, so, turn toward it, not away from it! Simply to move in this direction is always a political act; if we then look for what is political, what is radial even, in their work, then we are moving in the direction of coalitional theory making.

Contemporary Feminists Ought to Experiment in Liberatory, Coalitional Pedagogy!

Central to popular education approaches to social change is a process of coming to critical consciousness through collective analysis and critique…. Popular education challenges [the] relationship between "organizers" and organized. In defining and working together towards social change, we need to take up the authority of our own knowledge, the authority of our voice, and move with it, changing our situation as we see fit, after taking distance to engage in collective critical and complex mutual understanding. In popular education, we turn towards each other to do this work, jointly constructing a vision for our future. We determine its direction.

—MARÍA LUGONES AND CRICKET KEATING, *Educating for Coalition: Popular Education and Contemporary Political Praxis*

The classroom remains the most radical space of possibility in the academy....
I celebrate teaching that enables transgressions—a movement against and beyond boundaries. It is that movement which makes education the practice of freedom.

—BELL HOOKS, *Teaching to Transgress: Education as the Practice of Freedom*

Building on the insights of Pratt, Lugones, Keating, and others in relation to the assertion that a coalitional consciousness can be taught or cultivated in people, I want to close by posing one final suggestion: when teaching about intersectional feminism, we ought to consider *how the practice of teaching might be recast as a coalitional exercise in and of itself.* Putting the politico-ethical understanding of coalition elaborated by early US Women of Color coalition feminists in conversation with Paulo Freire's (1970) understanding of praxis in *Pedagogy of the Oppressed* and bell hooks's (1994) elaboration of it in *Teaching to Transgress*, I am proposing that we experiment with what we might understand as *coalitional pedagogy*, which shares much in common with what Keating and Lugones (forthcoming) call "coalitional popular education." A true "praxis," Freire tells us, is invested in "reflection *and* action upon the world in order to transform it" (Freire 1970, 51). Thus, for action to constitute a genuine praxis, one's actions must also "become the object of critical reflection" (66). It is precisely this interplay between what I have called the politics and ethics of coalition—and what Freire calls the reflection and action of praxis—that might shape an understanding of coalitional pedagogy as a *feminist praxis*. Such a praxis might also infuse the lessons above on dialogic analysis, existential transformation, and co-alitional theory making insofar as it might treat the classroom itself as a site for collectively generating theory.

To say that a coalitional pedagogy is a feminist praxis is therefore to suggest that the professor infuses both action toward and reflection on undermining interlocking oppressive forces into the very design of the course and into her approach within the classroom space by (1) being explicit (and transparent) about the political commitments that have shaped the design of her courses, including the syllabi associated with them, remembering that when constructing her syllabi she is are creating the very "citational chains" that defines her discipline; (2) continuing to (as feminist scholars have often done) decenter the authority of canonical white, male voices in favor of highlighting the unique knowledge and tactical know-how of the oppressed, including the unique know-how of *students* in the classrooms who sit at the intersection of multiple oppressions; which might also lead her to (3) decentering the teacher-as-leader model to teaching in favor of pedagogical practices that emphasize "learning with" as opposed to "teaching for" students (Freire 1970) while also complicating the teacher-student hierarchy to reveal the variety of ways in which students and teacher move in and out of oppressive relationships; (4) remaining committed to a "problem-posing" (Freire 1970) approach to teaching about intersectional social justice that continuously "asks the other question" (Matsuda 1996) as a way to help students learn to dialogically map intersectional oppressions; (5) embracing and experimenting with exercises in "'world'-traveling" (Lugones 2003) as a necessary part of this mapping process; and (6) encouraging and providing space within the classroom for critical reflection on exercises in "'world'-traveling" so that both students and teacher might embrace the existential transformation that results from this process.

Though these suggestions are only tentative at this point, it seems incumbent upon us as feminist scholar-activists to move our thinking in such directions; that is, to play with new liberatory pedagogies and to be explicit and intentional in the liberatory interventions we seek to make in our classrooms. Like many of the early US Women of Color coalition feminists and contemporary coconspirators engaged in these concluding remarks, I remain optimistic in relation to what we might do and affect in our roles as feminist educators.

Notes

Introduction

1 See Shireen Roshanravan (2010, 2014, 2018), Erica Townsend-Bell (2012), Chandra Mohanty (2003), María Lugones (2003), Romand Coles (1996), Ashley Bohrer, (2019), Karma Chávez (2013), and Zein Murib (2018).

2 The TWWA first started organizing in the late 1960s in response to the marginalization members felt in the Student Nonviolent Coordinating Committee (SNCC) on account of their race and gender. First forming as the Black Women's Liberation Committee within SNCC, these members soon became their own independent group, called the Black Women's Alliance, which changed its name to the TWWA when expanding its membership to Latinas and Asian American women (Burnham 2001).

3 One explanation for this could be that the 2017 special issue was not de-voted to a self-identified moment of coalitional activism in the way that the CLASSE special issue was. Additionally, a number of the articles included in the issue give some attention to the importance of collective resistance, solidarity, and alliance in the face of a Trump United States, and in so doing they cite important moments that we might read as those of intersec-tional coalitional activism, such as the Standing Rock movement and the Women's March (see Ferguson 2017; Baum 2017; Goodhart and Morefield 2017; Isabela Altamirano-Jiménez 2017). Unfortunately, however, much of this attention is limited either to the final paragraph or so of their remarks

or to brief comments made throughout the article. Exceptions here include Jodi Dean (2017) and Lia Haro and Romand Coles (2017).

4　This question is the subject of Palgrave Macmillan's thought-provoking edited book series, The Politics of Intersectionality.

5　See Murib and Taylor (2018a, 2018b); Taylor (2018); Osei-Kofi, Licona, and Chávez (2018); Murib (2018); Roshanravan (2018); and Keating (2018).

Chapter 1: From Rosa Luxemburg to the Combahee River Collective

1　Many critical race scholars and activists emphasize the connection between race and class. See, for example, Cornel West's edited collection of Martin Luther King Jr.'s writings and speeches (King 2015). For an excellent discussion of the intersectional roots of Marxism and the Marxist roots of intersectionality, see Bohrer (2019).

2　While they do not call this chain of equivalence a "coalition" (they instead call it a "Leftist hegemony"), and while they do not use the word *coalition* anywhere in the text outside of one instance of *coalesce* when describing the process of hegemonic articulation (Laclau and Mouffe 1985, xii), I am following Romand Coles (1996) in understanding hegemonic articulation as a form of *coalition* politics.

3　We see this especially in Lenin's texts such as *The Tasks of the Russian Social-Democrats* (1897), *What Is to Be Done? Burning Questions of Our Movement* (1902), *"Left-Wing" Communism: An Infantile Disorder* (1920), and *The State and Revolution* (1917). See Tucker (1975) and Lenin (1978).

4　See Carole Pateman (1988), Charles Mills (1997), and Joel Olson (2004) for good discussions of both the implicit and explicit patriarchal and racist motivations of Enlightenment ideals.

5　I should clarify that I do not disagree with the claim that ontology could provide the basis of politics. As I will argue in chapter 3, one of the greatest insights of US Women of Color coalitional feminism is their formulation of a *coalitional* identity that forms the basis of coalition politics. My problem with Laclau and Mouffe, therefore, does not reside with their willingness to present ontology as a possible basis for politics; rather, I take issue both with the notion that this would be a "fixed" identity and with the unmistakable inconsistencies that such a move engenders in the context of their argument.

6　The tension between the strict scientific socialism of Lenin and the spontaneous proletarian politics of Luxemburg is nicely captured by Georg Lukács (1968), who advocates putting these two components—organization or conscious control and spontaneity—in a dialectical relationship.

7　For Hegel, the dialectic is actually an unfolding of consciousness and spirit, not of society. This is what distinguishes Hegel's dialectic from Marx and Engels's *materialist* dialectic (Hegel 1988, 19–24).

1   It is worth noting that the other contemporary political theorists who en-
    gage with Reagon are almost exclusively feminist political theorists. Some
    of these include Bickford (2000), Brown (1993), and Honig (1994 and 2001).

2   While Debord uses the notion of "spectacle" to describe and critique the
    state of society, I am using it in the context of Butler's work to describe
    what she sees as the productive function of coalitions of sexual minorities.

3   Though I believe Coles develops an ethico-political understanding of coali-
    tion in his 1996 article, his use of the phrase "ethical-political *framework*"
    appears five years later. See Coles (2001, 489).

4   This theme appears over and over across Women of Color feminism lit-
    erature. Smith speaks of "principled coalitions" (Smith and Smith 1983,
    126). Barbara Ransby asserts that a "shared political vision" keeps bringing
    Women of Color feminists back together (Ransby 2000, 1216). bell hooks
    defines feminist solidarity simply as a shared political commitment to end-
    ing oppression (hooks 2000, 47). Nira Yuval-Davis and many others tell us
    that coalitional allies must be chosen based not on identity but on a shared
    political commitment (Yuval-Davis 1997, 126; Adams 1989, 32; Clark 1983,
    135). Charlotte Bunch concurs with Women of Color feminists in telling us
    that for coalitions to work—to do the hard emotional work of coalition—
    members must share a common political commitment (Bunch 1990, 50).

5   Patricia Hill Collins advocates a process of "ethical, principled coalition
    building" (Collins 2000, 38). bell hooks emphasizes an "ethical commitment
    to feminist solidarity" (hooks 1990, 92), telling us that "feminist ethics"
    is one of the most important dimensions of feminist struggle (99). Other
    feminists use a range of signifiers to emphasize this ethical dimension. By
    appealing to a language of love, community, home, family, and empathy
    within the context of discussions about coalition, many Women of Color
    feminists also evoke this ethical feature. Whether it is an emphasis on *love*
    for women of color as that which underpins collective work (Combahee
    1983, 267), a subtle reminder that "without *community* there is no libera-
    tion" (Lorde 1984c, 112; my emphasis), the conviction that "there is nothing
    more important ... than *home*" (B. Smith 1983b, xxi; my emphasis), or
    depictions of scholarly and activist coalitions of women of color as *families*
    (see Moraga 1983b, xix; and Anzaldúa 2009, 142), Women of Color feminists
    consistently appeal to an ethical language to describe coalition work.

6   I first drafted this book in late May 2020, as unrest across the country
    erupted in the wake of yet another police killing of an unarmed Black man,
    arrested and handcuffed for a petty and nonviolent crime. George Floyd
    died after almost nine minutes of excessive police force wherein an officer
    had him pinned to the ground, with his knee on Floyd's neck. In an eerily
    familiar scene of a Black man pleading for his life, alerting the officers to
    the fact that he "can't breathe," the cell phone footage of the incident

went viral, inciting large-scale protests across the United States. Throughout the first six nights of continued and escalating protest, met with at times excessively violent reactions from police, Trump's leadership was nowhere to be found. Instead, he continued with divisive tweets, at one point lambasting the media outlets for "fake news," and he did so on an evening when there was absolutely nothing "fake" about the very real protesting taking place on his doorstep (Milligan 2020). In addition to outright denial of what was occurring in the first week of protests, when he finally addressed the nation, his divisive rhetoric resurfaced with a vengeance, calling on local law enforcement to "dominate" the "looters" and "rioters" (refusing to affirm them as peaceful protestors) and not so subtly suggesting to his white nationalist supporters that they take matters into their own hands, ensuring them that he would protect their second amendment rights (Trump 2020). Predictably, in the weeks following his address to the nation, various disgruntled white nationalists confronted protestors, sometimes violently, with guns in hand.

7   Trump regularly used "immigration invasion" rhetoric to describe immigration at the United States' southern border. The gunman responsible for the mass shooting in El Paso, Texas, used the same language in his racist manifesto wherein he was explicit in his intention to target Mexicans. See Russo (2019) and Zimmer (2019).

8   Expressing frustration with lawmakers who advocated protecting immigrants from El Salvador, Haiti, and African countries, Trump questioned why the United States was providing shelter for people from these "shithole countries" (Dawsey 2018).

9   In this passage she is speaking of "unity." She later goes on to equate "coalition" and "unity" (Lorde 1984b, 142).

10 This central argument reappears across numerous empirical journal articles published since the 1980s (see Eisenstein 1991; Ludwig 1999; and Weeks 2009) and is one of the central findings in Stephanie Gilmore's (2008) historical account of second-wave feminist coalitions.

11 See Cole and Luna (2010), Hancock (2011), Carastathis (2013 and 2016), Chávez (2013), and the *New Political Science* authors for some of these articulations.

12 This social movement declared itself *le printemps érable* (Maple Spring) to align its efforts with those across the Arab world in 2011 and with a global resurgence of leftist resistance (Sorochan 2012).

13 These dominant voices include those of Gilles Deleuze and Félix Guattari, Jacques Derrida, Jacques Rancière, Alain Badiou, and Slavoj Žižek, among others. See my short discussion of this in the introduction.

14 For other accounts of Women of Color feminists unwilling to part with the metaphors of home and community, see Moraga (1983h, 106), Anzaldúa (1983d, 196; 2009, 142), Lorde (1984c, 112), and Walker (1983, 342).

15 The only authors who *possibly* lean toward political indeterminacy could be Osei-Kofi, Licona, and Chávez (2018). Here they argue that Maria Teresa Asplund's raised, clenched fist in the face of three hundred marching Swedish neo-Nazis operates as an unpredictable coalitional gesture. While they contend that the gesture was "coalitional" insofar as it represented, instantiated, and symbolized "embodied and/or performed and informed acts of solidarity and alliance" (140), they contend that both its "confrontational" and its unpredictable "relational" quality made it coalitional. Its "relational" quality speaks to its unpredictable reception by varied audiences that would encounter the gesture once the image went viral. They read this ambiguity as generative of coalitional possibilities. Here one might find resonances with coalition as spectacle. I should note, however, that they do not make the case for redefining coalition as unpredictable gesture. Rather, they choose to read a certain visual image, and the gesture behind it, as generative of collective solidarity. For this reason, I do not believe it invokes the poststructuralist orientation toward political indeterminacy that I have critically engaged here.

Chapter 3: Coalition from the Inside Out

1 Whether something called poststructuralist theory might be reconceived to loosen the stronghold of ontological unfixity, epistemological undecidability, and political indeterminacy in such a way that certain Women of Color coalition feminists (such as Anzaldúa, Sandoval, and Lugones, for instance) might now be included underneath its rubric is an interesting question. While such a project is not the one I wish to undertake here, it is certainly one provoked by my analysis.

2 Though Lloyd also uses the phrases "coalitional subject" (Lloyd 2005, 15) and "coalitional identity" (159) interchangeably with depictions of the "subject-in-process," the notion of coalitional identity (or coalitional self) that I develop here is distinct from Lloyd's, which falsely ascribes the quality of permanent unfixity to Anzaldúa's depiction of mestiza identity.

3 See Crenshaw (1991), Chung and Chang (1998), Burack (2004), Rowe (2008), Chavez (2013), and Carastathis (2013) for instances of referring to something called a coalitional identity. For feminist theorists who gesture toward a strong connection between identity and coalition politics, see Fowlkes (1997), Ackelsberg (1996), and Adams (1989).

4 See Barvosa-Carter (2001) and Barvosa (2008) for a similar rendering of the coalitional self.

5 I say "put in circulation by" because few early US Women of Color coalition feminist authors actually use the phrase "coalitional identity." Nevertheless, it is precisely their inclination toward theorizing identity as a kind of coalition that differentiates theories of multiple identity on offer by thinkers such as Anzaldúa, Lorde, and Lugones from contemporary articulations by thinkers such as Laclau and Mouffe, Butler, and those influenced by Deleuze

and Guattari, Derrida, and others. I am following Carastathis in naming this notion of identity a coalitional identity (Carastathis 2013, 960), though others have utilized similar phrases. See references in note 3 of this chapter.

6 See also Lugones's discussion of curdle-separation (Lugones 2003, 121–48), to which I turn shortly.

7 On coalitional consciousness, see also Keating (2005). On epistemological coalition, see Pryse (1998), Harding (1995), and Narayan (1989).

8 Somos Hermanas was a national solidarity project housed at the San Francisco Women's Building as part of the Alliance against Women's Oppression (AAWO) that formed originally as a multiracial delegation of lesbian and straight women to Sandinista Nicaragua in 1984 at the invitation of the Association de Mujeres Nicaragüenses Luisa Amanda Espinosa (AMN-LAE; the Association of Nicaraguan Women Luisa Amanda Espinosa). See Carastathis (2013, 943).

9 This is why, despite my strong sympathies with the political project he was attempting, Nicholas Tampio's (2009) endeavor to impose a Left-oriented direction to Deleuze and Guattarian coalitional assemblages seemed untenable to me. Inherent to Deleuze and Guattari's epistemology is a refusal of prescribed political directionality.

10 Though Sandoval refers to this guiding commitment to egalitarian social relations as an "ethical" commitment, it shares much with the notion of *politico-ethical* commitment that I develop in chapter 2. It is, she tells us, an "ideological code that is committed to social justice according to egalitarian redistributions of power across such differences coded as race, gender, sex, nation, culture, or class distinctions" (Sandoval 2000, 112). I continue to opt for the *politico*-ethical construction, emphasizing a self-reflexive political commitment, in an effort to foreground what I see as a unique aspect of US Women of Color coalitional feminism and to differentiate it from other contemporary articulations informed by a "neo-Nietzschean" turn to ethics as in Coles (1996) and Butler (2004, 2009).

11 I return to Roshanravan's treatment of disintegration in my discussion of the 2017 Women's March on Washington in chapter 5. Also see Barvosa (2008) for another brilliant account of Pratt's autobiographical coming to coalitional consciousness through the process of what Barvosa calls "self-craft" (Barvosa 2006, 175–206).

12 For another treatment of the self-reflexivity in Pratt's journey, see Martin and Mohanty (2003, 94, 101).

Chapter 4: Writing Feminist Theory, Doing Feminist Politics

1 These sections of the *Sisterhood* anthology are titled as follows: "The Oppressed Majority: The Way It Is"; "The Invisible Women: Psychological and Sexual Repression"; "Go Tell It to the Valley: Changing Consciousness"; "Up

from Sexism: Emerging Ideologies"; and "The Hand That Cradles the Rock: Protest and Revolt."

2 A focus on "sisterhood" in place of solidarity was typical of 1970s feminist anthologies. See Erica Townsend-Bell (2012, 138).

3 For a good discussion of the difference between additive and intersectional approaches, see King (1988).

4 For a good discussion of the ways in which racism, capitalism, and sexism intersect to control the reproductive capacity of women of color, see Roberts (1997).

5 For a discussion of the importance of the family to Black feminists, see Smith (1983a), hooks (1981; 2000), and Roberts (1997).

6 See Mohanty (2003, 106–23) for a critique of Morgan's second anthology, *Sisterhood Is Global: The International Women's Movement Anthology* (1984), on very similar lines.

7 See Andrea Canaan's essay, "Brownness," for a similar appeal to unity and wholeness (Canaan 1983, 234).

8 Exceptions here include contributions by bell hooks (1995), Angela Davis (1995), and Gloria Steinem (1995).

9 An important exception here is the essay by bell hooks wherein she considers how the intersection of racism and poverty may produce a need for beauty in the lives of Black people. She is careful to distinguish this need for beautiful things from the "hedonistic consumerism" of contemporary African American culture (hooks 1995, 161). Another exception is Danzy Senna's article wherein she self-reflexively finds her way back from power, or individualistic, feminism and to feminism as dismantling all oppressive forces (Senna 1995, 18–20).

10 By positioning her project *against feminism*, Walker's *Real* represents a radical shift from what we see in other third-wave anthologies such as Barbara Findlen's *Listen Up: Voices from the Next Feminist Generation* (1995). Unlike Walker, who seems most interested in moments in which a younger generation finds itself up *against feminism*, Findlen makes it clear that the essays appearing in her collection are those in which a younger generation first encounters sexism and patriarchy. While these instances will no doubt look different from the more overt forms of blatant sex discrimination of previous generations, the point of the collection is to allow a younger generation to articulate the different ways in which they confront patriarchy. "Many young feminists," she asserts, "describe growing up with the expectation that 'you can do anything,' whether that message came directly from parents or just from seeing barriers falling" (Findlen 1995, xv). "But there's a point," she continues, "where you realize that while you may indeed feel capable of doing anything, you can be stopped—because of sexism" (xv–xvi). It is these moments of encountering sexism that Findlen aims to capture in her anthology. Instead of contesting feminism, Findlen sets out to contest

patriarchy. What she asks of us is to listen to these younger voices and to be open to identifying patriarchy in new and unexpected places.

11 See hooks (2000, 29–31) for a good critique of lifestyle feminism.

12 Findlen's (1995) anthology is similarly laid out in this undifferentiated list format.

13 I need to self-reflexively name the many facets of my own privilege in this instance and problematize my use of the language of "privilege" to describe Walker. I am a white, Western, economically privileged, educationally privileged (having attended multiple private schools and colleges with the help of my parents, in addition to loans and fellowships), cisgender, heterosexual, able-bodied, forty-something woman. My privileges are numerous, indeed. My willingness to use the language of "privilege" in describing Walker (a Black woman) thus demands careful reflection. My use of "privilege" in this context is focused specifically on Walker's exposure to feminism. I am aware of and sensitive to the complicated and intermeshing forms of oppression that Walker likely confronts as a Black, Jewish woman (forms of oppression that aspects of my own privilege shelter me from). This is all the more reason, however, for why I am puzzled by Walker's reluctance to foreground interlocking oppressions in her anthology. My attempt to try to make sense of this absence is certainly imperfect, and I therefore welcome correction. Nevertheless, in this imperfect endeavor, I arrive at her *privileged feminism* (the fact of her exposure to feminism from such a young age, growing up, as she put it, in the "feminist ghetto" of her childhood) as that which leads her to believe that old-school feminist accounts of interlocking oppressions were passé and uninteresting.

Chapter 5: The Women's March on Washington and Politico-Ethical Coalitional Opportunities in the Age of Trump

Epigraph source: The quote from Mrinalini Chakraborty is from Tambe 2017, 228.

1 The first full draft of this manuscript was completed in summer 2020, amid the George Floyd antiracism protests sweeping the country.

2 This was a consistent finding in most coverage of the protests. See Harmon and Tavernise (2020); Iweala (2020); and Johnson, Fornek, and Cullotta (2020).

3 Think of the #BlackoutTuesday phenomenon wherein numerous people posted black squares on their social media platforms (Facebook, Instagram, Twitter) in an attempt to show support for and reflect on the protests surrounding the murder of George Floyd. See Coscarelli (2020).

4 See NASCAR's official statement: NASCAR, "NASCAR Statement on Confederate Flag," June 10, 2020, https://www.nascar.com/news-media/2020/06/10/nascar-statement-on-confederate-flag/.

5 See Trump's campaign ad, "Break In," at "Donald J. Trump for President: 'Break In.' Campaign 2020," *Washington Post*, July 21, 2020, https://www .washingtonpost.com/video/opinions/campaign-ads-2020/donald-j-trump-for -president-break-in—campaign-2020/2020/07/21/42e4f41a-4fca-4668-b9e9 -82381f9a8a3a_video.html.

Conclusion

Barbara Smith epigraph from "Racism and Women's Studies" quoted in *This Bridge Called My Back* (61); originally from a speech Smith gave at the 1979 NWSA conference and first published in *Frontiers: A Journal of Women's Studies* 5, no. 1 (1980): 48–49.

1 Cricket Keating and I have simultaneously taught similar versions of this course at our separate universities and created cross-classroom virtual world-traveling exercises for our students.

2 Though Lugones passed away in July 2020, Keating continues to theorize *with her* as she finishes their coauthored forthcoming manuscript *Educating for Coalition*.

References

Abner, Allison. 1995. "Motherhood." In Walker 1995a, 185–94.

Ackelsberg, Martha. 1996. "Identity Politics, Political Identities: Thoughts toward a Multicultural Politics." *Frontiers* 16, no. 1: 87–100.

Adams, Mary Louise. 1989. "There's No Place Like Home: On the Place of Identity in Feminist Politics." *Feminist Review* 31, no. 1: 22–33.

Agrawal, Nina. 2017. "How the Women's March Came into Being." *Los Angeles Times*, January 21, 2017.

Ahmed, Sara. 2017. *Living a Feminist Life*. Durham, NC: Duke University Press.

Albrecht, Lisa, and Rose Brewer, eds. 1990. *Bridges of Power: Women's Multicultural Alliances*. Philadelphia: New Society.

Alcoff, Linda Martín. 1997. "Cultural Feminism versus Post-structuralism: the Identity Crisis in Feminist Theory." In *The Second Wave: A Reader in Feminist Theory*, edited by Linda Nicholson, 330–55. New York: Routledge.

Alcoff, Linda Martín. 2015. "Linda Martín Alcoff." Interview by Chandra Mohanty and Linda Carty. *Feminist Freedom Warriors*, June 6, 2015. Video 1:03:33. http://feministfreedomwarriors.org/watchvideo.php?firstname=Linda&lastname=Mart%C3%ADn%20Alcoff.

Allyn, Jennifer, and David Allyn. 1995. "Identity Politics." In Walker 1995a, 143–56.

Al-Saji, Alia. 2012. "Creating Possibility: The Time of the Quebec Student Movement." *Theory and Event* 15, no. 3. https://muse.jhu.edu/article/484442.

Altamirano-Jiménez, Isabel. 2017. "Trump, NAFTA, and Indigenous Resistance in Turtle Island." *Theory and Event* 20, no. 1: 3–9. https://muse.jhu.edu/article/650858.

Althusser, Louis. 1965. *For Marx*. Translated by Ben Brewster. London: Penguin.

Althusser, Louis. 1971. *Lenin and Philosophy and Other Essays*. Translated by Ben Brewster. London: New Left Books.

Anzaldúa, Gloria. 1983a. "Foreword to the Second Edition." In Moraga and Anzaldúa 1983a.

Anzaldúa, Gloria. 1983b. "Introduction to Speaking in Tongues: The Third World Woman Writer." In Moraga and Anzaldúa 1983a, 163–64.

Anzaldúa, Gloria. 1983c. "Speaking in Tongues: A Letter to Third World Women Writers." In Moraga and Anzaldúa 1983a, 165–74.

Anzaldúa, Gloria. 1983d. "Introduction to El Mundo Zurdo: The Vision." In Moraga and Anzaldúa 1983a, 195–96.

Anzaldúa, Gloria. 1983e. "La Prieta." In Moraga and Anzaldúa 1983a, 198–210.

Anzaldúa, Gloria. 1987. *Borderlands/La Frontera: The New Mestiza*. San Francisco: Spinsters/Aunt Lute Books.

Anzaldúa, Gloria, ed. 1990. *Making Face, Making Soul/Haciendo Caras; Creative and Critical Perspectives by Feminist of Color*. San Francisco: Aunt Lute Books.

Anzaldúa, Gloria. 2002. "Preface: (Un)natural Bridges, (Un)safe Spaces." In Anzaldúa and Keating 2002, 1–5.

Anzaldúa, Gloria. 2009. *The Gloria Anzaldúa Reader*. Edited by AnaLouise Keating. Durham, NC: Duke University Press.

Anzaldúa, Gloria, and AnaLouise Keating, eds. 2002. *This Bridge We Call Home: Radical Visions for Transformation*. New York: Routledge.

Baillargeon, Normand, and Darin Barney. 2012. "To Misters Pratte, Duboc, Facal and All the Others Who Do Not Understand." *Theory and Event* 15, no. 3. http:// muse.jhu.edu/article/484444.

Bambara, Toni Cade. 1983. "Foreword." In Moraga and Anzaldúa 1983a, vi–viii.

Barvosa-Carter, Edwina. 2001. "Multiple Identity and Coalition Building: How Identity Differences within Us Enable Radical Alliances among Us." In Bysty-dzienski and Schacht 2001a, 21–34.

Barvosa, Edwina. 2008. *Wealth of Selves: Multiple Identities, Mestiza Consciousness and the Subject of Politics*. College Station: Texas A&M University Press.

Bates, Karen Grisgby. 2017. "Race and Feminism: Women's March Recalls the Touchy History." NPR, January 21, 2017. https://www.npr.org/sections /codeswitch/2017/01/21/510859909/race-and-feminism-womens-march-recalls -the-touchy-history.

Baum, Bruce. 2017. "Donald Trump's 'Genius,' White 'Natural Aristocracy,' and Democratic Equality in America." *Theory and Event* 20, no. 1: 10–22. https:// muse.jhu.edu/article/650859.

Beal, Frances M. 1970–75. "Double Jeopardy: To Be Black and Female." In *Black Woman's Manifesto*, edited by the Third World Women's Alliance, 19–34. New York: Third World Women's Alliance. https://repository.duke.edu/dc/wlmpc /wlmms01009.

Beal, Frances M. 1970. "Double Jeopardy: To Be Black and Female." In Morgan 1970a, 382–96.

Beltrán, Cristina. 2004. "Patrolling Borders: Hybrids, Hierarchies and the Challenge of *Mestizaje.*" *Political Research Quarterly* 57, no. 4: 595–607.

Bernstein, Leandra. 2017. "More Pro-life Groups Removed as Official Partners of the Women's March." *WJLA*, January 18, 2017.

Bevacqua, Maria. 2001. "Anti-rape Coalitions: Radical, Liberal, Black, and White Feminists Challenging Boundaries." In Bystydzienski and Schacht 2001a, 163–76.

Bickel, Christopher. 2001. "Reasons to Resist: Coalition Building at Indiana University." In Bystydzienski and Schacht 2001a, 207–19.

Bickford, Susan. 2000. "Constructing Inequality: City Spaces and the Architecture of Citizenship." *Political Theory* 28, no. 3: 355–76.

Black Women's Liberation Group. 1970. "Statement on Birth Control." In Morgan 1970a, 404–6.

Bliss, James. 2016. "Black Feminism Out of Place." *Signs* 41, no. 4: 727–49.

Bohrer, Ashley J. 2019. *Marxism and Intersectionality: Race, Gender, Class and Sexuality under Contemporary Capitalism.* Bielefeld: Transcript Verlag.

Bondoc, Anna. 1995. "Close, but No Banana." In Walker 1995a, 167–84.

Boothroyd, Sydney, Rachel Bowen, Alicia Cattermole, Kenda Change-Swanson, Hanna Daltrop, Sasha Dwyer, Anna Gunn, Brydon Kramer, Delaney M. McCartan, Jasmine Nagra, Shereen Samimi, and Qwisun Yoon-Potkins. 2017. "(Re)producing Feminine Bodies: Emergent Spaces through Contestation in the Women's March on Washington." *Gender, Place and Culture* 24, no. 5: 711–21.

Brewer, Sierra, and Lauren Dundes. 2017. "Concerned, Meet Terrified: Intersectional Feminism and the Women's March." *Women's Studies International Forum* 69: 49–55.

Brown, Wendy. 1993. "Wounded Attachments." *Political Theory* 21, no. 3: 390–410.

Bulkin, Elly. 1984. "Hard Ground: Jewish Identity, Racism, and Anti-Semitism." In *Yours in Struggle: Three Feminist Perspectives on Anti-Semitism and Racism,* by Elly Bulkin, Minnie Bruce Pratt, and Barbara Smith, 89–228. Ithaca, NY: Firebrand.

Bunch, Charlotte. 1990. "Making Common Cause: Diversity and Coalition." In *Bridges of Power: Women's Multicultural Alliances,* edited by Lisa Albrecht and Rose M. Brewer, 49–56. Philadelphia: New Society.

Bunch, Charlotte, Heidi Hartman, Ellen Bravo, Nancy Hartsock, Roberta Spalter-Roth, Linda Williams, and Maria Blanco. 1996. "Bringing Together Feminist Theory and Practice: A Collective Interview." *Signs* 21, no. 4: 917–51.

Burack, Cynthia. 2004. *Healing Identities: Black Feminist Thought and the Politics of Groups.* Ithaca, NY: Cornell University Press.

Burnham, Linda. 2001. "Working Paper Series, No. 1: The Wellspring of Black Feminist Thought." *Women of Color Resource Center.* Accessed March 2, 2021. https://solidarity-us.org/pdfs/cadreschool/fws.burnham.pdf.

Butler, Judith. 1990. *Gender Trouble: Feminism and the Subversion of Identity.* New York: Routledge.

Butler, Judith. 1995. "Contingent Foundations." In *Feminist Contentions: A Philosophical Exchange,* edited by Seyla Benhabib, Judith Butler, Drucilla Cornell, and Nancy Fraser, 35–57. New York: Routledge.

Butler, Judith. 2004. *Precarious Life: The Powers of Mourning and Violence*. London: Verso.

Butler, Judith. 2009. *Frames of War: When Is Life Grievable?* London: Verso.

Butler, Judith. 2011. "Bodies in Alliance and the Politics of the Street." In *#Occupy Los Angeles Reader* 13: 2–12. Accessed February 28, 2021. http://suebellyank.com /wp-content/uploads/2011/11/ola-reader-full.pdf.

Butler, Judith. 2015. *Notes toward a Performative Theory of Assembly*. Cambridge, MA: Harvard University Press.

Bystydzienski, Jill M., and Steven P. Schacht, eds. 2001a. *Forging Radical Alliances across Difference: Coalition Politics for the New Millennium*. London: Rowman and Littlefield.

Bystydzienski, Jill M., and Steven P. Schacht, eds. 2001b. "Introduction." In Bystydzienski and Schacht 2001a, 1–17.

Cabreros-Sud, Veena. 1995. "Kicking Ass." In Walker 1995a, 41–48.

Canaan, Andrea. 1983. "Brownness." In Moraga and Anzaldúa 1983a, 232–37.

Carastathis, Anna. 2013. "Identity Categories as Potential Coalitions." *Signs* 38, no. 4: 941–65.

Carastathis, Anna. 2016. *Intersectionality: Origins, Contestations, Horizons*. Lincoln: University of Nebraska Press.

Carroll, Tamar. 2008. "Unlikely Allies: Forging a Multiracial, Class-Based Women's Movement in 1970s Brooklyn." In *Feminist Coalitions: Historical Perspectives on Second-Wave Feminism in the United States*, edited by Stephanie Gilmore, 196–224. Urbana: University of Illinois Press.

Chappet, Marie-Claire. 2020. "Why White People May Feel Uncomfortable Right Now—and Why That's a Good Thing." *Glamour*, June 11, 2020.

Chávez, Karma. 2013. *Queer Migration Politics: Activist Rhetoric and Coalitional Possibilities*. Urbana: University of Illinois Press.

Chisholm, Shirley. 1972. "The Politics of Coalition." *Black Scholar* 4, no. 1: 30–32.

Chisholm, Shirley. 1983. "A Coalition of Conscience." Speech delivered at Greenfield High School, Greenfield, MA, October 3, 1983. https://awpc.cattcenter.iastate .edu/2017/03/09/a-coalition-of-conscience-oct-3-1983/.

Chrystos. 1983. "He Saw." In Moraga and Anzaldúa 1983a, 18–19.

Chung, Angie Y., and Edward Chang. 1998. "From Third World Liberation to Multiple Oppression Politics: A Contemporary Approach to Interethnic Coalitions." *Social Justice* 25, no. 3: 80–100.

Cisler, Lucinda. 1970. "Unfinished Business: Birth Control and Women's Liberation." In Morgan 1970a, 274–322.

Clarke, Cheryl. 1983. "Lesbianism: An Act of Resistance." In Moraga and Anzaldúa 1983a, 128–37.

CLASSE (Coalition large de l'Association pour une solidarité syndicale étudiante). 2012. "Share Our Future: The CLASSE Manifesto." *Theory and Event* 15, no. 3. https://muse.jhu.edu/article/484447.

Cole, Elizabeth, and Zakiya Luna. 2010. "Making Coalitions Work: Solidarity across Difference within US Feminism." *Feminist Studies* 36, no. 1: 71–98.

Coles, Romand. 1996. "Liberty, Equality, Receptive Generosity: Neo-Nietzschean Reflections on the Ethics and Politics of Coalition." *American Political Science Review* 90, no. 2: 375–88.

Coles, Romand. 2001. "Traditio: Feminists of Color and the Torn Virtues of Democratic Engagement." *Political Theory* 29, no. 4: 488–516.

Collins, Patricia Hill. 2000. *Black Feminist Thought: Knowledge, Consciousness, and the Politics of Empowerment*. 2nd ed. New York: Routledge.

Collins, Patricia Hill. 2015. "Intersectionality's Definitional Dilemmas." *Annual Review of Sociology* 41: 1–20. https://doi.org/10.1146/annurev-soc-073014-112142.

Combahee River Collective. 1983. "A Black Feminist Statement." In Moraga and Anzaldúa 1983a, 210–18.

Cook, Anthony. 2015. "The Ghosts of 1964: Race, Reagan, and the Neo-conservative Backlash to the Civil Rights Movement." *Alabama Civil Rights and Civil Liberties Law Review* 6, no. 81: 81–119.

Coole, Diana. 1993. *Women in Political Theory: From Ancient Misogyny to Contemporary Feminism*. Boulder: Lynne Rienner.

Coscarelli, Joe. 2020. "#BlackoutTuesday: A Music Industry Protest Becomes a Social Media Moment." *New York Times*, June 2, 2020.

Crenshaw, Kimberlé. 1991. "Mapping the Margins: Intersectionality, Identity Politics, and Violence against Women of Color." *Stanford Law Review* 43, no. 6: 1241–99.

Crenshaw, Kimberlé. 2015. "Why Intersectionality Can't Wait." *Washington Post*, September 24, 2015.

Cuomo, Chris. 2020. "Here's the Proof of Systemic Racism in the U.S." *Cuomo Prime Time*, CNN, June 12, 2020. https://www.cnn.com/videos/politics/2020/06/12/closing-argument-systemic-racism-us-economy-kudlow-cpt-vpx.cnn.

davenport, doris. 1983. "The Pathology of Racism: A Conversation with Third World Wimmin." In Moraga and Anzaldúa 1983a, 85–90.

Davis, Angela. 1989. "Interview with Angela Davis." By Terry Rockefeller and Louis Messiah. *Eyes on the Prize, II: Interviews*, PBS, May 24, 1989. http://digital.wustl.edu/e/eii/eiiweb/dav5427.0115.036marc_record_interviewer_process.html.

Davis, Angela. 1995. "Afterword." In Walker 1995a, 279–84.

Davis, Angela. 1997. "Interview with Lisa Lowe; Angela Davis: Reflections on Race, Class, and Gender in the US." In *The Politics of Culture in the Shadow of Capital*, edited by Lisa Lowe and David Lloyd, 303–23. Durham, NC: Duke University Press.

Davis, Angela. 1998. "Interview with Angela Davis." PBS *Frontline*. Accessed February 27, 2021. https://www.pbs.org/wgbh/pages/frontline/shows/race/interviews/davis.html.

Davis, Angela, and Kum-Kum Bhavnani. 1989. "Complexity, Activism, Optimism: An Interview with Angela Davis." *Feminist Review* 31, no. 1: 66–81.

Davis, Angela, and Elizabeth Martínez. 1994. "Coalition Building among People of Color." *Inscriptions* 7. https://culturalstudies.ucsc.edu/inscriptions/volume-7/angela-y-davis-elizabeth-martinez/.

Davis, Angela. 2016. "Angela Y. Davis." Interview by Chandra Mohanty and Linda Carty. *Feminist Freedom Warriors*, February 27, 2016. Video 0:50:08. http://

feministfreedomwarriors.org/watchvideo.php?firstname=Angela%20Y
.&lastname=Davis.

Davis, Angela, and Keeanga-Yamahtta Taylor. 2016. "Freedom Is a Constant Struggle." University of Chicago Postelection Lecture, November 16, 2016. https://
www.chicagoreader.com/Bleader/archives/2016/11/21/watch-angela-daviss
-entire-postelection-lecture-at-the-university-of-chicagos-rockefeller-chapel.

Davis, Eisa. 1995. "Sexism and the Art of Feminist Hip-Hop Maintenance." In
Walker 1995a, 127–42.

Dawsey, Josh. 2018. "Trump Derides Protections for Immigrants from 'Shithole'
Countries." *Washington Post*, January 12, 2018.

Dean, Jodi. 2017. "Not Him, Us (and We Aren't Populists)." *Theory and Event* 20,
no. 1: 38–44. https://muse.jhu.edu/article/650861.

Debord, Guy. 1994. *The Society of the Spectacle*. Translated by Donald Nicholson-
Smith. New York: Zone.

Deggans, Eric. 2020. "'Me and White Supremacy' Helps You Do the Work of Dismantling Racism." NPR, July 9, 2020. https://www.npr.org/2020/07/06/887646740
/me-and-white-supremacy-helps-you-do-the-work-of-dismantling-racism.

Deleuze, Gilles, and Félix Guattari. 1987. *A Thousand Plateaus: Capitalism and Schizophre-
nia*. Translated by Brian Massumi. Minneapolis: University of Minnesota Press.

DeLombard, Jeannine. 1995. "Femmenism." In Walker 1995a, 21–34.

Dunbar, Roxanne. 1970. "Female Liberation as the Basis for Social Revolution." In
Morgan 1970a, 536–56.

Edgar, David. 1981. "Reagan's Hidden Agenda: Racism and the New American
Right." *Race and Class* 22, no. 3: 221–38.

Eisenstein, Zillah. 1981. "Antifeminism in the Politics and Election of 1980." *Feminist Studies* 7, no. 2: 187–205.

Eisenstein, Zillah. 1991. "Privatizing the State: Reproductive Rights, Affirmative
Action, and the Problem of Democracy." *Frontiers* 12, no. 1: 98–125.

Eisenstein, Zillah. 2016. "Zillah Eisenstein." Interview by Chandra Mohanty and
Linda Carty. *Feminist Freedom Warriors*, April 30, 2016. Video 0:57:57. http://
feministfreedomwarriors.org/watchvideo.php?firstname=Zillah&lastname
=Eisenstein.

Eisenstein, Zillah. 2017. "Revolutionary Imaginaries in a Time of Women's Marches."
Zillah Eisenstein, February 2, 2017. https://zillaheisenstein.wordpress.com/2017
/02/02/revolutionary-imaginaries-in-a-time-of-womens-marches/.

Eisenstein, Zillah. 2019a. "The Making of a New Anti-racist Feminist Working
Class." *Feminist Wire*, January 31. https://thefeministwire.com/2019/01/
the-making-of-a-new-anti-racist-feminist-working-class-feminism4the99/.

Eisenstein, Zillah. 2019b. "Why March: Women's March/es till Trump Is Gone."
Medium, January 16, 2019. https://zillaheisenstein.medium.com/why-march
-womens-march-es-till-trump-is-gone-8db1dacdce56.

Elam, Diane. 1994. *Feminism and Deconstruction: Ms. en Abyme*. New York: Routledge.

Emejulu, Akwugo. 2018. "On the Problems and Possibilities of Feminist Solidarity:
The Women's March One Year On." *IPPR Progressive Review* 24, no. 4: 268–73.

Felsenthal, Julia. 2017. "These Are the Women Organizing the Women's March on Washington." *Vogue*, January 10, 2017.

Ferguson, Michaele. 2017. "Trump Is a Feminist, and Other Cautionary Tales for Our Neoliberal Age." *Theory and Event* 20, no. 1: 53–67. https://muse.jhu.edu /article/650863.

Findlen, Barbara, ed. 1995. *Listen Up: Voices from the Next Feminist Generation*. New York: Seal Press.

Firestone, Shulamith, ed. 1968. *Notes from the First Year*. New York: Radical Feminism.

Firestone, Shulamith, ed. 1970. *Notes from the Second Year: Women's Liberation; Major Writings of the Radical Feminists*. New York: Radical Feminism.

Fisher, Dana R., Dawn M. Dow, and Rashawn Ray. 2017. "Intersectionality Takes It to the Streets: Mobilizing across Diverse Interests for the Women's March." *Science Advances* 3: 1–8.

Fowlkes, Diane L. 1997. "Moving from Feminist Identity Politics to Coalition Politics through a Feminist Materialist Standpoint of Intersubjectivity in Gloria Anzaldúa's *Borderlands/La Frontera: The New Mestiza*." *Hypatia* 12, no. 2: 105–24.

Freire, Paulo. 1970. *Pedagogy of the Oppressed*. Translated by Myra Bergman Ramos. New York: Bloomsbury.

Furman, Laura. 1970. "'A House Is Not a Home': Women in Publishing." In Morgan 1970a, 73–75.

Fuss, Diana. 1989. *Essentially Speaking: Feminism, Nature and Difference*. New York: Routledge.

Gagliardi, Barbara. 1981. "West Coast Women's Music Festival." *Big Mama Rag*, November, 1981. http://revolution.berkeley.edu/assets/SS_AnnotateFix_West -Coast-Womens-Festival.pdf.

Gallop, Jane. 1992. *Around 1981: Academic Feminist Literary Theory*. New York: Routledge.

Garcia, Alicia. 2017. "Our Cynicism Will Not Build a Movement. Collaboration Will." NFG, January 26, 2017. https://www.nfg.org/news/our-cynicism-will-not-build -movement-collaboration-will.

Gilmore, Stephanie, ed. 2008. *Feminist Coalitions: Historical Perspectives on Second-Wave Feminism in the United States*. Urbana: University of Illinois Press.

Glassman, Carol. 1970. "Women and the Welfare System." In Morgan 1970a, 112–27.

Gökariksel, Banu, and Sara Smith. 2017. "Intersectional Feminism beyond U.S. Flag Hijab and Pussy Hats in Trump's America." *Gender, Place and Culture* 24, no. 5: 628–44.

Goodhart, Michael, and Jeanne Morefield. 2017. "Reflection Now! Critique and Solidarity in the Trump Era." *Theory and Event* 20, no. 1: 68–85. https://muse .jhu.edu/article/650864.

Goodman, Amy. 2020a. "Feminist Scholar Barbara Smith on Identity Politics and Why She Supports Bernie Sanders for President." *Democracy Now!*, February 12, 2020. https://www.democracynow.org/shows/2020/2/12.

Goodman, Amy. 2020b. "The US Functions with White Supremacy as Its Engine: Here's How We Dismantle It." *Democracy Now!*, September 11, 2020. https://www.democracynow.org/2020/9/11/barbara_smith_ending_white_supremacy.

Gossett, Hattie. 1983. "Who Told You Anybody Wants to Hear from You? You Ain't Nothing but a Black Woman." In Moraga and Anzaldúa 1983a, 175–76.

Gramsci, Antonio. 1971. *Selections from the Prison Notebooks*. Edited and translated by Quintin Hoare and Geoffrey Nowell Smith. London: Lawrence and Wishart.

Gramsci, Antonio. 1995. *The Southern Question*. Translated by Pasquale Verdicchio. West Lafayette, IN: Bordighera.

Green, Emma. 2020. "What to Know about Women's March 2020." *Atlantic*, January 17, 2020.

Grossman, Zoltan. 2001. "'Let's Not Create Evilness for This River': Interethnic Environmental Alliances of Native Americans and Rural Whites in Northern Wisconsin." In Bystydzienski and Schacht 2001a, 146–62.

Grosz, Elizabeth. 1994. "Identity and Difference: A Response." In *Critical Politics*, edited by Paul James, 29–34. Melbourne: Arena.

Hancock, Ange-Marie. 2011. *Solidarity Politics for Millennials: A Guide to Ending the Oppression Olympics*. New York: Palgrave Macmillan.

Haraway, Donna J. 1990. "A Cyborg Manifesto: Science, Technology, and Socialist-Feminism in the Late Twentieth Century." In *Feminism/Postmodernism*, edited by Linda Nicholson, 190–233. New York: Routledge.

Harding, Sandra. 1995. "Subjectivity, Experience, and Knowledge: An Epistemology from/for Rainbow Coalition Politics." In *Who Can Speak? Authority and Critical Identity*, edited by Judith Roof and Robin Wiegman, 120–36. Urbana: University of Illinois Press.

Harmon, Amy, and Sabrina Tavernise. 2020. "One Big Difference about George Floyd Protests: Many White Faces." *New York Times*, June 12, 2020.

Haro, Lia, and Romand Coles. 2017. "Eleven Theses on Neo-fascism and the Fight to Defeat It." *Theory and Event* 20, no. 1: 100–115. http://muse.jhu.edu/article/650866.

Hartsock, Nancy. 1985. *Money, Sex, and Power: Toward a Feminist Historical Materialism*. Boston: Northeastern University Press.

Hegel, G. W. F. 1988. *Introduction to the Philosophy of History*. Translated by Leo Rauch. Indianapolis: Hackett.

Hobson, Sheila Smith. 1970. "Women and Television." In Morgan 1970a, 76–83.

Honig, Bonnie. 1994. "Difference, Dilemmas, and the Politics of Home." *Social Research* 61, no. 3: 563–97.

Honig, Bonnie. 2001. "Culture, Citizenship, and Community." *Polity* 33, no. 3: 479–85.

hooks, bell. 1981. *Ain't I a Woman: Black Women and Feminism*. Boston: South End Press.

hooks, bell. (1984) 2000. *Feminist Theory: From Margin to Center*. Boston: South End Press.

hooks, bell. 1990. *Yearning: Race, Gender, and Cultural Politics*. Boston: South End Press.

hooks, bell. 1994. *Teaching to Transgress: Education as the Practice of Freedom*. New York: Routledge.

hooks, bell. 1995. "Beauty Laid Bare: Aesthetics in the Ordinary." In Walker 1995a, 157–66.

Howard, Judith, and Carolyn Allen. 2000. "Editorial: Feminisms at a Millennium." *Signs* 25, no. 4: xiii–xxx.

Hull, Gloria T., Patricia Bell Scott, and Barbara Smith, eds. 1982. *All the Women Are White, All the Blacks Are Men, but Some of Us Are Brave: Black Women's Studies*. New York: Feminist Press.

Indigenous Action. 2014. "Accomplices Not Allies: Abolishing the Ally Industrial Complex." May 4, 2014. https://www.indigenousaction.org/accomplices-not -allies-abolishing-the-ally-industrial-complex/.

Iweala, Uzodinma. 2020. "White Signs at Black Protests." *Vanity Fair*, June 5, 2020.

Jackson, Jesse, Rev. 1984. "The Rainbow Coalition." Speech delivered, San Francisco, July 17, 1984. http://www.speeches-usa.com/Transcripts/052_jackson.html.

Johnson, Jennifer, Kimberly Fornek, and Karen Ann Cullotta. 2020. "Suburban Protests against Racial Injustice Awakened Many White Residents. Allies Hope They Follow Through." *Chicago Tribune*, June 29, 2020.

Johnson, Merri Lisa, ed. 2002. *Jane Sexes It Up: True Confessions of Feminist Desire*. New York: Four Walls Eight Windows.

Jones, Beverly. 1970. "The Dynamics of Marriage and Motherhood." In Morgan 1970a, 49–66.

Jones, Lisa. 1995. "She Came with the Rodeo (an Excerpt)." In Walker 1995a, 253–66.

Joreen. 1970. "The 51 Percent Minority Group: A Statistical Essay." In Morgan 1970a, 39–48.

Joyce, Fay S. 1984. "Jackson Criticizes Remarks Made by Farrakhan as 'Reprehensible.'" *New York Times*, June 29, 1984.

Karp, Marcelle, and Debbie Stoller, eds. 1999. *The BUST Guide to the New Girl Order*. New York: Penguin.

Keating, AnaLouise. 2002. "'Charting Pathways, Making Thresholds' ... A Warning, an Introduction." In Anzaldúa and Keating 2002, 6–20.

Keating, Cricket. 2005. "Building Coalitional Consciousness." *Feminist Formations* 17, no. 2: 86–103.

Keating, Christine (Cricket). 2018. "The Politics of Everyday Coalition-Building." *New Political Science* 40, no. 1: 177–83.

King, Deborah. 1988. "Multiple Jeopardy, Multiple Consciousness: The Context of a Black Feminist Ideology." *Signs* 14, no. 1: 42–72.

King, Martin Luther, Jr. 2015. *The Radical King*. Edited by Cornel West. Boston: Beacon.

King, Noel. 2020. "What Systemic Racism Means and the Way It Harms Communities." NPR, July 1, 2020. https://www.npr.org/2020/07/01/885878564/what -systemic-racism-means-and-the-way-it-harms-communities.

Klar, Rebecca. 2020. "Poll: Majority Supports Removing Confederate Statutes from Public Spaces." *Hill*, June 12, 2020.

Laclau, Ernesto, and Chantal Mouffe. 1985. *Hegemony and Socialist Strategy: Towards a Racial Democratic Politics*. London: Verso.

La Rue, Linda. 1970–75. "The Black Movement and Women's Liberation." In *Black Woman's Manifesto*, edited by the Third World Women's Alliance, 35–48. New York: Third World Women's Alliance. https://repository.duke.edu/dc/wlmpc /wlmms01009.

lee, mary hope. 1983. "On Not Bein." In Moraga and Anzaldúa 1983a, 9–11.

Lenin, Vladimir Il'ich. 1978. *State and Revolution: Marxist Teaching about the Theory of the State and the Tasks of the Proletariat in the Revolution*. Westport, CT: Greenwood.

Littlebear, Naomi. 1983. "Dreams of Violence." In Moraga and Anzaldúa 1983a, 16–17.

Lloyd, Moya. 2005. *Beyond Identity Politics: Feminism, Power, and Politics*. London: Sage.

Lorde, Audre. 1982. *Zami: A New Spelling of My Name*. Berkeley, CA: Crossing Press.

Lorde, Audre. 1984a. "Age, Race, Class, and Sex: Women Redefining Difference." In Lorde 1984f, 114–23.

Lorde, Audre. 1984b. "Learning from the 60s." In Lorde 1984f, 134–44.

Lorde, Audre. 1984c. "The Master's Tools Will Never Dismantle the Master's House." In Lorde 1984f, 110–13.

Lorde, Audre. 1984d. "An Open Letter to Mary Daly." In Lorde 1984f, 66–71.

Lorde, Audre. 1984e. "Scratching the Surface: Some Notes on Barriers to Women and Loving." In Lorde 1984f, 45–52.

Lorde, Audre. 1984f. *Sister Outsider: Essays and Speeches*. Berkeley, CA: Crossing Press.

Lorde, Audre. 1984g. "The Uses of Anger: Women Responding to Racism." In Lorde 1984f, 124–33.

Lorde, Audre. 1984h. "Uses of the Erotic: The Erotic as Power." In Lorde 1984f, 53–59.

Ludwig, Erik. 1999. "Closing in on the 'Plantation': Coalition Building and the Role of Black Women's Grievances in Duke University Labor Disputes, 1965–1968." *Feminist Studies* 25, no. 1: 79–94.

Lugones, María. 1987. "Playfulness 'World'-Traveling and Loving Perception." *Hypatia* 2, no. 2: 3–19.

Lugones, María. 1990a. "Hablando cara a cara/Speaking Face to Face: An Exploration of Ethnocentric Racism." In Anzaldúa 1990, 46–54.

Lugones, María. 1990b. "Structure/Anti-structure and Agency under Oppression." *Journal of Philosophy* 87, no. 10: 500–507.

Lugones, María. 1991. "On the Logic of Pluralist Feminism." In *Feminist Ethics*, edited by Claudia Card, 35–44. Lawrence: University Press of Kansas.

Lugones, María. 1994. "Purity, Impurity, and Separation." *Signs* 19, no. 2: 458–79.

Lugones, María. 1995. "Hard-to-Handle Anger." In *Overcoming Racism and Sexism*, edited by Linda Bell and David Blumenfeld, 203–17. Lanham, MD: Rowman and Littlefield.

Lugones, María. 2003. *Pilgrimages/Peregrinajes: Theorizing Coalition against Multiple Oppressions*. Lanham, MD: Rowman and Littlefield.

Lugones, María, and Elizabeth Spelman. 1983. "Have We Got a Theory For You! Feminist Theory, Cultural Imperialism, and the Demand for 'the Woman's Voice.'" *Women's Studies International Forum* 6, no. 6: 573–81.

Lugones, María, and Cricket Keating. Forthcoming. *Educating for Coalition: Popular Education and Contemporary Political Praxis*. Albany, NY: SUNY Press.

Lukács, Georg. 1968. *History and Class Consciousness: Studies in Marxist Dialectics*. Translated by Rodney Livingstone. Cambridge, MA: MIT Press.

Luxemburg, Rosa. 2004a. "The Mass Strike, the Political Party, and the Trade Unions." In *The Rosa Luxemburg Reader*, edited by Peter Hudis and Kevin Anderson, 168–99. New York: Monthly Review Press.

Luxemburg, Rosa. 2004b. "Women's Suffrage and Class Struggle." In Luxemburg 2004a, 237–42.

Lynch, Gayle. 1970–75. "Introduction." In *Black Woman's Manifesto*, edited by the Third World Women's Alliance. New York: Third World Women's Alliance. https://repository.duke.edu/dc/wlmpc/wlmms01009.

Lynes, Krista Geneviève. 2012. "Poetic Resistance and the Classroom without Guarantees." *Theory and Event* 15, no. 3. https://muse.jhu.edu/article/484451.

Mallory, Tamika. 2018. "Wherever My People Are Is Where I Must Be." *Newsone*, March 7, 2018. https://newsone.com/3779389/tamika-mallory-saviours-day/.

Mangan, Dan. 2020. "NASCAR Bans Confederate Flag at All Events and Properties." *CNBC*, June 10, 2020.

Manning, Erin. 2012. "Propositions for Collective Action; Towards an Ethico-Aesthetic Politics." *Theory and Event* 15, no. 3. https://muse.jhu.edu/article/484452.

Marso, Lori. 2006. *Feminist Thinkers and the Demands of Femininity: The Lives and Work of Intellectual Women*. New York: Routledge.

Marso, Lori. 2017. *Politics with Beauvoir: Freedom in the Encounter*. Durham, NC: Duke University Press.

Martin, Andrew. 2020. "White People, if Talking about Racism Makes You Uncomfortable; Good. Embrace That Discomfort." *Medium*, June 7, 2020.

Martin, Biddy, and Chandra Mohanty. 1986. "Feminist Politics: What's Home Got to Do with It?" In *Feminist Studies/Critical Studies. Language, Discourse, Society*, edited by Teresa de Lauretis, 191–212. London: Palgrave Macmillan.

Marx, Karl. 1970. *A Contribution to the Critique of Political Economy*. Edited by Maurice Dobb. Translated by S. W. Ryazanskaya. Moscow: Progress.

Marx, Karl, and Friedrich Engels. 2004. *The Communist Manifesto*. Edited and translated by L. M. Findlay. Peterborough, ON: Broadview.

Matsuda, Mari. 1996. *Where Is Your Body? And Other Essays on Race, Gender, and the Law*. Boston: Beacon.

McCall, Leslie. 2005. "The Complexity of Intersectionality." *Signs* 30, no. 3: 771–800.

McSweeney, Leah, and Jacob Siegel. 2018. "Is the Women's March Melting Down?" *Tablet*, December 10, 2018. https://www.tabletmag.com/sections/news/articles /is-the-womens-march-melting-down.

Milligan, Susan. 2020. "Trump Accused of Inciting Protestors as George Floyd Demonstrations Reach the White House." *U.S. News and World Report*, June 1. 2020. https://www.usnews.com/news/national-news/articles/2020-06-01 /trump-accused-of-inciting-protesters-as-george-floyd-demonstrations-reach -the-white-house.

Mills, Charles. 1997. *The Racial Contract*. Ithaca, NY: Cornell University Press.

Minkowitz, Donna. 1995. "Giving It Up: Orgasm, Fear, and Femaleness." In Walker 1995a, 77–86.

Mohanty, Chandra. 1984. "Under Western Eyes: Feminist Scholarship and Colonial Discourses." *boundary 2* 12, no. 3; 13, no. 1 (Spring/Fall): 338–58.

Mohanty, Chandra. 1991. "Cartographies of Struggle: Third World Women and the Politics of Feminism." In *Third World Women and the Politics of Feminism*, edited by Chandra Mohanty, Ann Russ, and Lourdes Torres, 1–50. Bloomington: Indiana University Press.

Mohanty, Chandra. 1995. "Feminist Encounters: Locating the Politics of Experience." In *Social Postmodernism: Beyond Identity Politics*, edited by Linda Nicholson and Steven Seidman, 68–86. Cambridge: Cambridge University Press.

Mohanty, Chandra. 2003. *Feminism without Borders: Decolonizing Theory, Practicing Solidarity*. Durham, NC: Duke University Press.

Mohanty, Chandra. 2006. Foreword to Sangtin Writers and Nagar 2006, ix–xv.

Mohanty, Chandra. 2013. "Transnational Feminist Crossings: On Neoliberalism and Radical Critique." *Signs* 38, no. 4: 967–91.

Mohanty, Chandra, and Biddy Martin. 2003. "What's Home Got to Do with It? (with Biddy Martin)." In Mohanty 2003, 85–105.

Moraga, Cherríe. 1983a. "Refugees of a World on Fire: Foreword to the Second Edition." In Moraga and Anzaldúa 1983a.

Moraga, Cherríe. 1983b. "Preface." In Moraga and Anzaldúa 1983a, xiii–xx.

Moraga, Cherríe. 1983c. "Introduction to Children Passing in the Streets: The Roots of Our Radicalism." In Moraga and Anzaldúa 1983a, 5.

Moraga, Cherríe. 1983d. "For the Color of My Mother." In Moraga and Anzaldúa 1983a, 12–13.

Moraga, Cherríe. 1983e. "Introduction to Entering the Lives of Others: Theory in the Flesh." In Moraga and Anzaldúa 1983a, 23.

Moraga, Cherríe. 1983f. "La Güera." In Moraga and Anzaldúa 1983a, 27–34.

Moraga, Cherríe. 1983g. "Introduction to And When You Leave, Take Your Pictures with You: Racism in the Women's Movement." In Moraga and Anzaldúa 1983a, 61–62.

Moraga, Cherríe. 1983h. "Introduction to Between the Lines: On Culture, Class, and Homophobia." In Moraga and Anzaldúa 1983a, 105–6.

Moraga, Cherríe, and Gloria Anzaldúa, eds. 1983a. *This Bridge Called My Back: Writings by Radical Women of Color*. 2nd ed. New York: Kitchen Table/Women of Color Press.

Moraga, Cherríe, and Gloria Anzaldúa. 1983b. "Introduction." In Moraga and Anzaldúa 1983a, xxiii–xxvi.

Moraga, Cherríe. 2017. "Cherríe Moraga." Interview by Chandra Mohanty and Linda Carty. *Feminist Freedom Warriors*, February 25, 2017. Video 1:04:43. http://feministfreedomwarriors.org/watchvideo.php?firstname =Cherr%C3%ADe&lastname=Moraga.

Morales, Rosario. 1983a. "I Am What I Am." In Moraga and Anzaldúa 1983a, 14–15.

Morales, Rosario. 1983b. "We're All in the Same Boat." In Moraga and Anzaldúa 1983a, 91–93.

Morgan, Robin, ed. 1970a. *Sisterhood Is Powerful: An Anthology of Writings from the Women's Liberation Movement*. New York: Vintage.

Morgan, Robin. 1970b. "Introduction: The Women's Revolution." In Morgan 1970a, xv–xlvi.

Morgan, Robin. 1984. *Sisterhood Is Global: The International Women's Movement Anthology*. New York: Feminist Press at the City University of New York.

Murib, Zein. 2018. "Unsettling the GLBT and Queer Coalitions in US Politics through the Lens of Queer Indigenous Critique." *New Political Science* 40, no. 1: 165–76.

Murib, Zein, and Liza Taylor. 2018a. "Feminism in Coalition: Rethinking Strategies for Progressive Politics across Difference." *New Political Science* 40, no. 1: 113–18.

Murib, Zein, and Liza Taylor. 2018b. "Conclusion to Feminism in Coalition: Rethinking Strategies for Progressive Politics across Difference." *New Political Science* 40, no. 1: 184–85.

Nagar, Richa. 2006. "Introduction: Playing with Fire; a Collective Journey across Borders." In Sangtin Writers and Nagar 2006, xxi–xlvii.

Narayan, Uma. 1989. "The Project of Feminist Epistemology: Perspectives from a Nonwestern Feminist." In *Gender/Body/Knowledge: Feminist Reconstructions of Being and Knowing*, edited by Alison M. Jaggar and Susan R. Bordo, 255–69. New Brunswick, NJ: Rutgers University Press.

Nicholson, Linda. 1994. "Interpreting Gender." *Signs* 20, no. 1: 79–105.

Nietzsche, Friedrich. 1998. *On the Genealogy of Morality*. Translated by Maudermarie Clark and Alan J. Swenson. Indianapolis: Hackett.

Norman, Brian. 2006. "The Consciousness-Raising Document, Feminist Anthologies, and Black Women in 'Sisterhood Is Powerful.'" *Frontiers* 27, no. 3: 38–64.

Norris, Pippa, and Ronald Inglehart. 2019. *Cultural Backlash: Trump, Brexit, and Authoritarian Populism*. Cambridge: Cambridge University Press.

Norton, Eleanor Holmes. 1970–75. "For Sadie and Maude." In *Black Woman's Manifesto*, edited by the Third World Women's Alliance, 1–8. New York: Third World Women's Alliance. https://repository.duke.edu/dc/wlmpc/wlmms01009.

Obie, Brooke. 2017. "Woman in Viral Photo from Women's March to White Female Allies: 'Listen to a Black Woman.'" *Root*, January 23, 2017. https://www

.theroot.com/woman-in-viral-photo-from-women-s-march-to-white-female
-1791524613.

Olson, Joel. 2004. *The Abolition of White Democracy*. Minneapolis: University of
Minnesota Press.

Osei-Kofi, Nana, Adela C. Licona, and Karma R. Chávez. 2018. "From Afro-Sweden
with Defiance: The Clenched Fist as Coalitional Gesture." *New Political Science*
40, no. 1: 137–50.

Parker, Pat. 1983. "Revolution: It's Not Neat or Pretty or Quick." In Moraga and
Anzaldúa 1983a, 238–42.

Pateman, Carole. 1988. *The Sexual Contract*. Stanford, CA: Stanford University
Press.

Pratt, Minnie Bruce. 1984. "Identity: Skin Blood Heart." In *Yours in Struggle: Three
Feminist Perspectives on Anti-Semitism and Racism*, edited by Elly Bulkin, Minnie
Bruce Pratt, and Barbara Smith, 9–64. Ithaca, NY: Firebrand.

Pratt, Minnie Bruce. 2015. "Minnie Bruce Pratt." Interview by Chandra Mohanty
and Linda Carty. *Feminist Freedom Warriors*, May 6, 2015. Video 0:49:27.
http://feministfreedomwarriors.org/watchvideo.php?firstname=Minnie%20
Bruce&lastname=Pratt.

Presley, Rachel E., and Alane L. Presswood. 2018. "Pink, Brown, and Read All Over:
Representation at the 2017 Women's March on Washington." *Cultural Studies—
Critical Methodologies* 18, no. 1: 61–71.

Pryse, Marjorie. 1998. "Critical Interdisciplinary, Women's Studies, and Cross-
Cultural Insight." *Feminist Formations* 10, no. 1: 1–22.

Puar, Jasbir K. 2007. *Terrorist Assemblages: Homonationalism in Queer Times*. Durham, NC: Duke University Press.

Puar, Jasbir K. 2012. "'I Would Rather Be a Cyborg Than a Goddess': Becoming-
Intersectional of Assemblage Theory." *philoSOPHIA* 2, no. 1: 49–66.

Quintero, Sofia. 2001. "'Isms' and AIDS: Transforming Multicultural Coalitions into
Radical Alliances." In Bystydzienski and Schacht 2001a, 91–106.

Rancière, Jacques. 2004. *The Politics of Aesthetics: The Distribution of the Sensible*.
Translated by Gabriel Rockhill. London: Continuum.

Ransby, Barbara. 2000. "Black Feminism at Twenty-One: Reflections on the Evolution of a National Community." *Signs* 25, no. 4: 1215–21.

Reagon, Bernice Johnson. 1983. "Coalition Politics: Turning the Century." In
B. Smith 1983a, 343–56.

Rich, Adrienne. 1986. "Notes Toward a Politics of Location." In *Blood, Bread, and
Poetry: Selected Prose, 1978–1985*, 210–31. New York: W. W. Norton.

Richardson, Bradford. 2017. "Black Lives Matter Resentful of Peaceful, Favorable
Women's March against Donald Trump." *Washington Times*, January 24, 2017.

Roberts, Dorothy. 1997. *Killing the Black Body: Race, Reproduction, and the Meaning of
Liberty*. New York: Vintage.

Rose-Redwood, Cindy Ann, and Reuben Rose-Redwood. 2017. "'It Definitely Felt Very
White': Race, Gender, and the Performative Politics of Assembly at the Women's
March in Victoria, British Columbia." *Gender, Place and Culture* 24, no. 5: 645–54.

Roshanravan, Shireen. 2010. "Passing-as-If: Model-Minority Subjectivity and Women of Color Identification." *Meridians* 10, no. 1: 1–31.

Roshanravan, Shireen. 2014. "Motivating Coalition: Women of Color and Epistemic Disobedience." *Hypatia* 29, no. 1: 41–58.

Roshanravan, Shireen. 2018. "Self-Reflection and the Coalitional Praxis of (Dis)Integration." *New Political Science* 40, no. 1: 151–64.

Rowbotham, Sheila. 1979. "'The Women's Movement and Organizing for Socialism." In *Beyond the Fragments: Feminism and the Making of Socialism*, by Sheila Rowbotham, Lynne Segal, and Hilary Wainwright, 21–156. Boston: Alyson.

Rowe, Aimee Carrillo. 2008. *Power Lines: On the Subject of Feminist Alliances*. Durham, NC: Duke University Press.

Russo, Amy. 2019. "Trump Ran Facebook Ads Decrying an Immigrant 'Invasion.'" *City Watch*, August 8, 2019.

Sandoval, Chela. 1982. "Feminism and Racism: A Report on the 1981 National Women's Studies Association Conference." Oakland, CA: Center for Third World Organizing.

Sandoval, Chela. 1984. "Comment on Krieger's 'Lesbian Identity and Community: Recent Social Science Literature.'" *Signs* 9, no. 4: 725–29.

Sandoval, Chela. 1990. "Feminism and Racism: A Report on the 1981 National Women's Studies Association Conference." In Anzaldúa 1990, 55–74.

Sandoval, Chela. 2000. *Methodology of the Oppressed*. Minneapolis: University of Minnesota Press.

Sangtin Writers and Richa Nagar. 2006. *Playing with Fire: Feminist Thought and Activism through Seven Lives in India*. Minneapolis: University of Minnesota Press.

Schacht, Steven, and Doris Ewing. 2001. "Feminist Women and (Pro)Feminist Men: Moving from an Uneasy to a Radical Alliance." In Bystydzienski and Schacht 2001a, 191–206.

Schram, Sanford. 2013. "Occupy Precarity." *Theory and Event* 16, no. 1. https://muse.jhu.edu/article/501861.

Schultz, Jason. 1995. "Getting Off on Feminism." In Walker 1995a, 107–26.

Scott, Joan. 1997."Deconstructing Equality-versus-Difference: Or, the Uses of Poststructuralist Theory for Feminism." In *Feminist Social Thought: A Reader*, edited by Diana Meyers, 758–70. New York: Routledge.

Senna, Danzy. 1995. "To Be Real." In Walker 1995a, 5–20.

Shapiro, Ari. 2020a. "Interrupt the Systems; Robin DiAngelo on *White Fragility* and Anti-racism." NPR, June 18, 2020. https://www.npr.org/2020/06/17/879136931/interrupt-the-systems-robin-diangelo-on-white-fragility-and-anti-racism.

Shapiro, Ari. 2020b. "'There Is No Neutral': 'Nice White People' Can Still Be Complicit in a Racist Society." *All Things Considered*, NPR, June 9, 2020. https://www.npr.org/2020/06/09/873375416/there-is-no-neutral-nice-white-people-can-still-be-complicit-in-a-racist-society.

Sides, John, Michael Tesler, and Lynn Vavreck. "The Electoral Landscape of 2016." *Annals of the American Academy of Political Science* 667, no. 1: 50–71. https://doi.org/10.1177/0002716216658922.

Siegel, Deborah L. 1997. "The Legacy of the Personal: Generating Theory in Feminism's Third Wave." *Hypatia* 12, no. 3: 46–75.

Simons, Margaret. 1979. "Racism and Feminism: A Schism in the Sisterhood." *Feminist Studies* 5, no. 2: 384–401.

Smith, Barbara, ed. 1983a. *Home Girls: A Black Feminist Anthology*. New Brunswick, NJ: Rutgers University Press.

Smith, Barbara. 1983b. "Introduction." In B. Smith 1983a, xxi–lviii.

Smith, Barbara. 1989. "A Press of Our Own Kitchen Table: Women of Color Press." *Frontiers: A Journal of Women's Studies* 10, no. 3: 11–13.

Smith, Barbara. 2016. "Barbara Smith." Interview by Chandra Mohanty and Linda Carty. *Feminist Freedom Warriors*, May 3, 2016. Video 0:56:38. http://feministfreedomwarriors.org/watchvideo.php?firstname=Barbara&lastname=Smith.

Smith, Barbara. 2017. "Barbara Smith." In K.-Y. Taylor 2017, 29–69.

Smith, Barbara. 2020. "I Helped Coin the Term 'Identity Politics': I'm Endorsing Bernie Sanders." *Guardian*, February 10, 2020.

Smith, Barbara, Caitlin Breedlove, and Amy Sonnie. 2020. "The Women's March Feminist Future Series: Feminism beyond White Supremacy; Where We Have Been and Where We Need to Go." July 30, 2020. Video (of webinar) 1:20:12. https://www.youtube.com/watch?v=RwJPqk9YvJc.

Smith, Barbara, and Beverly Smith. 1983. "Across the Kitchen Table: A Sister-to-Sister Dialogue." In Moraga and Anzaldúa 1983a, 113–27.

Smith, Dorothy. 1987. *The Everyday World as Problematic: A Feminist Sociology*. Boston: Northeastern University Press.

Snyder, Claire. 2008. "What Is Third-Wave Feminism? A New Directions Essay." *Signs* 34, no. 1: 175–96.

Snyder-Hall, Claire. 2010. "Third-Wave Feminism and the Defense of 'Choice.'" *Perspectives on Politics* 8, no. 1: 255–61.

Sorochan, Cayley. 2012. "The Quebec Student Strike: A Chronology." *Theory and Event* 15, no 3. https://muse.jhu.edu/article/484441.

Spivak, Gayatri Chakravorty, and Sarah Harasym. 1990. "Practical Politics of the Open End." In *The Post-colonial Critic: Interviews, Strategies, Dialogues*, edited by Sarah Harasym, 95–112. New York: Routledge.

Squires, Judith. 1999. *Gender in Political Theory*. Cambridge: Polity.

Steinem, Gloria. 1995. "Foreword." In Walker 1995a, xiii–xxiii.

Stockman, Farah. 2017. "Women's March on Washington Opens Contentious Dialogues about Race." *New York Times*, January 9, 2017.

Stockman, Farah. 2018. "Women's March Roiled by Accusations of Anti-Semitism." *New York Times*, December 23, 2018.

Sutherland, Elizabeth. 1970. "An Introduction." In Morgan 1970a, 423–25.

Tambe, Ashwini. 2017. "The Women's March on Washington: Words from an Organizer; an Interview with Mrinalini Chakraborty." *Feminist Studies* 43, no. 1: 223–29.

Tampio, Nicholas. 2009. "Assemblages and the Multitude: Deleuze, Hardt, Negri, and the Postmodern Left." *European Journal of Political Theory* 8, no. 3: 383–400.

Tanner, Leslie B., ed. 1971. *Voices from Women's Liberation*. New York: New American Library.

Taylor, Jocelyn. 1995. "Testimony of a Naked Woman." In Walker 1995a, 219–38.

Taylor, Keeanga-Yamahtta, ed. 2017. *How We Get Free: Black Feminism and the Combahee River Collective*. Chicago: Haymarket.

Taylor, Keeanga-Yamahtta. 2019. "Bernie Sanders' Democratic Socialism Speech Was a Landmark." *Jacobin Magazine*, June 18, 2019.

Taylor, Keeanga-Yamahtta. 2020a. "Episode 19: Building Coalitions (with Keeanga-Yamahtta Taylor)." *Hear the Bern*. https://berniesanders.com/podcast/ep-19 -building-coalitions-w-keeanga-yamahtta-taylor/.

Taylor, Keeanga-Yamahtta. 2020b. "Until Black Women Are Free, None of Us Will Be Free." *New Yorker*, July 20, 2020.

Taylor, Keeanga-Yamahtta. 2021. "A Black Lives Matter Founder on Building Modern Movements." *New Yorker*, January 18, 2021.

Taylor, Liza. 2018. "Coalition from the Inside Out: Women of Color Feminism and Politico Ethical Coalition Politics." *New Political Science* 40, no. 1: 119–36.

Tesler, Michael. 2016a. *Post-racial or Most-Racial? Race and Politics in the Obama Era*. Chicago: University of Chicago Press.

Tesler, Michael. 2016b. "Views about Race Mattered More in Electing Trump Than in Electing Obama." *Washington Post/Monkey Cage*, November 22, 2016.

Tolentino, Jia. 2017. "The Somehow Controversial Women's March on Washington." *New Yorker*, January 18, 2017.

Townsend-Bell, Erica E. 2012. "Writing the Way to Feminism." *Signs* 38, no. 1: 127–52.

Trump, Donald. 2015. "Presidential Announcement Speech." Delivered June 16. Published in *Time* by Time staff, June 16, 2015. https://time.com/3923128 /donald-trump-announcement-speech/.

Trump, Donald. 2020. "Read: President Trump's Rose Garden Speech on Protests." CNN *Politics*, June 1, 2020. https://www.cnn.com/2020/06/01/politics/read -trumps-rose-garden-remarks/index.html.

Truth, Sojourner. 2004. "Ain't I a Woman?" In *Voices of a People's History of the United States*, edited by Howard Zinn and Anthony Arnove, 128. New York: Seven Stories.

Tucker, Robert C., ed. 1975. *The Lenin Anthology*. New York: Norton.

Turney, Shad, Frank Levy, Jack Citrin, and Neil O'Brian. 2017. "Waiting for Trump: the Move to the Right of White Working-Class Men, 1968–2016." *California Journal of Politics and Policy*, May 18, 2017. Institute of Governmental Studies, University of California at Berkeley. https://escholarship.org/uc/item/1cq9k81z.

TWM (The Women's March). 2017a. "The March." https://www.womensmarch.com /march.

TWM (The Women's March). 2017b. "Unity Principles." https://womensmarch.com /mission-and-principles.

TWM (The Women's March). 2020a. "Defund Statement." Accessed July 27, 2020. https://womensmarch.com.

TWM (The Women's March). 2020b. "Women's Response to COVID-19." Accessed July 27, 2020. https://womensmarch.com.

Vasquez, Enriqueta Longauex. 1970. "The Mexican-American Woman." In Morgan 1970a, 426–32.

Walker, Alice. 1983. "Only Justice Can Stop a Curse." In B. Smith 1983a, 339–42.

Walker, Rebecca. 1992. "Becoming the Third Wave." Ms., January–February.

Walker, Rebecca, ed. 1995a. To Be Real: Telling the Truth and Changing the Face of Feminism. New York: Anchor.

Walker, Rebecca. 1995b. "Being Real: An Introduction." In Walker 1995a, xxix–xl.

Watson, Janell. 2012. "Butler's Biopolitics: Precarious Community." Theory and Event 15, no. 2. https://muse.jhu.edu/article/478357.

Webb, Veronica. 1995. "How Does a Supermodel Do Feminism: An Interview with Veronica Webb." In Walker 1995a, 209–18.

Weeks, Kathi. 2009. "'Hours for What We Will Work': Work, Family, and the Movement for Shorter Hours." Feminist Studies 35, no. 1: 101–27.

Williams, Maxine. 1970–75. "Black Women and the Struggle for Liberation." In Black Woman's Manifesto, edited by the Third World Women's Alliance, 9–18. New York: Third World Women's Alliance. https://repository.duke.edu/dc/wlmpc/wlmms01009.

Winfrey, Oprah. 2020. "Spotlight: Where Do We Go from Here?" Oprah Winfrey Network. Aired June 9 and June 10 on Discovery. https://www.oprah.com/app/where-do-we-go-from-here.html.

Wolf, Naomi. 1995. "Brideland." In Walker 1995a, 35–40.

Wong, Nellie. 1983. "When I Was Growing Up." In Moraga and Anzaldúa 1983a, 7–8.

Woodson, Leroy, Jr. 1986. "Angela Davis." Los Angeles Times, March 2, 1986.

Wortham, Jenna. 2017. "Who Didn't Go to the Women's March Matters More Than Who Did." New York Times, January 24, 2017.

Yang, Allie. 2019. "Women's March Co-president Tamika Mallory Discusses Controversial Relationship with Louis Farrakhan." ABC, January 14, 2019.

Yuval-Davis, Nira. 1997. Gender and Nation. London: Sage.

Zimmer, Ben. 2019. "Where Does Trump's 'Invasion' Rhetoric Come From?" Atlantic, August 6, 2019.

Zivi, Karen. 2004. "Who or What Are We? The Identity Crisis in Feminist Politics." Polity 36, no. 2: 323–40.

Index

Anzaldúa, Gloria, 5, 93, 138, 141, 147, 181, 187, 199, 251n5; and Angela Davis, 225–26; and Barbara Smith, 227; *Borderlands/La Frontera*, 26, 116, 125–26; on home, 152n14; "La Prieta," 124; on mestiza consciousness, 27, 114, 116, 124, 128–30, 144–45, 253n2; and poststructuralism, 253n1; role in *Bridge*, 14–15, 18, 29, 151–52, 163–66, 173–76; and theories of identity, 20, 25, 28, 108–9, 114–18, 123–33, 172–73, 253n5; on theory in the flesh, 21; *This Bridge We Call Home*, 185–86. See also *This Bridge Called My Back: Writings by Radical Women of Color*

Arab Spring, 75
Arbery, Ahmaud, 223
Asplund, Maria Teresa, 253n15
assemblage, 97; in Butler's work, 9, 75–76; in Deleuze/Guattari's work, 27, 254n9; in Puar's work, 25, 96, 99, 113–14, 122, 139
Association de Mujeres Nicaragüenses Luisa Amanda Espinosa (AMNLAE), 254n8
Ayala, Alma, 173

Badiou, Alain, 2, 252n13
Bajpayee, Vibha: *Playing with Fire*, 29, 153, 186–88, 243
Bambara, Toni Cade, 166, 188
Barvosa-Carter, Edwina, 1, 14, 21, 108, 138, 201, 253n4, 254n11; *Wealth of Selves*, 20
Bates, Karen Grisgby, 208
Baum, Bruce, 249n3
Beal, Frances, 56, 64, 237; "A Black Woman's Manifesto," 60; "Double Jeopardy," 12, 61–62, 159–60, 225, 231
Beauvoir, Simone de, 236
Beltrán, Cristina, 26, 28, 138–39; "Patrolling Borders," 128
Bickel, Christopher, 93–94, 97
Bickford, Susan, 251n1
Biden, Joe, 233
bird's eye view, 16, 27–28, 136, 139, 176, 181–82, 243
birth control, 158–60
Black liberation, 158–59, 205, 235, 249
Black Lives Matter (BLM), 90, 143, 192, 201, 215, 222, 227–29, 232, 234, 237, 241; Vancouver chapter, 193

#BlackLivesMatter, 201
Black nationalism, 34
#BlackoutTuesday, 256n3
Black Panther Party, 68, 234, 236
Black Women's Alliance, 249n2. See also Third World Women's Alliance (TWWA)
Black Women's Liberation Group: "Statement on Birth Control," 159
Bland, Bob, 191–92, 203–6, 208, 213, 215, 220–21
Bliss, James, 13
bodies in alliance, 74–77, 98
Bohrer, Ashley J., 23, 58, 62, 64, 94, 104, 249n1, 250n1; *Marxism and Intersectionality*, 14, 34–35, 55–56, 122
Boothroyd, Sydney, 193
bourgeois feminism, 155
bourgeoisie, 38, 40, 48, 51, 54, 155
Brewer, Sierra: "Concerned, Meet Terrified," 210
Brooklyn College, 228
Brown, Connie, 155, 251n1
Bulkin, Elly, 213, 215; *Yours in Struggle*, 212
Bunch, Charlotte, 6, 251n4
Burack, Cynthia, 14, 17, 29, 127, 184, 253n3; *Healing Identities*, 150–51
Butler, Judith, 11, 26, 104, 114, 122–23, 125, 127, 129, 136, 148, 243, 253n5, 254n10; on assemblage, 9, 75–76; "Bodily Vulnerability, Coalition Politics," 98; on coalition, 2, 8–9, 24–25, 68–69, 71–79, 82–83, 94–101, 108, 118, 139, 176–77, 179, 185, 251n2; *Frames of War*, 74, 94; *Gender Trouble*, 74, 78, 95, 114; on indeterminacy, 75, 96, 176; on interlocking systems of oppression, 95; on performativity, 116; and poststructuralism, 2, 109, 111, 116, 119, 177, 194; *Precarious Life*, 74, 76–77; on solidarity, 2, 98, 100; on undecidability, 95; on unfixity, 9, 71, 73, 75, 78, 95, 108, 129
Bystydzienski, Jill M.: *Forging Radical Alliances across Difference*, 91–92

California: San Francisco, 26, 178, 254n8; Yosemite, 69
calling out, 60–61, 113, 166, 200, 211, 213
Canaan, Andrea, 255n7

Canada: Quebec, 1–2, 96; Vancouver, 193
Carastathis, Anna, 1, 26, 104, 108, 252n11,
    254n8; on coalition, 128–29, 146, 253n3,
    253n5
cartography, 116, 135, 176, 181, 199, 243
Carty, Linda E., 225–26, 228, 237, 243
caste, 186–88
chain of equivalence, 36, 43–45, 250nn1–2
Chakraborty, Mrinalini, 194, 197, 204
Chang, Edward, 253n3
Chávez, Karma, 14, 20–21, 73, 249n1, 250n5,
    252n11, 253n3, 253n15
Chisholm, Shirley, 10, 14–15, 24, 151,
    161–62, 195; 1972 presidential run, 5,
    67; on coalition, 5, 67–69, 82, 85, 133,
    227–28, 235
choice feminism, 153, 179
Christian, Barbara, 141
Christianity, 28, 142, 144, 222
Chrystos: "He Saw," 169
Chung, Angie Y., 253n3
Cisler, Lucina, 158–60
citation, 33, 93, 95, 117, 128, 141, 220, 249n3;
    of Audre Lorde, 91; of Bernice Johnson
    Reagon, 25; of Combahee statement, 34;
    feminist politics of, 241–46
Clarke, Cheryl, 227
class antagonism, 39–40, 52, 54
class consciousness, 23, 41, 50, 53
classism, 155–56, 163, 178
Clinton, Hillary, 192, 232–33
coalition, definition, 4–5, 119
coalitional consciousness, 14, 21, 27–28,
    103, 109, 137, 177, 211, 246, 254n11; and
    Bridge, 153, 162, 166, 169–71, 173; and
    Chela Sandoval, 18–19; Cricket Keating
    on, 28, 226, 238–39, 254n7; definition,
    16; and identity, 25–26, 28, 106–49; and
    Marxism, 27; and WMW, 201, 209, 214
coalitional discourse, 17, 21, 29, 150–51
coalitional identity, 14, 16, 21, 107, 110, 118,
    148, 152, 200, 213, 250n5, 253n3; Anna
    Carastathis on, 253n5; Bernice Johnson
    Reagon on, 107; Carmen Vázquez on,
    133; Cherríe Moraga on, 167, 172; defini-
    tion, 26; Gloria Anzaldúa on, 28, 117,
    124, 127, 131; Minnie Bruce Pratt on, 28,
    142, 144–46; Moya Lloyd on, 253n2
coalitional pedagogy, 245–47

coalitional scholarship, 14, 19–21, 149, 243;
    Bridge as, 17–18, 28–29, 150–88, 242
coalitional selves, 16, 26, 123, 137–41, 148,
    253n2, 253n4; and Bridge, 165–69; Gloria
    Anzaldúa on, 28, 127–30, 173; Minnie
    Bruce Pratt on, 144–47, 201; and WMW,
    201, 210
coalition analytic vs. alliance analytic, 20–21
coalition as ethical community, 9–10, 24–25,
    68, 71–72, 76–78, 95, 101, 160
coalition as Left hegemony, 36, 41
coalition as politico-ethical encounter, 72
coalition as spectacle, 10, 24, 71, 181, 184,
    253n15; Judith Butler on, 9, 25, 74–78,
    95, 101, 108, 139, 176–79, 185
Coalition large de l'Association pour une
    solidarité syndicale étudiante (CLASSE),
    2–3, 6, 25, 96–97, 249n3
coalition of conscience, 68, 226–28
coalition of one, 128–29, 133, 146
coalition risk-taking, 240
coauthorship, 18, 85, 170, 186, 212, 226, 243,
    257n2
coconspirators, 228–30, 232, 237, 240, 243,
    247
Cole, Elizabeth, 252n11
Coles, Romand, 25, 36, 71, 72, 79–87, 100,
    104, 249n1, 249n3, 250n2, 251n2, 254n10
collaboration, 17, 29, 100, 173–74, 176, 185,
    187, 193, 236
collective drag, 9
Collins, Patricia Hill, 56, 92, 141, 251n5
Combahee River Collective, 12, 14, 44–45, 72,
    108, 113, 197, 205, 229; "Black Feminist
    Statement," 23, 26, 33–34, 59–60, 63,
    85, 115, 120–21, 165, 195, 227, 232; and
    Black Lives Matter, 227–28, 237; on co-
    alition, 5, 62, 73, 78, 85–87, 94, 97, 103,
    123; on identity politics, 26, 34, 59, 115,
    120–21, 235; on interlocking systems of
    oppression, 11, 60, 62–64, 121, 195; on
    intersectionality, 63–66; on intersec-
    tional Marxism, 15, 23–24, 33–35, 38, 60,
    231–32
Communism, 34, 38–40, 41, 47–48, 50, 53,
    56, 58, 63–64
Confederacy, 223
consciousness raising (CR), 15, 18–19, 63, 86,
    132, 174, 240

Garza, Alicia, 192–93, 210–11, 234; *The Purpose of Power*, 232
gender justice, 196
Georgia, 145
Germany, 52
Gilmore, Stephanie, 252n10
Glassman, Carol, 158
Global North, 242
Global South, 122, 242
Goldman, Emma, 169–70
Goodhart, Michael, 249n3
Goodman, Amy, 229
Gramsci, Antonio, 36, 42–43, 46
Green, Emma, 216, 219
Grimké, Sarah and Angelina, 145
Grosz, Elizabeth, 109, 111
Guardian, 233
Guattari, Félix, 2, 8, 115, 117, 136, 176, 252n13, 253n5; on assemblage, 27, 115, 254n9; on diagramming, 134–35; on minoritarian becomings, 16, 27

Haiti, 252n8
Hampton, Fred, 68–69
Hancock, Ange-Marie, 1, 252n11
Harding, Sandra, 254n7
Harmon, Amy, 256n2
Haro, Lia, 249n3
Hartsock, Nancy, 139
hatred, 89, 91, 126, 146, 200; hatred politics, 3–4, 30, 90, 94, 190, 201, 222, 224, 236, 251n6, 252nn7–8
Hear the Bern, 234–35
Hegel, G. W. F., 48, 250n7
hegemonic articulation, 36–37, 42–46, 250n2
hegemony, 244; hegemonic white feminism, 99, 132, 191, 193; Left, 36–37, 47, 65, 250n2
Herndon-De La Rosa, Destiny, 194
heterosexism, 60, 64, 86, 143, 156–57, 163
heterosexuality, 60, 69, 121, 163, 222, 231, 256n13
historical materialism, 48
Hobson, Sheila Smith, 159
home, 126–27, 229, 251n5, 252n14; and Black feminism, 86–88, 120; and coalition, 69, 79–83, 86, 92, 99, 101–2, 105, 107, 166–68
homophobia, 165, 213, 215, 227
Hong, Grace Kyungwon, 205

Honig, Bonnie, 251n1
hooks, bell, 141, 180, 204, 225, 231, 255n5, 255n8; *Ain't I a Woman*, 226; on beauty, 255n9; on feminist advocacy, 194–97, 233; on feminist solidarity, 251nn4–5; on lifestyle feminism, 256n11; on sisterhood, 156; *Teaching to Transgress*, 246
Hull, Gloria T., 5, 29; *But Some of Us Are Brave*, 18, 141, 151
human rights, 195–96
hybridity, 128, 139

identity-based group politics, 26, 109, 120, 122
identity politics, 90, 107, 114, 117, 140, 227, 241; alternatives to, 30, 137, 190; *versus* coalition, 95; Combahee River Collective on, 26, 34, 59, 115, 120–21, 235; essentialist, 27, 45, 113, 120, 137; and WMW, 195–96, 217–18
Illinois: Chicago, 6, 68, 94, 138
indeterminacy, 3, 22, 112, 177, 253n1, 253n15; alternatives to, 14, 53, 62, 71, 93–94, 99, 102–3, 108–9, 189; and coalition, 7, 14, 62, 71, 73, 109, 181; Ernesto Laclau/Chantal Mouffe on, 8, 36–37, 51–53, 55, 62; Judith Butler on, 75, 96, 176
Indiana University, 93, 97
Indigenous Action Media, 229
Indigenous Peoples, 11, 103, 122, 193, 195–96
inessential coalitions, 108, 127
interlocking systems of oppression, 19, 44–45, 65, 93, 200, 234; and anthologies, 18; Ashley J. Bohrer on, 104; Barbara Smith on, 165; and *To Be Real*, 177, 179, 183, 256n13; Bernice Johnson Reagon on, 197; Chandra Mohanty on, 101, 171, 172; Cherríe Moraga on, 164; and coalition, 5, 7, 10, 14–15, 21, 25, 68, 78, 82–84, 97, 123, 164–65, 199, 246; Combahee River Collective on, 60, 62–64, 121, 195; and Donald Trump, 90; Gloria Anzaldúa on, 175; and intersectionality, 11, 64, 231–32, 235; Judith Butler on, 95; and the master's tools, 91; Minnie Bruce Pratt on, 142; Rosa Luxemburg on, 55; TWWA on, 62–63, 226; and WMW, 30, 190, 195, 202; and Women of Color analytic, 4

intersectionality, 7, 10, 14–15, 18, 22, 26, 30, 66, 71–72, 103–4, 134, 187, 235–42, 249n3; and 2016 presidential election, 232–34; *versus* additive politics, 255n3; Angela Davis on, 6, 225–26; bell hooks on, 255n9; and *To Be Real*, 178, 181–82; Bernice Johnson Reagon on, 25, 84; and Black Lives Matter, 227–29; and *Bridge*, 166, 184; Combahee River Collective on, 34–35, 65, 121–22, 231; definition, 11–12; and interlocking systems of oppression, 11, 64, 231–32, 235; intersectionality crisis, 8, 23, 108; intersectional wedge, 24, 38, 47, 54–65; Jasbir Puar on, 13, 96, 113–15, 137; Minnie Bruce Pratt on, 145; and pedagogy, 246–47; and poststructuralism, 110; precursors to, 34; and reproductive rights, 255n4; and Rosa Luxemburg, 47, 54–56, 65, 107; Shirley Chisholm on, 5; and *Sisterhood*, 156, 159–61; Sojourner Truth on, 12; and WMW, 189–91, 193–97, 201, 204, 208–24. *See also* intersectional Marxism
intersectional Marxism, 14–15, 23–24, 33–36, 64, 65, 250n1
Israel, 213–15, 219
Ivy League, 178
Iweala, Uzodinma, 256n2

Jackson, Jesse, 68–69, 82, 214, 223
Jefferson, Margo, 209–10
Jewish feminists, 212
Johnson, Abby, 218
Johnson, Jennifer, 256n2
Jones, Beverly, 158
Jones, Claudia, 56, 66; "An End to the Neglect of the Problems of the Negro Woman!," 58–59
Jones, Lisa, 179–80; "Rodeo Caldonia High-Fidelity Performance Theater," 179–80
Jordan, June, 187, 227
Joreen, 158
Joseph, Gloria: *Common Differences*, 226

Kautsky, Karl, 41
Keating, AnaLouise: *This Bridge We Call Home*, 185–86

Keating, Cricket, 1, 14, 31, 73, 103, 235, 237, 240, 250n5, 257n1; "Building Coalitional Consciousness," 226; on coalitional consciousness, 28, 226, 238–39, 254n7; *Educating for Coalition*, 226, 234, 238–39, 242–43, 245–46, 257n2
King, Deborah, 56, 255n3
King, Martin Luther, Jr., 250n1
Kingston, Maxine Hong, 167
Kitchen Table: Women of Color Press, 151–52, 162, 173

Laclau, Ernesto, 35, 44–45, 54, 64, 69, 71, 97, 104, 112, 118, 127, 136, 148, 250n5, 253n5; on indeterminacy, 8, 36–37, 51–53, 55, 62; on Marxism, 7–8, 14–15, 23, 27, 36, 41–42, 46, 51, 63, 65; on unfixity, 8, 10, 24, 27, 36–37, 41–43, 46–47, 52–53, 55, 108
La Escuela Popular Norteña (EPN), 243
La Rue, Linda, 61; "A Black Woman's Manifesto," 60
Latin America, 70
Lenin, Vladimir, 35, 37, 49–50, 52, 54–55, 58, 62–65, 136, 176, 250n3; on scientific socialism, 16, 23, 27, 38–41, 46–47, 51, 250n6
Levinas, Emmanuel, 76–77
Lewis, Jill: *Common Differences*, 226
liberal feminism, 114
liberalism, 46, 114
Licona, Adela, 73, 250n5
lifestyle feminism, 29, 153, 176, 179–81, 185, 256n11
lines of flight, 135
Littlebear, Naomi, 168
Lloyd, Moya, 26, 108–9, 127, 129, 148, 195, 253n2; *Beyond Identity Politics*, 111–20
Lorde, Audre, 14–15, 18–19, 92–93, 137–38, 146–47, 165, 171, 195, 237, 252n14, 253n5; "Age, Race, Class, and Sex," 124; and Black Lives Matter, 227; on coalition, 5, 25, 72–73, 78, 88–91, 95, 97–99, 102–5, 108, 123, 125–33, 197–206; and Kitchen Table: Women of Color Press, 162; "Learning from the 60s," 89; "The Master's Tools Will Never Dismantle the Master's House," 91, 98; "An Open

Letter to Mary Daly," 98, 110, 112–14, 117, 163, 202, 244–45; *Sister Outsider*, 24, 26, 88; "The Uses of Anger," 89; and WMW, 240

Lowe, Lisa, 177

Ludwig, Erik, 252n10

Lugones, María, 14, 21, 31, 103, 108–9, 114, 135, 145, 191, 201, 204, 206, 235, 237, 249n1, 253n1, 253n5; on curdle-separation, 137–38, 221, 254n6; *Educating for Coalition*, 226, 234, 238–39, 242–43, 245–46, 257n2; "Have We Got a Theory for You!," 139, 170; on pedestrian theorizing, 21, 27, 115, 134, 136, 141, 244; *Pilgrimages/Peregrinajes*, 19, 107, 133–34, 198, 200, 243; "Purity, Impurity, and Separation," 137–38; on resistant writing, 175–76; on traveling, 28, 131, 143, 170, 199–200, 219, 240

Lukács, Georg, 50, 250n6

Luxemburg, Rosa, 27, 48, 57–60, 62–63, 92, 132, 239; and intersectionality, 23–24, 47, 54–56, 65, 107; "The Mass Strike, the Political Party, and the Trade Unions," 23, 49–51, 55–56; on spontaneity, 23–24, 35, 37, 41, 46–47, 50–55, 65, 250n6; "Women's Suffrage and Class Struggle," 52, 54–55, 64

Lynch, Gayle, 61; "A Black Woman's Manifesto," 60

lynching, 57, 145, 241

Lynes, Krista Geneviève, 96, 98

Mallory, Tamika D., 191, 198, 203, 211–16, 220–21

Manning, Erin, 96

Maple Spring, 1–3, 96, 252n12

March on Washington for Jobs and Freedom (1963), 193

Marso, Lori, 236

Martin, Biddy, 254n12

Martínez, Elizabeth "Betita," 56

Marx, Karl, 34, 38, 56, 250n7; *The Communist Manifesto*, 38–39, 47–50, 52; *A Contribution to the Critique of Political Economy*, 38–39, 47

Marxism, 17, 30, 107–8, 148, 151; Ashley J. Bohrer on, 104; Claudia Jones on, 58; Combahee River Collective on, 15,

23–24, 33–35, 38, 60, 231–32; Ernesto Laclau/Chantal Mouffe on, 7–8, 14–15, 23, 27, 36, 41–42, 46, 51, 63, 65; Gloria Anzaldúa on, 124; intersectional, 14–15, 23–24, 33–36, 64, 65, 250n1; Judith Butler on, 95; Rosa Luxemburg on, 23–24, 27, 37, 46–47, 49–51, 55–56, 63–65, 107; Vladimir Lenin on, 38–40, 47, 49–50, 54–55, 63, 65, 136. *See also* post-Marxism

#MaskUp, 222

Massachusetts: Boston, 33, 178, 208

McCain, Meghan, 220–21

Mexico, 11, 90, 125–26, 130, 138, 252n7

Million Man March (1995), 204

Million Women March (1997), 204

Mills, Charles, 250n3

minoritarian becomings, 16, 27, 136

misogyny, 3, 30, 143, 179, 227–28. *See also* patriarchy

Mock, Janet, 192

Mohanty, Chandra Talpade, 14, 26, 31, 108, 187–88, 225–26, 228, 235, 237, 249n1, 254n12, 255n6; on coalition, 73, 94, 105, 107, 121–23; on depoliticization of theory, 241–42; on dialectical materialism, 239; *Feminism without Borders*, 19, 25, 101, 243; "Feminist Encounters," 99; on identity, 235; on interlocking systems of oppression, 101, 171, 172; on solidarity, 99–102, 104, 238, 242, 245; "Under Western Eyes," 244–45; on Women of Color (term), 4

Moraga, Cherríe, 5, 14, 31, 147, 197, 225–27, 233, 237–38, 252n14; on 2016 presidential election, 232; "For the Color of My Mother," 168–69; "La Güera," 169–70; "Refugees of a World on Fire," 173; role in *Bridge*, 15, 18, 21, 29, 151–52, 163–76, 181, 186. See also *This Bridge Called My Back: Writings by Radical Women of Color*

Morales, Rosario, 163; "I Am What I Am," 168

Morefield, Jeanne, 249n3

Morgan, Robin: *Sisterhood Is Global*, 99, 255n6; *Sisterhood Is Powerful*, 29, 153–62, 165, 173, 176–78, 184, 186–87, 254n1

Mouffe, Chantal, 7, 35, 44–45, 54, 64, 69, 71, 97, 104, 112, 118, 127, 136, 148, 250n5, 253n5; on indeterminacy, 8, 36–37, 51–53, 55, 62; on Marxism, 7–8, 14–15, 23, 27, 36, 41–42, 46, 51, 63, 65; on unfixity, 8, 10, 24, 27, 36–37, 41–43, 46–47, 52–53, 55, 108

Murib, Zein, 14, 73, 103, 249n1, 250n5

Nagar, Richa: *Playing with Fire*, 29, 153, 186–88, 243

Narayan, Uma, 254n7

NASCAR, 223

"Nasty Woman" shirts, 203

National Policy Roundtables, 103

National Women's Studies Association (NWSA), 15, 18, 132, 174, 226, 243

Nation of Islam, 204; Saviour's Day, 215

neoliberalism, 2–3, 7, 11, 96, 231, 236–37, 242

neo-Nazis, 253n15

New Mexico, 243

New Political Science (NPS), 104, 252n11; Feminism in Coalition symposium, 25, 73, 94, 102

New Wave Feminists, 194

New York City, 168, 178, 203, 212

New Yorker, 232

New York Times, 209

New York University, 180

Nicaragua, 254n8

Nicholson, Linda, 6

Nieto-Gómez, Anna, 56

Nietzsche, Friedrich, 36, 72, 125, 127, 254n10; *On the Genealogy of Morality*, 111

nomadic science, 134, 136, 140

nonaggression, 68–69

nongovernmental organizations (NGOs), 186

Norman, Brian, 153

North Carolina, 142–43

Norton, Eleanor Homes, 61; "A Black Woman's Manifesto," 60

Obama, Barack, 3, 227

Ocasio-Cortez, Alexandria, 234

Occupy Wall Street, 75

Ohio: Akron, 11

Olsen, Tillie, 167

Olson, Joel, 250n3

Oluo, Ijeoma, 192

Omar, Ilhan, 234

ontological entrapment, 30, 217, 219, 229

ontology crisis, 8

oppositional consciousness, 27, 129, 132, 135–36, 140

Osei-Kofi, Nana, 73

overdetermination, 13, 41–43, 113

Palestine, 203, 212, 215

Palgrave Macmillan, 250n4; The Politics of Intersectionality series, 250n4

Parker, Pat, 68

Parti libéral du Québec, 2

Pateman, Carole, 250n3

patriarchy, 157, 210, 232, 250n4; Combahee River Collective on, 60; hetero-, 231, 234; and Marxism, 34, 64; racialized, 12, 57, 160; Rebecca Walker on, 182, 255n10; Rosa Luxemburg on, 54–55. *See also* misogyny

pedagogy, 245–47

pedestrian theorizing, 21, 27, 115, 134–37, 141, 176, 182, 244

Peoples, Angela, 192, 202–3, 209

Perez, Carmen, 191, 203, 211–13, 215–16, 218–20

police defunding, 222

political crisis, 8

political science, 2, 3, 6, 91. See also *New Political Science* (NPS)

politico-ethical coalition politics, 14–16, 22–23, 92, 118, 141, 148–49, 156, 178, 181, 184, 223–24, 230, 237, 246; and Audre Lorde, 90–91; and Barbara Smith, 88, 107–10; and Bernice Johnson Reagon, 24–25, 71–72, 78–85, 91, 98–99, 101–2, 151, 229; and *Bridge*, 29, 151–54, 161–77, 185–88; and Chandra Talpade Mohanty, 73, 100–102; and Chela Sandoval, 132, 254n10; choosing, 94–105; and Christopher Bickel, 93–94; and coalitional identity, 26; and Combahee River Collective, 24, 45, 87; and Cricket Keating/María Lugones, 238–40; and Minnie Bruce Pratt, 28, 110, 142–43, 146; and TWWA, 45; and WMW, 30, 189–91, 194, 199, 203, 207–13, 216–17

politics of the future, 96

politics of the open end, 96

post-Marxism, 7, 14, 23–24, 30, 35–36, 38, 69, 72, 151, 189

postmodern feminism, 6, 99, 119

postmodernism, 6, 99, 119, 122, 244

poststructuralism, 25, 109, 130, 177, 241, 253n1, 253n15; alternatives to, 16, 20, 22, 104, 109–23, 139, 194; critiques of, 7–8, 10–11; and Maple Spring, 2–3

Pratt, Minnie Bruce, 14, 25, 31, 108, 110, 116, 171, 199, 211, 226, 235–40, 246; and Black Lives Matter, 228–29; on coalitional identity, 28, 142, 144–46; on coalitional selves, 144–47, 201; "Identity: Skin Blood Heart," 5, 28, 142–47, 228; and self-reflexivity, 142–44, 147, 165, 172, 204, 254nn11–12; *Yours in Struggle*, 212

praxis, 93, 101, 103, 140, 200, 246

precariousness, 9, 58, 61, 74, 76, 90, 95; *versus* precarity, 77

precarity, 9, 30, 68, 71, 74–75, 95, 98; *versus* precariousness, 77

Presley, Rachel, 205

Presswood, Alane, 205

privileged feminism, 178, 182

pro-life/anti-abortion politics, 194, 197, 217–18, 220–21

proliferation of struggles, 7, 35–36

Pryse, Marjorie, 254n7

Puar, Jasbir, 11, 25–26, 97, 99, 104, 115, 117, 121–23, 135–37, 139; "I Would Rather Be a Cyborg than a Goddess," 13, 113–14; *Terrorist Assemblages*, 96

Puerto Rico, 5, 133, 138, 158–59, 167–68, 173

pussy hats, 193, 217

racial justice, 196, 223, 233

racist capitalism, 12, 61

racist sexism, 56, 61

rainbow coalition, 68

Ramsheela: *Playing with Fire*, 29, 153, 186–88, 243

Rancière, Jacques, 2, 252n13

Ransby, Barbara, 251n4

Ray, Rashawn, 191

Reagan, Ronald, 4, 161, 226–28

Reaganomics, 4, 7, 68, 236

Reagon, Bernice Johnson, 5, 12, 14, 19, 110, 113, 123, 127, 133, 142–43, 146, 157, 168, 177, 195, 197, 236, 240, 251n1; "Coali-

tion Politics," 15, 24–25, 69–72, 78–108, 132, 151, 198, 230; on home, 69, 79–83, 86–87, 92, 99, 101–2, 105, 107, 120; and politico-ethical coalition politics, 24–25, 71–72, 78–85, 91, 98–99, 101–2, 151, 229; principles of coalition, 79–80, 84

receptive generosity, 25, 79, 83

Reed, Carolyn, 183

reproductive justice, 4, 196

reproductive rights, 160, 208

Republican Party (US), 4

resistant writing, 175–76

revolutionary feminism, 140

Roberts, Dorothy, 255nn4–5

Rose, ShiShi, 202–3, 206–8, 210, 217

Roshanravan, Shireen, 4, 14, 73, 103, 108, 145, 200–201, 204, 249n1, 250n5, 254n11

Rowe, Aimee Carrillo, 20–22, 253n3

RU486, 182

Russia, 40, 49–50, 56, 57; Nicholaiev, 53

Russian Revolution (1905), 49, 57

Russo, Amy, 252n7

Sanders, Bernie, 223, 234

Sandinistas, 254n8

Sandoval, Chela, 14, 17, 25, 108–9, 115, 174, 253n1, 254n10; on coalition, 5, 18–19, 28, 132, 136–37, 139–41, 151; on consciousness raising, 15; "Feminism and Racism," 18, 129, 131–32, 243; *Methodology of the Oppressed*, 18–19, 132; Moya Lloyd on, 127; on oppositional consciousness, 27, 129, 132, 135–36, 140; on Women of Color (term), 4

Sangtin Writers: *Playing with Fire*, 29, 153, 186–88, 243

Sarsour, Linda, 191, 203–4, 208, 213, 215

Schacht, Steven P.: *Forging Radical Alliances across Difference*, 91–92

Schlack, Julie Wittes, 208–9

Schram, Sanford, 75, 96

scientific materialism, 37–40, 47, 50, 52

scientific socialism, 16, 23, 27, 37–41, 46–47, 51–52, 54, 63, 65, 250n6

Scott, Joan, 109, 111

Scott, Patricia Bell, 5, 29; *But Some of Us Are Brave*, 18, 141, 151

second-wave feminism, 180, 252n10

Seitz, Jane, 155